Marching to the Drums

Other Books by Ian Knight

The Anatomy of the Zulu Army
Brave Men's Blood: The Epic of the Zulu War
By the Orders of the Great White Queen: Campaigning in Zululand through the
   Eyes of the British Soldier
Fearful Hard Times: The Siege and Relief of Eshowe (with Ian Castle)
Go to your God like a Soldier: The British Soldier Fighting for Empire
Great Zulu Commanders
Great Zulu Battles
Nothing Remains but to Fight: The Defence of Rorke's Drift
The War Correspondents: The Anglo-Zulu War (with John Laband)
Warrior Chiefs of Southern Africa
Zulu: The Battles of Isandlwana and Rorke's Drift
The Zulu War: Then and Now (with Ian Castle)

Monographs

Boer Wars (1): 1836–1898
Boer Wars (2): 1898–1902
British Forces in Zululand 1879
Colenso 1899
Rorke's Drift 1879
Queen Victoria's Enemies (1): Southern Africa
Queen Victoria's Enemies (2): Northern Africa
Queen Victoria's Enemies (3): India
Queen Victoria's Enemies (4): Asia, Australasia and the Americas
Zulu, 1818–1906
The Zulus
The Zulu War: Twilight of a Warrior Nation (with Ian Castle)

Marching to the Drums

Eyewitness Accounts of War
from the Kabul Massacre
to the Siege of Mafikeng

Edited by Ian Knight

GREENHILL BOOKS, LONDON
STACKPOLE BOOKS, PENNSYLVANIA

Marching to the Drums
first published 1999 by Greenhill Books, Lionel Leventhal Limited,
1 Russell Gardens, Park House, London NW11 9NN
www.greenhillbooks.com
and
Stackpole Books, 5067 Ritter Road, Mechanicsburg, PA 17095, USA

British Library Cataloguing in Publication Data
Marching to the drums : eyewitness accounts of war from the Kabul
massacre to the siege of Mafikeng
1. Great Britain. Army – History 2. War – History – 19th century
I. Knight, Ian, 1956–
355.3'0941

ISBN 1–85367–372–2

Library of Congress Cataloging-in-Publication Data
Marching to the drums : eyewitness accounts of war from the Kabul
massacre to the siege of Mafikeng / edited by Ian Knight.
p.   cm.
Includes bibliographical references (p.) and index.
ISBN 1-85367-372-2
1. Military history, Modern--19th century. I. Knight, Ian, 1956–.
D361.M36 1999
355'.009'024--dc21   99-35088
                                                 CIP

Typeset by Wyvern 21, Bristol, England
Printed and bound in Great Britain by
Creative Print and Design (Wales), Ebbw Vale

Contents

List of Illustrations and Maps

Illustrations (pages 161–76)

Maps

The World at War
1837–1902

Date	The British Empire at War	The Rest of the World
1839–42	First Afghan War Opium War, China	
1841–44		French campaigns in Algeria
1845–46	First Maori War, New Zealand	
1846	First Anglo-Sikh War	Mexican/American War
1846–47	Seventh Cape Frontier War, South Africa	
1848		'Year of Revolutions', Europe
1848–49	Second Anglo-Sikh War	
1850–53	Eighth Cape Frontier War, South Africa	
1851–65		Taiping Rebellion, China
1852	Second Burma War	
1854–56	Russian War (Crimea, etc)	
1856–60	Dagu Forts expeditions, China	
1857–58	Indian Mutiny	
1857–59		French campaigns, north Africa
1859–84		French conquest of Indo-China
1860–72	Second Maori War, New Zealand	
1861–65		American Civil War
1863–86		U.S./Apache Wars

1865–89		Plains Wars, USA
1866		Prussian/Austrian War
1868	Abyssinian expedition	
1870		Franco-Prussian War
1873–74	Asante campaign, West Africa	
1877–78		Russo-Turkish War
1878–80	Second Afghan War	
1879	Anglo-Zulu War	
1881	Transvaal War (First Boer War)	
1882	Egyptian expedition	
1884–99	Sudanese campaigns	
1885–92	Third Burma War	
1892		French expeditions, West Africa
1894–96		Italian/Abyssinian War
1898		Spanish/American War
1899–1900		Boxer Rebellion, China
1899–1902	Anglo-Boer War	

Introduction
by Ian Knight

For much of the nineteenth century, the voice of the ordinary British soldier, who served in the ranks on the far-flung boundaries of the Empire on which the sun never set, was seldom heard, even by his own countrymen.

This was ironic, since it might be argued that more than just the military muscle of the Empire rested on the broad and often-bloodied back of the red-coat. The Empire expanded slowly and inevitably along lines of world-wide trade, and the profits from mercantile expansion fuelled the emerging industrial revolution and the rise of the middle classes at home. It was not strictly true, as the old saying had it, that trade followed the flag; often, the flag followed trade. As King Cetshwayo of the Zulu ruefully observed, 'first comes the trader, then the missionary, then the red soldier'. Traditionally, British geographers liked to colour red on the globe those new areas added to British influence; and red could scarcely be a more appropriate colour, for seldom was imperial expansion executed without bloodshed. Thousands of indigenous inhabitants died resisting the imposition of what the British liked to consider 'progress' and 'civilisation'; and thousands of British soldiers died, too, executing policies which originated in the far-off centres of Imperial administration. The world may have moved on today, and come to regard the ideology and politics of Empire in a jaundiced light, but that does not detract from the sacrifice of generations of soldiers and administrators who paid the ultimate price for what they believed to be their duty. From the rain forests of West Africa to the heady mountains of Tibet, from the gold-fields of Australia to the Balkans, there were few parts of the world which did not produce their sad crop of forlorn crosses that were forever England.

Yet only late in the history of the British Empire did the public at home come to express any sense of appreciation for what their army had achieved and endured on their behalf. Queen Victoria was on the throne for so long that her realm underwent huge social changes during her reign alone. When she came to power in 1837, Wellington was still Commander-in-Chief, and the young officers who had served under him against Napoleon in the Peninsula, or in

Belgium at Waterloo, had grown to become conservative and cliquish generals under his patronage. The Iron Duke had firm views on the natural order of the society; officers were drawn from the gentry, who were born to exercise authority, while the ordinary soldiers – recruited from the impoverished, illiterate, usually unemployed and often desperate labouring class – were still widely regarded as the 'scum of the earth'. For at least the first half of the nineteenth century, the standing of the army in civilian society was so low that many families considered it a greater shame to lose a son into the army than to see him sent to prison. And indeed, the lot of the ordinary soldier in the early Victorian period has little to commend it to modern eyes. Soldiers enlisted for long periods – twenty-five years, which often so exhausted them that they were fit for nothing else upon their discharge – and could expect to spend years at a stretch in remote imperial garrisons, a prey to all manner of strange diseases which thrived in crowded and insanitary barracks. The daily routine was one of repetitious drill, and soul-destroying boredom, which many soldiers sought to escape in the cheap drink supplied within the barracks by licensed contractors. Any lapse of discipline was liable to be punished by rigorous use of the infamous 'cat o'nine tails'. Active service offered at least the chance of excitement, adventure, and possibly prize money, but it was paid for with the physical hardship of long marches over inhospitable terrain and often in appalling weather, and punctuated with bouts of ferocious violence, often conducted, in the days before rifled muskets, at brutally close range. Medical facilities were limited, surgery savage, and disease inevitable.

The civilian public in Britain had little experience of military life, beyond the sight of soldiers drinking, brawling and whoring in the public houses which thrived in garrison towns. Nor did it have much idea of the soldier's trade, for there had been no serious military activity on British soil since Culloden and the collapse of the '45. It was not until the advent of the first illustrated papers in the 1840s that the literate middle classes, at least, were able to gain some insight into the activities of their own armies. Even then, forty years before it was possible to reproduce photographs in the press, their impressions of the conflicts which charted the growth of the Empire were inevitably stilted. The pictures – engravings, based on drawings made on the spot – were carefully sanitised, and the texts written to reassure, often ripe with indignant with tales of insults offered to the British Crown by minor potentates beyond the borders, and righteous with tales of punitive expeditions and gallant heroism.

Yet the advent of the illustrated press set in motion a process which would change not only the relationship between the army and civilian society, but the nature of the British army itself. The exposure by Russell of *The Times* and others of the deadly muddle and inefficiency of the Crimean campaign (1854–56) – which was no worse than most campaigns of the Napoleonic era, but simply more reported – focused political and public attention on the army in a way it never had before. The result was an erratic but ultimately comprehensive pro-gramme of reforms which made the army of 1900 – at the end of the Great Queen's reign – scarcely recognisable from the one she had inherited, and which mirrored important shifts in civilian society. While huge social gulfs still existed between officers and men, the worst excesses of corporal punishment had been abandoned, living conditions were greatly improved, educational levels were far higher, along with the efficiency and effectiveness of the army in the field.

These changes were introduced against a background of almost constant war-fare. For an institution usually characterised – with some justification – as being inherently conservative and hide-bound, the late Victorian army was called upon to be remarkably flexible in the field. From the 1860s to 1902 it was required to fight enemies as varied as the Maoris of New Zealand, the Asante ('Ashanti') of West Africa, the Chinese, the Mahdists of the Sudan, Pathan tribesmen on the North-West Frontier, the Zulu and the Boers. While the army was usually under-strength, ill-informed and badly supplied in the field – circumstances which inevitably produced a fair share of disasters – only one campaign over that period resulted in consistent military and political defeat, the Transvaal revolt of 1881. Even the Anglo-Boer War (1899–1902), which has passed into popular mythol-ogy as an example of the unimaginative use of inappropriate strategy and obsolete tactics, was actually a military victory, in which British troops learned – eventually – how to outmanoeuvre, pin-down and exhaust into submission a highly mobile and resourceful enemy.

All of these campaigns were reported in the British press. By the 1870s, editors had come to realise that the appetite of the reading classes for tales of military adventure overseas was almost inexhaustible. Readers thrilled with horror at the stories of disasters like Isandlwana or Maiwand that unfolded over their break-fast table – complete with highly inaccurate but pleasantly satisfying images of the dastardly foe – or swelled with pride at the news of some gallant stand at an exotic and unpronounceable spot on the very fringes of empire. By 1880, the illustrated papers had produced a new class of journalist to pander to this taste, the 'special correspondent', who travelled the world's trouble-spots, sending back vivid accounts of the mayhem around them, and which often included their own adventures centre-frame.

For most of the Victorian period, then, the British public had a decidedly un-realistic appreciation of the realities of the warfare of their age. War was a bold, glorious, 'Boy's Own' adventure, waged by a resolute, manly, thin red line of heroes – at least until the universal adoption of khaki in the late 1880s – whose image seemed curiously at odds with the reality of the roistering drunks they still encountered outside home barracks.

The Victorian view of warfare was all the more unrepresentative because it included almost no perspective from the vast majority of common soldiers. Wars were reported by professional journalists, or by amateur correspondents among the army itself, who were almost always officers, for whom writing was an increasingly fashionable pursuit. And while the occasional letter from a private soldier was sometimes published at home – more often in the local rather than the national press, where it would be of more interest to his friends and family – full-length memoirs were almost always confined to the officer class. While literacy levels rose enormously between 1870 and 1900, few ordinary soldiers were capable of the sustained effort necessary to write a book, and there was, in any case, little market for them. Those that were published were usually rare stories of the author's rise through the ranks – such as Sir William Robertson's *From Private to Field Marshal* – or were intended to appeal to a particular dedicated market, such as Edward McToy's essay on the virtues of temperance on campaign, *A Brief History of the 13th Regiment in South Africa during the Transvaal and Zulu Difficulties.*

That the voice of the Other Ranks was so rare adds particular interest to the eye-witness accounts included in this volume. All are accounts by ordinary soldiers or, at best, NCOs; unlike more recent anthologies, these were published during the soldiers' lifetimes. The majority of these accounts are drawn from a series which appeared in the monthly *Royal Magazine*, between 1905 and 1911, under the series title 'Survivors' Tales of Great Events'. The series was the result of interviews conducted by staff writers, chiefly Walter Wood, who specialised in military and naval subjects, and focused on a number of dramatic incidents which had been head-line news over the previous sixty years.

Most were military, and almost all of them *British* military (though there were accounts of famous actions from around the world, such as Gettysburg and Sedan), though there were also a number of tales of sea-faring adventure, shipwreck, and civilian disasters such as colliery explosions, earthquakes and riot.*

The range of subjects selected for the present volume reflects the contemporary bias. Already, by 1905, the hey-day of Victorian military adventure was receding. The Great Queen was dead, and many of the events described had taken place at least a generation before, and were already assuming the qualities of a heroic by-gone era. The choice of interviewees reflected the level of popular interest in particular subjects at that time, and it is interesting to note that this has remained broadly similar to those of today. The series began with Private Alfred Henry Hook's account of Rorke's Drift – still arguably the most famous battle of the Victorian era, nearly a century after his interview – and went on to consider the Crimea, India, the North-West Frontier and South Africa in some depth. In some cases, the same campaign might be covered by two or three interviews of different participants; this was particularly true of the Crimea and

* For a full list of the 'Survivors' Tales' series from *The Royal Magazine*, see James Bancroft's article, 'Survivors' Tales of Great Events', in *Soldiers of the Queen*, the Journal of the Victorian Military Society, Issue 91, December 1997.

Sudan campaigns. Other campaigns, such as the wars against the Maori in New Zealand, or the Abyssinian campaign, received token coverage, limited to a single interview, which reflected then, as now, the lack of popular interest in the subject, rather than its historical importance. The series of costly campaigns waged on the Eastern Cape Frontier in South Africa, for example, which required one of the heaviest British military commitments of the Victorian era prior to the Crimean War, was represented solely by the famous story of the sinking of the transport *Birkenhead*.

The stories were interpreted for publication in a style which suited the time; brisk, stirring, and patriotic. His style is consistent throughout the interviews, yet it never entirely stifles the authentic voice of his subjects, which often speaks clearly to the reader, even now, of the unpalatable realities of the soldier's life in the nineteenth century. They also speak much of the opinions and attitudes of the time. It was not the duty of the ordinary soldier to question the wisdom of his political masters, or the strategies of his military ones, nor did many question the assumption that the British cause was essentially righteous. Few Victorian generals cared to explain their objectives to their men, and the view from the ranks was inevitably a narrow one, confined by ignorance and a sense of moral superiority. Yet it is interesting to note that most of the men interviewed spoke of their enemies with a respect born of an acknowledgement that they, too, were courageous men, who were usually fighting to defend their country against a foreign invader. Only in the accounts of the Indian Mutiny are their traces of the feelings of racial hatred and vengeance, provoked by initial rebel attacks on British civilians, which made this campaign unusually bitter and vicious.

Of course, it is true that many of these accounts were written years after the events they describe. While the most recent of them – the events of the Anglo-Boer War – were still fresh in the participants' minds, some, like the Mutiny itself, had taken place more than half a century before. The modern reader must make allowance for fading memories, and wonder to what extent the interviewer filled any gaps. By way of comparison and to add a different perspective on some events, accounts of some of the same actions have been added which appeared in *The Strand* magazine in the 1890s. Although useful, however, the *Strand's* series was both shorter and more limited in scope, confining itself to the accounts of men who had won the Victoria Cross in action.

Yet all of these accounts remain remarkably fresh. They are an important collection of first-hand historical material, and they provide a remarkably vivid insight into the human experience of Victorian warfare.

The 'Survivors' Tales of Great Events' series was illustrated by Stanley Wood, a popular illustrator of military subjects, then at the height of his powers. Stanley Wood's pictures were the visual equivalent of the text; designed to stir the blood of Englishmen who had probably never heard the clash of cold steel, or seen a shot fired in anger. Wood's style was extremely animated, and his pictures are

replete with manly heroes, defying the odds with blazing eyes and fixed bayonets; cavalrymen charge full-pelt straight towards the observer, eyes wild, hooves
thundering and nostrils flaring. A number of Wood's original illustrations are
included in the present work, as they add immeasurably to the flavour of the text;
by way of a contrast, some more sober images of the same conflicts have also
been added.

This book grew out of my study of the Victorian soldier on campaign, *Go To
Your God Like A Soldier*. In writing a book which attempted to encapsulate so
much of the experience of the Victorian soldier, I came to feel a tremendous
sympathy for what the ordinary man in the ranks endured in the name of Queen
and country, and to realise how little his voice was heard. One might no longer
believe in the causes for which so many of his wars were fought, but one can
only respect his courage, endurance and astonishing adaptability. I hope this
book offers a readily accessible insight into his world, a world which was very
different – and much tougher – than our own, but which continues to shape our
lives on the very eve of the 21st century.

My acknowledgements here must largely mirror those in the earlier book. I
owe much to an association with the Victorian Military Society which has lasted
for more than twenty years. In particular, I must single out the Society's re-
enactment group, the Die-Hard Company, who have made the drill and
appearance of the mid-Victorian soldier come alive to myself, and so many others.
In particular, I cherish our experience together in Zululand in January 1999, when
we staged a re-enactment of the battle of Isandlwana on the field, as part of the
anniversary commemoration. The image of the Die-Hards skirmishing through
the green summer grass at the foot of Mount Isandlwana, dressed as the 24th
regiment, is likely to remain a moving one for a very long time to those who were
lucky enough to witness it. Among the individuals who have helped and supported my research I must especially thank Lieutenant Colonel Ian Bennett, who
has been unstinting in his advice about military matters which have confused this
mere civilian, and Michael Barthorp, who has shared some of his life-time's work
on the uniforms of the army in the field with me. Bryan Maggs has once again
allowed me access to his remarkable collection of Victorian photographs. As
usual, Keith Reeves and Ian Castle have been a most useful sounding board,
while my wife Carolyn and son Alexander have continued to tolerate that dreadful phrase – 'I can't, I've got work to do' – with remarkable good humour.

I have not meddled with the original accounts or their contemporary editing,
and the opinions they contain remain those of their time. I have very occasionally substituted words that have offensive overtones today. Victorian renditions
of foreign place names are sometimes at variance with modern orthography; I
have not altered place names in the eye-witness material, but have adopted modern spellings in my commentary, such as Panjab for Punjab, Asante for Ashanti,
Dagu for Taku and Mafikeng for Mafeking.

Select Bibliography

The campaigns waged by the British army between 1837 and the end of the Anglo-Boer War have resulted in literally thousands of books, ranging from contemporary eye-witness accounts to modern sociological studies. It would be both pretentious and a physical impossibility to list them here. A brief over-view of further reading can be found in the author's *Go To Your God Like a Soldier*, the following list merely identifies some more recent studies of the various campaigns described in this book, which might be a useful place to start for the new reader in the field.

General

Haythornthwaite, Philip, *The Colonial Wars Source Book*, London, 1995.
Knight, Ian, *Go To Your God Like A Soldier: The British Soldier Fighting For Empire*, London, 1996.
Spiers, Edward, *The Army and Society 1815–1914*, London, 1980.

The Crimea

ffrench, Blake, *The Crimean War*, London, 1971.
Lambert, Andrew, *The Crimean War: British Grand Strategy 1853–56*, Manchester, 1990.
Mollo, John, *The Valley of Death*, London, 1991.

Indian Mutiny

Hibbert, Christopher, *The Great Mutiny: India 1857*, London, 1978.
Ward, Andrew, *Our Bones are Scattered: The Cawnpore Massacres and the Indian Mutiny, 1857*, London, 1996.
Stokes, Eric, *The Peasant Armed: The Indian Revolt of 1857*, Oxford, 1986.

Afghanistan

Barthorp, Michael, *The North-West Frontier: British India and Afghanistan, a Pictorial History 1839–1947*, Poole, 1982.
Heathcote, T.A., *The Afghan Wars 1839–1919*, London, 1980.
Robson, Brian, *The Road to Kabul: The Second Afghan War 1878–1881*, London, 1986.

Abyssinia

Bates, Sir Darrell, *The Abyssinian Difficulty: The Emperor Theodorus and the Magdala Campaign of 1867–68*, London, 1979.
Myatt, Frederick, *The March to Magdala: The Abyssinian War of 1868*, London, 1970.

New Zealand

Belich, J., *The New Zealand Wars and the Victorian Interpretation of Racial Conflict*, London, 1979.
Gibson, T., *The Maori Wars: The British Army in New Zealand 1840–1872*, London, 1974.
Ryan, Tim, and Bill Parham, *The Colonial New Zealand Wars*, Wellington, 1986.

China

Beeching, J., *The Chinese Opium Wars*, London, 1975.
Mann, Michael, *China 1860*, Salisbury, 1989.

Asante (Ashanti)

Lloyd, Alan, *The Drums of Kumasi: The Story of the Ashanti Wars*, London, 1964.
Myatt, Frederick, *The Golden Stool: An Account of the Ashanti War of 1900*, London, 1966.

Egypt and the Sudan

Barthorp, Michael, *War on the Nile: Britain, Egypt and the Sudan 1882–1898*, Poole, 1983.
Harrington, Peter, and Frederic A. Sharf, *Omdurman 1898: The Eye-Witnesses Speak*, London, 1998.

Robson, Brian, *Fuzzy-Wuzzy: The Campaigns in the Eastern Sudan*, Tunbridge Wells, 1990.

Symons, Julian, *England's Pride: The Story of the Gordon Relief Expedition*, London, 1965.

Zulfo, Ismat Hasan, *Karari: The Sudanese Account of the Battle of Omdurman*, London, 1990.

South Africa

Castle, Ian, *Majuba: Hill of Destiny*, London, 1996.

Emery, Frank, *The Red Soldier*, London, 1978.

Knight, Ian, *Brave Men's Blood: The Epic of the Zulu War*, London, 1990.

Knight, Ian, *Nothing Remains But To Fight: The Defence of Rorke's Drift*, London, 1992.

Knight, Ian (ed.), *By The Orders of the Great White Queen: Campaigning in Zululand, 1879, through the Eyes of the British Soldier*, London, 1993.

Laband, John, *Rope of Sand: The Rise and Fall of the Zulu Kingdom in the 19th Century*, Johannesburg, 1995 (published in the UK as *The Rise and Fall of the Zulu Kingdom*).

Lee, Emanoel, *To the Bitter End: A Photographic History of the Boer War*, London, 1985.

Mostert, Noel, *Frontiers: The Epic of South Africa's Creation and the Tragedy of the Xhosa People*, London, 1992.

Pakenham, Thomas, *The Boer War*, London, 1979.

Pemberton, S. Baring, *Battles of the Boer War*, London, 1964.

Reitz, Denys, *Commando: A Boer Journal of the Boer War*, London, 1933 (many reprints)

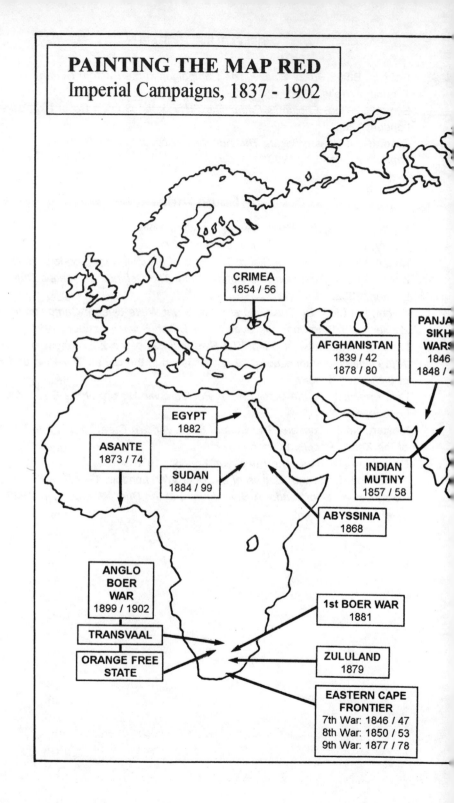

PAINTING THE MAP RED
Imperial Campaigns, 1837 - 1902

CRIMEA
1854 / 56

AFGHANISTAN
1839 / 42
1878 / 80

PANJA
SIKH
WARS
1846
1848 /

EGYPT
1882

ASANTE
1873 / 74

SUDAN
1884 / 99

INDIAN
MUTINY
1857 / 58

ABYSSINIA
1868

ANGLO
BOER
WAR
1899 / 1902

TRANSVAAL

ORANGE FREE
STATE

1st BOER WAR
1881

ZULULAND
1879

EASTERN CAPE
FRONTIER
7th War: 1846 / 47
8th War: 1850 / 53
9th War: 1877 / 78

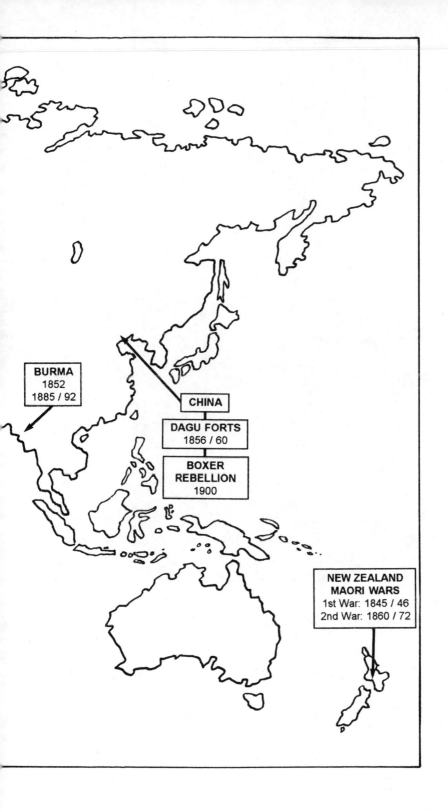

BURMA
1852
1885 / 92

CHINA

DAGU FORTS
1856 / 60

BOXER
REBELLION
1900

NEW ZEALAND
MAORI WARS
1st War: 1845 / 46
2nd War: 1860 / 72

1. The Crimea

When Queen Victoria came to the throne in 1837, the British army was already embroiled in protracted colonial entanglements around the world. A war on the Cape Frontier in southern Africa – the 6th – had recently been brought to a close, but a further outbreak was brewing. French settlers in Canada had broken into open revolt against British authority, while in New Zealand tension between Maori groups and British settlers was leading inexorably to war. In India, British interests on the North-West Frontier would shortly lead them to embark on the disastrous expedition to the Afghan capital, Kabul.

Yet while all of these campaigns preceded the Crimean War (1854–56), none was comparable in impact. The Crimean War was a watershed in the history of the British Army, a time when old practices and theories were tested in a new and terrible crucible, and found wanting; found wanting, moreover, in the full glare of press publicity, which exposed the army's failings to politicians and public at home in a way which had never happened before. For this reason, the Crimean War was without doubt the most crucial campaign of the early Victorian period.

In many ways, however, it was untypical of British military experience of the period. It was not, like all the other wars of the 1840s and '50s, waged to enlarge or secure colonial possessions; it was that rarity of the Victorian period, an essentially European war. It was waged by armies who fought and – for the most part – thought along European lines, who were armed, uniformed, and equipped in a European manner, and who followed broadly similar tactics. Indeed, there was little to differentiate it from the great clashes of the Napoleonic Wars forty years before, except that improved weaponry added a new destructive twist on the battlefield.

Moreover, the war arose out of issues of grand imperial strategy, not, as was so often the case, local expediency. The flash-point was an obscure religious quarrel in Jerusalem, but the war's origins lay in a deep-seated British fear of Tsarist Russia. While Russia had been hailed as a great ally in the distant days of the struggle against Napoleon, this had given way to suspicion of Russian motives as Russia had begun to expand her possessions in central Asia at the expense of the ailing Ottoman empire. To Britain, it seemed that the Russian drive through Asia had one ultimate goal; to threaten British interest in India. Indeed, fear of Russian intervention in Indian affairs, conducted through neighbouring Afghanistan – which spawned fifty years of spying adventures in remote mountain chiefdoms, the so-called 'Great Game' – remained a cornerstone of British policy throughout the nineteenth century.

By 1850, Russia was exerting considerable pressure on Ottoman Turkey. An argument between the Orthodox and Catholic Churches over access to the Holy sites in Jerusalem led to Britain and France aligning themselves against Russia, and when in 1853 Russia launched an invasion of the Turkish-held Balkans, Britain and France declared war in support of the Turks.

Yet the allies' objectives at the start of the war remained confused. France and Britain intended to launch an attack on Russia to ease pressure on the Ottoman Empire, but had no very clear idea of where that attack should take place. British and French troops embarked for the Black Sea – before the war was over, Britain had committed almost half her military strength to the campaign – but even as they sailed their generals were uncertain as to their plans. The expedition landed at Varna, only to find that the Russians withdrew their troops from the Balkans shortly thereafter. Still keen to make a demonstration, however, the allies decided to strike at the Russia port of Sebastopol, in the Crimean peninsula. The expedition landed, unopposed, at the ominously named Calamita Bay on 14 September 1854. Few of the allied generals had any idea of the geography of the peninsula, or the dispositions of the Russians. Indeed, most of the British generals were woefully inexperienced in modern warfare; most were in their mid-60s, and had last commanded troops under Wellington. They had little experience of commanding large formations, such as brigades and divisions, and were not used working to working together. These shortcomings, together with the almost complete breakdown of the British supply system, were to have an enormous impact on the subsequent campaign.

Let Sergeant-Major J. Parkinson of the 11th Hussars take up the story of those first confused days in the Crimea, and of the first major clash with Russian forces along the Alma river on 20 September. The story appeared in *The Royal Magazine*, where it was noted that Sergeant Major Parkinson served in the Crimea 'from first to last', and later took part in the famous charge of the Light Brigade. In later life, Parkinson put his military experience to good effect, and enlisted with the mounted police in London, and later with the Birmingham Police Force.

Publisher's note: throughout this book, original eye-witness accounts are set in a different typeface, to distinguish them from the editor's commentary.

The Battle of the Alma

Through the surf which broke and murmured on the shore, each man struggling with two horses, sometimes in the water, sometimes on the rafts, cold and drenched – that was how we landed in the Crimea. Our regiment was nearly nine hours in getting from the transport to the shore – yet it got there safely, and even if we shook and shivered in our soldier finery, that was better than being at the bottom of the sea, which some of the foreign troops had reached instead of the land.

We belonged to the Light Brigade – yes, I went through the Valley of Death with the Six Hundred – and we bivouacked as best we could. We had three days' rations, but no commissariat, and we got through the first miserable night in the land of the enemy as best we could. We wrapped ourselves in our cloaks and lay down and tried to sleep, but there was no rest for most of us. To begin with, there was the excitement of actual campaigning, and we did not know what was going to happen.

As a matter of fact, the very first night in the Crimea a remarkable thing resulted from the natural nervousness of the new troops in a new campaign. War is like most other things – you have to get used to it; it is full of surprises, too, and we received our baptism of fire in a very strange way.

Some of us were bivouacking, and some of us were sent at once on outlying piquet, as the cavalry in the Crimea called it; outpost duty, as the term now is.

I rode out with my comrades of the 11th Hussars towards the direction in which we knew the Russians must be. About half-a-mile from us our French allies were still landing from their ships. Suddenly, to our amazement, the darkness of the night was broken by flashes of fire, and the stillness was disturbed by the crackle of small arms.

What had happened? Who were firing on us? It could not be the Russians, because they were inland; it could not be our own comrades, who even in their excitement could not have opened fire on their own piquets, knowing where we were. There was only one explanation, and that was that the French, hearing but not seeing us, knowing that the Russians were in our direction, had mistaken us for the enemy and had instantly begun to pepper into us! And so in truth it was.

The very first shots that were fired in the Crimea were fired by our friends and allies.

We were in a desperate case. We knew that the potters were our allies, and we were thus prevented from retaliating; yet it was no pleasant thing to come by such an early and inglorious death.

What did we do? What could we do but dismount a good deal quicker than we had mounted, and shelter behind our saddles and our horses until the real truth dawned on our assailants. And providentially that was very soon, for they knew from the non-return of their fire that they were blazing away at friends. We heard the welcome and the soothing sound of 'Cease fire!' But the French had drawn some blood at least, because two or three of our horses were wounded. The precarious luck of war had saved us from death under fire before even a Russian had been seen.

That incident was mere comedy. We were soon enough to get more than our fill of the gloomy horrors of a long and woefully mismanaged war.

Our friendly baptism was swiftly followed by the first brush with the enemy himself, and a plunging into the sensations of meeting in the flesh the men of whom we had heard and talked so much, but had not yet beheld.

We had a day in which to settle down. Then early in the following morning we marched off in skirmishing order in front of the brigades of infantry, with two troops of Horse Artillery in our rear. It was a time for thrilling emotions, for eager anticipations, for a man to test himself and find out of what stuff he was made. Here we were, almost as soon as we had set foot in the Crimea, marching to seek the enemy, with every probability of a speedy finding.

The hours passed on, and the afternoon was wearing; then, abruptly and dramatically, we met the foe – and that part of it in which we as cavalrymen were so intensely interested – the Cossacks, of dreaded memory.

It was a wonderful first meeting of combatants. We came together; we knew that we were mortal enemies. Still we advanced without firing, drawn to one another as if magnetised, until we were near enough to laugh at each other. Not more than a hundred and fifty yards separated us; yet it was not until this short distance intervened that we crushed our mutual curiosity, remembered that we were there to fight and not to stare, and suddenly and simultaneously opened fire.

You might suppose, from our closeness to each other, even allowing for the nervousness and disorder which are inseparable from a first engagement, that there would have been blood enough and to spare shed in this opening meeting; yet it is an extraordinary fact that, although we were firing into each other for at least twenty minutes, not a man amongst us was hurt – only one was struck, and that was a trooper who was hit on the foot by a spent bullet!

And how did this come about, you ask? Well, you must remember that I am talking of fifty years ago, when a very slow-firing and imperfect carbine was in use – a weapon which even the smartest of men could not discharge more than once in two minutes. We fired from ten to twelve rounds of ammunition from the saddle – there was no dismounted firing by cavalry during the whole of the war. Nowadays two such forces so near to each other would suffer mutual annihilation in a few moments; but then, of course, they would never get so near except for sabre work.

But the Russians were not so fortunate as we had been. They shed blood to some extent, for the Horse Artillery dashed up and began firing, and the enemy retreated with the loss of several men. Grape and canister proved far more deadly than the carbine.

It was a striking opening to the war, and the effect of it upon us was remarkable, too. Our men stood their ground coolly – astonishingly calmly, indeed, considering that almost without exception they were young men – most of them youths, in fact – fresh from England. I believe this freedom from fear, when the firing had really begun, was due to the fact that no one was hurt. A feeling of great confidence was aroused, and our spirits rose to a high pitch.

If this was war, where were its horrors? They were to be revealed to us in all their nakedness only a day later by Alma river.

We of the Light Brigade were in a starving state, for by this time our three days' provisions had gone, and we had nothing to eat or drink. But Providence and energy – and again the luck of war – saved us from too much suffering. We were bivouacking on that night before the first great battle in the Crimea at a village called Bulganac. It was now forlorn and deserted, but some ducks and poultry, and a few sheep and pigs, had been left in the hurry of evacuation by the villagers, and we raided and captured them and roasted them over our camp fires as best we could, which was indifferently, as we had no cooking utensils. It was a welcome meal, and all we had to eat till the battle was over.

That was a memorable and fateful night. The battlefield was an arena of about five square miles, a valley commanded by two ranges. We, the Allies – British, French, and Turks – were in the valley; the Russians, equalling us in strength, were mustered in the hills. The object of the fight was to overcome and drive them away, and to do that the heights had to be stormed and captured.

Who that went through it can ever forget that night before the battle? It was dreary because of the intense cold and our own unreadiness for it – no tents, no comforts, no commissariat, none of the things which are needful nowadays to make your troops ready for contest; we had been dumped down on shore and hurried up to meet the Russians. But our gloomy bivouac ended when the morning broke – a cold, grey, misty morning which was in keeping with our spirits. Swift disease had carried off many of us in the night – yet there was no time for mournful contemplation. The players were mustered for the great game of death and triumph, and the game began with a general advance of the Allies at something after one o'clock, when the sun was high and hot.

A river and village ran parallel with each other under the first range of heights – a narrow river and a mean mud village. The miserable buildings had been filled with straw and other quickly-burning things – why, we did not learn until the battle opened, then the village burst into flames and smoke, and we saw that the purpose was to mask the fire of the Russian batteries, which immediately began to flash and boom in the hills.

Simultaneously with the outbreak of the fire in the huts and hills the British infantry forded the Alma, and began that desperate journey which those who could view it as we from our position saw it – the Light Brigade was posted on the left flank, ready for a swoop when the enemy should be broken – never hoped to see accomplished.

The Russian guns in the heights – there were 180 of them – roared and re-echoed, crashed and roared again. The valley below was torn with shot and shell, the troops were ploughed into, and the earth was thrown up about them. Men fell, slain or wounded – the first fruits of the war that was now raging in grim earnest – and it looked as if the red regiments would never reach the heights, and never scale and carry them. Yet they steadily drew nearer, gaining courage as they went. They never flinched from their purpose, never hesitated to obey that order which was always the 'Advance!' Covered by our own artillery fire, with chosen men picking off the gunners in the hills, the infantry forced its way by sheer cohesive strength, impelled by an unfaltering courage, to the burning village.

In face of such overwhelming odds it seemed incredible that the victory could be won at all, still more unlikely that at such an early stage of the engagement there should be a chance of knowing how the fight would end; yet, in my judgment, even then the turning point had been reached, for if troops could get across that ball-swept vale, surely they could not be held at bay when their blood was up, and the time for storming with the bayonet came!

It was marvelous and thrilling to watch these raw, untrained lads push steadily on in face of such determined odds. On that field of battle no man could see more than part of the fight – not more than part is ever seen by any individual; but the Light Brigade were able to witness as much of the engagement as anybody, and a fascinating panorama it was, too.

There was the undulating plain between the hills and the sea, intersected by the river; on it, in the battle-smoke, were the brigades of Allies, rolling in red ranks towards the heights. Many of the masses of troops were very solid, some of the regiments were widely scattered. Colours were flying bravely in the thick air, officers were loudly encouraging their men, the men themselves were shouting as they advanced, and with it all there was the ceaseless, dull crash of artillery, and the constant rattle of musketry. And there were those other noises also which begin with every fight – the shrieks

of the wounded and the groans of the dying – noises which are mercifully
mingled with the greater din of battle, or men could never face each other
in war. Combatants were shot dead by gun or musket; others were hideously
wounded. Still the ranks were kept together, still the Colours were held on
high, and the waving swords of the officers flashed in the grey smoke and
the gleams of sunshine.

There were a few – there always are, I think, in battle – whose hearts
failed them, and who managed to fall out and stay behind in the confusion;
but with these rare exceptions the redcoats panted on and up, and at last
there came the great moment when the first of them were in the very batteries
of the Russians. That was little more than an hour after the fight began –
a grand result, indeed, when you bear in mind that the heights were considered impregnable, and that the Russians calculated that, even if they were
constantly and desperately assailed, and fell at all, they could not be reduced
and taken in less than six or eight weeks. So sure were they of this that,
behind the second range of heights, they had built towers from which they
could comfortably watch the daily operations of the Allies.

The river, rugged ground, ruined buildings, burning huts, gardens, vineyards – all these and other obstacles had been safely passed, in defiance of
the Russian gunners and sharpshooters; now the very hills were reached, and
the hardest trial of the battle came. Could human courage stand the fire from
the very muzzles of the weapons and afterwards face the steel of the defenders? Could human strength, taxed so heavily by the desperate advance across
the open that men could scarcely speak, survive that final call to mount the
heights and drive the brave and sullen grey coats off?

The answer was first given by one of the British regiments – the 23rd
Royal Welsh Fusiliers. They stormed the Great Redoubt, the principal bat-
tery, and with Colours flying rushed with the bayonet upon the defenders.
One of the Colours was planted in the earthwork by Ensign Anstruther, and,
in the very act of fixing it in token of victory, the gallant subaltern fell dead.
The Colours dropped with him, and his blood was dyeing their silken folds.

Would his followers waver? Would they rally? For already the 23rd had
suffered terribly, and there is a limit to endurance. The answer to the unspo-
ken question was given instantly. Colour-Sergeant O'Connor snatched
the Colours from the stiffening hands, and, raising them triumphantly afresh,
he put new heart of grace into the 23rd. During the rest of the day he per-
sisted in carrying the precious trophy he had saved, although he himself
was shot through the chest. Afterwards he was given the Victoria Cross –
one of the very first to be won – and he rose to General's rank. He is living
still.

But the Great Redoubt was not yet wholly mastered. The enemy was
retreating, but he was dangerous still, and it was necessary to cripple him

as he went. The guns were already limbering up, and one of them was just about to drive off when Captain Edward Bell of the 23rd shouted to his company: 'Take that gun, lads!' He dashed forward as he spoke, outran his men, seized the leading horse, and actually, single-handed, made the gun a prize. He also was given the Cross for his valour.

Seven Crosses were won at the Alma, and most of them for gallantry about this period of the battle. There was Lord Wantage who, when his Scots Fusilier Guards wavered because the odds seemed hopelessly against them, stood rock-like against the Colours, and rallied his men; there was Sergeant John McKechnie, who in that supreme moment also raised his rifle and shouted: 'By the centre, Scots! By the centre! Look to the Colours, and march by them!' Sergeant John S. Knox and Private Reynolds, too, were awarded the decoration for rallying the regiment that day – a rare quartette of honours; and there was another hero in Sergeant John Park, of the 77th Regiment, who gained the Cross for many acts of courage at the Alma.

While these few men were doing things which won them lasting glory, the brave fellows who fought and bled and died and whose names have been forgotten, even if they were ever known, were holding grimly to their work, firing when firing was possible, falling back on sabre or bayonet when steel was needed, and never flinching from the death which played about them, never turning from the stern purpose of winning those frowning heights. They were thrilled and stimulated by the knowledge of success, encouraged by the capture of the Great Redoubt, heartened by the raising of the British Colours in the very stronghold of the foe.

Every soldier will tell you that there is nothing more demoralising than to be inactive under fire. It is more than human flesh can endure to remain a mere target, getting all the fire and giving none. In this respect at least war makes man unselfish. We of the Light Brigade were very much in that position, for we were within range of the Russian guns, and in the line of fire of some of the artillery. The result was that round shot from the heights plumped into us from time to time, and made us jump, I can tell you. But a special Providence appeared to watch over us, because we suffered no casualties worth mentioning.

I have told you that there were a few waverers – was ever a battle fought which had not some, at least, of them? – but there were noble heroes, too, humble soldiers, who fought as well as the very best, and for whom there was nothing at the finish but a soldier's grave. I do not think that the Alma made a truer hero than a Foot Guardsman whom I saw. Early in the fight he was wounded, yet he would not leave the ranks; he would not fall out; he would hold on until he sank. He tried to keep up with his regiment, and for a little while he did so, supported by his courage and excitement, but, more than all, his sense of duty. Then he was overcome by loss of blood, he dropped behind, he lagged, he lost his place. The regiment rushed on and left him – it could do nothing else.

The brave Guardsman had done his duty, and he could do no more. To reach the heights was hopeless, impossible; to fall, with horse artillery and cavalry sweeping the plain, was to run a serious risk of being killed by hoofs or crushed by gun-wheels. He could just walk, and he used his last remaining strength to come towards us and find refuge in our ranks. He advanced a little, he gained ground slightly, he came slowly nearer, and we were ready to receive him with a cheer of friendship and protection. Then, almost in the midst of those who could have helped him, saved his life, perhaps, he fell on that too bloody field. A shot had struck him, and he never moved again.

The general wish amongst the men of the Light Brigade before we received the order to advance was to get into action; but, of course, as cavalry, we could not work until the first range of heights was taken, and the Russians driven out into the open, where we could get amongst them. So we had to bide our time, and wait as patiently as we could – and that was not very patiently with some of us.

I vividly recollect the case of my old – nay, I must say, young – comrade, George Wootton, a Cheltenham man, who was riding on my left in the ranks. The excitement of battle suddenly overcame him – he was at all times rather emotional – and seized with an overwhelming wish to be in the thick of the fight, he made as if he would dash straight out of the ranks. Just as he was talking wildly a shell from the heights struck the ground not more than ten or a dozen yards in front of us. Wootton's terrified horse reared straight up, and would literally have gone over if we had not caught hold of the reins, and managed to keep him down and calm him. That sobered George for the time, and he got plenty of opportunity to work off his agitation a few minutes later.

Poor George! He was killed in the charge of the Light Brigade five weeks later. It was said amongst us then that his excitement was his undoing, for, overcome by it, he rode out of the ranks, and rushed to meet the doom which was certain to any solitary horseman in that fatal valley.

So far I had been a witness of the horrors and excitement of a battlefield from a distance. Now I was plunged into the thick of the conflict, and abruptly confronted by all the dangers of a stricken field. At such a time the incidents of war make a far deeper impression on your mind than those with which you make acquaintance as a veteran, even as the earliest happenings in one's life stand out more clearly than the later events.

One thing in particular I recall. The Horse Artillery had fired two rounds from each gun, and were advancing across the valley, the Light Brigade following them. As we rode after the retreating masses I saw a Russian lying on the ground, apparently dead. Not knowing that the cavalry were following the guns, he turned over on his side.

Then I saw that he had his rifle underneath him, and that he had raised it and fired at one of the men, who was riding on the back of a gun-carriage. The man was badly wounded, and the Russian was instantly killed by one of our troopers as we rode past. If he had remained still he would have been unhurt, for no British sabre would have been raised to cut him down. His was not the only case of treachery that day – there were many others; and we became sadly accustomed to this feigning of death in the Crimea by Russians who were scarcely wounded at all, so that they could bring down at least one of the Allies.

We kept up the pursuit until we were ordered to halt, and in spite of all that has been said about the feebleness of the harrying of the flying Russians, I think, as I have always thought, that if once they had pulled themselves together and rounded on us we should have been destroyed, and the heights would have been recaptured, because there were such hosts of them, and the advantages they possessed were so great.

I can assure you that at the beginning of the battle I had little doubt as to the result, and that was that we should be compelled to abandon our attempt, and that victory, if it came at all, would be long delayed.

Yet all my gloomy fears had vanished long before we were recalled from the vale between the ridges, and knew that within three hours the first great, glorious victory of the Crimea had been won.

We had suffered heavily – the brave old 33rd Foot had lost nineteen sergeants in killed alone, mostly slain in defence of the Colours, and many British officers had perished.

The dead lay thick about the valley and in the hills, yet we were exuberant enough when we bivouacked on our first, hard-won, stern battlefield, and by our camp fires told and heard of the strange things that had been done and seen. We listened to the tales of French plundering, and listened all the harder because we ourselves had been forbidden to loot; and we heard of the curious discoveries, in the abandoned rifle-pits, of small barrels of a Russian drink called arrack, and of black bread and provisions which were plentiful enough to last six weeks. The British soldier of the Crimea was equal to almost any drink, but even he would not have been proof against the arrack, supposing he had been allowed to take it, which he was not; and so the spirit was emptied out of the casks and allowed to run to waste.

Victory is very much like other novelties. After the excitement comes the reaction; and there were none of us so callous as not to feel the effects of the battle before the morning came. Those were hard days, remember, when troops went forth to kill more deliberately than now, I think, because they were not so highly educated; for education, let people say what they will against it, is a great humaniser.

Besides, our weapons were cruder and more cruel, and hosts of poor fellows, who in these days would be saved by the skill of the surgeons, were then left to a certain fate. There was no help for it. Appliances were scarce, and the wounds that were inflicted by the old, big bullets were much more terrible than the clean perforations of to-day.

Even as we were rejoicing over our success, there were those of our own side, and amongst the Russians, too, who were vainly calling for the help which could not be afforded to them. The hot day was followed by the bitter night, and through heat and cold they had to lie on the field of battle. Thus, many who had survived the engagement itself succumbed before the day broke. And our own hot blood, too, was cooled, so that there was many a sorrowful heart amongst us when the flush of victory had passed.

You may liken our case to that of fighters with a great conflagration. While the flames are raging all is thrill and commotion, there is no time or inclination to count the cost, or contemplate the havoc which is being wrought; but when the fire has died away, and nothing but the charred timbers and gutted walls are left, how great the contrast, how cooled the spirits of the fighters! So it was with us by Alma River, and I do not minimise the courage of any of the troops engaged when I say that even then, at the very beginning of the war, there were those who would gladly have laid down their arms and hailed the tidings of peace.

And how much more gladly they would have welcomed such intelligence if they could have foreseen the sufferings and horrors which the Crimea had in store for them! Lucky, indeed, it was that for the present they were mostly possessed with the intoxication of a great and crushing victory.

The joy of triumph was succeeded by the gloom of burial. For two days after the battle we were burying our dead in the riflepits, and our wounded were collected and taken into hospital or on board ship. The rifle-pits were covered in and we left our fallen sleeping on the heights which they had won.

Two years later, as one of Lord Gough's escort, I visited the battlefield again. The vineyards were there, the broken ground, the ruined village, the murmuring river – all seemed strangely unchanged.

Yet there was one new thing. When we marched from the Alma the rifle-pits were raw with new earth. The earth was seen no longer – for man-high grass was softly waving over our comrades' graves.

The battle of the Alma had proved a significant allied victory, although the nature of their attack – in the open, across steeply rising ground – had led to heavy casualties. Nevertheless, the battle had effectively cleared the road, for the

Russian garrison retired into Sebastopol. Just a few days after the battle, the allies resumed their advance.

Their route led them to approach Sebastopol from the north, but the Russians had anticipated this, and had heavily fortified the port's northern defences. Instead, the allies swung wide of the Russian position, and circled round to approach Sebastopol from the less well-defended south. Unknown to the allied generals, the Russian commander, Prince Menshikov, at the last minute decided not to risk being invested in Sebastopol, and slipped away with the bulk of his command into the Crimean interior. This was a risky move, and the British almost blundered into the Russian rear-guard as it moved across their front, but the Russians were successful. By the time the allies surrounded Sebastopol, they found it guarded by just 16,000 men, with a much larger army, commanded by Menshikov, poised menacingly to their rear.

In surrounding Sebastopol, the allies effectively occupied the entire Sebastopol peninsula, with the exception of the port itself. With free access to the coastline, the allies selected the supply bases which would effectively shape their lines of communication. While the French, however, secured two open beaches to the west, the British commander, Lord Raglan, opted for the port of Balaclava to the south. Although superficially this had much to recommend it – it consisted of a narrow inlet commanded by hills on all sides – it soon proved far too small for the task in hand, and would remain hopelessly congested throughout the war.

By this time the Russians had extended their fortifications across the southern approaches to Sebastopol, and the allies had lost any chance of mounting a decisive attack. Instead, they began construction of a system of siege lines which effectively cut off Sebastopol from the interior.

Prince Menshikov, meanwhile, had been steadily reinforced by troops shipped to the Crimea from across the Sea of Azov to the east. Circumstance had placed the British lines nearest his own position, and Menshikov soon realised that the British were weakest along their lines of communication. Indeed, the defences of the port of Balaclava itself largely rested on a series of hastily-constructed redoubts lying along a ridge to the north of the inlet. These were lightly manned by Turkish troops and British artillery.

On 25 October Menshikov swept down on the redoubts from the east, rolling them up one by one, with little resistance. Only when Russian cavalry tried to advance on Balaclava itself were they checked by a resolute stand from Sir Colin Campbell's 93rd Highlanders – the famous 'thin red streak, tipped with steel'. A further Russian cavalry movement was countered by a determined charge from the British Heavy Cavalry Brigade. Menshikov at this point seems to have decided to cut his losses, and to withdraw from the field, carrying away British artillery abandoned in the redoubts.

The stage was now set for one of the most famous incidents in Victorian military history. To British observers on the rising ground towards Sebastopol, including

Lord Raglan, it seemed that the Light Cavalry Brigade, drawn up in reserve at the foot of the heights, were ideally placed to intercept the Russian withdrawal by attacking their flank, and to recover the guns. Orders were sent to instruct the Light Brigade to advance; tragically, from the foot of the heights, the intention of these orders was none too apparent to the Brigade commanders, Lord Lucan and Lord Cardigan, whose view was restricted by folds in the ground. From their perspective, the only guns visible were Russian batteries lying at the far end of a valley ahead of them. Urged on by Lord Raglan's ADC, Captain Nolan, the Light Brigade began to move forward; not, as Raglan had intended, to harass the Russian flank, but straight up the heavily-defended 'valley of death'.

Fifty years later, one of the veterans of the Light Brigade, H. Herbert of the 4th Light Dragoons, described the battle to the *Royal Magazine.**

The Charge of the Light Brigade

The object of the Russians was to capture Balaklava Harbour, and so bring about the loss of our base. But the harbour was strongly fortified on the heights surrounding it; and in addition a frigate was moored broadside on at the top of the harbour, so that she was able to sweep the surrounding country with her guns.

We thought we were to attack the Russians on October 22nd or 23rd, 1854, but we did not do so until the 25th, the day of the charge. Of course our staff must have observed a movement amongst the Russians, whom they could see through their glasses; but to us, with the naked eye, they were invisible. We had been continually standing to our horses, and were doing so during the greater part of the 24th, returning to our camp late at night. It was the custom on active service in those days to turn out and stand to our horses for two hours before daybreak, and on the 25th we turned out about four o'clock. The weather was cold and miserable, and we had slept on the ground under our tents, fully dressed and armed. We had nothing to eat or drink before turning out.

The Light Brigade was formed up not far from where the charge afterwards took place. It consisted of the 4th Light Dragoons, 8th Hussars, 11th Hussars, and 13th Light Dragoons, all of which are now Hussar regiments, and the 17th Lancers.

Our pickets suddenly gave the alarm that the Russians were attacking,

* By way of personal details it was stated that Mr Herbert had risen to the rank of Sergeant during his time in the army. When he left he started business as a builder, and worked for twenty years 'until misfortune overtook him'. In later life he worked as a night-watchman. For ten years he was chairman of the Balaklava Relief Committee, which sought to help veterans of the battle who had fallen on hard times.

and we advanced across the plain to the three British redoubts which were the object of the Russian attack. The redoubts were manned by a few British artillerymen and Turks. The Russians abruptly loomed up out of the dull grey of the morning, and immediately shells and cannon-balls were falling amongst us, and screaming over our heads.

As I sat on my horse I took particular notice of the Russian lines as they advanced to attack us; and I have often thought that they resembled the keys of a piano under the fingers of a clever player. Some of the keys seem to fall out and reappear rapidly; and so it was with the Russian ranks as our artillerymen played upon them — only the keys which disappeared did not come up again. A great many of the Russians fell, dead or wounded, as they advanced.

Very soon we found that the Russians had carried the redoubts, for the guns — our own guns — were turned upon us. As soon as the redoubts were taken, we saw the Turks rushing out of them and tearing pell-mell down the eminences and across the plain towards us. I remember how freely our men cursed them, and how little the Turks seemed to care whether they were cursed or blessed. As they flew past they shouted to us, 'Bono, bono, Johnny!' meaning 'Good, good' — they called all Englishmen in the Crimea Johnny, but our men shouted back, 'No Bono!' and swore fearfully.

The I Battery of the Royal Horse Artillery had already dashed up and gone past us in magnificent style, and had opened fire on the Russians. Shortly afterwards I saw Captain Maude, commanding the battery, carried away to the rear, with either an arm or a leg — I think it was a leg — shattered.

As soon as our commanders found that the Russians had got our range from the redoubts we retired back upon our own camp, which was towards Balaklava. There was a large plain extending from these redoubts, so that we had a good level surface to ride on.

We retired, the shot and shell playing on us continuously. The Russians at the same time advanced their cavalry — masses of them, and some of them remarkably handsome regiments, too. Amongst them were hussars dressed in light blue.

While we were retiring across the plain, the Russians following, the Heavy Brigade, under Sir James Yorke Scarlett, prepared to charge. The Heavy Brigade consisted of the Scots Greys, the Inniskilling Dragoon Guards, the Royal Dragoons, and the 4th and 5th Dragoon Guards. At first the Russian cavalry were galloping down the hill, but the sudden appearance of the 'Heavies' stopped them, and they came on at a walk. Sir James instantly swept on, dashed into them, and with his 600 men scattered 3000 Russians.

The Heavy Brigade advanced splendidly, and made a grand charge. They went right through the enemy, and at the same time the guns were supporting them with a smart and telling fire. We were a little bit too much to the left to see the charge itself fully; but we could hear the din of the fight.

If the Light Brigade had dashed on the Russians' right flank and followed up the terrific charge of the 'Heavies' there is no doubt, I think, that we could have annihilated the Russians on the spot. It was a grand opportunity for the Light Brigade; but it was lost.

After this there was a lull in the fight, and we thought the battle was over. We were ordered to take ground to the left, and reached some rising ground at the top of the valley, where we halted.

We next proceeded to dismount, and stood to our horses for some time. A few men were able to take a snack of something to eat, but only those who had saved part of the last rations issued on the previous day, for on that morning we had turned out in a violent hurry, and there was no time to do little odds and ends of work that had been overlooked.

For instance, the straps under my trousers were still unbuttoned, because in the hurry of mounting I had had no time to secure them. The riding and galloping about had made me very uncomfortable. There were no jackboots in those days – soldiers are very differently provided for in these times, I can assure you – and my trousers had wriggled up my legs.

I said to a comrade of mine, a young fellow from Birmingham, named Fletcher: 'Tom, will you button up my straps for me?'

He willingly obliged, and was just finishing the job when Captain Nolan galloped up to Lord Lucan.

What passed between Captain Nolan and Lord Lucan I cannot pretend to know, because I was not close enough to hear anything; but at any rate Lord Cardigan shouted: 'Stand to your horses, men! Prepare to mount! Mount!'

The trumpeters of the different regiments sounded these orders, and we sprang into our saddles.

The order was then given: 'The Light Brigade will advance!'

We knew one thing – we knew what was expected of us, for two or three days before the charge Lord Lucan had addressed us, saying: 'Keep your horses well in hand, men, and obey your officers; but when you get in amongst the Russians, skiver them well!'

As he spoke he gave us with his own sword an illustration of what he meant – which was pointing and cutting with the weapon.

Lord Lucan had previously served in the Russian army. He was a regular fire-eater. Lord Cardigan and he were a well-matched pair in that respect.

We knew that we were going into something pretty desperate; but we did not realise what was in store for us. Not a soul suspected that.

The advance began. We had not got more than two or three hundred yards when the Russians bellowed fire from three batteries of guns, with ten guns in a battery. There were ten on our left, ten on our right, at a distance of about a mile, and ten at the bottom of the valley, with their muzzles pointing directly at us. All these batteries were field guns, and very much superior to ours.

The batteries poured in a fearful fire from these three quarters – straight ahead and on our right and left; and, in addition, there must have been great numbers of Cossacks and infantry in ambush on our right, because from that direction also a murderous fire was coming.

Rushing into the 'jaws of death' like that our men dropped from their saddles by dozens. Some were wounded, some were killed on the spot, and fell out of their saddles. There were cases of man and horse being literally blown to pieces by shells.

Soon after we had started, the wild rush of the living men was accompanied by maddened horses with emptied saddles.

The first man to fall in the charge was the officer who, rightly or wrongly, had brought the order for it – Captain Nolan. He was ripped up the breast by a piece of shell and fell from his horse with terrible cries; but his foot got fixed in the stirrup and he was dragged for a considerable distance. Our own major – Major Halkett – was struck by a shell, or a cannon-ball, full in the chest and killed on the spot.

Very soon afterwards, my own chum, Tom Fletcher, was shot. He was a brave soldier and a splendid horseman; but the heavy fire was disorganising us, and he got a little behind me in his dressing – that is to say, he was not level with me in the line. I shouted: 'Keep up, Tom!' The words were no sooner out of my mouth than I heard a whizz and a thud, and a bullet which had just grazed me struck him in the back of the head. But he held on, wounded though he was, and fought till he was taken prisoner. He lived for a little while, but died not long afterwards in the Crimea.

The Light Brigade was advancing in three lines – the 13th Light Dragoons and the 17th Lancers forming the first, the 4th Light Dragoons and 11th Hussars the second line, and the 8th Hussars the third. Lord Cardigan was in command, and led the first line; Colonel Douglas led the second, and Lord George Paget the third. The 17th had lances, the rest of us carried swords, although as light cavalry we had been through the lance exercises.

From our starting-point to the place where the farthest guns – those at the lower part of the valley – were stationed was at least a mile and a quarter; and for the whole of that distance we rode through a perfect blaze of fire. So terrible was the flanking fire on our right and left, that when we had reached the bottom of the valley there were not more than about one hundred men remaining mounted.

We literally flew at the batteries; but by the time we got to the guns the first line of the Brigade had melted away. It had been almost annihilated by shot and shell.

When we reached the battery we found that the gunners and drivers had limbered up their guns and were slowly retreating. We galloped up and surrounded them as well as we could with our shattered numbers, and stopped them from going.

Then the most terrible part of the whole mad business came. The gunners tried to escape from the fury of our men by crawling under the guns; but the drivers had not time to get away from their horses. They were sabred as they tried to dismount, and a good many of our own men dismounted and struck the Russians under their own guns or routed them out at the point of the sword. At such a time nothing could escape – men had no time to think, and the very horses were cut and stabbed and killed. So far as my own recollection goes there was not a man or horse who escaped alive in the whole of the battery.

Many of our men were fighting dismounted, their horses having been killed by fire or steel. Some of them performed prodigies of valour, amongst them being Sam Parkes, a private of my own regiment. When we were mixed up with the guns Parkes was on foot, his horse having been killed. He was surrounded by Russians, and fought like a demon. In a curious way he got level with his officer, for he disobeyed an order. He was going for a Russian, and for some reason the officer shouted: 'Spare him, Sam!'

But Parkes was far too busy looking after his own skin, and the Russian had to go. He fought as long as he could, and then had to take his choice between surrender or being cut to pieces. He surrendered and was made prisoner, but not until his sword had been smashed by a shot. The Russians kept him for twelve months, then he was released, and was awarded the Victoria Cross for valour during the fight. For many years he lived at the Marble Arch, where he was the attendant.

Six Victoria Crosses were given for the charge of the Light Brigade, and three for the 'Heavies' – nine in all. No fewer than three of them went to the 17th Lancers.

We had captured the guns fairly enough, and for a short time they were actually in our possession; but the Russians were seen to be hurrying up large bodies of troops to rob us of the fruits of our charge. The enemy was seen by our officers.

Lord George Paget shouted to Colonel Shewell, commanding the 8th: 'We must rally on the Lancers, men!' evidently believing that a body of Lancers had advanced to our support. He was at that time looking up the valley – the 'Valley of Death.'

One or two of our men, amongst them a sergeant called Andrews, shouted back, 'But they're Russian Lancers!' Then Lord George replied that we must hold together and cut our way through them; and the order was given to go about and retire.

That, indeed, was the only thing we could do, because it was clear that the handful of men who were still lucky enough to be living could do nothing against the Russian masses who were now in motion against us.

To stay where we were was to be cut to pieces – and for nothing – inasmuch as we had no supports, and could not take the guns away. As for supports, it was fortunate, in a way, that we were without them; for if they had advanced they would have been served in the same way as the Light Brigade. There would have been no help for it, because the odds were so overwhelmingly against us.

When we went about we made for the Lancers, whom we now saw clearly enough. They were drawn up in a line right across the valley, not far from the points at which the flanking batteries on our right and left were placed.

Our horses were utterly winded, and terribly distressed with the galloping and charging down the valley for more than a mile. It was impossible to get them to go very fast; but the remnants of the five regiments obeyed the order to hold together, and went at the Russian Lancers.

As we came back I saw the officers commanding the Russians waving their swords, as if they were trying to bring the flanks of the Lancers round, so as to hem us in; but they seemed to me either to be afraid to move, or not to know what their officers were driving at. It was, of course, a disgraceful thing that they allowed a single man of us to get back again down the valley. Strictly speaking, not a soul in the Light Brigade should have been permitted to return, in view of the superior numbers of the enemy, their freshness, and our own exhausted state.

We rushed in amongst them, and there was a renewal of the cutting, slashing, pointing, and parrying of the earlier part of the fight. There was no fancy work, but just hard, useful business, and it fulfilled its object, for we cut our way through the opposing lancers.

There was a repetition of a savage thing that happened as we dashed down in the beginning – the Russian batteries continued to blaze away even when we were mixed up with their own people, and destroyed friend and foe alike. It was merciless butchery so far as their own soldiers were concerned, though it was fair enough in our case, as we were the object to be destroyed.

In addition to this artillery fire we had to bear the fire of the hundreds of Cossacks who were hovering on our flanks. Many a man who had gone through the charge in safety fell before the Cossacks' fire.

The charge had caused us to be scattered and utterly disorganised and separated, so that we retreated pretty well anyhow and as best we could.

Many a friend was missing, and some that I thought I should never see again were found. There was one amongst them, a member of my own troop, that I did not expect to set eyes on, but I overtook him during our retreat.

I saw that something was wrong, as he was terribly pale, so I said: 'Hello, Bill, what's the matter? Are you hurt?'

He said: 'Yes, I am; I'm shot through the foot.'

'Here, old boy,' I told him, 'you must get out of this. Hang on to the saddle and give me the reins. I'll get you through.'

I did get him through luckily, and when we were safely back I saw him taken off his horse. He was removed to one of the hospital ships in Balaklava Harbour, doctored, and invalided home. He wrote me a letter afterwards to say that he had heard I had got my first step towards being a general. So I had – I had been promoted to corporal.

A few lucky ones amongst us got safely back – and a melancholy return it was! Ages seemed to have passed since we charged down the valley, and yet the whole of the desperate business had been done well within half-an-hour.

We staggered in, some singly, some in twos, and some in threes; and the way we were met and cheered and helped showed how stunned those were who had been left behind, and had seen us going on an undertaking that looked like sheer madness and certain death for every man and horse.

The fire which had pretty well destroyed us had caused the Heavy Brigade some further losses, as they were on the slope behind us, and in the line of fire. That we should have suffered even more than we did at the finish is certain if it had not been for the action of some French cavalry, who advanced and silenced some of the Russian guns.

We were back at last – but what a handful! When we turned into our tents at night some of them were perfectly empty, for not a single man belonging to them was alive; while others, which had sheltered twelve soldiers in the morning, now held only two. The camp seemed quite deserted, and the shadow of death lay heavy upon it. Some of our brave fellows were, we knew, prisoners in the hands of the Russians, because their horses had been shot down, they were themselves wounded, and escape was impossible; but most of the missing were dead.

Between six and seven hundred of us had charged down the valley; when we were mustered for the roll-call it was found that half were missing, and when the final returns were prepared, it was shown that in that charge of a few minutes' duration 247 officers and men had been killed or wounded or were missing, while of the horses 475 had been killed and forty-two were wounded.

A never-to-be-forgotten night followed the day of the charge. The survivors turned into the tents, exhausted and miserable; but all the same I know that there was not a man who had come out of the charge who thought he had done anything more than his duty, and if the rest of the Light Brigade had been ordered to form up again for another charge not a man would have disobeyed.

Fully dressed and armed, with horses saddled and picketed to the ropes, we turned into our tents, and lay down to try to sleep. A wild and disturbing thing happened. In the middle of the night we were startled by a terrible shouting and commotion. The officers were halloing, and the guards were shouting 'Turn out! Turn out! The Russians are upon us!'

We roused up and rushed out of the tents to our horses. As we were getting the bits into their mouths I heard an officer shout: 'By —, men, turn out, or we shall be cut to pieces!' Almost as he spoke, a hundred or a hundred and twenty horses galloped madly right into our camp; but, luckily, although they were Russian, they were riderless. They were loose horses which had stampeded. All we had to do was to capture them as best we could.

On the morning after the charge, our men who had been taken prisoners by the Russians were paraded before the Russian general, Liprandi, who spoke very good English. He asked the men if they had had anything to eat, and was astonished when they said they had charged on empty stomachs. He gave them plenty to eat and drink, and saying that he thought they would, no doubt, like to write to their mothers and wives and sweethearts, he had them provided with ink and pens and paper.

He asked, 'What did you men have to drink this morning before you came down in the charge?'

They told him, 'Nothing.'

'Oh,' he said, 'I thought you were all drunk or mad!'

Then an Irishman said to him: 'By —, General, if we'd had anything to drink we should have had half Russia by this time!'

The general laughed and answered: 'Well, my man, if they were all like you, I believe you would!'

I do not remember the case of the butcher of the 17th Lancers, who, you say, joined his regiment fresh from the shambles, and rode through the charge with his pole-axe; but I can tell you of a case as amazing in its way, and one which shows the brutal discipline of the Crimea period.

There was a man in our regiment named Fox. When the order to advance was given he was on duty in the camp. He rushed to his horse, rode in the charge, and came safely back. And to what? The cat! He was court-martialled for leaving his post without orders and sentenced to receive fifty lashes.

The remnant of the 4th was paraded for the degrading and monstrous punishment, and Fox was tied to the wheel of a forge-cart. One of the farriers took a cat-o'-nine-tails and gave twenty-five strokes. At that time, when flogging was in vogue in the army, one man never gave more than twenty-five lashes, then a new man and a fresh cat were obtained.

When half the punishment had been given, the colonel said: 'Hold! I will forgive you the other twenty-five.' Fox, who was an Irishman, answered: 'Oh, don't. Please, colonel, I don't want to be beholden to you for anything. I'll take the other twenty-five!' The colonel said sternly: 'Silence, sir,' and had him marched off to the hospital marquee. The balance was never given. Fox was a desperate character, and a rough customer to deal with, it was true; but he was a fine soldier, and, considering what he had gone through, his punishment was out of all proportion to his crime.

After Balaklava we were under the command of the French general, D'Allenville, at Eupatoria. We tried very hard to get the Russians to have another brush with us, but they would never face us again.

It has always been a disputed point as to whether the trumpets sounded the 'Charge!' or not. The order was, 'Walk!' then 'Trot!' The men found that they were passing through such a murderous fire that they all wanted to get at the enemy as soon as possible. Accordingly they began to gallop, and from the gallop they broke into the charge. But I never heard any 'Charge!' sounded, and other survivors bear me out in this statement.

Such was the interest in the story of the Charge of the Light Brigade that a number of other survivors were also asked at various times to give their stories. In 1891, *The Strand* magazine ran a series of eye-witness accounts called 'Stories of the Victoria Cross'. Unlike those in *The Royal*, most of these accounts were limited to a paragraph or two, and their value now is limited. One of the longest and most vivid accounts was that of Troop-Sergeant-Major John Berryman, 17th Lancers, however, who won the VC – which had only recently been instituted – for saving the life of an officer during the Charge. His account confirms Mr Herbert's description of the chaos and confusion of the battle.

The Light Brigade at Balaclava

'Gallop!' was the order as the firing became general. And here a discharge from the battery in our front, whose guns were doubly shotted, first with shot or shell, and then with case, swept away Captain Winter and the whole division on my right. The gap was noticed by Captain Morris, who gave the order, 'Right incline,' but a warning voice came from my coverer in the rear rank (Corporal John Penn), 'Keep straight on, Jack; keep straight on.' He saw what I did not, that we were opposite the intervals of the guns, and thus we escaped, for the next round must have swept us into eternity. My attention here was attracted to James Melrose, a Shakespearian reciter, calling out, 'What man here would ask another man from England?' Poor fellow, they were the last words he spoke, for the next round from the guns killed him and many others. We were then so close to the guns that the report rang through my head, and I felt that I was quite deaf for a time. It was this round that broke my mare's off hind leg, and caused her to stop instantly. I felt that I was hit, but not till I dismounted. Seeing that the mare's leg was broken, I debated in my own mind whether to shoot her or not, when Captain Webb came up to me, and asked me, was I wounded? I replied, 'Only slightly, I thought, in the leg, but that my horse was shot.' I then asked, 'Are you hurt, sir?' He said that he was, and in the leg, too; what had he better do? 'Keep to your horse, sir, and get back as far as you can.' He turned, and rode back. I now caught a loose horse, and got on to his back, but he fell directly, the brass of the breast-plate having been driven into his chest. Seeing that there was no hope of my joining the regiment in the *mêlée*, and the 11th Hussars being close upon me, I moved a little to the right, so as to pass through the interval between the squadrons. Both squadrons closed in a little, and let me pass through. I well remember that Sergeant Gutteridge was the right guide of the 2nd squadron. Finding that Captain Webb had halted, I ran to him, and on inquiries found that his wound was so painful that he could not ride any further. Lieutenant George Smith, of my own regiment, coming by, I got him to stand at the horse's head whilst I lifted the captain off. Having accomplished this, I assisted Smith to mount Webb's horse, and ride for a stretcher, taking notice where we were. By this time the Russians had got back to their guns, and re-opened fire. I saw six men of my own regiment get together to recount to each other their escapes. Seeing their danger, I called to them to separate, but too late, for a shell dropped amongst them, and I don't think one escaped alive. Hearing me call to these men, Captain Webb asked what I thought the Russians would do?

'They are sure to pursue, sir, unless the Heavy Brigade comes down.'

'Then you had better consult your own safety, and leave me.'

'Oh no, sir, I shall not leave you now.'

'Perhaps they will only take me prisoner.'

'If they do, sir, we will go together.'

'Don't mind me, look to yourself.'

'All right, sir; only we will go together, whatever happens.'

Just at this time I saw Sergeant Farrell coming by. I called to him. He asked, 'Who is it?' When told, he came over. I said, 'We must get Captain Webb out of this, for we shall be pursued.'

He agreeing, we made a chair of our hands, lifted the Captain up, and found that we could carry him with comparative ease. We had got about 200 yards in this manner, when the Captain complained that his leg was very painful. A private of the 13th being near, Malone, I asked him would he be good enough to support Captain Webb's legs, until we could procure a stretcher? He did so, and several of the officers passed us. Sir G. Wombwell said, 'What is the matter, Peck?' (Captain Webb's nickname.)

'Hit in the leg, old fellow. How did you escape?'

'Well, I was unhorsed and taken prisoner, but when the second line came down, in the confusion I got away, and, seizing the first horse I could, I got away, and I find that it is Morris's.'

Sir W. Gordon made the same inquiry, and got the same answer. He had a very nasty cut on the head, and blood was then running down his face. He was carrying his dress cap in his hand. We had now reached the rear of the Greys, and I procured a stretcher from two Infantry band boys, and a young officer of the 'Greys' gave me a 'tourniquet,' saying that he did not know how to apply it, but perhaps I might. I put it on the right thigh, and screwed it up. Doctor Kendal came here, and I pointed out what I had done, and asked was it right?

'I could not have done it better myself; bring him along.'

I and Farrell now raised the stretcher and carried it for about fifty yards, and again set it down. I was made aware of an officer of the Chasseurs d'Afrique being on my left by his placing his hand upon my shoulder. I turned and saluted. Pointing to Captain Webb, but looking at me, he said: —

'Your officer?'

'Yes.'

'Ah! and you sergeant?' looking at the stripes on my arm.

'Yes.'

'Ah! If you were in French service, I would make you an officer on the spot.' Then, standing in his stirrups and extending his right hand, said: —

'Oh! it was grand, it was *magnifique* but it is not war, it is not war.'

This officer was General Morris. We resumed our patient, and got to the doctors (Massy and Kendal). I saw the boot cut off and the nature of the wound, the right shin bone being shattered. Farrell made an exclamation, and I was motioned to take him away. I told him that I should go and see the end of it. He said that he was too exhausted to do any more. Finding a horse in the lines, I mounted him, although the animal belonged to the 4th Light Dragoons, and thus dropped in behind the Duke of Cambridge, and heard what passed. The Duke, speaking to Lord Cardigan, said: —

'Cardigan, where's the Brigade, then?'

'There,' said Cardigan.

'Is that all of them? You have lost the finest Brigade that ever left the shores of England.'

A little further on he spoke to Captain Godfrey Morgan (Lord Tredegar): —

'Morgan, where's the regiment, then?'

'Your Royal Highness, that is all of them!'

'My poor regiment, my poor regiment!'

I now took my place in the ranks, and, in numbering off, being on the extreme left, I counted 22. We fell back during the night, and, being dismounted, I, with my servant, was left behind. I suffered intensely with my head, and got a napkin and tied it as tightly as possible round my brows. I also had time to examine my wound, which was inside the calf of my leg. A small piece about the size of a shilling had been cut clean out of my leg; but except that the blood had run into my boots, I felt but very little inconvenience from it. Cold water bandage was all I used; but, unfortunately, scurvy got to it, and it was a long time healing.

Despite the devastation of the Light Brigade, Balaclava must be accounted a British victory, of sorts, because Prince Menshikov's attempt to deprive the British of their supply depot had been defeated. Nevertheless, the battle made little impact on Menshikov's ability to mount offensive actions, and less than a fortnight later he combined with the Sebastopol garrison to make a serious attempt to dislodge the British siege lines.

The allied lines did not completely cut off Sebastopol, since on the far right – the British sector – the lines fell just short of the Tchernaya river. This allowed one road to the Russians, which ran along the valley, and who were therefore able to maintain communications between the town and Menshikov's forces in the interior. A little after dawn on 5 November, a combined force of 40,000 Russians mounted a surprise attack on the British right flank. Under cover of a heavy mist, they advanced from the Tchernaya valley, up the steeply rising ground which led to the British position. The terrain here was extremely broken, scarred by deep, narrow ravines, and covered here and there with patches of bush. Just above the ruins of the deserted village of Inkerman, the Russians struck the outlying British pickets, but the local British commander, realising the danger of his line being rolled up, rushed forward reinforcements rather than withdraw his pickets. There then began the most confusing, desperate, and hard-fought battle of the war. With both sides hurrying men into the melee, the battle dissolved into a series of piecemeal fights which raged up and down the slopes for most of the day. It was impossible to retain coherent formation, and command of the battle devolved upon regimental commanders, company officers, and often NCOs. Much of the fighting took place in a nightmare world of fog and smoke, where visibility was often limited to a few yards, and where every foot of ground was contested at bayonet point, with rifle-butts, or with stones and even fists. The brunt of the fighting fell to small groups on both sides, who were required to mount fierce attacks or stubborn defences, often at their own initiative. For this reason, Inkerman is often described as a 'soldiers' battle'. Sergeant Patrick Conway, of the Royal Artillery, was in the thick of the fight, and left a vivid account of its unique character.

Inkerman: The Soldiers' Battle

Sunday morning – a dense fog, driving rain, bitter cold, and black darkness. That was November 5th, 1854, when, on the heights of Inkerman, eight thousand ragged, starving British soldiers awaited the assault of forty thousand Russians, who advanced in the assurance of a swift and crushing victory.

The reveille had sounded, but the ring of the bugle was almost a mockery to famished and disease-stricken troops who had been so long on duty in the trenches that sleep was nearly a forgotten blessing. The notes heralded a long and bloody struggle on a battlefield so limited that the whole front of it did not extend more than three-quarters of a mile. Fifty thousand men were to fight furiously for hours, and at the end of their encounter fresh forces were to come into the fray, so that when the day was done the field of combat was a reeking shambles.

Many famous regiments and units were at Inkerman; but none, although I say it, was more distinguished than my own, G Battery, of the Royal Artillery. We were noted even in a body that had covered itself with glory since it landed in the Crimea; and of all the officers who had gained renown not one was more entitled to distinction than my own brave and beloved commander, Captain Turner.

Look at that framed printing on the wall – it is extracts from Kinglake's 'Invasion of the Crimea,' and tells you what the great historian thought of my superior officer. It also tells of some of the things I did myself at Inkerman and elsewhere. Yes, it fills me with pride, and helps me to bear the affliction – rheumatism from the Crimea – from which I have suffered for nearly half-a-century, and which now holds me to my bed a cripple.

My battery was posted on a height where we were open to the fire not only of the Russian artillery on land, but also of the guns of warships in the harbour, as well as the desperate onslaughts of the Russian infantry.

A fine battery we made, with our four nine-pounders and two twenty-four pounder howitzers – the composition of a field battery in those days. They were very good guns, superior to the weapons of either the Russians or the French; and Captain Turner was a born artillerist. I am not alone in saying that his marvellous handling of his battery that day had much to do with turning what seemed like a sure defeat into a brilliant and historic victory.

We were plunged into the fight almost before we could realise what had happened. It was a straightforward struggle – a fierce hurling of brave and merciless masses against a foe as resolute and stubborn. Sheer love of life, the instinct of self-preservation, if nothing else, would have held us to our duty, for we knew that if once we were broken or abandoned our position, we and the day were lost beyond redemption.

Time after time, in that cold, clammy fog, the Russian hordes advanced; time after time they were driven back. They came towards us with their Colours flying and their drums beating, with the voices of their officers encouraging them, and with the clerical assurances that had been given them of a triumph which would end the war. And in a land of so much suffering what greater incentive could they have than that?

In the grey light the grey masses rolled upon us, and they melted as they came, for we destroyed them with both guns and rifles. Repeatedly they crossed the ravine which lay between the two armies, and struggled with all the stubborn valour of their race to annihilate us. It was a perfect hell of fighting, and it seemed as if nothing could save us from destruction.

Repeated charges had been made; men had fallen in their hundreds on both sides, and the field of conflict was littered with the dead and dying. Yet neither side gave way, no sign of surrender was given. It was hard, terrific pounding, and the hardest pounder was to be the winner. That much was certain when the battle had been raging long enough to supersede the fog of Nature with the stifling smoke of battle.

So hideous was the carnage that at last our infantry were ordered to lie down, for in shelter was their only hope of safety.

The Russian columns seemed never to lessen or be affected. Men went down, but other men took their places; battalions were annihilated, but fresh battalions were pushed forward as if from some magic forces. They had new blood, you see, to make up for their losses; but as for us, we were powerless. We had no reserves, and when a unit was destroyed its place was not filled. There were only eight thousand of us, remember; while the Russians were at least five times as strong.

Two of our battery sergeants, those who commanded Nos. 1 and 2 guns, were sent to order our infantry to lie down. We saw them go – and we saw them blown to atoms before they could obey their orders.

It was a terrible and thrilling time, Nos. 1 and 2 were dead, and I was No. 3, and so it happened that when my comrades had fallen Captain Turner called upon me to volunteer to try and do that which they had failed to accomplish.

Death appeared assured – but who at such a time, and especially a soldier, thinks of death or cares for it?

The Russians were almost at our very throats, and to keep them back it was imperative that we should fire case-shot – that is, shot which scatters at very close quarters, fan-like, and destroys all human life that is within its reach. But if our infantry did not lie down they would be annihilated as well as the enemy. Such was the position when my officer addressed me.

'Conway,' said Captain Turner, 'I want you to make your way to the first mounted officer you meet, and ask him to gallop along the line and order his men to lie down, so that I can fire case-shot into the Russians.'

I carried out his order, then returned to my battery, and we fired with common case over the heads of our own troops, who were lying down. I do not exaggerate when I say that the advancing Russians fell like corn before the reaper. Not even their valiant infantry could withstand that storm of bullets. They wavered, they became confused, they lost heart – and before they could recover, the British battalions had sprung to their feet and hurled themselves upon them.

Only eight hundred yards separated the two forces at that stage of the battle, and in that short space there was awful carnage. A hundred Russian guns and thirty-six of our own pieces of artillery were booming deafeningly, and with it all there was the everlasting rattle of musketry.

But when the furious assaults had been repulsed, there came a strange calm. The crashes and rattling died away, and it was known that on both sides the ammunition was giving out. That did not mean cessation of the fighting – far from it. Cold steel was now needed, and it was when the bayonet and sword were wielded with such savage force that the most appalling stages of the deadly struggle came.

For a breathing space it seemed almost as if we might claim victory, and see a finish to the fight; but for a breathing space only. Scarcely had the Russians been driven back when they were upon us again, and this time they got to our very guns.

My battery was divided into two halves – the Right Half and Left Half, Nos. 1, 2, and 3 guns forming the Right Half, and Nos. 4, 5, and 6 the Left Half.

When the Russian infantry swooped upon us we were practically defence-less, for, as I have said, our ammunition was exhausted, and we were waiting for the French gunners to come up. The Russians loomed out of the fog, and such was their determination, so great were their numbers, and so weakened were we in Turner's Battery, that for a few moments the enemy actually took possession of the Left Half.

So swift and overwhelming was the rush that our gunners were butchered where they stood, and the horses were killed or maimed on the spot. How could it be otherwise when horse and man were helpless?

But mark what happened with some of our brave fellows. They had seen too much of war to die tamely, and although they had no weapons of any sort yet they did not lose heart. They were stalwart men, with plenty of muscle and lots of pluck, and they were fighting for life itself, too, which is the greatest of all our treasures, so they fell on the Russians with their fists, and pounded them so mercilessly and savagely that the men with the rifles and bayonets actually bit the earth.

Some of them, I am certain, went down as much because of amazement as through the violent practice of the noble art of Tom Sayers. More than one fist-fighter snatched a Russian weapon and bayonetted or clubbed his man before he could rise to his feet again. It was no time for asking or giving quarter; and many acts were committed that day by Russians which put them quite beyond the pale of mercy.

In that fierce *mêlée* many stirring deeds were done, and there were many instances of valour and devotion. Men forgot their privations, and pulled themselves together to the end that they might save the situation, in their country's interests, and because they wished to keep their private honour unsullied. Turner's battery was famous, and it could not afford to have its reputation tarnished. That wonderful *esprit de corps*, let scoffers say what they will, has a marvellous effect at a time of peril.

For the few minutes during which the guns were held by the enemy, there was such a struggle as I had not seen before in the Crimea, nor during the rest of the war did I witness anything to exceed it in determined and ruthless ferocity. Horses, guns, and men were jumbled up in that confined and reeking battle-space, and on the thick air arose the awful confusion of a struggle to the very death.

Fists are useful weapons, especially when they belong to such gunners as ours; but of what avail are mere flesh and blood against a long bayonet at the muzzle of a rifle?

Men were borne down and slain – cruelly slain – on the wet ground, mixed up with the guns and limbers and hideous *débris* of the fight. The Russian shot had done terrible mischief to our weapons, and now even the wheels were shot away and the ammunition-waggons shattered into wrecks. The grey-coated legions showed no mercy, and in their frenzy clubbed and bayonetted almost every man they could reach.

One or two rare exceptions they made, and the rarest was in the case of a brave sergeant named Henry, who commanded No. 6 gun. Henry was a fine fellow, and was wearing his tunic, a somewhat gorgeous garment, which made him look like an officer. I myself was fighting in my blue guernsey shirt, having thrown my fine jacket off, so that I should be freer in my movements.

Convinced that Henry was an officer, the Russians set to work, not to kill him, but to take him prisoner, so that they could get the reward of so many roubles which was offered for every British officer captured. Henry fought like a fiend, slashing at them with his heavy sword, and sweeping them away in deadly fashion. They could have killed him twenty times over; but they spared him, merely playing to the point of exhaustion. At last he fell, fighting and undaunted still, and they rushed in upon him, and surrounding him as best they could in that condition, gently bayonetted him about the arms and shoulders. He resolutely defied them, and refused to yield; but by very force of numbers they made him prisoner and dragged him away from our shambles of a battery.

I saw what it was happening, and knew what his fate would be. Three men had hold of him, and when just beyond the guns they put him down and left him on the sodden ground to get an escort, so that they could carry him safely to the Russian lines.

It was more than flesh and blood could endure to see my comrade dragged away like that. I looked swiftly around me and saw with thankfulness that some, at any rate, of our men survived.

I called upon two brave fellows to go with me, and sword in hand we dashed away from the guns and hurried after Henry. One of the men was shot dead almost as soon as we began our rush, but the two of us – myself and Jim McGrath – ran to the spot where Henry was lying. Startled by this unlooked-for development, his captors had halted and turned upon us; but we had more than our fists, and with our swords we slew them.

One of the Russians, who were maddened at seeing their prize so nearly taken from them, rushed upon and lunged at me with his bayonet; but I was swifter with my own steel, and he fell.

Terrible blows are given at a time like that, and I remember that I smashed the fellow's arm. He dropped his musket. Instantly McGrath picked the weapon up and killed the Russian with it, driving the bayonet through his body. Then the two of us fell upon and destroyed a Russian who was stubbornly holding Henry to the ground – trampled ground that was like a puddle with the rain, and red with blood.

Henry, almost unconscious, did not understand what was taking place, and when he first saw me he cried:

'Hello, are *you* a prisoner, too?'

'No,' I shouted; 'we've come to rescue you.'

Henry made some sort of objection, but I cut it short by hoisting him on my back and carrying him to our own guns again. I was a strong man then – one of the strongest in my battery. He was terribly cut, and I was wet with his blood when I got him into safety again. Jim, like myself, received the Gold Medal from the French Emperor, and Henry got the Victoria Cross and a commission in the Land Transport Corps, which is now the Army Service Corps. I, too, was offered a commission, but I did not take it. My ambition did not lie in that direction. They removed Henry to a sheltered place, where the surgeons were doing their dreadful but humane work, and I did not see him for many years. Then I came across him at Aldershot, he a captain and me a sergeant still; and many a pleasant jibe did he cast at me for being such a fool, as he put it, as to refuse promotion.

My own battery had suffered dreadfully. Twenty of our men were killed, and thirty-six were wounded. The horses suffered just as much. Out of 280, only thirty-seven were effective at the finish of the fight. Most of the poor creatures were killed; and as for those that were living, the greater number had to be destroyed.

But you can best understand what our losses were when I tell you that my battery alone heavier casualties than all the rest of the artillery put together. We were on the apex of the hill – Shell Hill, as it was appropriately called – and we were a target for all the Russian gunners.

We had been engaged from an hour before daylight, fighting continuously, and it seemed as if the end of the battle would never come, and as if the grey-coated legions were numberless. It seemed, too, more than once as if the success on which our hearts were set could never be ours, for our battery was shattered and our ammunition was done. Yet even then, I am certain, no such thought as surrender entered the minds of any one of us in Turner's battery.

No, it was a case of fighting to the bitter end, and we did everything we could to stave off disaster. The gunners, the actual fighters of the guns, were dead or wounded; very well, there were still the drivers. So the drivers were hurried up and their whips gave place to swords, and they did as best they could until, late in the day, the French troops came up and took the brunt of the battle off our shoulders. Our Allies themselves suffered very heavily, and, indeed, so great were our losses that even when it was known that we had won the day and scored a glorious victory, there was not heart enough left in any one of us to admit of rejoicing. Who could exult on such a stricken field?

The dead were lying in their thousands, and throughout that awful night most of us who still lived were busy in the heartbreaking work of collecting the wounded and carrying them to the operating places.

But if we had no cause for open rejoicing, we had at any rate the deep, quiet satisfaction of knowing that we had done our duty, and that because we had stuck to our guns and fought the good soldier's fight Inkerman had been made a great victory for the Allies instead of being a defeat which would have meant the ending of the war in favour of the enemy. That is the way I look at it.

Many distinguished officers were present on that great day. Four of high rank were numbered with the dead. Amongst the living who did fine work was the late Duke of Cambridge. I had many talks with him in those far-off Crimean days; and in later years, when his Royal Highness visited at the Hospital, he never failed to see the old gunner, who was wheeled in his invalid chair on to the parade ground.

One day the Duke, after chatting with me, turned and said to the officers who were standing near him: 'This is Sergeant Conway, the man who frightened Prince Gortchakoff and all the Russian army at Inkerman!'

The battle of Inkerman cost the Russian army 11,000 killed, wounded or captured. The British lost nearly 2500 killed and wounded, and the French 880 casualties. The effect of the battle was to paralyse the Russian forces, for such losses seriously undermined their ability to make further such assaults, and the war settled down to a grim stalemate of trench warfare. Both sides made occasional probes, forays and trench raids, but neither were able to dislodge the other from their lines. The situation became further complicated towards the end of November 1854 by the onset of the Crimean winter. The British, in particular, had expected the war to be over long before, and had made no provision for the biting cold and snow which now swept across the peninsula. The commissariat arrangements, which had scarcely coped at the best of times, collapsed completely. It was just a few miles from Balaclava harbour to the siege lines, but in poor weather, with inadequate transport, and with the harbour itself hopelessly congested, the chain of supply broke down completely. In the cramped and insanitary trenches there was a desperate shortage of food and warm clothing; disease soon took hold, while many men suffered the agonies of frost-bite. Troops sent out from Britain to make good the losses often fell sick as soon as they were exposed to these conditions, and had to be sent home again.

Yet the allies clung to their positions, and conditions eased with the coming of spring in 1855. Encouraged by the decision of Sardinia to enter the war against Russia, the allies made an inconclusive demonstration against the Russian army, still lurking in the interior, in May. Yet the forces inside Sebastopol remained as secure as ever. In an attempt to drive them out, the allies mounted two major attacks on key defensive positions. The French attacked a stone tower – the Malakoff – which dominated their sector, while the British assaulted a deep earthwork which they had christened 'the Redan'.

The attacks on these strongpoints foreshadowed the costly and futile battles of WW1, more than sixty years later. The assault parties were assembled in front-line trenches, then had to make a dash across several hundred yards of no-man's land, which was broken by obstacles, and swept by rifle fire and canister shot. Among the assault parties in both actions was Private William Kimberlin, of the 7th Royal Fusiliers.

Sebastopol: The Storming of the Redan

It is a great and memorable anniversary, for it is the 18th of June, 1855, exactly forty years since Waterloo was fought. Forty years ago the French and British met in that immortal struggle under Wellington and Buonaparte. See what wondrous changes time has wrought! Here, fighting side by side against a common enemy, are Englishmen and Frenchmen, both awaiting the signal to storm the keys to that great fortress which is called Sebastopol. There the frowning Malakoff Tower is the target for the French; here the grim Redan awaits the onrush of the English. And this allied assault, they say, has been planned so that a glorious victory may take the sting from the bitterness of an Emperor's downfall and the crushing of a nation's army forty years ago.

But I am only a plain British soldier. I do not understand these matters, which are settled by the general and the rest of the officers. My only business is to obey orders to storm the Redan, and to remember that the watchword is 'Forward!'

So now that I am in front of the Redan I am able to look about me and note things fairly calmly. The Redan by this time is an old friend, so is the Malakoff. The difference between them is great, for while the Malakoff – a great round white stone tower – has been there from the beginning of the bombardment of Sebastopol five months before, the Redan has grown up out of nothingness. So have many of the defences of the Russians and the allies, because a peculiarity of this war has been that the two forces have been constantly working towards each other under cover of the trenches which they have made.

Redan, you know, is a word used by engineers to indicate the simplest sort of field-work, and its purpose is to defend the approach to any given place, building, bridge or town.

The Redan at Sebastopol has been formed by throwing up the earth in an immense thick wall, or parapet, about fifteen feet high. There are two long stretches of the wall, each extending for about seventy yards. In the middle is a sharp point called a salient, jutting out towards you like the bow of a ship. This salient is about seventeen feet high.

The whole of the Redan grins at you with guns. That is not all. In front of it is an enormous ditch, eleven feet deep, and from fifteen to twenty feet wide. In front of that again, is a *chevaux-de-frise*, a hedge of spikes and bayonets and swords. In front of this again is a stretch of very rough sloping ground, and something like 400 yards from the Redan itself are the trenches which we have made to shelter ourselves from the Russian fire, and to cover us as we work our way day after day, like moles burrowing, near enough to make it possible to deliver a fierce sudden rush. Let me complete this mental picture by telling you that on each side of us, right and left, there is a ravine. So even the simple watchword 'Forward!' is hardly needed, since we cannot go on either side, and we cannot go back.

This storming of the fort would be like a tremendous obstacle race at any time, and thrilling enough even if we were all no more than friendly competitors. What will it be, then, to rush up that rough slope to the ridge where the Redan is, packed with troops and bristling with guns? The fight will be hard, but the prize is magnificent – Sebastopol itself! for if the Redan and the Malakoff and the rest of the fortifications, which are not so important, fall, the allies cannot be kept out.

There are three columns of us Englishmen – sappers, skirmishers, ladder parties and woolbag men, with storming parties, reserves, and workmen. The woolbagmen – we can call them that, though some carry bags of hay, are to try and fill parts of the ditch, then the ladders are to be planted, and we are to swarm up into the Redan and take it. In the three columns there are about 6000 officers and men, and all are crowded together in a very little space, waiting for the signal to advance. There are amongst us some very young officers who are in later years to become famous and get the highest promotion possible for fighting men. There is a young midshipman with the sailors who is later to go into the army, and who is now Field-Marshal Sir Evelyn Wood, V.C.; and there is a young Engineer who is to become Commander-in-Chief of the British Army – Field-Marshal Viscount Wolseley.

We have marched at Sunday midnight from our cantonments to the trenches – two miles under the shelter of the entrenchments which we have made for our own protection. We have been crouching and crowding for two hours, waiting for the Monday's dawn.

My officers and comrades are about me. There is the brave Colonel Yea, of my own regiment, the 7th Royal Fusiliers. He is commanding No. 3 column, and they have made him a brigadier-general. No man is more beloved in all the British regiments, because none has shown more consideration for his soldiers. Colonel Yea is a hard fighter, too, and has seen as much of death and suffering as most of us. It is he who at the Alma said, with tears in his eyes: 'There, look there! That's all that remains of my poor Fusiliers! A colour is missing but, thank God, no Russian has it!' We carried colours into battle in those days, and they are with us here, at the foot of the little hill which is crowned by the Redan. Colonel Yea is standing, alert and bold, a glorious picture of a fighting man, waiting for the signal for the simultaneous storming. His left hand – I see him now – is on his scabbard, his right is on his sword-hilt.

The fight has now been opened by the stormers, and we of the bayonets are awaiting the order to advance.

Suddenly the signal comes. There is a scrape and swish of steel as Colonel Yea whips out his sword, a flash of a blade, and the loud ringing voice of our chief as he shouts: 'Follow me, men!'

Remember that!

'Follow me!'

That was the spirit of the best of them, those who led the way to death or victory. And for the most part the men, the old hands, those who have been scorched in the fire of battle, obey. If there are those who hold back,

the raw recruits, the unnerved, what of it? Has it not been so in every fight
– and did not Wellington himself say that not every man who wore the
soldier's uniform was a hero? And you must remember that it is reported
that the Redan is mined, that the ground will explode under our very feet,
even if we reach it, and that there are those amongst us who have seen the
Russians mercilessly slay our helpless wounded.

We have, as I have told you, a mere strip of ground to cover – only a few
hundred yards – and we dash after or with our officers, dash as best we can,
but mostly helter-skelter, because there is no keeping to a programme at a
time like this.

I see one thing only, the Redan, in front and above us, on the ridge. I am
filled with only one desire, to reach the parapet, and get the dreadful business
over. And why not? It is sweeter to live than die, and although I have faced
death in every hideous shape since I landed in the Crimea I never cease to
dread it and to shrink from its shadow.

Now it is a very inferno in that small space. The guns burst in our very
faces; the packed Russians blaze at us with musketry. Every yard, every foot,
every inch, it seems, of that rough ground which lies between us and the
Russians, that open space which we must cross before we win the fight, is
torn by shot and shell and ball. There are officers present – our Commander-
in-Chief, Lord Raglan, amongst them – who remember the Peninsula and
Waterloo, who saw the storming of Badajoz and Rodrigo, in the days when
British soldiers made a trade of fighting, and were at it year after year for
half-a-dozen years. And these veterans say that the fusillade is worse than
even Badajoz.

I cannot speak for that; but I do know that at the Alma, at Inkerman, at
Balaklava – at no previous battle have I seen anything to match it.

We rush along, through the rank grass, over the rough, broken ground,
reckless of the gravel-pits, ignoring the trenches; panting, shouting, jostling,
cheering, in the track of the stormers and woolbagmen and laddermen who
have gone ahead.

What happens instantly? Dazed though we may be, and numbed to most
things, we know that our colonel has fallen. I am very near him and see him
fall – not ten paces has he covered since his sword swished and his clear voice
rang. Now he is lying dead in front of the Redan, riddled by rifle bullets.
Dead! And he has escaped death so often!

Near the colonel is our sergeant-major – Bacon, they call him, a fine man
and a gallant soldier. His place is at the head of the regiment, and he is
passing me to get there and to lead us into the Redan, if human effort can
accomplish it. I dimly see his figure in the battle-smoke, pressing onward in
the turmoil. He stops abruptly and falls without a cry. That again is a hideous
happening, for a grape-shot has struck his neck and the head is nearly severed.

So the colonel and the sergeant-major are gone – the heads of the regiment. Fate is merciless to us. Our adjutant, Hobbs, another fine soldier, is killed as we advance – but why prolong the list of the slain? There are many, and no ranks suffer more than the commissioned. We know of and notice these things, although in battle you know little and most that happens is unnoticed.

You have seen an engine trying to start with a heavy load or on slippery rails? Every ounce of steam goes into the cylinders, and the wheels whirr round on the lines; but the locomotive does not move, the train stands still.

So are we in front of the Redan. We strive, madly, savagely, and with all our hearts and souls to get at the enemy, for the sooner we are at steel-grip with him the sooner we shall see the end of this rain of metal, this ploughing and destroying of our ranks, this covering of the earth with our dead and wounded; but we melt before the crashing guns and crackling muskets and are thrown back from the parapet and the salient.

I have told you of the Bluejackets, who are the woolbagmen and the laddermen. I could not tell you half enough of the gallant way in which they rush with their burdens, drag their bags and their ladders, and get them to the parapet. Up go the ladders against the rough crude walls of earth, and up swarm some of the sailors and stormers – a few who have escaped the fire which sweeps across the ground like hail. They climb like acrobats and fight like fiends, but they are overwhelmed in what promises to be the moment of victory, and are either killed as they jump into the Redan or are hurled back into the yawning ditch.

Now we think of nothing but our task, we hear nothing but the order 'Forward!' It is follow your leader – and we do our best. Many have been numbered with the commanding officer, the adjutant, the sergeant-major, and the rest; you have to go on – there is no going back. And so, against the fence of steel and iron, and into the ditch we go and dash for the ladders.

How is it done? I cannot tell you. How are many things accomplished when the blood is hot? You have your orders and you obey. That is all. And there is always the discipline and emulation which make men do the seemingly impossible.

We do not remember or notice much, but we do not forget that our allies, the French, are storming the Malakoff, and we do not want to fail when they succeed.

So we continue. It is terrible, deafening, bewildering. We are for ever striving and winning nothing – the human waves of us hurling like breakers on the shore, against the Redan – and crumbling just as the water does. As well might we cast ourselves against the cliffs which defy the sea.

We fight furiously on, hoping against hope that we shall win – then suddenly we know the truth, that the assault on the Redan has hopelessly failed, that we are repulsed – beaten, if you like, defeated, and that the Russians are the victors.

So the unwilling bitter order is issued, and we withdraw from the ground which is strewn with our dead and more than ever torn with shot, and we re-form in the trenches from which we have sallied in the hope of glorious victory.

It is the mournful right of a beaten enemy to hoist the flag of truce, and under cover of that signal of temporary mercy we go out to the Redan again and gather up our dead and wounded. Then the horrors of a fight are manifest. There is no thrill of battle, no clash of steel, no whizz of bullet, no crash and roar of gun, and no wild tingling of the blood. There is awful stillness, broken only by the groans of the dying and the louder cries of those who will live – and be maimed for ever.

The brave commanding officer is lying where he fell, and we see that seven bullets have struck him. Swift, too, has been the end of other officers and men, as their attitudes and faces show – but there are many soldiers on that bloody spot who have died hard, very hard; and more who are dying harder still.

Two hours only for the truce – the burial and the bringing in of the wounded; then we are enemies again, and resume the grim bombardment of the fortress which seems as if it would never fall.

We count up our losses. They are heavy – ninety-nine officers and nearly fifteen hundred men killed and wounded – one officer in fifteen. And we estimate our gains – which are nothing.

So we have to start afresh and pound away at the Redan with big guns until we can storm the fort again. And as the days go by, we in the ranks gradually learn what is being said in higher quarters – that the plan of the attack on the Redan was bad, and the carrying out of it worse.

It is nearly three months later – September 8th – and we are in front of the Redan again, at noon this time, huddled in the trenches, waiting for the signal of attack. It is very much a repetition of the disastrous storming of June 18th; but we have the benefit of our bitter experience, and profit by it. Here, again, for those of us who care to think, there are plenty of gloomy subjects, for the ground on which we stand and over which we are to fight once more is a veritable cemetery. But there is a consciousness that now, indeed, the only word is 'Forward!' There is no going back.

We lie down in our trenches while our batteries and the Russian batteries pound each other, and while the French storm the Malakoff afresh. They are to be luckier than the English, because they catch their enemy unprepared, taking his noonday rest after eating and drinking.

The signal that we are to attack comes with the hoisting of a flag. Then it is 'Advance!' and 'Forward!' once more, and we are in the thick of the fight. Again a man loses his individuality, and becomes a member of a desperately striving band of soldiers.

It is June 18th over again; but not so fatal, not so terrible, not so bloody. We are more lucky, too, and I am one of those who manage, God alone knows how, to get as far as the deep, wide ditch through that amazing hail of missiles.

The ground, remember, is hard, and there is a constant rattling of metal upon it – a death-rattle, in very truth. And that storm is broken at little intervals by a savage squall, as it seems, of grape-shot.

Picture the sight you have often witnessed of a hailstorm in a paved roadway. The hail patters down, does it not? That represents rifle-fire. Then there is a scream of wind, and the ground is swept with a volley of hail. You have seen it? You understand? The pattering is the ceaseless rifle-fire; the volleys are the crashes of grapeshot at a murderous range.

We rush ahead, I know not how, and tumble, helter-skelter and pell-mell, into the ditch. Then there are the ladders to climb, to swarm up, and the work with the bayonet to be done at the top.

Fancy yourself rushing the side of an ordinary house, scrambling up a ladder, and fighting for your footing at the top. You are pushed or shot or bayoneted, or thrown from your footing and your grip, and struggle in a hell-heap in the ditch, which has become like a vast grave. How can men do it? How do they live at all through such a time? Again, I say, I cannot tell you. I am only a soldier, and the order is 'Forward!'

'Advance!' and my duty is to obey.

I am in the ditch, I say, and I mean to be in the Redan, which has threatened and defied us so long. There is shouting, struggling, ordering, wild confusion, a furious pressing onward. The dead and wounded are thick about me. Men have fallen under their ladders or bags, officers, who have been leading and encouraging, are still and silent; but there is no time to think or look or stop. Victory is so near at last that we may snatch it.

My furious advance is checked. I am struck and crippled by a spent grapeshot, and am knocked out of the fight and present knowledge of the battle.

I am taken, after many hours, into hospital, and next day I have to make room for men who are more dangerously hurt. I am fit for duty of some sort, and I am told off for it.

Eh? What is that? Where am I to go? Into Sebastopol itself!

Then I know that the Redan has fallen at last; that it has become ours; that we have really taken it, but have been forced to evacuate it for want of reinforcements.

I know that that resistless storming has succeeded, that British troops have actually gained the parapet, have won the Redan, and are holding it. And I hear that because the reinforcements have not come, because our men are not strong enough to hold the fort, the Russians take heart of grace and furiously rush back upon them. There is a mad dash for the ladders and a headlong overbalancing of officers and men into the ditch.

To advance has been terrible enough, but to retire is infinitely more awful. That is always the case, and this is no exception. In the scramble to escape from the hard-won Redan there is this tumbling back into the ditch, and amongst the fixed bayonets and drawn swords, too. Some tumble on to these pitiless blades, and of their wounds who shall tell? How shall I describe them? Others are crushed by the mere weight of falling bodies upon them. And to add to the horrors of it all, the Russians mount the parapet afresh and hurl stones, grape-shot, muskets with fixed bayonets, and even live shells, into the very midst of the struggling writhing human mass.

But even the sullen, patient, gallant, stubborn Russians have had enough of it, and during the night they abandon the Redan. Perhaps they might have held it still – but what of that? The Redan has fallen, and fallen because we have pounded it remorselessly during all these long months, and desperately stormed it twice. Just under 2500 officers and men have been killed or wounded, and in two hours – heavier losses than we had at Inkerman in six; so that these two stormings have cost us more than 4000 casualties.

But what of the price? The Redan is ours, and we are satisfied. When the morning of the 9th comes the war is over, for Sebastopol, after such a siege as they say has never been known in history, has fallen. Even while it is burning and the Russians are hurrying out of it by water the victors – sometimes English, French, and Turkish, arm-in-arm together, are roystering about the ruined streets and are singing gladly 'No more trenches!'

The war is ended – and I am very glad, for battle, famine, cold, and disease have claimed the lives of a vast number of Englishmen. And there are the French and Turkish losses, too – and on the other, the Russian, side the gloomy, grey-coated troops from the strange big country which is once again at war as I talk with you – and fighting for her very life. In Sebastopol itself we count their dead by hundreds – is there not in one large room alone seven hundred, many of them lying just as the surgeons had left them after amputations?

But that is the fighting of fifty years ago. Let me finish in a cheerier strain.

Of that enforced withdrawal for the second time from the Redan we are reminded in a very curious way. The Turks have a habit of saying to us, 'No bono,' when they mean that a thing is no good, and our French allies, when we meet, as we often do, jeer at us because of our failure and shout, 'No bono, Redan!' We are stung into answer, and remembering that June 18th, forty years before, we shout back 'No bono Waterloo!' which always knocks the conceit out of them.

That, of course, is fifty years ago – and we were soldiers of the tough old school. They are different now, because times have changed – and they tell me it is better so.

The capture of the Redan persuaded the Russians to abandon Sebastopol in good order, and effectively brought the siege to a close. In truth, however, the focus of the war was already shifting away from the Crimea. The Russians launched a major attack into Turkish Armenia, where the city of Kars resolutely stood against them. Assisted by British advisers, the defenders of Kars held out for five months before starvation finally forced them to submit. The British responded by stepping up naval attacks on Russian coastal towns, bombarding the port of Odessa, and patrolling the Russian Pacific coast.

Sebastopol, meanwhile, proved a disappointing prize. The defenders had held out for 349 days – just short of a year – but the allies had gained little by entering the town, beyond gaining the shelter of the abandoned Russian barracks as another winter loomed.

By the spring of 1856, the war seemed increasingly directionless, and both sides seized upon the offer of Austria to mediate. Peace was agreed at the Treaty of Paris in March 1856. Under its terms Russian warships were banned from the Black Sea, while the territorial integrity of the Ottoman Empire was guaranteed. By the middle of 1856 the last British troops had been withdrawn from the Crimea.

The war had cost the British army 1933 men killed in action, 1921 dead from wounds, and a staggering 15,724 dead from disease. Moreover, the unprecedented publicity given to the army's failings had created the first serious pressure for reform, and ensured the first staggering steps in the long journey away from the outmoded systems of the Napoleonic wars, and towards the recognisably modern twentieth-century army which characterised the late Victorian era.

2. India and Afghanistan

If the Crimean War was the single most influential campaign in the history of the early Victorian army, the British preoccupation with India would prove one of the most consistent means of its employment.

When Queen Victoria ascended the throne in 1837, India was already the most valuable possession in the canon of the British empire. Directly, or ruling through local allies, Britain controlled an area of 1.6 million square miles, and her sway extended from the borders of Burma in the east, to the Indus and Satlej rivers in the west. British rule affected the lives of over 400 million people, and the need to secure India internally, or protect it from external threats, dominated British foreign policy throughout the nineteenth century.

The origins of British power in the region were strictly mercantile. In 1600 Queen Elizabeth I had granted the East India Company a monopoly of trade across half the world, between the Cape of Good Hope and Cape Horn. This monopoly allowed the British Crown to benefit from the activities of merchant adventurers while maintaining a safe political distance. The great prize was the enormously profitable spice trade with the Indies, and rival British, Dutch, Portuguese and French trading concerns sought to control it. Forming alliances with local rulers within India, they brought their wider political rivalries with them, provoking a series of struggles which ultimately saw the British victorious, and left the Company the dominant power within the sub-continent. Much of India was nominally under the control of the Mughal empire, but by 1837 the last of the Mughal emperors was little more than a Company pensioner, and many apparently independent Indian princes were only able to rule with Company approval.

The Company ruled India through three self-contained Presidencies – Bombay, Madras and Bengal – each of which maintained an establishment of regular troops, raised by the Company from among the Indian population, and officered by Europeans. The Company's armies were trained, equipped and uniformed along European lines, and were infinitely more powerful than the semi-feudal forces maintained by independent Indian rulers.

In 1837, the Company's main strategic preoccupation was with its western border. Here, the plains of the Indus gave way to the rugged foothills of the Afghan massif in an area which had traditionally been used as the gateway to India by succeeding generations of invaders. Although more than 2000 miles separated the Indus from the nearest outposts of the Russian empire in central Asia, Britain remained obsessed with the idea that the Tsar might one day try to oust the British by mounting an invasion through Afghanistan. Nor was this idea entirely without foundation, for although it was inherently unlikely that a nineteenth-century Russian army could have mounted an expedition to the Afghan capital at Kabul, none-the-less Russian diplomats undoubtedly sought to influence events on the borders through the agencies of local rulers.

In 1839, the British insecurity regarding the North-West Frontier of India resulted in her undertaking a campaign which would prove one of the most disastrous of the century.

In 1810 a palace coup in Afghanistan had ousted the incumbent ruler, Shah Shuja, and seen him replaced with a rival, Dost Mohammed. In 1828, Russia had intervened in Persian affairs to establish a pro-Russian Shah on the throne. In 1837, Persia, with Russian support, attacked the western Afghan town of Herat. The Company was concerned that Dost Mohammed had neither the capacity, nor, perhaps, the will, to resist the Russian incursion, and decided to shore up its own influence by rescuing Shah Shuja from the obscurity of exile, and returning him to his throne. Little was known of Afghan politics, and it was widely believed that the Afghans would welcome the restoration of their legitimate ruler, or, if they did not, they would be unable in any case to resist an army organised along European lines.

The British expedition consisted of 37,000 men, a mixture of Company and Queen's – British regular – troops, supported by an enormous baggage train. Refused permission by an astute local ruler from using the most direct route into Afghanistan – the Khyber pass – it advanced in February 1839 by way of the independent amirates of Sind in the south. This seems to have caught the Afghans off-guard, and the British forces were able capture a succession of Afghan towns with only token resistance. On 7 August Shah Shuja made a triumphal return to the Afghan capital, Kabul, and the head of the British army. It seemed that the expedition had been a complete success.

In fact, however, the outward signs of Afghan submission were entirely misleading. Dost Mohammed had fled to the hills with his charismatic son, Akbar Khan, from where he rallied the fierce hill tribes to his support. In Kabul, the British garrison settled down to enjoy the pleasures of garrison life, unaware that their European attitudes and morals were causing deep offence to the city's Moslem population. The first signs of the impending crisis surfaced in 1841, when the British decided not only to withdraw part of their garrison, but also to cancel subsidies they had agreed to pay to the hill tribes. A brigade commanded by Sir

Robert Sale marched out of Kabul on the road to India, only to be attacked along the road by indignant tribesmen. Sale retired on the fortified town of Jellalabad, but as he did so a serious rising broke out in Kabul. Two British envoys were murdered in quick succession, and a large force of Afghans collected outside the town. The commander of the British garrison, the elderly Major General Elphinstone, decided to abandon Kabul and retire to India. He had with him some 4500 troops – including one battalion of Queen's infantry, the 44th Regiment – but was hampered by over 12,000 camp followers, including the wives of many of his British officers. Elphinstone began his retreat on 6 January 1842, and despite assurances from Akbar Khan granting him safe passage, Afghan marauders immediately fell upon his stragglers.

Within a week, the Kabul garrison had been utterly destroyed. Pressing on in bad weather across rugged terrain, the column came under increasing pressure from Afghan bands. Elphinstone seemed paralysed by the crisis, and it was left to junior commanders to organise some form of defence. On the second day of the retreat, as many as 2000 camp followers and 500 soldiers were slaughtered as they struggled through the narrow Khurd-Kabul Pass. The following day Elphinstone accepted Akbar Khan's offer to send the women into safe keeping. As the garrison collapsed into a pathetic, shambling mob, only a handful of soldiers under resolute officers managed to stay together. On the 13th the survivors of the 44th made a gallant stand on a rocky hill not far from the village of Gandamak; scorning Afghan offers of surrender, they were overwhelmed and either killed or captured. Just one man, a surgeon, William Brydon, escaped the slaughter to carry the news to 'Fighting Bob' Sale's garrison at Jellalabad.

Curiously, it was one of the *Royal Magazine*'s interviewees who was on sentry go at Jellalabad, and who first spotted the forlorn spectre of Brydon ('Bryden' in these accounts) approaching in the distance. Sergeant Edward Teer of the 13th Light Infantry was, by that time, the sole survivor of the Jellalabad garrison, and his account not only paints a telling picture of the events of the 1st Afghan War and the sufferings of the Jellalabad garrison, but also suggests something of the hardships of life in the early Victorian army.

The Cabul Massacre

The Cabul disaster of 1841 was 'the heaviest and most shameful which had ever befallen our arms in Asia.' Hatred of the restored native sovereign, and the deplorable incapacity of our commanders, caused the fanatical Afghans to rise against the British, who then occupied Cabul.

The commanders were assassinated, and the British were forced to leave the city. About 5000 British troops and 12,000 camp followers and women and children tried to retreat to Jellalabad, not a hundred miles away, but only accessible through gloomy mountain passes which were thick with snow. Of that large body only a few survived as prisoners, and only one soul, the famous Dr. Bryden, reached Jellalabad. Every other creature was butchered by the merciless Afghans.

It is a remarkable fact that the narrator of this story, Sergeant Edward Teer, a veteran who is close upon his ninetieth year, was the sentry who saw Dr. Bryden – that 'Remnant of an Army' immortalised by Lady Elizabeth Butler – approach the fort, and challenged him when he rode up to claim its shelter.

Let your imagination take you back for more than sixty years to the early forties, and to that wonderful land whose very name suggests unnumbered battles and incalculable booty – India.

Cabul – city of blood and treachery and intrigue – is on the very outskirts of our Indian Empire, in the heart of the hills, and it was occupied by British troops, who were so sure of their position that most of them who were married had been joined by their wives and families, as if the city were actually an Indian station. Profound peace was supposed to reign, and yet the Afghans were plotting to remove the hated Feringhees, who, they said, treated them, a proud and warlike race, as if they were dirt, and treated their women even worse.

Suddenly the signal was given for an appalling butchery. The streets of the city were filled with armed tribesmen clamouring for vengeance. They demanded the life of Sir Alexander Burnes, the British Envoy-elect. He tried to pacify them, and offered a heavy bribe for his own life and his brother's. A hillman, who pretended friendship, guaranteed to take them into safety if they would disguise themselves as natives. They did so, but, as soon as they had left their house, the traitor made them known, and they were cut to pieces.

That was the beginning of ruthless work with fire and sword and musket. From that day onward, the rioters were reinforced by fierce hillmen, who hurried forward so that they might share in the plunder and revenge. Just before Christmas-day, Sir William Macnaghten, the envoy, who had tried to overcome the deceit of the Afghans with deceit of his own, was found out and treacherously murdered, and there was nothing left but to try to retreat to Jellalabad, and seek the protection of the British and native garrison there under the brave Sir Robert Sale.

Six hostages were demanded by the Afghans, and amongst those who were left were Lady Sale and her daughter-in-law, Mrs. Sturt. The sick and wounded were left also, and then, at nine o'clock on the morning of January 6th, 1842, began that retreat which is without parallel in our annals.

Snow had fallen heavily, and was a foot deep even on the regular track. The disheartenened, dejected army slowly picked its melancholy way through

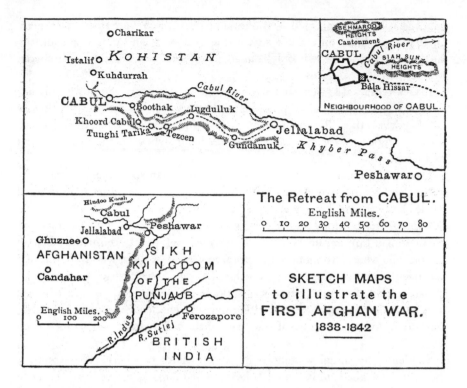

The Retreat from CABUL.

SKETCH MAPS
to illustrate the
FIRST AFGHAN WAR.
1838-1842

snow and slush, escaping from a pitiless enemy into a country as merciless. The women and children were carried in doolies, guarded by a score or two of cavalry and infantry.

It was like a gigantic wounded animal crawling on the face of the wild, barren country, with every part exposed to ceaseless danger. Long, indeed, before the rearguard left Cabul the bloodthirsty Afghans had fallen upon it, and the snow was dotted with corpses.

Only five miles were covered in the course of that unspeakably depressing day. Then came a night of unmitigated suffering and horror. The intense frost killed many starving men and women and little ones, while Afghan knives and bullets claimed many more. Only a few tents remained, and these were used for the women and children and two or three of the commanders, amongst them General Elphinstone, the chief.

Near Cabul is the Little Cabul Pass, which must be traversed before Jellalabad is reached. It is a gloomy, terrible road at best, but infinitely awful now when that long, straggling, despairing body of human beings was hurrying into its forbidding mouth. Well indeed might they have fancied that they were entering the jaws of death or hell, for as they gained its portals the hillmen hovering in the cliffs above fired incessantly, and hurled rocks upon them. There was a helter-skelter hurry through the pass to reach the open plain beyond.

Fighting valiantly, the rearguard and the gunners were slain in the pass, and so overwhelming were the onslaughts of the barbarous assailants that on the morning of the 9th fewer than a thousand fighting men were left alive, while thousands of camp followers had been massacred and all the baggage plundered.

A halt was made, and in sheer despair the list of hostages was lengthened. With them were transferred all the women and children and the wounded officers. Another long pass was traversed on the 10th, which was a repetition of the butchery and outrage and plunder of the previous days, so much so, that only two hundred and fifty white men emerged, every native soldier being killed or dying of famine or exhaustion.

Yard by yard, night and day, the survivors struggled on despairingly, their pathway through the snow being marked by the bodies of the dead or dying. So they continued, ever hoping to reach Jellalabad, until they came to a cleft in two enormous walls of rock. Into this fatal chasm they forced their way – only to find that their path was blocked by tree-trunks and branches of the prickly holly-oak. While struggling to overcome this unexpected obstacle the writhing troops and followers were shot down from above, and the gloomy hills re-echoed with the hideous yells of Afghans, who rushed in upon them with their cruel knives and put the finish to their work of butchery.

Even yet a few of the soldiers escaped from the pass into the open country beyond; but salvation was denied them, and nothing more appalling has been pictured in regimental annals than the last stand of the British soldiers in those fatal hills – prominent amongst them being the old 44th Foot, now the Essex Regiment.

Three men, indeed, struggled onward until they were within a few miles of Jellalabad, but they were overtaken and killed, and only Dr. Bryden, after a week of unexampled sufferings and horrors, rode on his exhausted horse into the fort – 'remnant of an army,' indeed! He alone had effected the retreat to the friendly fort, although about a hundred and twenty men, women, and children were living as prisoners in the keeping of Mohammad Akbar, the man who had treacherously shot Macnaghten dead.

Now let Sergeant Edward Teer go on with the story.

I had left Cabul only two or three weeks before the general rising against the British and the murder of the leading officers, and had gone with my regiment, the 13th Light Infantry, to Jellalabad, where Sir Robert Sale, as second in command, was at the head of a brigade. We had been forced to fight our way from Cabul, and fight so hard that one bit of the march,

through a pass only ten miles long, took us thirteen hours to cover. We had
to drive the hillmen off at every step. I potted at them steadily, being encouraged by a staff officer whom I afterwards knew to be Captain Havelock, and
who in later years became one of the heroes of the Mutiny.

Soldiering was soldiering in those days – one of my first sights in Candahar,
before going to Cabul, was seeing an Afghan blown to pieces from a gun,
for the trivial offence of spitting in the face of an English soldier! I had been
ill with sunstroke and had just left hospital, and, oh! how sick it made me!
They put a board across the muzzle, the man was tied to it, and then board
and victim were blown to bits when the gun was fired.

As if our marching and sufferings on the way from Cabul to Jellalabad
were not enough, we had to escort a dozen prisoners of the 13th who had
been court-martialled and sentenced to transportation to Van Diemen's Land,
but our general released them on the way, on his own responsibility. Those
were the days of old John Company, remember, before India was actually
taken over by the Crown.

We left Cabul on October 8th, but did not enter Jellalabad until
November 14th. The Afghans were close upon our heels, harrying us,
and had got into the fort ahead of us, but we drove them out and
worked without ceasing to strengthen the city and hold it until we were
relieved.

Until we were relieved! That was the pity and the irony of it!

We had taken the fort, and now the tribesmen were gathering to wrest
it from us. We were waiting for relief, for reinforcements, and from the very
people who were themselves compelled to fly and try to seek refuge with us
in Jellalabad!

But of all those terrible happenings we knew nothing. We deluded ourselves into the comforting belief that help was coming, and were we not justified, for had we not heard that General Elphinstone was leaving Cabul?
We, who had covered the same route, knew how long it took an army
to get from Cabul to Jellalabad, and we reckoned up the days as only prisoners
who are craving for their liberty count them.

Now came the saddest and most thrilling day that has marked my life,
nor have I known a more momentous one in all my days of soldiering and
adventure.

It was January 13th, two months after we had entered the fort, and I was
on sentry duty on the walls over what we called the Cabul Gate. At such a
time, in such a place, imprisoned in an enemy's fort in the heart of that
enemy's country, the unbidden thought arose, as it had arisen so often lately:
'Will the promised relief never come? Shall we never again hear the welcome
sounds of English voices, never more behold the bronzed and resolute
faces of the British soldiers, the faces that mark the men whose lives are

always threatened and in peril?' No human being who has not been in such a desperate case can know or understand the craving that possesses one who was placed as I and the rest of us were placed – on the very outskirts of the world, with nothing to mark one weary day from another but the tale of death or work or suffering.

The yearning question had been put a hundred times, and as often answered. See the relieving force? Have the reinforcements with us? Of course we should! Had it not been ordered that an army should be sent to us, and were not orders such as that at all times carried out when British troops received them?

Surely our help was near! Surely the hateful plains which were everlastingly the same would be brightened with the glorious scarlet of those old and distant days before khaki had been even dreamt of as a fighting colour for our soldiers.

'Ah! What was that?' Even as I thought like that while looking from my post towards that spot where I knew the relieving force must first be seen, I saw a moving object! It was a mere speck, but the speck grew larger and still larger until it was revealed as a man on horseback. That I knew, and I knew as surely that the man was not an Afghan, because the Afghans' clothing was a dirty white, and his was black.

A very tumult of excitement and conjecture filled me. I watched his coming with a gaze that never faltered – never left him, and all the time, as man and horse grew more distinct, what could I think except that here was an advance messenger to bring the glad tidings of approaching British reinforcements?

The solitary horseman rode towards the fort. It was like a dream to watch him coming out of nothingness – a thing so small in a country so vast, a creature so helpless in a land where cruel tribesmen swarmed.

On he came until he was only 200 yards from the fort. Then he dismounted and knelt down behind a little bit of garden wall – for fragments of a wall had been left, just enough to cover a man, and giving shelter to the stranger who had ridden up. From that protecting spot he scanned the fort, and God alone knows what his feelings must have been to see a British sentry standing out against the Indian sky.

Then, and not till then, when I saw that the lonely rider was an Englishman and a fugitive, I gave the alarm. How did I raise it, you ask? Well, at such a time a sentry cannot and does not always act according to a cut-and-dried instruction.

I was full of wonder and excitement, and I turned towards the inside of the fort and shouted:

'There's a European behind a bit of the garden wall! He is dismounted!'

On hearing that amazing cry the officers rushed out and scrambled on to the walls. They saw that the fugitive was a fellow-countryman, and that he was utterly exhausted. They signalled to him to advance, and more than that, they rushed forward to succour him, and two of them 'linked' him into our place of refuge. His horse – so badly wounded that it died next day – was brought in, too. That was when we had opened the gate of the fort and lowered the only drawbridge we possessed – one which spanned a trench we had dug outside the walls.

Not until then did we learn the too terrible truth – that this worn-out man whose very looks inspired a melting pity, was Dr. Bryden, a British Army doctor, and that he was the only survivor of the army which had left Cabul to join us.

He alone, this fugitive who had seemed to come from nowhere, was left of a force which numbered nearly sixteen thousand souls!

'Remnant of an army' indeed!

Human nature is prone to selfishness, and perhaps the feeling that at the outset possessed most of us was one of bitter disappointment that no relief could come from the quarter to which we had looked; but whatever selfishness there might have been was swallowed up in sympathy for this lonely fugitive, and grief for the slain – and worse – away in the gloomy passes. The doctor had fallen into good hands indeed, and no pains were spared to bring him round.

What a night it was which closed that awful day! At dusk the buglers were told off to the city walls – for what? To sound the 'Advance and assembly!' To send the message of welcome and safety ringing over those barren plains and amongst those pitiless hills, to sound those clear and stirring notes which would have been so gladly heard by those whom death had made silent for ever.

Was ever anything more pitiful than this invitation to the wanderers to come into the fold?

There were none of us who did not see the deep significance of it all, and none more clearly saw it than our commanding officer, who went to the buglers and sorrowfully told them that he never expected to hear the resurrection bugles, 'for,' he added, 'these are the resurrection bugles for General Elphinstone's army. There is not another man of them left alive!'

And so we knew when the doctor told his story.

First we heard that he had parted company from three other officers only eight miles from Jellalabad, and next morning we sent out a party to find them. We discovered the bodies of two, and carried them into the city, where we buried them; but the third was never accounted for.

Of the gloomy stories which he told, none moved us more than his narrative of the death of General Sale's son-in-law, Captain Sturt, who had married Miss Sale in Cabul just before the disastrous retreat, and whose bride was amongst the hostages left behind. Captain Sturt was informed that a European woman was lying dead in the snow, and that a child, which was still alive, was by her side. 'We must save that child!' cried Captain Sturt, and, reckless of his own life, he dashed forward – reckless, I say, because the work of massacre was going on, and on every side men and women and children were falling in the snow under the Afghan knives.

As the captain picked the child up he was shot through the heart, and fell dead.

The mother's name was Stokes, and she was married to a private in the 13th. She was one of three soldiers' wives – unhappy creatures! – who had come out from England and been taken up to Cabul. The Afghans sent the child in to us some time afterwards. It was greatly disfigured by tattooing. I remember it well, because it was in a tent next to mine and used to keep me awake at nights by shouting, in either Hindustani or the Afghan tongue. Poor little creature! Who can wonder if it had bad dreams, remembering what it had gone through?

For six sad nights our buglers sounded the 'Advance and assembly' from the walls, then we ceased to hope that stragglers from the vanished army would answer the call, and after that the bugles rang no more.

We held out in the city against the Afghans for six long months, and defied all their efforts to crush us.

But there is only one outstanding thing that I am going to tell about, and that was a happening so terrible and nerve-destroying that I have never hesitated to say that I would rather fight in a hundred battles than live through that catastrophe again.

On February 18th there was one of those mysteries of Nature which in those days few men could understand. The air was so full of electricity that the sentries could not hold their muskets, and had to stand beside them, for to touch metal of any sort was to have the body thrilled with countless needle-pricks.

This was awesome enough in the daytime, when man's courage is at its highest, but it was unendurable at night. There was the sense of an overwhelming danger, and with it the helplessness of perfect ignorance. Not even the officers could explain the mystery, and we could only wait fearfully for a solution. In the darkness, the electric force played round the tips of the bayonets, making balls of ghostly flame.

These dreadful signs disappeared with the night, and, soldier-like, we forgot our fears and went about our work.

But just before noon next day there was a strange, unearthly noise like thunder. Instantly we thought that the enemy had outgeneralled us, and had sprung a mine to encompass our destruction; then we knew that no work of man had startled us.

Believe me, the very earth heaved like a stormy sea, aud the great mountains near us literally danced.

In that time of peril we thought the hills would fall upon and bury us.
As it was, we were hurled to the ground, and when, in speechless fear, we
staggered to our feet again, we reeled like drunken men. We clutched each
other and never spoke a word, but there was not a blanched face on which
was not written the word 'Lost!'

The earthquake, for such it was, lasted about eighteen seconds, and
destroyed in a flash of time our heavy labours of four months. Our works of
defence – how puny against such a mighty power! – were shattered; some
of the native troops were buried in the hospital, which collapsed, and some
were injured. The earthquake was guilty of some strange freaks, too, for it
hurled one of our officers and a man who was bargaining with him for a pipe
through some piled arms, but by extraordinary luck the two escaped being
cut to pieces by the bayonets.

While we were standing about in groups, awed and silent, the brave
Havelock said solemnly: 'Now, men, that is the voice of the great "I Am,"
telling us not to put our trust in big guns and mud walls, but to trust in
Him, our God!' I learnt to venerate the name of that great soldier, and none
the less because when he had spoken like that he added: 'At the same time,
we must get the guns up!'

And get to work we did. We patched up our defences and replaced our
guns, and as for the period when we were at the mercy of the foe, we were
spared his onslaughts because he, too, had suffered, and had abandoned the
siege for a while so that he could run home and repair his shattered villages.

For two more weary months we held the fort against the whole of the
Afghan army, which had the captured English guns to use, while we had no
help from anywhere. There was a friendly chief amongst them who suddenly
galloped up to our walls, threw himself from his horse and jumped into the
ditch, marvellously escaping the shower of bullets which followed him. When
we got him inside we found that he had brought gold for our use and was
quite weighted down with it. He remained with us throughout the rest of
the siege.

We had the excitement of our sorties, and the sending of spies. One of
these spies, dispatched by Havelock, had his message hidden in a cake. The
Afghans caught him, and by way of warning to those who might try to do
the same, they choked him with his own cake before our eyes. But desperate men can never be deterred, and at last a spy got safely through, with his
cypher dispatch hidden in a quill.

Then came a solemn night when we were to risk everything in the forlorn attempt to rush from the city upon the enemy, to capture that food
without which we must surely perish. We knew how desperate the effort was

considered when we received orders that all who wished to make their wills
must have them ready for attestation at midnight, when company officers
would witness them and company pay-sergeants would issue paper for the
purpose. But there was not paper enough for all, and I was amongst those
whose wills were left unmade.

We sallied forth and conquered, for we put the enemy to flight and seized
his provisions, and not only that, but his standard. It was Sergeant White,
of the 13th, who took it, and he got £20 a year pension for taking the flag,
which was sent to the Tower of London.

Then, on April 17th, there came to our relief the Army of Revenge, and
words cannot describe the exultation in our hearts as we saw the redcoats
coming.

And was our welcome any the less joyful because our bands mounted those
mud walls from which I had challenged 'the remnant of an army' and played
the deliverers in with 'Oh! but you're a long time a-comin'?

The massacre of the Kabul garrison provoked a stiff British response. A relief
force under the command of Major-General Pollock was assembled at Peshawar,
on the Indian border. Pollock advanced into Afghanistan by the most direct route,
the Khyber Pass, brushing aside Afghan resistance as he did so. Indeed, Pollock
was among the first British officers to realise that the key to defeating the Afghans
in their own territory lay in adopting their own tactics; in driving the Afghans off
the heights, and seizing the commanding ground on the hills above them, Pollock
pioneered the guiding principle of frontier warfare – that of 'taking the high ground'.

Pollock's orders were simply to extricate the surviving garrisons from
Afghanistan, but he contrived to spend several months rampaging through the
country, wreaking revenge for the massacre of the Kabul garrison, and, indeed,
securing the safe release of some of the prisoners held by the Afghans. It was
not until October 1842 that British troops finally withdrew from Afghanistan.

Yet despite the work of Pollock's 'Army of Retribution', the 1st Afghan War
had proved a complete disaster. The attempt to place a compliant ruler on the
Afghan throne had failed – Shah Shuja had been murdered as soon as the British
garrison first abandoned Kabul, and Dost Mohammed had returned in triumph –
and the blow to British prestige had been enormous. The British were compelled
to allow events in Afghanistan to take their own course for more than thirty years.

Instead, the Company's response was to extend direct control up to the very
borders of Afghanistan. This necessitated the dispossession of two independent
states: the amirates of Sind, to the south, along the lower reaches of the Indus
river, and the Kingdom of Lahore, beyond the Satlej to the north.

The acquisition of Sind proved straightforward enough. General Sir Charles
Napier was entrusted with the task, which he achieved by provoking the Amirs
with a treaty he knew they could not accept. When a British outpost in southern

Sind was attacked, Napier rushed 2600 troops across the border, and dispersed the Amirs' forces after a sharp fight at Miani on 17 February 1843. When, after further fighting, the Amirs enquired what terms Napier would offer, he replied 'Life and nothing more. And I want your decision by 12 o'clock, as I shall by that time have buried my dead and given my soldiers their breakfast'. The Amirs submitted.

The Kingdom of Lahore, however, was never likely to be such a walk-over. The kingdom had emerged early in the nineteenth century under the command of the dynamic and ruthless Maharaja Ranjit Singh, who had used the Sikh faith as an instrument to forge a common identity among his followers. Sikhism was originally a reformist Hindu sect, but it had acquired a militant edge during its early days, when its followers were persecuted by the Moslem Mughals, and its teachings encouraged adherence to military ethics and discipline. Working upon this philosophical foundation, Ranjit Singh had employed European mercenaries – mostly French veterans of the Napoleonic Wars – to raise and train a formidable army. Known as the Khalsa, the Sikh army consisted of a core of trained regular troops, uniformed along similar lines to the Company's forces, supported by a large force of troops armed and trained in the traditional Indian manner.

Ranjit Singh had been astute enough to maintain good relations with the Company, while at the same time ensuring his own political independence. In 1839, however, he died, and the Kingdom of Lahore was split with bitter faction-fighting among his successors. After a period of confusion, the Khalsa emerged as the most powerful political force within the kingdom. Anti-British feeling within the army was encouraged by generals who, taking their cue from the Afghan debacle, saw a raid into Company territory as a means of furthering their political ambitions. In 1845, the Khalsa crossed the Satlej, and besieged the Company outpost at Ferozepore. Its exact motives for embarking on the campaign remain obscure; at its most simple, it is possible that the expedition was little more than a raid en masse.

The Company responded by hurrying an army under Sir Hugh Gough to the front, and the stage was set for some of the toughest battles yet fought by British troops on Indian soil. The character and discipline of the Sikh army was such that the battles of the 1st Sikh War were essentially Napoleonic struggles, played out in the heat of north-western India. Gough attacked the Sikhs in a series of brutal slogging-matches – Mudki, Ferozeshah, Aliwal, Sobraon – gradually driving their concentrations back beyond the Satlej. His success in each battle was largely dependent of the willingness of his infantry to maintain assaults in the face of skilful and heavy Sikh artillery fire. John Howton was present in the ranks of the 50th Regiment throughout most of these battles. Recalling the events more than fifty years later, his account blurs the distinction between individual battles in what was, in any case, as the interviewer commented, 'practically one continuous struggle'.

The First Sikh War

We were charging for the guns.

I was young, and full of life and strength – and I had spiked guns at Punniar in '43. So there was a familiar look about the grinning muzzles, and the sort of invitation to come on that no British soldier could resist.

And we did charge, too, in those hard fighting days in India, when most things depended on the bayonet. Colours flew, bullets whistled, steel flashed, smoke choked us, thirst tortured us – yet whenever the bugles rang out the wild 'Charge!' a fierce 'Hurrah!' was shouted and we tore along, sweating and panting in our stiff and sweltering uniforms. And we nearly always got there.

I was rushing on with my brave old regiment, the 50th, on the right of the British line. The Sikh intrenchments were ahead of us, the Sikh guns were belching death, the Sikhs themselves were daring and defying us.

What a mad confusion it was!

The intrenchments were only forty yards away; we were nearly in them, almost within steel touch of the warriors of the Sutlej, who had conquered even the Afghans. I was rushing ahead, strong on my legs, sound in my lungs, seeing nothing but the gunners and the guns, wanting nothing but to be in amongst them.

Suddenly, owing to a shock which I did not know then, and which I have never understood since, I fell to the ground and lost my senses. How long I remained unconscious I cannot say, but perhaps not more than a few moments. When I came round, I saw that my cap was lying just in front of me, and that the regiment was forging on, still towards the intrenchments.

I looked up at the batteries, and saw a great, bearded Sikh waving his sword and shouting to his men to keep the hated *feringhees* off and destroy them. I looked at my musket and saw that it was loaded. 'Well,' I said to myself, 'before I get up I'll have a trial shot.' I stretched myself on the sandy plain and took a nice, steady aim. Whether my bullet went home or whether it was somebody else's, I cannot say, but the moment I fired the Sikh disappeared. Then I jumped up and ran on to rejoin my section, fourteen or fifteen men.

Marvelous is the luck of war!

I had been struck down, which seemed bad fortune indeed; yet even as I rushed back to my comrades they were destroyed by a shower of grape-shot from one of the guns. All were killed or wounded except the sergeant – Godwin they called him – who was left standing.

'Come on!' he shouted, and the pair of us, sole survivors of our section, dashed onward for the intrenchments. I had plucked up wonderfully, and I was the first to reach them. I staggered blindly on and slipped down a sandy bank six or eight feet deep, which they had built up with a few planks; then I struggled up the opposite sloping side to a twelve-pounder gun which was mounted in their battery.

I got my arm round the muzzle and ducked my head under the very mouth. Instantly there was a terrific flash and a deafening roar. The gun had been fired, and my cap had gone with the ball, but my head was left on my shoulders. Yet so close was I to the explosion that for three weeks I was deaf owing to the jar of the recoil.

But I was in amongst the guns. I had now a footing in the embrasure, and where I had got two or three more quickly followed, and larger bodies after them. In that way, with our successful charge, we finished the work of the field artillery and the rocket battery.

We formed a sort of half-moon round our trophies, and the Sikhs, knowing that they could not recover their guns, began to retire from the intrenchments. This was Sobraon, remember – I am not talking about the battles in order, but as they come into my mind; and since they all made what was really one great fight, it does not matter.

Well, when the Sikhs began to leave their stronghold they had only one way of escape left open to them, and that was across the Sutlej, a broad, swift river in their rear. A bridge of boats had been thrown over the stream, and it was towards this and safety that the enemy pressed forward in hurrying, disordered thousands.

Safety seemed assured for them, yet they met their doom just when they felt most secure, for our engineers had been at work on the bridge, and when it was blocked up with flying fugitives, the very middle of it was blown into the air. The Sikhs who were nearest the intrenchments pushed on, not knowing what had happened, regardless of the noise and shouts, and by sheer weight of bodies drove hundreds of their fellows into the yawning chasm. So it happened that at Sobraon, where thirteen thousand Sikhs perished or were wounded, men by regiments, who had not received a shot or scratch in the battle, died unexpectedly in the water.

Ah, yes! It was a great fight, a stubborn battle, a chapter of thrilling things, and abounding in those strange incidents which do not seem to come about in warfare nowadays, because times and men are so different. In those days there was no Victoria Cross, yet soldiers did not do lesser deeds because there was no bronze recognition of their valour. They took up fighting as their life's trade – once a soldier always a soldier was a pretty general rule; and there was no chance for a young man who had scarcely learnt to march talking about having a claim on his country because he had served it.

But I must not moralise. I must get back to the guns and the Sikhs and the battle. We had our own regimental Colours, and many a fierce fight in those old days was waged around them. It was our duty to defend them to the last, and we were always just as keen to seize the enemy's. We clung to and preserved our own, and when the fight was over we found that we were a third Colour to the good. It was captured in a gallant way, and, by reason of one of those strange things which are done in time of war, the wrong man got credit for the performance.

The Sikh Colour was wrested from the enemy by a brave fellow named Leonard Hale – exactly how or where I do not know and nobody could tell. But he had it and he came up with it and made a rambling, excited statement about it. He wanted to take it to the spot where our own regimental Colours were, and he was making his way towards them when one of the officers, Lieutenant White, stopped him and told him he could not reach the place. 'If you will give it to me,' he said, 'I will take care of it.' And so Hale delivered up his Colour, and that was the last he had to do with it, for Mr. White got his name down for it, and poor Hale was knocked completely out.

There was another man who took another Colour – McCabe, of the 61st – but he was sharper than Hale, and stuck to it until he planted it alongside the Colours of his own regiment. Mark the difference in men's fortunes. He got a commission for his performance, and was posted to the 18th Royal Irish. I saw him when he came from China with them. The 61st were always great friends of the 50th.

I have been putting the cart before the horse a bit, beginning with Sobraon when I should have started with Moodkee; but I suppose that is because a man at times would rather look at the finish of a great and heavy enterprise than at the start or middle. We can, however, work back a little and speak of a few of the many things I saw and heard, and of some of the famous men who were then either at the summit of their fame or winning their spurs. Among the latter was Havelock, brave and true as he always was until he died in the Mutiny – here, there, and everywhere, escaping death in the most wonderful manner.

It was Havelock who, at Moodkee, brought back a native regiment that had turned tail, bitingly telling them that the Sikhs were in front and not behind. There was Sir Robert Sale, who was mortally wounded at Moodkee, Sir Hugh Gough, and, above all in my recollection, Sir Harry Smith. What a soldier he was! What a fighter! What a swearer! What a friend! And how the whole Army worshiped him! South African towns to-day remind you of what he did there and in India – Harrismith, Ladysmith, Aliwal North, and so on. He was a stern disciplinarian, but he tempered swift and awful justice with a mercy that saved many a humble soldier's life.

There was the distressing case of poor Jim Harris. He had been on duty for two whole days and nights – lots of us had to do that during the whole of our short but terrible campaign. Harris was a good soldier, but after all he was only a man. In spite of his excessive duty, he was put on again for the third consecutive night. In such a climate, with such work to do, this burden was more than he could bear. He marched to his post, and fell down in a dead sleep – he did not lie down, but literally thudded to the earth. When the officer went round to see that the sentries were alert and at their posts, he found poor Harris sleeping. They roused him, and put him in the rearguard for the night.

Next morning the sentry was taken before Sir Harry, sad enough, for he knew that he had been guilty of a crime for which in those days there was only one punishment.

'Ah! my poor fellow,' said Sir Harry, 'I am sorry enough for you; but you know that for such a crime as this you must die.'

The sentry – he was a very young fellow – looked piteously around him; but he could say nothing, and did not try to speak just then.

'Have you any excuse or explanation to give?' Sir Harry asked. 'Can you say why you went to sleep at your post in the presence of the enemy?'

Harris pulled himself together.

Any man can speak when he has to plead for the life that is likely to get short shrift.

'I can only say this, sir,' he answered. 'I was on duty for the third night in succession. But I didn't fall asleep, sir. I simply dropped to the ground. I don't even remember it, I was so tired.'

'Fetch the sergeant of the guard!' thundered Sir Harry. 'Now,' he said, when the sergeant came, 'how is it that a man was put on duty for three successive nights? Surely there were enough men to share the work without going to such extremes as this? How is it?'

They could not answer him. Then he had the orderly-sergeant of Harris' company before him, probing the thing to the very heart; but the Colonel put a sort of stopper on.

'I am very sorry, Sir Harry,' he said, 'so sorry that I feel as if I would like to be shot myself; but there has been foul play.'

'Yes,' replied Sir Harry, 'foul play and bad management.'

Then he turned to the prisoner again. 'My lad,' he said, in kinder tones, 'you have been guilty of a very terrible crime; but you have been imposed upon, and I shall forgive you.'

So the prisoner was set free, and we were almost as glad as he was, because he was a nice boy, a very nice boy. Poor fellow! he did not enjoy his pardon long. We went into action again soon after that, and he was killed.

It was things like this that made Sir Harry worshiped by all the men. There were other reasons why we loved him, too. Like the good commander he was, he always gave his soldiers his first consideration. He liked the barrack and battlefield calls well enough, so did we; but he loved as well, when we were on those long, hot, dusty marches, which were more dreaded than meeting the enemy, to order the buglers to sound the glorious 'grog' call, or the call for meat and drink and bread to be served out. And it was woe, indeed, for the quartermasters if they weren't ready or began to offer excuses. I saw one of them come trembling up when the little Scotch bugler – 'Rush 'Em' we nicknamed him – had sounded the 'grog' call. The quartermaster said he had no grog available, because he had nowhere to put it.

'Nowhere to put it!' shouted Sir Harry. 'Why, your—fat carcase is big enough to store all we've got! Go and find it, or by—I'll sling you up to the topmost branch of the highest tree as a warning!'

It is wonderful what a few words in season from the right quarter will do. He went and got the grog from somewhere.

No, it was useless for any officer to shuffle about with excuses when Sir Harry had ordered a certain thing to be done. He knew that the welfare of his division depended on its proper feeding – we had such marches as had never been known in India since Wellington made his name there.

We had, in my regiment, a sort of link with the Iron Duke, too – a survivor of the Peninsular War. This was Lieutenant-Colonel Sir Thomas Ryan, who was then nearly sixty years old. He was severely wounded at Sobraon, and died a few days later at Simla.

One evening, after a terrible day, when most of us were nearly dead with fatigue, and thirst, and hunger, Sir Harry rode up and said: 'I think you fellows look very hungry. We'll have a double allowance of bread and beef and grog to-night.' He told someone to fetch the quartermaster, and the quartermaster came.

'Issue a double allowance of rations and grog, Mr. Moore,' he said.

'Oh, dear me, Sir Harry!' moaned the quartermaster. 'Look at the expense!'

'What the — has that got to do with you?' shouted Sir Harry. 'You haven't got to pay it!' And without another word the quartermaster turned his fat old pony round and wobbled off, I can tell you.

I think everybody has been agreed that one of the most extraordinary things about this stubborn Sikh war, this famous quartette of battles of the Sutlej, which in just over seven weeks smashed the finest native army in India, and gave the Punjab to England, was the number of guns which the enemy had, and the number that we spiked or captured or destroyed.

Spiking the guns! Why, it became so common that, when we had charged into the batteries and driven the Sikhs away, we used to get our ramrods, drive the point into the touch-hole and snap off the ramrod, leaving the gun useless. The authorities meant to supply us with proper gear for the work – hammers and nails: but we never got them. Like many other things, these did not come up from Delhi till the worst of the war was over.

At Ferozeshuhur and at Aliwal we got gun-spiking enough to rejoice the heart of a military glutton. Ferozeshuhur was a frightful two-days' fight, December 21st and 22nd – it made a sorry Christmas for many a man and many a home. We had been in the thick of it on the first day, and Sir Harry said on the second morning, when we were going to renew the battle: 'You will be in the third line to-day, because you were in the hottest of it last night.'

Well, I daresay we should have kept to that instruction all right, but even a general's orders cannot always be obeyed. It was a harassing night – one Sikh gun in particular worried us, a 32-pounder, which kept dropping pills in amongst us and doing heavy mischief. For instance, all the horses of one of our batteries were destroyed, so at daylight, in spite of what Sir Harry had said, we were desperately keen to get level with the guns again. We made towards them, growing more and more excited as we advanced. We pushed ahead until we were within a few, a very few, yards of the enemy. We were going blindly on, helter-skelter, with, as it seemed, no guiding hand, no master mind, amongst us. How was it, I wondered, that, although we were so near to the batteries, there was no one to give us the magic word to rush them? Almost as soon as the thought flashed through my mind there was a wild, mad shout of 'Charge!' followed by 'Hurrah!' as madly. Then it was a dash and a rush again, and at a bound we were in amongst the guns, and they were ours.

Now, the curious thing is that no one knew who had given the order to charge – all we could find out was that in the intense excitement somebody had rapped the word out – and we had obeyed. That came well on the other deviation, for instead of being in the third line we were in the very first again, and Sir Harry told us pretty luridly what he thought about us. But, all the same, I do not think that in his heart of hearts he blamed us very much for our disobedience, because, you see, we were in his own division, and he never liked his pet regiments to get left. All's well that ends well, but it might have finished very badly for us, seeing that only a little band of fifty made the charge, and the Sikhs could have rolled us up without feeling it. Luckily for us they hadn't stopped to count.

At Aliwal, as you know, there was a very famous charge by the 16th Lancers, and some fine gun-spiking. One of the last of the Aliwal troopers and one of the last of the officers have just died. The trooper, Mares, rode in the charge with his regiment, got up to the guns, spiked some of them, and galloped safely out. This was a very desperate encounter, because, although we had scored two great victories and driven the Sikhs over the Sutlej, we were too much weakened and exhausted to follow up our successes, and our having to wait for reinforcements led the enemy to believe that we had become more or less panic-stricken. So they recrossed the river and gave us battle.

Aliwal itself was a village which stood on the plain, and as we advanced to storm it and dislodge the enemy it did not look bigger than a house or an umbrella. We were about eleven thousand opposed to fifteen, but some of the fifteen thousand were hillmen who were not very plucky fighters, and they bolted and left the Sikhs to it. I cannot say that we were very sorry for that, for by this time we knew what brave, desperate fellows we had to fight – warriors who gave no quarter and did not ask for it.

Sir Harry – Aliwal was his own particular fight – led us on and handled us magnificently. We were in fine form, too, seeing that as soon as our spies had come in and told us that the enemy was ready to meet us, Sir Harry had ordered meat and bread and grog to be served out to us immediately. He knew that a British Army fought best on its stomach.

We were plunged into the thick of the fight, the infantry forging on towards the masses of Sikhs. We saw that the 16th Lancers were posted on the left of the line. We were going steadily at our work when we heard a terrific commotion, a noise which rose above all other noises of the battle.

First the trumpets sounded, then our own bugles rang – and we opened out to let the 16th thunder over the plain to charge the Sikh guns. They shook the very earth as they galloped through and past us, with wild shouts of 'Hurrah!' and 'Hurrah for England!' And, believe me, they had a foe who was worthy of the finest cavalry that ever carried lance. Before the charge the Sikhs had hurled away their muskets, and with their swords and shields had rushed upon the horsemen.

The Lancers were met with an awful fire; but they drove into the very heart of the Sikh masses, broke them up, scattered them, and captured or spiked their guns. A poor little trumpeter, who was one of the very first to reach the enemy, was literally blown to pieces. Not a fragment of him, not even a particle of his clothes, was ever found.

The Lancers drove the Sikhs away, but the broken masses formed up again about three hundred yards off, and defied us afresh.

Sir Harry dashed up to one of the field artillery officers. 'Abbott,' he said, 'we can't have them there. Warm them up a bit. Shift them.' And Captain Abbott did warm them, too. They found the heat too much, and so they sullenly withdrew across the river, leaving more than fifty guns with us. Two of their guns they saved, and actually got them over to the other side; but Lieutenant Holmes, who belonged to an irregular cavalry regiment, and Gunner Scott, a horse artilleryman, forded the river, spiked the guns – they were 12-pounders – and got safely back again.

Romance as well as blood entered largely into that long-past fighting in India. A great many French officers, veterans of the Napoleonic wars, whose very souls were wrapped up in campaigning, had entered the service of the

Sikhs, glad enough of any chance to fight against their old enemy. A few renegade Englishmen, too, were serving with the Sikhs.

In the very hottest of the battle at Aliwal the captain of my company, Captain J. B. Bonham, shouted: 'Hallo! Who's this coming towards us?' He pointed to a strange figure which was emerging from the battle-smoke, the figure of a man who obviously wanted to surrender. 'Thompson,' shouted the captain to a sergeant, 'go and meet him. Bring him in.'

The sergeant ran up and took his man, and piloted him to the rear-guard. He proved to be a very remarkable person, an Englishman named Potter, or Brown, I forget which, who had deserted from the East India Company twenty years before and had joined the Sikh army. He was now a general of the Sikh artillery, and was taken before our Commander-in-Chief, who had had letters from Brigadier Wheeler showing that he had wished to give himself up, but had been advised by the Brigadier that he could do greater service by remaining in his present position, and waiting till the war ended. Then, when matters had been settled, he was again brought before the Commander-in-Chief, who gave him the command of the new contingent.

After the fight was ended an extra guard was put over the prisoner in the evening, until Sir Harry should be able to see him.

When Sir Harry entered the guard-tent he began to make short work of such a man, and promised that he should be hanged from a tree first thing next morning. But apparently certain things were told him which made him waver or hesitate, or, at least, wish that some higher officer would deal with the matter. So he dispatched one of our fleet camels to the Commander-in-Chief, who was not far away, and the order came back for the man to be spared. Then it came out that he had been a very valuable ally for us, and had been in communication with the English to our great advantage. One of the very last things he did before bolting to us to rejoin his old countrymen – which was his first chance – was to have the Sikh guns so trained that the shot, instead of ploughing through our ranks, killing and wounding us, buried themselves harmlessly in the earth about a dozen yards in front of us.

The destruction of the Sikh concentrations at Sobraon in February 1846 effectively broke the Khalsa, and in March the Kingdom of Lahore submitted to the Company. The Sikh army was dissolved, and Company officials were distributed around the kingdom to administer it on behalf of the British.

Yet the kingdom was not truly defeated. Most of the fighting had taken place east of the Satlej, on Company territory, and large parts of the kingdom had neither been occupied nor pacified. Many members of the Khalsa felt that they had not been defeated by their enemy, but rather betrayed by their own high command. Their discontent found expression in the murder of two Company officials at the city of Multan in April 1848. The Company immediately hurried troops to Multan, but even as they did so members of the Khalsa rallied to oppose them. By the end of the year much of the Panjab was in open revolt.

The 2nd Sikh War had much in common with the first. Once again, Sir High Gough was given command of the Company's forces, and once again the fighting dissolved into a series of brutal slogging-matches. Gough found his advance blocked by Sikh artillery at Ramnaggar on the river Chenab on 22 November, and was forced to withdraw, slipping round the Sikh flank instead. On 13 January 1849 he blundered into a large Sikh concentration, which was well-placed on rising ground above the village of Chillianwallah. The subsequent battle was remarkable for two reasons; it was one of the most brutal battles of the entire Sikh Wars, and it was notable for the misfortunes which befell one of the Queen's battalions, the 24th Regiment. The 24th were ordered to take a Sikh battery at bayonet point, and suffered tremendous casualties as a result, including the loss of their Colours. Chillianwallah achieved a special place in the folklore of the 24th, an example of extraordinary courage in the face of folly; thirty years later, they recalled it to memory to wish themselves better luck in a campaign which, as it would turn out, brought them even greater suffering – the Anglo-Zulu War of 1879.

The story of Chillianwallah was told to the *Royal Magazine* by a survivor from another Queen's battalion, Sergeant J. Ford of the 61st Regiment. To set Ford's story in the context of the hard campaigning of the war in western India, Wood commented that between November 1845 and November 1850, the 61st marched 5295 miles, sometimes covering forty miles a day.

Chillianwalla: A Jungle Battle

Scorching heat by day, freezing cold by night – heat so fierce that men dropped dead in the ranks, cold so intense that comrades perished in their sleep – always marching, often over choking plains, ankle-deep in sand, carrying your crossbelt with sixty rounds of ammunition and your musket in your hands; with few tents, no comforts, little water, scanty rations – that was our training for the jungle fight at Chillianwalla.

And all for fivepence a day – when you got it, which you did when there were no stoppages. But there were many British soldiers under old John Company Bahadur who had never a penny due to them when they had paid for new boots and other equipment which they were forced to have to ply their trade of fighting. Yes, fivepence daily was our reward in wealthy, lazy, deadly India – so that John Company, despite his boundless riches, was not more liberal as a master than John Bull proved when the Honourable Company's troops became Imperial soldiers.

We had marched from Cawnpore, glad beyond telling to escape from a city which in eight months had claimed the lives of 89 men, 74 children, and 26 women of my regiment. Marching, suffering, fighting – that was our lot; but what did it matter, so that we got clear of the unhealthiest city in India?

Being tall and stalwart, I was in the Grenadier Company of my regiment, and the grenadiers in those days took the place of honour as the flank companies, and were distinguished by their bearskin headdress and the 'wings,' which you now see only on the shoulders of bandsmen. We were big, heavy men, and those who were smaller and lighter called us 'The Sandbags' – but was there ever a post of honour that was not belittled by those who did not fill it? We got level with the scoffers by calling them 'The Buffers.'

Through sandy desert and dense jungle we had forced our way to Chillianwalla, where between 30,000 and 40,000 Sikhs, with 62 guns, were waiting for us. They were in a formidable position and had advantages of which Lord Gough was ignorant when he resolved to attack it. In guns they equaled us; in troops they were two to one. They had a double line of intrenchments; in front of their position were obstacles such as boughs to cripple our cavalry work; in the rear was a rock like a precipice, down which we were at liberty to tumble if we carried their stronghold. But their greatest protection and our worst barrier was the jungle thereabouts – the jungle into which they lured us, and where many of our men were destroyed while they were as helpless as game in a battue.

We had been slow in getting into touch with the enemy, but now that we were face to face, and our old Commander-in-Chief had inspected us and told us how we were to fight, we knew that it would not be long before we were in the death grip. It was wonderful to notice the different ways in which men looked at things – some carelessly, even recklessly; some with a strange fear or overwhelming foreboding – but all consumed with eagerness to be up and doing and get the terrible tension over.

You have heard of people having a premonition of death? Those who will may scoff at it, but I know too well how true it is; and even in those far-off days, before the Crimea and the Mutiny were talked of, I had been a witness more than once of its fulfilment. You notice and remember these things most when they come nearest home to you, and a case came very closely home to me at Chillianwalla. There was a special friend of my own, by name George Hanlin, who had been with me in my company for nine years.

On the night before the battle we had walked to the regimental bazaar or market. We knew that the fight could not be long delayed, because already we had seen the enemy's camp very plainly. Most of us, indeed, were glad to think that we were so soon to measure strength – and I was in the majority. I had escaped death in so many terrible forms already – cholera, dysentery, and the hundred and one swift dooms of the East – that I could almost afford to laugh at muskets, guns, and steel, and I dwelt with a light heart on the prospects of the morrow.

Not so my friend. He was gloomy and disturbed, and when I said, as we returned: 'I think we shall have a bit of a brush with the enemy to-morrow, George,' he answered: 'Do you think so?'

'Yes,' I told him.

'Then,' he said solemnly, 'if we do, I'm sure to be killed.'

I tried to laugh his fears away. 'Why so?' I asked.

'Because I am,' he replied, and with that – a woman's reason and a fatalist's – I had to be content.

I could laugh and argue as I liked, but my words had no effect on him. He was positive, and, I believe, resigned – can it be that at such a time there comes to some of us the power of seeing into the unknown and comprehending the unfathomable? – and, talk as I would, and did, I could not cheer him or remove his conviction.

'No,' he repeated positively; 'I shall be killed. I know it, and I want you to take charge of my things and the few rupees I have.'

What could I do but promise? I gave him my word – and, oh! the solemnity of that night before the battle, the thoughts of home and far-off England, that possessed even the most reckless of us. And the grim sensations when the night fell and the hospital-sergeant came to our tent and issued bandages to the pay-sergeant – myself – with rough instructions how to put them on a wounded leg or arm!

That confirmed my friend's gloom; but, as for me, I went about my business and took things easily. I made up my accounts – for I was at all times methodical – even to the preparation of a balance-sheet between my company officer and myself. That took me until nearly midnight. Then I slept till five in the morning, when the *réveillé* sounded, and we all turned out, struck our tents and loaded up the elephants with them, and put our bedding on the camels. Two hours later we were ready to march – such a march as I had never before seen and was never again to know, even in India.

We went at it through the thick jungle and over ditches and hedges, on and on until we were near the Sikh outposts. Again we halted, and a dram of grog and a pound of beef were issued to each man. Half-an-hour's rest, then on again until noon, when we heard the first growl of the combat.

There was a crash in front of us, a flash of flame, a cloud of smoke, and the boom of artillery.

It was the opening music of our jungle battle.

But that was only, after all, an affair of outposts, and we were suffered to remain in peace on a space of open ground outside the jungle which we of our division had reached. From the spot where we piled our arms not one of the enemy was to be seen; so some of us lay down to sleep, while others kept awake and idled, too restless to repose.

I was sleeping peacefully when I was galvanised into life and action. What had happened?

What was the meaning of the scattering of our piled arms, the furious beating of our drums, the wild rushing of men, the hoarse shouting of our officers, the galloping of aides-de-camp? And, above all, what was the meaning of that terrific cannonade almost, as it seemed, in the midst of us?

The soldier's instinct gave the answer. This was the real battle at last.

As soon as I awoke I dashed for my musket, and fell into my place in the line that was already advancing to charge the enemy.

Grape and canister screamed about us – wildly for the present; but we had only covered a hundred yards when a round shot shattered the head of my comrade Hanlin.

His prophecy had come true – and with terribly dramatic emphasis, for of all who fell on that desperate field he was the first to be slain.

Our company officer turned round for an instant.

'We can do nothing for him?' he shouted. 'Come on!'

'No, sir, nothing,' I shouted back. 'He's as dead as a door-nail.'

Then we were struggling ahead again into the hail of missiles, with the earth around us becoming such a shambles that we could scarcely move without walking over fallen comrades. My company was thinned frightfully, for even early in the battle a third of its members were killed or wounded.

As we advanced I noticed one of many instances of the way in which the British soldier will keep his place in the ranks even when he is dangerously or mortally wounded. A comrade named Mason was lagging behind.

'What's the matter, Jim?' I said.

'I think I'm shot in the body,' he answered.

'Then you'd better fall out,' I told him.

'Not I,' he said; 'I shall be better directly.'

With that he pulled himself together and hurried up to his place in the front rank, like the brave fellow he was. He had scarcely done so, and had not even fired a shot, when he fell dead. Afterwards it was found that he was right, and that he had been fatally wounded by a shot in the lower part of the body.

When the fire of war is burning in your veins you will do things that in cold blood are impossible. How, if we had had time to think, could we have obeyed the orders to advance over ground every yard of which was a death-trap? It is hard enough work to go ahead across smooth ground, with nothing to oppose you, and when the air is clear and fresh; how hard, then, in an Oriental country, under a blazing sun, at the hottest time of the day, laden like beasts of burden, and, when we were not ploughing through sand, forcing our way through the swamp and jungle to get at the enemy, who were mowing us down with their guns and picking us off with their small-arms?

You can picture our case to some extent by imagining troops operating over a patch of country in England, advancing to the charge across land thick with high grass and broken up with ponds and swamps. At the best the progress would be slow; in circumstances like ours it equaled only a crawl. Yet in some way we went ahead, struggling through the jungle towards the Sikhs, for there was no going back, and the sooner we got to their position the quicker we should reach the end of the fight.

The jungle sheltered some of us from the fire; others it shielded from the sun when they were struck down, while it offered protection to many a poor wretch who crawled into its shade from the open where he had been wounded.

That passage through the jungle made many breaks and gaps in our line as we advanced, and by the time we were through it many companies had been reduced to sections; but we were clear of it at last, and got our chance to return the fire which already had destroyed so many of my comrades. We of the 61st gave it as hot as we got it, and the cannonading was terrific. A very inferno of artillery fire confronted us, but we had clear ground to rush across, and over it we went; to the muzzles of a battery of twenty guns. We dashed up and took them, and it seemed as if already we were to score a victory, because we had done the seemingly impossible.

It was at this thrilling stage of the battle that two sharp contrasts were afforded of the behaviour of troops in action. As it is with individuals, so it is with regiments; the one will show the extreme of courage, the other the utmost cowardice. The first quality was displayed by the 24th Regiment, now the South Wales Borderers; the second by a crack British cavalry regiment, which had greatly distinguished itself not long before, and did the same afterwards, when it found itself again. The 24th belonged to the 5th Brigade, and this was ordered to advance by Lord Gough, who was somewhat hasty tempered. The 24th were as fine and brave a lot of troops as I ever saw, and to tell them to advance was to set a spark to powder.

They rushed on, never stopping, forging over the dusty ground, forcing their way through the jungle, advancing until they were only eighty yards or so from the Sikhs. The danger and misfortune of their position was that they had to force their passage blindly, because they could not see the enemy towards whom they advanced. Then, in the twinkling of an eye, the open space they had gained was strewn with the mangled forms of British soldiers, for the Sikhs had opened fire from masked guns, and with grape and canister at point-blank range mowed the 24th down by sections.

It was an appalling slaughter, an unexpected and fatal check.

We were very near them, and I saw the whole dreadful drama, the hail of grape and canister, the blotting out of a regiment, as it seemed, the shattered ranks which but a moment before had been so strong and steady. Lieutenant-Colonel Brook, commanding the 24th, was slain as he encouraged his men in the attack; Brigadier-General Pennyquick was killed, too, and on that fatal field, where many mighty deeds were done, I saw none nobler than the hopeless effort of the brigadier's son to save his father's life. He was a young ensign, a mere youth, but he fought like a lion over his father's prostrate body, and fell only when he was cut to pieces.

On that great day, renowned for ever in the annals of the 24th, thirteen of their officers and 227 men were killed, and ten officers and 300 men were wounded. Almost exactly thirty years afterwards the 24th were annihilated by the Zulus at Isandalwana, and the story is told that just before the butchery the officers of the two battalions met, and, having a few bottles of wine left, they jokingly drank the toast: 'That we may have better luck and not get into such a — mess as we did at Chillianwalla!' A few hours later not one of the toast-drinkers was left alive.

But while the 24th at Chillianwalla did so bravely, some of the cavalry were seized with panic and bolted, tearing madly over the ground, caring for nothing but their own skins. They dashed over our wounded, and many a man who would have survived the enemy's bullets was killed by the hoofs of his own comrades' horses.

It is not well to talk too much of that part of the affair; but afterwards, when Sir Charles Napier inspected the regiment, he said some icy things, and the colonel went and committed suicide in his bathroom.

A worse punishment than that was given by those of us who had been in the fight and had seen what happened. Trust the British soldier for choosing the right way to show his liking or contempt – and many a crack cavalryman wished that he had stayed on the battlefield when he writhed under the taunt: 'Who turned their horses' tails to the enemy at Chillianwala?'

While the 24th were being destroyed in such wholesale fashion the 61st continued their advance. We had this great advantage, that the ground over which we were working was more open than the area of operations of the 24th. We could see our objective pretty clearly, and that was a Sikh battery here and another there – the guns being distributed in pairs and threes. At them we went. With a rush and a cheer we were upon them and in the midst of the gunners. It was short work to spike the weapons, shorter still to dispose of the artillerymen when once we could get the bayonet in.

The Sikhs were fierce and desperate fighters and splendid swordsmen. They did not show a sign of defeat until they recognised that the position which they had considered impregnable had been stormed and taken by the British and native troops. Then they began to withdraw, to pull themselves out of the wild *mêlée*, and seek the shelter of a safer place.

Many of their guns were ours, many more, which we could not bring away, we made useless; but because of our losses we were not able to clinch our victory for the present, so, after a short bout of one of the most ferocious battles ever waged in India, we were got together by our officers, slowly returned over the field, and made ready to pass the night.

That fatal afternoon passed, and the night came, bringing with it one of the heaviest rainstorms I had ever seen, accompanied by incessant thunder and lightning. In such a lurid setting we piled our arms, then set about a task which was infinitely worse than anything we had yet accomplished, and that was to collect our wounded and bring them in for the surgeons. Yet even then we were not so far overcome that we could not raise three rousing cheers when our old chief, Sir Colin Campbell, rode past our shattered regiment. It was said afterwards that his leadership of the 61st decided the action and saved the British Army; while the Duke of Wellington declared that our performance was one of the most brilliant exploits ever performed by that Army.

The commissariat was close at hand – so close that one of the camels laden with rum was struck by a round shot at the beginning of the battle, and, poor brute, wounded though he was, carried his two barrels of spirit for hours afterwards. Pay-sergeants were ordered to attend for grog, and I claimed the full allowance for my company's casualties. But nobody wanted rum, and the mournful and incessant cry was: 'Water! Water!' from the wounded – and the pity of it was that there was not a drop of water available.

Never can I forget that night after the battle. The air was rent with the groans and cries of the sufferers, and the more terrible sounds from those who were in the hands of the surgeons. Men who had passed unscathed through combat, who had borne themselves unflinchingly, quailed at the sights they witnessed on and about the rough tables which the doctors used. One man in particular was so overcome by what he saw that he went into hospital and died.

Merciful though the surgeons' work was, yet it was more hideous than the havoc of the battle, for in the one there was passive endurance in full consciousness, in the other the excitement of the contest, and, often enough, ignorance of the fact that injury had been sustained. The dim lights of lamps and candles, the lightning flashes showing for an instant the whole ghastly spectacle, the crashing thunder, the pitiless deluge of rain, the harassed surgeons working furiously, the cries, the groans – above all, the unutterably appealing looks of stricken men whose turn was coming – this was war stripped of its thrill and pomp.

In the jungle and on the open ground, when the day broke, I came across the dead and wounded wherever I turned. In the night some of the injured had fallen into the hands of the enemy, who gave no quarter, and it had not

been possible to find others. There were veterans and recruits in all sorts of
strange positions, some looking as if they were sleeping, others hideously
contorted. Of the living, most of the veterans were grim and reconciled, but
it was from the youngsters that the most heartrending prayers and appeals
came – and many a lad, with the freshness of home still on his face, was
calling for his mother.

At one spot I saw a fine Sikh who had attacked a British infantryman.
Sword in hand he had rushed upon his enemy just as the charge was being
rammed home, and while the ramrod was still in the barrel. The infantryman had seen that he could not reload in time to fire, so he had pulled the
trigger, and the ramrod was shot through the Sikh's face and head. Yet in
spite of his awful wound, the noble fellow never flinched or murmured; he
made no sound when I bent over him. He was carried to the surgeons, and
died as soon as they had drawn the ramrod out. In another place a British
soldier, badly wounded, laughed and chatted as he was carried from the field;
at the same time he complained of pain in his hands – yet both his arms
had been shot away.

Next day, when we buried our dead, the rain continued, deepening our
misery. Worst of all, perhaps, was that sad final ceremony. In two trenches
alone, which our sappers and miners dug, we buried 197 of the 24th and
fourteen of the 61st; then, thank God, there was work to do in intrenching
ourselves, and in the stress of labour we forgot our woes.

At last the sun came out again, and – such is soldiering – we laughed and
joked almost as if there had been no fighting – laughed when a horse broke
loose and galloped through the camp, with ropes and pegs flying about his
heels, or when a man barked his shins in the darkness, or a camel snapped
viciously, or when a new elephant, which did not fancy work, stampeded
with its huge load of camp equipage or gunny-bags.

The heat of battle vanished, the days passed quickly, and – the enemy
retreated from Chillianwalla. We started after him, our band playing as we
left 'St. Patrick's Day in the Morning.' For a whole month we and the enemy
kept in sight of each other, until he gave us battle once more at Goojerat.
This time we conquered him completely, pursuing him from mid-day until
dark. He left us his camp, baggage, ammunition, and fifty-three guns – and
our loss was only one-third that which we suffered in our jungle fight.

In both battles I escaped injury; but I was wounded not long afterwards
in a little affair with the Afridis, who were giving England trouble not long
ago. We were out skirmishing at the time, and saw a man on a camel with
a swivel gun – rather like a little ship of war let loose on land.

'I'm going to have a shot at that chap,' I said, and three of us rushed up
to within about forty yards, quite expecting an easy capture. But before we
could get our muskets up the swivel gun was fired, and the three of us went

down. I was shot in the leg, one of my comrades was shockingly wounded in the face, and the third was bowled over so badly that he could not live. He puzzled the doctors for a long time. Then they found that one of his brace buttons had been driven into him.

The Company's campaigns in western India effectively extended their control up to the foothills of Afghanistan, but they were among the hardest British troops had yet fought on Indian soil. Although the British regulars of the Queen's regiments had been heavily involved – and, indeed, some of the Company's troops were Europeans – the burden of conquest had nonetheless fallen heavily on the Company's Indian troops. Indeed, India could never have been conquered by the British without the complicity of some of her own subjects. Yet the extent of the Company's dependence on its Indian troops would become all too apparent when, in 1857, the army of the Presidency of Bengal turned against its masters, precipitating a bitter struggle in which the survival of British authority in India itself was at stake.

The so-called 'Great Mutiny' was both a military protest and a nationalist rising. It was started by Company troops who had legitimate grievances with their officers, and the discontent soon spread among the Indian gentry and landlords who felt the loss of independence which had come with Company rule. The rebels, both civil and military insurgents, looked to the person of Bahadur Shah, the last Mughal emperor, an ageing recluse in his palace at Delhi, to provide a figure-head, who conjured up for them the image of a pre-colonial golden age of Indian independence. Yet the rising was never a national one; it was confined almost entirely to the Bengal Presidency, and even here many Indians chose to adhere to British rule, rather than chance their luck with the rebels.

The military mutiny had been sparked off by the Company's attempt in 1856 to replace the smooth-bore muskets carried by its Indian sepoys with the new Enfield rifle. To load the new rifle, it was necessary for a soldier to bite the end off a waxed paper cartridge. Against a background of growing discontent over other conditions of service, the story spread among the Bengal army that the waxed paper contained animal fat. Since the cow was a sacred animal to the Hindus, and the pig an unclean one to the Moslems, this act carried a risk of great ritual defilement to both the two main groups who made up the bulk the Company's ordinary soldiers. Once the story took hold, it soon came to be believed that this was part of a wider European attempt to destroy indigenous religious practices to pave the way for Christian evangelism.

Mutiny was an accepted means of protest among Indian armies in the eighteenth and nineteenth centuries, and it was common for troops to express their discontent by refusing pay, or by disobeying their officers. The disturbances of 1857, however, were far more severe, both in terms of immediate action, and of their consequences. When troops were issued with the new rifle, most refused to accept it, and their commanding officers reacted with varying degrees of sympathy or harshness, according to their inclination. Some offered to replaced the offending cartridges with ones waxed in harmless vegetable fat; others bullied and shamed their men in front of their officers. A few isolated acts of violence gave no hint of the storm that was brewing; on Sunday, 9 May 1857 the 3rd Light Cavalry and 11th and 20th Native Infantry, stationed at the important garrison town of Mirath (Meerut), on the Grand Trunk Road which linked Calcutta in the east to the Panjab in the west, not only refused the new cartridges, but attacked their officers. Joined by the bazaar mob, mutinous sepoys slaughtered every European they encountered, and over the following few weeks the rising spread throughout the garrisons across northern India.

Private Joseph Bowater of the 6th Dragoon Guards was present in Mirath when the mutiny broke, and his account of the shock, horror and confusion felt by the European community was still vivid when he recalled his experiences nearly half a century later.

The Outbreak of the Indian Mutiny

From Gravesend with my regiment I sailed to Calcutta by the long sea route; from Calcutta I and the rest of us went by 'Mother Ganges' – India's sacred river – to Meerut, nearly a thousand miles away. Fresh from England, I had just settled down to army life under old John Company when the storm of the Mutiny burst. There were murmurs of it as soon as I reached Meerut, which was one of the principal stations in the country, because there had been many complaints that the British authorities were trying to degrade the caste by forcing the native troops to use cartridges which were greased with the fat of sacred or unclean animals. Secret messages had been sent from place to place in *chupattis*, which are native loaves of bread, and in lotus flowers.

Natives and Europeans were almost evenly matched at Meerut, although the advantage was with the natives. Amongst them were the 3rd Bengal Light Cavalry, the first regiment to break out into open revolt, and to set the spark to that awful flame which spread like wildfire. A troop of the 3rd was ordered to load and fire with new cartridges. Out of ninety men only five obeyed. The eighty-five were court-martialed at once, and sent to prison for five or more years. That was on Friday, May 10th, 1857. On the Saturday, the prisoners were put in irons and sent into the gaol at Meerut, and there were those of us who supposed that the mischief had been finely throttled at the very outset. How little we knew of the cunning, widespread plot which had been hatching in secret Oriental ways!

Then that Sunday came which was to sear itself on my memory as if it had been branded with a burning-iron. The morning went, taking the church parade with it; the hot, dull, lazy afternoon wore on, and the time approached for evening service. I had got through with my own worship, and the 60th Rifles were making ready for theirs, turning out with side-arms only. The officers were either preparing for church or dressing for riding or walking. There were a few ladies – officers' wives – and children, and these, too, were busy in the same way. In a word, there was peace in Meerut and a sense of security, in spite of all the ugly rumours.

Then the sleeping volcano of the rebellion burst into eruption.

There was a sudden rising of the 3rd Bengals, a rush to the horses, a swift saddling, a gallop to the gaol – which had no European guard – a breaking open of the gates, and a setting free, not only of the mutineers who had been court-martialed, but also of more than a thousand cut-throats and scoundrels of every sort. Simultaneously the native infantry fell upon and massacred their British officers, and butchered the women and children in a way that you cannot describe. Gaolbirds, bazaar riff-raff, and Sepoys – all the disaffected natives in Meerut – blood-mad, set about their work with diabolical cruelty, and, to crown their task, they fired every building they came across.

In the twinking of an eye, Meerut had changed from the perfect peace of a Sabbath evening to the noise and horror of a bloody field.

The British cavalry lines, where we were quartered, were some distance from the native cantonments, from which we were separated by rough and broken ground. It was over this hard country that one of the officers who had escaped from the massacre galloped up, and told us what had happened. But we already knew that something serious, something terrible, was on foot, and the colonel was even now on horseback, and had given the order to saddle, arm, and mount instantly. It had been scarcely necessary for the trumpets to sound the 'Alarm.'

If you remember our peaceful state, the suddenness of the rising – there is little doubt that the incident of the court-martial at Meerut had unexpectedly hastened the outbreak – you will understand that it was a work of some time and difficulty to get our squadrons ready for action. It was not a case of mere smartness for parade, but a matter of life and death, of issuing ball ammunition and doing the score-and-one important things which are necessary in making ready for battle. At least a couple of hours passed before we rode quickly out of our lines to fight the first fight of the Mutiny.

There has been, I know, harsh criticism because of what seemed to be an undue delay; but the critics have lost sight of the fact that when the Mutiny began we had not got half the horses broken in – some of them had never been saddled, even; and as for the troops, they were mostly like myself, raw lads fresh from home, dumped down in a strange country in the midst of a strange race, whose very lives and methods were deep mysteries to them.

You can imagine my feelings – fresh from England, and plunged straight-way into unexpected war. The circumstances could not have been more dramatic, more terrible; for as we rode off it was dark, and the darkness was reddened with the flames that rose from burning buildings. The still Sabbath, too, had been made hideous with the noise of fighting. All was horror and confusion, and scarcely a man of us knew what to do. But, even then, just as we were going forth to begin that long campaign, there were evidences of a belief in high quarters that the rising was only local and would die as swiftly as it had been born. For instance, General Hewett, who com-manded at Meerut, rode out in front of us and said: 'Men, don't fire on my poor, sober Sepoys. They will come back again to-morrow and be sorry for what they have done.' Yet, almost while that was being said, a handful of the officers and wives who had escaped the butchery ran breathlessly up to us, claiming our protection. Claim, indeed! There was no need to beg for that defence which every man would have given even at the cost of his life.

It was dusk, as I have said, when we rode from our lines, thinking that we should make straight for the very spot where fire and sword and musket were doing their work; but, instead of that, we turned away from the burn-ing buildings and hurried towards the Delhi road, because already many of the mutineers were marching to that city, India's ancient capital, and the rebels' rallying ground, to join hands with their fellows. We got in amongst a few of them with our sabres, then the 'Halt!' abruptly sounded, and we turned and rode back into Meerut, helped by the light of the moon, which had now risen.

We were just in time to share in the last of the struggle in Meerut itself, and to take a hand with the 60th and the Horse Artillery in saving the few Europeans who had managed to escape. All was turmoil, terror, and excite-ment – a blind groping after security for life and the station. Most of the mutineers were flying towards Delhi, but there remained the hordes of released prisoners, the bazaar loafers, the fanatics, and all the scoundrels who congregate in such a place at such a time. All that we could do was to shoot and sabre when we got the chance, and to gather together our poor fugi-tives, comfort them as best we could, mount guard over them, and take as many prisoners as we could lay our hands on.

The first thing I saw when I had time to look about at all was a sight which sickened and unmanned me then, and which has never failed to fill me with a furious grief when I have recalled it. And that was the spectacle of native bullock carts slowly coming up towards us, bearing the mangled forms of our gentle ladies and their little children – ladies who were laugh-ing lightly but an hour or two ago, children who were playing at their mothers' knees as recently.

Helpless and unprotected, they had been attacked even as they were getting ready for their Christian worship, or as they were resting in the cool of evening after the heat of an Indian day. Regardless of sex, in spite of their appeals for mercy, deaf to the piteous cries of the little ones, the mutineers had done their monsters' work.

Massacre itself would have been terrible enough; but they had not been satisfied with that, for to murder they had added outrage and nameless mutilation; and not the most callous of us could gaze unmoved upon the bullock-carts which bore their burdens to the hospital. Hospital, I say; but the building was really the theatre, and – the irony of it! – that very Monday evening a tragedy was to have been performed there by some of those who were now laid out in it.

I made my little effort of salvation. I saw a child, still living, one who had managed – God alone knows how – to get away. I rushed towards her, picked her up, carried her in my arms to the hospital, and lingered for just one sorrowful moment to learn her fate. Was she also stricken mortally, like the silent forms in the bullock-carts, or were that pallor and unconsciousness the inevitable results of the terrors of the rising? I put her down and bent over her, whispering words of hope and courage.

I raised her very gently to bid her be of good cheer and remember that she was amongst friends and soldiers. Then, with a sudden load of heaviness upon my heart, I put her down again, for my little, gently-nurtured maid had passed away as I tried in my poor way to soothe her. A rebel's bullet had pierced her brain. My soul rises in anger even as I speak of it – and it is nearly fifty years ago. Still the cry for vengeance surges through me now, as fiercely as it moved me then. Remember that, and the other, nameless things, when I shall come to tell you of the judgment that we meted out to mutineers and murderers.

Many of us – and I amongst them – throughout that long, sad night went round with sword and carbine, and from all sorts of lairs we turned out looters, murderers and mutineers, some with lighted torches in their hands. Meanwhile there was incessant strife, and wherever we looked we saw the darkness pitted with musket fire, as the Europeans came across the rebels.

Morning dawned at last – and what a mournful morning it was! What sights the day revealed, which it would have been a mercy for the darkness to hide for ever! Wherever we looked there was the same scene of blood and devastation. Meerut was a mass of smouldering ruins, and here and there, in the *débris* where they had met a nameless death, or in the open where they had been pitilessly slaughtered as they fled for refuge, were the corpses of men, women, and children.

There, where he had rushed out and implored his Sepoys to be loyal to their Queen, I saw the body of Colonel Finnis, commanding the 11th Native

Infantry, riddled with a score of bullets; there, struck down and cut to pieces as she tried to fly towards the European lines, I came across the wife of another officer of the same regiment; but, worse still, in another spot I beheld all that was left of the wife of the adjutant, who, before she was shot and cut to pieces, had had her clothes set on fire by men who were no longer human. And here and there I saw the still forms of little children.

Even in times of greatest horror there is found some gleam of comfort, some slender cause for joy. We found it on that fatal morning – and in a quarter, too, where, remembering how solidly banded the natives were against us, we might not have expected it, though, to be sure – and thank God for it – we found it.

Some of the *ayahs*, had risked their lives for their charges, and to do that they had combined the love of a woman with the craft of an Oriental. They had circumvented even the cunning of the mutineers, and, because of what they did, a few at least of the little ones were alive and well when day broke. Resourcefulness and courage had preserved a handful of Europeans as well, for by hiding in gardens or obscure corners, and even by swiftly disguising themselves as natives, they had survived the outbreak, and saved themselves until they could steal or rush for safety to our camps of refuge.

Upon the incidents of that heartbreaking morning I need not dwell – you can imagine them for yourself. Terrible though they were they were only the forerunners of thousands more before the Mutiny was crushed. We had to bestir ourselves in many ways – to protect the living and bury the dead. That last gloomy task was done without delay. Those who had been massacred were interred by the chaplain, and afterwards the other bodies, as they were discovered, were buried.

Peace of a sort fell upon Meerut again. The bulk of the mutineers were already at Delhi – they had made a hard forced march in the night, the cavalry helping the infantry – and we did not for the present follow them. But we strengthened Meerut, a few of the disaffected natives returned to their allegiance, and we had as reinforcements about a thousand Ghoorkas. Other companies of natives were ordered to Meerut, but they mutinied, murdered their commanding officer as soon as they arrived, and set off for Delhi. We were wide awake by that time, though, and we followed and killed or captured most of them.

Those of the mutineers who had not gone to Delhi set themselves to work with all the cunning of the native to annihilate us. First they tried to lure us into surrender, with the promise of safe conduct to the coast, so that we could sail for England. We laughed at their proposal, and kept them at bay with the report we spread that Meerut was undermined, and that at the first sign of their advance we would blow it up. This drove a good many of them away, but those who were left tried to bribe our water-carriers to poison the wells, which were our only source of supply. But, keen as we were in this direction, we lost sixteen poor fellows by poisoned water, and only stopped the diabolical mischief when we placed sentries over the wells.

Plots to destroy us sprang up ceaselessly. No sooner was one defeated than another replaced it, and just when we thought that we were able to rest from the attempts to poison us, we discovered another scheme of mischief. This was not against us human beings, but against our horses.

The mutineers resolved to steal down amongst us in the dead of the night and hamstring the poor creatures; then, indeed, we might have said farewell to safety. We heard of the plot – we managed to learn most of their intentions – and we prepared for them. We removed our native grooms – the *syces* – and kept watch over the horses ourselves. It was a thrilling bit of work, I can tell you, and made a tremendous demand on our pluck and courage. It seemed, indeed, as if we had not men but devils to deal with, for the mutineers came up literally like snakes – and in the dead of night, too.

Put yourself in our shoes for a little while, transport yourself to that gloomy station, with its unnumbered horrors, and you will understand why we jumped nearly out of our skins at every sound. We were not veterans, mind you, but raw recruits.

There was on one particular night a strange noise near me, a stealthy something which I could not understand, a noise which was not walking, nor crawling, nor running; but a wriggling or gliding over the ground towards me and my precious horse. In spite of myself I shivered and trembled, just as a man will who is afraid of ghosts, although he does not believe in them. The sound came nearer, it was at my very feet. I fell upon the thing, which I could hear but could not see – and instantly I grasped a long, naked, oiled body – a knife-armed mutineer, who was wriggling up like a serpent to hamstring my horse. I closed with him, and furiously tried to hold him; but he slipped through my hands as easily as a greased pole. He was almost free, nearly on his feet and away, leaving his knife behind. But my blood was up; I made a last effort. I gripped the sliding shins, brought him up by the ankles, and —

Well, some of them were dealt with on the spot, and some were taken to the gallows or the gun.

Those were the days of strong men, strong measures, and swift and stern retaliation. A terrible evil had arisen, and only desperate remedies, ruthless retribution, could cure it. The remedies were promptly found – or some, at any rate, and the chief and most awful of these was death itself. Circumstances needed stern examples, and steps were taken to carry out the judgments of the courts-martial on the prisoners in a way that should leave a lasting memory.

There were two methods of inflicting death – the gallows and the gun;

and it was in keeping with things that these means should be in fullest operation at the very beginning of the Mutiny, and on the spot where the Mutiny
had started. So at Meerut, on a piece of rising ground, which we came to
know as Gallows Hill, we built a big wooden structure. It was a thing with
which both Europeans and natives became familiar enough in India while
the Mutiny lasted.

The scaffold was a simple enough contrivance. A number of broad stairs
led up to the floor, which was laid on upright timbers at the corners; above
the floor, or drop, was the beam, which in our case was made to hang six
men. And the mutineers were executed six at a time, day after day, for many
days, by the troops in turn, so that we all had a hand in the work. The prisoners were bound and blindfolded, led up the steps, and arranged on the
drop. Those of us who fixed the ropes round their necks, pulled the bolts,
and the drops fell, the whole of the bodies remaining in sight, as the bottom
of the scaffold was open. The custom was to draw the bolts at six o'clock in
the morning, and leave the silent forms suspended until six o'clock at night.

This was the death that was dealt out to the mutineers who might be
called civilians. For those who were soldiers, and had been false to their oaths,
a more imposing doom was chosen. This was the blowing from the guns of
the artillery. Awful as the hanging was, it was not and could not be so dreadful as the other form of punishment. To add to its terrors the mutineers were
blown away a score at at time – for we had many prisoners, and I remember that once we had five hundred awaiting execution.

Those who were doomed to the guns were stripped to the waist; then each
was bound to the muzzle, which was at the small of the back, and their arms
were fastened to the wheels on each side. There they were bound – twenty
guns behind, twenty mutineers in front, with the port-fires burning in the
gunners' hands. Then, when the word of command was given, there was a
simultaneous crash, and a dense cloud of stifling smoke in which the forms
or limbs could be often seen – though, as a rule, the trunks remained with
the guns. But appalling though the death was, yet it was mercifully swift
and sure.

But I must not surfeit you with horrors. Let me turn from these gloomy
subjects for a moment or two to the lighter side of the Mutiny – for there
is no war which has not its humours – before I take you from Meerut to
Delhi. You will recollect that I was speaking of our faithless friends, the 3rd
Bengal Light Cavalry, who started the Mutiny. Well, as they were mounted,
and we were mounted, we naturally had a deep mutual interest, not to say
fascination.

In those days the two of us were posted not far away from each other,
some of the 3rd still making a pretence of loyalty even when their comrades
had mutinied. We trusted them as far as we could see them, which, in truth,

was no great distance. We were constantly on the watch to get more than level with them; but they were as artful as the Evil One, and it seemed as if a chance would never come to us. We wanted to cripple them as much as possible at the least cost.

But how? Not by charging down upon them, or by inciting them to attack us, but by strategy or craft, whatever you like to call it. And some genius amongst us hit upon a proper way to do it, too, for we managed to get the 3rd lured on to a hurried dismounted parade by raising a false alarm: and as soon as they had tumbled out and formed up, we swooped down on their horses and brought them triumphantly away. Not much of the clash of arms about a trick like that, perhaps, but it was a brilliant little success, because just in proportion as the 3rd were weakened by the loss of their horses, so we were strengthened by their acquisition. And we wanted horses badly.

There was another little incident which had its humour – and remember that the humour of war differs greatly from that of peace. I am anticipating a little; but when we were outside Delhi we were suddenly rushed by the 9th Native Lancers. Everything was in their favour, because they managed to bring about a perfect stampede in our camp. There was plenty of scattering and commotion as the result of their performance; yet when the raid was over, and the 9th had got away faster than they came, we found that the only casualty to their credit was an old native woman, who was grinding 'gram,' for our horses.

She was killed, poor old soul, but I am afraid that our chief feeling was one of amusement. You find it hard to credit that, maybe; but there were many things of the same kind which, however grim in themselves, had the reverse of depressing our spirits in the Mutiny. I will mention a case that was a good deal noticed at the time, although I did not myself see it. I have spoken of the Ghoorkas – terrible little blood-thirsty fellows they were, and are, glorious fighters and splendid allies, so long as they are kept in their right places. Well, their weapon, then, as it is now, was the dreaded *khookri*, that big, curved knife which will slice off a limb as easily as you can slice a turnip with your sabre.

There had been a fight in a village, and the usual routing of mutineers from all sorts of nooks and corners in mud huts and other buildings. One hut was passed by a couple of our infantrymen, and as they were going away a mutineer who had been hiding in a dark corner and had escaped unseen, thrust his head out of the window, which was only a few feet above the pavement. He was too much interested in chuckling and watching the men depart to turn his head, or he would have seen that two other infantryman and a Ghoorka were just round the corner by the window. Like a flash the Ghoorka sprang silently forward, seized the mutineer by the hair, whipped out his *khookri*, and literally, before the victim knew what was happening, his head had been slashed off. And – such is war's perverted humour – the two infantrymen were so intensely tickled by the performance that it was ten minutes before they could stop laughing enough to handle their muskets and march off to rejoin their comrades.

Let us get before Delhi.

We held Meerut for three weeks, until all was quiet and we were masters there. Then two squadrons left for the siege of the ancient capital of India, a splendid city of vast riches, seven miles in circumference, guarded by strong walls with nine gates. These were on the three land sides, the fourth side being protected by the Jumna. It was to this great fortress that the mutineers had fled from Meerut.

Then the Mutiny spread, and the few Europeans in the city were massacred just as barbarously as their fellow-creatures in Meerut.

Well, there came at length the great day when we finally assaulted and captured Delhi.

Silently, without so much as a bugle or a trumpet sound, our troops were mustered soon after midnight. They bided their time till daybreak; then there was a desperate and prolonged attack, the blowing up of the Cashmere Gate, which had been long in preparation for explosion, the rushing in of our victorious and revengeful infantry, and the following of the cavalry to crown the work of capture and retaliation.

Delhi was ours at last, at heavy cost, and into our hands had fallen the Eastern potentate who had been proclaimed king, with his palace, his wives, his eunuchs, and all his belongings.

There was amongst us, outside Delhi, an officer who had won the love of his soldiers as thoroughly as he had awed the mutineers, a man whose daring courage made him famous even in that band of heroes which the Mutiny gave England, a man whose very name was worshiped by the troops.

This was Major Hodson, of Hodson's Horse.

It was Hodson who dashed into the Royal palace and secured the surrender of the king, who was a very old man, and his favourite wife. That in itself was a marvelous performance, for the ex-monarch was still surrounded by many of the mutineers; yet it was tame compared with what Hodson did afterwards – an act which gave rise to many bitter criticisms.

The King was spared – I was one of his escort when he was banished from India – because Hodson had his orders on the point; but there were two sons and a nephew of the King who had been the chief movers in the massacre of women and children in Delhi four months before. They had fled from the city and taken refuge in an enormous royal tomb six miles away. First thing next morning Hodson, accompanied only by his second in command and a hundred faithful Sikhs, rode hard towards the tomb.

When he reached it he found that in and about it were five or six thousand of the mutineers who were quite ready to defend the princes against two white officers and a hundred sowars. Undaunted, Hodson sent a messenger to demand the unconditional surrender of the princes, and at last, unwillingly enough, they came out in a bullock cart, believing that as the King had been spared their lives would be preserved.

Hodson promptly made them prisoners, then actually returned to the huge tomb and commanded the mutineers to lay down their arms, swearing that he would shoot the first man that moved!

There was perfect silence, and such was his wondrous power over Asiatics that it acted like a spell upon them and they obeyed. For two hours he and his second and four men collected the arms of about three thousand; then, and not till then, did he leave the tomb and overtake the princes, who were by this time about a mile away, slowly going back to Delhi.

What happened then was as dramatic as it was unexpected. Hodson halted his troop, told them that the princes were the men who had originated the rebellion and given orders for the European women and children to be foully butchered, and that he had determined that they should die. He ordered them to get down from the cart and strip to the waist. Then, as they remounted and huddled in the vehicle, he shot them dead with his own carbine.

After that he took the bodies into Delhi and ordered them to be placed side by side in the most public street, and there I saw them on the very spot where they had done the deeds for which they suffered death.

That was Hodson's way of teaching retribution.

Terrible punishments you say, all these that I have named?

Yes; but remember what the crimes had been.

The fate of three cities came to symbolise the progress of the rebellion to both sides. At Kanpur, the British garrison under General Wheeler had retired to two exposed brick-built barrack buildings outside the town when the rising broke. For nearly three weeks Wheeler conducted a forlorn defence, until it became apparent that his position was hopeless. At the end of June 1857 he accepted an offer of safe conduct from the local leader of the rebel coalition, a dispossessed Mahratta prince known as the Nana Sahib. Wheeler's men – together with a large number of civilians – marched out of their barracks to the nearby river Ganges, where the Nana Sahib had provided boats to take them to safety. As they reached the river's edge, however, the rebels opened fire. Whether this was the result of planned treachery, or simply of the unbearable tension of the moment, has never been satisfactorily decided, but the result was a massacre. Most of Wheeler's men were slaughtered in the shallows, and over 200 women and children were taken prisoner.

Once it became clear that the rebellion was drawing in towards Delhi, British troops were rushed to the area. They proved unable to defeat the growing rebel concentration, however, and instead established a camp on a long, dry ridge overlooking the city. For the best part of three months they held on, nominally besieging the rebel capital, but in fact all but under siege themselves.

The rising also proved particularly severe in the state of Awadh (Oudh), which the Company had only recently annexed, and which was still unreconciled to British rule. When the rising broke out, the British commissioner, Henry Lawrence, sallied out from the Residency in the capital Lucknow, only to be severely defeated by rebel forces outside the town. The British hurried back to the Residency, and were promptly besieged by rebel forces.

The fate of Kanpur, Delhi and Lucknow would decide the success of the rebellion. To the rebels, the capture of the British positions there would give an enormous boost to their cause, as well as effectively neutralising the Company's armies in Bengal. Conversely, the British desperately needed to cling to these remaining bastions of their authority, which provided a military focus for their attempts to quash the rising. In due course, British troops, hurried to Bengal from across India, would fight their way through to Kanpur, only to find that the rebels had slaughtered the British prisoners the day before the troops arrived. This terrible deed was apparently committed in the hope of discouraging the British, but in fact it worked the relief column into a fury of retribution, and the war entered a new and particularly brutal phase, as British troops attacked rebels and civilians alike in punishment for the horrors of Kanpur. In September, the first British troops forced their way through to Lucknow, only to find that they did not have sufficient strength to relieve the siege, and could do little more than reinforce the garrison. It was to be two further months before fresh troops arrived at Lucknow and lifted the siege.

The 'Survivors' Tales of Great Events' series not unnaturally devoted several interviews to veterans of the Mutiny, which remained a controversial issue throughout the nineteenth century. Among them, one, unusually, came from an officer, Lieutenant General McLeod Innes, of the Royal Engineers. As a junior officer, Innes had served throughout the siege of Lucknow, and had won the VC later in the Mutiny.

The Defence of the Residency at Lucknow

'When I joined at Lucknow early in 1857,' said General Innes, 'there was irritation in the district, owing to the presence of robber bands, the remains of the chronic bandit warfare of this province; but there was not a whisper of sedition, though the cartridge business, to which the Mutiny has been attributed, was causing anxiety in Calcutta and at Umballa.

'The first event of importance was the arrival of Sir Henry Lawrence a few days after I joined. On May 12th news reached him of the risings at Meerut and at Delhi, which began the war of the Mutiny. Sir Henry at once realised the gravity of the danger, and his work and correspondence became overwhelming, including, as it did, advice to out-stations, and to Sir Hugh Wheeler at Cawnpore, the detachment of troops in all directions, the strengthening of the military position so as to control the native force at the Lucknow cantonments, and finally the occupation of the Muchi Bhown as a fort or stronghold to overawe the city and its great mosques and buildings.

'The prominent feature of the Muchi Bhown was an old, massive-looking pile, of castellated appearance, about a hundred yards square. It was perched on a natural eminence about thirty feet above the adjacent streets and roads. On one side of the pile were large and airy arcaded halls, but the rest of the rooms were unsuited for use except by natives or for stores. All the roofs were flat with parapet walls.

'I was appointed engineer to the fort, and instantly began to clear the place, which was a work of several days. It is impossible in a limited space to go into detail concerning the engineering work generally, or my own particular share in it; but I may mention that I prepared sites at both ends of the position at the Muchi Bhown for some of the heavy guns which had been brought in from the old arsenal in the city. Next day the native force in the Muchi Bhown was increased, and I began preparations for roofing and converting into powder and ordnance magazines two large, old, dry reservoirs, which had been superseded by very good wells.

'Again, on the top of the highest parapets, bordering and commanding the streets, I added two bricks to their height with six-inch gaps at every yard, and laid in those gaps the worthless popguns which had been brought in from the arsenal. These weapons were of no real use whatever, and their employment was a mere trick; but the deception was perfectly successful, for the apparent view from the surrounding streets was that of a circuit of grinning parapet, filled with small guns at close intervals. Indeed, the rumour gained credence that this was an armament of three hundred guns – and very telling it was on the populace! The rumour was the more readily credited because no one but selected artisans and Sikh sepoys was allowed in these mysterious upper regions.

'By May 23rd the position had become secure; its garrison being six companies, including one of the 32nd Foot, now the 1st Battalion Duke of Cornwall's Light Infantry. I continued extending the accommodation for both European and native troops and for prisoners of rank and station, for hospitals, and for the quickly-growing accessory wants – accommodation which was sorely needed, and which, even before the siege, had many heavy calls upon it.

'On the night of May 30th the long-threatening storm burst, and the Mutiny broke out in cantonments. The British forces had been kept intensely on the alert, and were fully ready for the rising when it came off.

'The mutinous sepoys broke out from their lines at evening gun-fire. They scattered over the cantonments, sought out, gutted, and burnt down the officers' houses, and fired their muskets towards the British camp, where the 32nd were drawn up, with some artillery, ready for action. They murdered the officer in charge of the main picket.

'Next morning the mutineers were attacked and dispersed, and were pursued for about ten miles. The rising was followed on the 31st by an attempt of some conspirators in the city to join the mutineers; but they were crushed and scattered.

'Strong steps were needed and were instantly taken, for on June 1st I had erected gallows outside the city gate of the Muchi Bhown, and on them the mutineers who had been taken prisoners and convicted of murder or treason were hanged. These stern measures, however, had little or no effect on the rising, for every day news came of fresh mutinies at out-stations. Fugitives arrived and had to be accommodated either in the Muchi Bhown or the Residency, and they were generally accompanied by more or less faithful sepoys, which did not lighten our trouble in the beleaguered posts.

'Numerous men of rank and influence, but of doubtful loyalty, were brought in, and kept under more or less close confinement, and, at the same time, some who were criminals of position, including two or three of the deepest dye, parricides and others, like the Rajah of Toolseepore. This state of things continued for three weeks.

'By June 20th there were rumors of the mutineer regiments of Oudh and Rohilkund showing signs of concentrating for some common rendezvous to our north-east, and I learnt, on the other hand, that there were numerous isolated friendly bodies of natives; that food and cattle were pouring in to us from every direction; and that our position at the Residency, not a mile off, was being formed into a ring fence, and prepared for an all-round siege. Swarms of workmen were busy at the Residency, putting it into a state of defence; and there were enlivening and exhilarating feelings arising from the knowledge that this was being vigorously done, as well as from the continuous movement of the storing of carts and elephants which brought in supplies to help us all to face and endure the impending siege.

'Meanwhile my works at the city front went on in full vigour, crowds being busily employed. There was not yet a sign of difficulty, of anxiety of any kind, till June 30th, when we heard of the enemy's approach, and we officers had sat down to breakfast as usual. Presently I heard an occasional cannon shot, but no heavy firing, when suddenly our old havildar (native sergeant) of the Pensioners, entered the room, and told Major Francis, who was in command, that our troops were returning, driven back by the enemy in much superior force.

'I was no sooner outside to see how matters were going, than I found that this news had reached the workpeople also, and that they had all stampeded. I made everything as snug as possible, and especially examined and completed any shortcomings in the two new magazines (which had now been filled with powder and arsenal stores), and posted a sentry at the semaphore to report at once any signalling from the Residency.

'Presently our officers and men began to arrive from the fight which had taken place at the village of Chinhut, in which our force had been practically routed by overwhelming numbers. The 32nd, being prostrated by the heat, had lost 100 men; but the retirement was, otherwise, under control, and the troops rejoined the two positions.

'In an hour or so the whole of our force was collected in the Residency and the Muchi Bhown; but the enemy, who followed up hard, were checked by the guns of those two positions. But they crossed the river by the iron and stone bridges, the bridge of boats, and otherwise during the day and in the darkness of the night, and next morning both our positions were closely surrounded by the mutineers. Early in the forenoon the semaphore called us to "Attention," and I read off, letter by letter, the message, "Retire tonight at twelve; blow up well." A council was at once held, with closed doors, and arrangements were discussed and settled in full detail for the retirement ordered.

'During the previous night the native artillery drivers had fled, and so the gun-teams had to be driven by officers. The State prisoners, as well as the sick and wounded, were to be secured on the artillery waggons, and the guns that were to be left behind were to be spiked at the last moment. As the rearguard left, the ordnance officer, Lieutenant Thomas, was to fire the train which was to explode the magazines a few minutes later.

'We of the council proceeded quietly to take the preliminary steps assigned us, no one else being told of it. Meanwhile the one matter of chief moment – the preparations for the blowing up of the two magazines – was equally quietly begun by Lieut. Thomas. At six o'clock all the sentries were doubled, and the strictest guard was organised against the possibility of any idea of our intentions getting outside. As a fact, not a whisper of them ever reached the enemy, and whilst we were preparing for the move at midnight, our howitzers and mortars were firing at intervals on the gardens and spaces occupied by the enemy between the two positions.

'By eleven o'clock the guns, etc., which were to accompany us, were very quietly formed up in due order on the lower plateau where the exit gate was, and the several sections of the party, including the State prisoners and hospital, found their proper places in the order of the procession. Lieutenant

Thomas had been preparing his two magazines for the explosion, and had arranged a system of fuses that should take fifteen minutes to burn through.

'As the hour of midnight struck, I saw the Eastern Gate thrown open, and the head of the column start on what, in my heart, I thought would be a hopeless march, and rode up to Thomas with orders to light his fuse. He and I then moved down together to the rear of the column. Then I pressed my way forward, amazed beyond measure at not hearing a shot or row of any kind, and found, on reaching the entrance to the Residency grounds below the Redan (a ride of 1000 yards) that the head of our column was actually reaching the Redan Gate itself!

'As I began riding up the Redan Road a shot pealed forth from the Redan Battery, fired under a mistaken idea of the gunner that Sir Henry's order, "Open the gate," was "Open with grape." Fortunately no harm was done.

'Then the extraordinary truth became known – that the mutineers, who had been surrounding this position all day, had disappeared for a frolic in the city! The whole of our force was therefore able to enter the Residency position, and did enter it, without loss of any kind whatever.

'Sir Henry asked me fully of our measures, and was overjoyed at the completeness of the evacuation of the Muchi Bhown. Then all at once he exclaimed: "But why have you not blown it up?" No sooner had he spoken than there was a great shake of the earth, a thunderous report, an increase of darkness, and then an intense blaze, for the Muchi Bhown magazine had been successfully exploded!

'We were all now, in the early hours of July 2nd, concentrated in full force in the Residency intrenchments, prepared to hold it to the death.

'Sir Henry's happiness was intense, and his closing words were: "Till now, Innes, we owe our lives to you; from now, all will rest with Fulton," implying that the speciality of the defence was an Engineer officer. And so, with a buoyant heart, in the very small hours of the morning, I joined our engineer party in the house called Anderson's Post. Later on, but still very early in the morning, I was hailed by Sir Henry, and accompanied him round the position.

'That was the last I saw of our brave and beloved leader.

'In another hour he was mortally wounded. Already one shell had burst in the room in the Residency which he had chosen for himself. After returning to his apartment at the close of his round of inspection, a round in which he impressed on every man his duty to hold out to the death, and in which he steadied every soul in the garrison by his own noble example and dauntless courage, another shell entered and burst. Sir Henry was mortally wounded by the explosion, and two days later he died, to the intense grief of all, myself in particular, for he was to me more than a friend – he was a father.

'After this heavy and almost irreparable loss, the life of the defence cen-
tred in Captain Fulton, of the Madras Engineers. Many were the gallant souls
who departed, either killed or dying of wounds or disease; but our greatest
loss after Sir Henry was Fulton, who was killed by a round shot in Gubbins'
Bastion, eleven days before Havelock joined hands with us.

'His skill, energy, and wonderful resourcefulness had won the love and
confidence of all, and it is not too much to say that his cheerful presence
and the sight of his shrewd and resolute face did more than any score of
other men to keep up our spirits. His appearance was the signal for all of us
to be up and doing. Fulton was a crack shot, and did great execution amongst
the enemy's sharpshooters.

'Once a friend of his cried out to him, while they were firing at the enemy,
"There are two men at the loophole!" Fulton fired at the spot indicated, and
next day it was reported that two men had been killed by one shot at this
particular loophole – one of them being a native officer who commanded the
post.'

Let us now leave the general's story for a moment or two, so that we may
picture the state of things in the Residency. By this time the mutineers have
completely hedged the Residency in; they are at least twenty deep all round,
and not the boldest man in the beleaguered garrison believes that there would
be a chance of escape, of cutting through the bloodthirsty and cruel besiegers
with the bayonet, by even the most desperate and courageous forlorn hope.
Day follows day, each bringing its gloomy tale of death and the heavier pall
of burial.

For every day there is the tribute to the grave – every day except one,
and that is to become pitifully memorable because it is not marked by either
death or burial! Many deaths there have been, some of brave and loving officers, of gently-nurtured women, who have uncomplainingly taken the places
of the cowardly servants who fled at the beginning of trouble. These women
have discharged all the unattractive duties which fall on those who live and
move in close and pestilential quarters in an Eastern city, for since the siege
began the women and children have been sheltered in the inner courts and
lower storeys of the buildings, where the bullets cannot penetrate. These non-
combatants have been rigidly forbidden to stir from their retreats, and to
this care is due the fact that they are practically immune from the danger
of the mutineers' fire.

At the beginning of the siege there were 240 women and 270 children,
but at the end of the eighty-seven days, during which the banner of Britain
is kept flying, it is to be found that of the women three have been killed
and eleven have died, while of the children no less than one-third have
perished. These losses have been due to hardships and exposure and want
of comforts; but not to lack of actual food, for the care of Sir Henry has

secured the entire garrison against that. His wisdom and foresight, indeed, have overshadowed all else, and amongst all the deaths in that heroic garrison none was greater nor more bitterly deplored than his. But the sound of his voice was still heard, and often in hours of darkest gloom and deepest despair his thrilling words were re-echoed – and nobly obeyed – 'Never surrender!'

The garrison, then, is rigidly, and, as it seems, hopelessly beleaguered; the enemy, cunning, resourceful, pitiless, is working at his mines, so that he may reach the Residency and blow it up, with all the hated white people who are prisoners within its stifling walls. He has no mercy even for the sick and dying children, or the despairing and heartbroken mothers who tend them and try to stave off a greater and more ruthless enemy.

To meet and thwart the purpose of the mutineers Lieutenant Innes and the rest of the Engineers are steadily working at their counter-mines, so that the enemy may be destroyed as he burrows underground. There is amongst the defenders the constant loss by death, the ceaseless prostration due to illness, the never ending miseries which mark such a stubborn siege as this, and the agony of deferred hope to crush the most sanguine spirit, the endless watching for the help that does not come, just as castaways at sea scan the horizon for a sight of steam or sail.

But it is this very expectation of relief which makes it possible to hold out, to go on making mines and sorties, to defy the savage enemy to the bitter end, for it is known that Sir Henry Havelock and Sir Colin Campbell, as well as Sir James Outram, are working up to the salvation of the garrison.

A wonderful and daring exploit has electrified the heroic band who hold the Residency. Thomas Henry Kavanagh, who went to Lucknow with Lawrence, who knows the natives and the city thoroughly, has disguised himself as a native, has bravely plunged into the midst of the mutineers, made his way through them at the peril of an awful death, has joined Sir Colin, and is now guiding him back to Lucknow. Outram and Havelock have succeeded in reaching the Residency by September 26th, but the garrison is not to be actually relieved until a few weeks later, when Sir Colin's force will cut through the incircling besiegers, avoiding the miles of deadly narrow lanes leading to the Residency – lanes through which Outram had fought his way at heavy loss – and, directed by Kavanagh, he will reach the Residency by way of Dilkoosha Park, and thereby avoid much loss to the British troops.

To resume the General's narrative: – 'It was only by degrees that I mastered the mutually defensive features of the posts – my chief duty continuing to lie at the Redan. It soon became obvious that the enemy were making it, somehow or other, their chief point of attack. So, one night, I donned some garments, which had been dyed black, crept out of the Redan, crawled along to the open ground well to its front, and then right and left;

but I could detect no mischievous sound or sight of any kind. As it turned out, the enemy were mining, but had not yet reached half-way up.

'Again, on the night of the 18th, a native being seen lying dead in front of the Baily Guard Gate, we opened it slightly, and I crawled out with a rope and fastened it round the body, which on being hauled in was found to be that of a woman; but no letter or anything of importance was found on her.

'On the morning of July 20th came the first, and the greatest, all round attack by the whole strength of the enemy, The look-out at the top of the Residency had warned us that the enemy's movements showed something to be impending, and I was taking a snatch of breakfast when a great roar and earthquake, followed at once by a furious artillery and musketry fire, announced a grave assault.

'The earthquake meant the explosion of a mine by which the enemy thought they would ruin the Redan Battery; but its site was, even now, at only half the proper distance; so the attempt was innocuous. The enemy's attacks were very bold at first, especially against the Cawnpore Battery, and were continued all day, but without any success. So we rejoiced greatly.

'The enemy having now started mining, we forthwith began preparatory defensive and counter operations. These went on without intermission to the end of the siege, which was marked by three great attacks, at intervals of about three weeks.

'The third and longest stage of the siege was notable for one exceptional mining operation. The most mischievous post held by the enemy was Johannes' House, which it had been intended to include within our own defences, but which was lost to us by the suddenness of the start of the siege. It was specially mischievous because it fired straight down our principal road, was held by picked marksmen, and had done much fatal damage.

'I had shortly before clambered up, in the night, by a ruined staircase, *outside* a small post, next Anderson's, called De Prat's Shop, in full view of our watchful enemy, and had found the roof covered with much valuable material and implements, such as picks, shovels and tools of all sorts, and tarpaulins. I had thrown them all over the edge into the interior, and now, with these available, Fulton assigned me the unique task of blowing up Johannes' House! Here was an exceptional enterprise and a feather in my cap.

'To plan the operation properly I had to get on to the top of the building we called the Martinière, and, crawling along the inside of the outer parapet, and extending a measuring tape all along it, take bearings, from the shotholes, of the two ends of the enemy's post.

'I thus ascertained, and was able to plot accurately, the lie of the enemy's post relatively to our own. Having done this, I started my gallery (main mine) at a level well below the road outside, from a point which I calculated to be exactly opposite the middle of Johannes' House; drove that gallery straight underneath the building till I judged it to be a point more than six feet inside it, then drove two other galleries from that point, right and left, each twelve feet long, and then two very short branches from each of them, right and left, at the ends of which were the four points at which to lay my four charges. These were each of 100 lb. The rest of the work was quickly finished, and all was ready by the very small hours of August 21st.

'By the first streak of dawn the troops were all ready for a sortie, and we began a fusillade against Johannes' House to attract the enemy into it. When it was well filled, I lighted the fuse, and sixty seconds later the house heaved upwards, the walls fell outwards, its crowded garrison lay dead or dying on the ground, and our sortie party cleared the adjacent houses.

'Our Cawnpore battery was thus freed from the scorpion that had hitherto been stinging and paralysing it, and it could now sweep and protect the whole front to well beyond Gubbins' Post.

'On September 5th the third and last all-round attack on us was made. This was the first occasion on which we saw amongst the enemy other than regular sepoys. These were men with matchlocks, spears, and bows and arrows, either Talukdars' clansmen, or men of an aboriginal tribe called Pasees, and a very strange, old-world appearance they presented, too.

'On the 22nd I was told that our most effective messenger, Ungud, had arrived with letters from Outram and Havelock, telling of their approach to the Alum Bagh, and thence to our relief. The next day we heard their royal salute fired at the Alum Bagh.

'On the 24th there was a lull, while they were arranging for the next day's movements.

'We heard firing all day on the 25th without being able to judge of its site, while the town population to our east were ceaselessly and in crowds fleeing north across the Goomtee. Then suddenly we heard firing near us on the east. Our friends had been circling round the east of the city, and just as dusk was coming on, Havelock's foremost troops came sweeping down the two streets leading to the Baily Guard Gate and the Cawnpore Battery!

'Our reinforcement – practically our relief – had been effected!

'In the course of that evening I met a few of my old friends and brother officers, and till midnight I was in the roads outside, which the relieving party had traversed, helping to bring in the wounded. After about four hours' sleep I was out again, bringing in others of the wounded; but at daylight I was attached to a party which was to sortie from Innes' Post and clear out any enemy that might be lurking in the long grass on that front.

'At first no one was to be seen, but I plunged into and through the long grass, and emerged after a few yards into the open. Lawrence's party had not followed me, but instead of them, a party of sepoys in undress uniform emerged, running down towards the road below.

'Then suddenly they turned to the left, on which, thinking they belonged to our party, I called out to them: "No – halt! Turn to the right!" Thereupon they halted, turned round, and blazed away at me, but did not hit me. I fired my revolver at them, but it never went off, the powder having got wet during the night's work.

'I was now transferred to the Chuttur Munzil, under Major Crommelin. This was the new position extending eastward on the river front.

'My work under my new chief was, I found, to be almost entirely restricted to mining operations, to their initiation and control, and the guidance and supervision of the young and inexperienced officers and men appointed to the work.

'Disconnected attacks occupied us till October 8th, by which time I was able to carry out a systematic defence with the newly-trained troops and followers. But it was against a most persistent series of attacks. Not only were there sixteen separate and distinct aggressive mines carried out against us, but some were of unprecedented length.

'Our defensive measure against this very extensive mining attack was the construction of 1100 yards of mining galleries – which either stopped or broke into the enemy's mines. One of them was so long, that though it had not reached its aim, the Hirn Khana (deer house), it had to be stopped, as the miners could not breathe in it.

'Of the many minor incidents of the siege I will mention two or three. One of the enemy's shots caught the end of a punkah-fringe and tore down most of it. Being checked while doing this, the shot got a circular motion and whirled round a young officer of the 32nd, its final impact breaking his leg and causing his death. Another shot smashed the leg of a chair on which a lady was sitting and brought her to the ground. Then the shot was caught in her dress, unrolled itself, and ran along the floor without doing further harm. Another shot grazed the temple of a young Engineer officer who was asleep, broke the skin, and plunged into a treasure-chest beyond; while a further shot cut through the pillow on which a Fusilier officer was sleeping and broke the leg of a bed next him.

'I may also tell of an amusing incident in which I was concerned. The end of our mine was a long distance from its mouth, and was reached by a succession of bends and zig-zags. The enemy's miners were quite close to ours, and working very cautiously with trowels instead of picks. I had placed one of my men at each bend for prompt communication and support, and had been waiting an apparently interminable time for the breaking in of the enemy. I had heard their voices, and at last became aware of a speck of light.

'Remaining quite still, I soon heard whispering begin; then suddenly

rison and give up the Residency. However sound the measure, we of the old
garrison were very angry, as if our honour were touched – we who had so long
kept the flag of England flying from our tower and held the enemy at bay.'

The decisive fighting of the war, however, took place outside Delhi. The British
position on the ridge had been steadily reinforced – particularly by Sikh troops
raised in the Panjab which, crucially, remained loyal to the Company – until, by
the middle of September, the British felt able to make an assault on the city. The
Kashmir Gate – one of the principal entrances to the city, which had been bricked
up and barricaded by the rebels – was blown by Engineers, and storming parties surged into the city streets. The fighting was particularly brutal, as the British
made no distinction between rebel combatants and civilians. Sergeant Thomas
Pearce of the 9th Lancers was among those who saw Delhi fall, and his account
reveals the full fury of the British attack, and the reasons for it.

The Siege and Storm of Delhi

I was in the Army for nearly a quarter of a century; I took part in twenty-one campaigns and battles, big and little, and of them all I consider that the siege and storm of Delhi was the worst. I do not except the bloody jungle fight of Chillianwalla, the severe action at Goojerat, or the relief of Lucknow, in all of which I shared, for the work in front of Delhi was so long, so hard, and was done in such an awful climate – the climate of the deadly Indian summer, and the almost unendurable miseries that are inseparable from tropical heat.

It was a war of revenge – even the most charitable amongst us did not make any secret of that simple motive – revenge and punishment for the inhuman slaughter of our fellow soldiers and, which was infinitely worse, our women and little children. There had been butchery at Meerut and Delhi, and atrocities everywhere throughout the district. Whatever the failings of the British soldier may be he never overlooks or forgives a wrong which is done by an enemy to English women and English children, and far less than the atrocities of the Mutiny were needed to make him carry out the resolve to give no quarter to the rebels.

No mercy was deserved, none was given, yet throughout the war I never knew of a case in which a British soldier sought revenge on a native woman or child. They were just as carefully spared as the men were ruthlessly destroyed.

It was with this feeling of vengeance in my heart that I marched towards Delhi, the headquarters of the mutineers, the ancient city which they were holding, where already they had murdered all the English people they could lay their hands on, and where they fortified themselves and defied us.

One sight I saw before I got to Delhi which was to burn itself for ever in my memory, and which is as clear now, fifty years afterwards, as it was then, and that was the 'slaughter-house wells' of Cawnpore, as we called the dreadful spot where between 120 and 130 women and children were cut to pieces by the mutineers. Gentle women and little children had been murdered, and worse, by the inhuman rebels; butchered in a shed, and then dragged out and thrown into the dry well in the compound or courtyard.

I saw the building where the murders were done, and in the compound I looked down the well, which was choked with the mangled bodies of our countrywomen and the little children. The ground and the earth were still red, and everywhere were ghastly signs of the massacre. The strongest men amongst us broke down when we beheld the pitiful evidence of Nana Sahib's treachery, and the feeblest called aloud for vengeance. If at any time throughout the long weary months of fighting and siege work a man faltered in his resolution he braced himself up again when he recollected that awful sight,

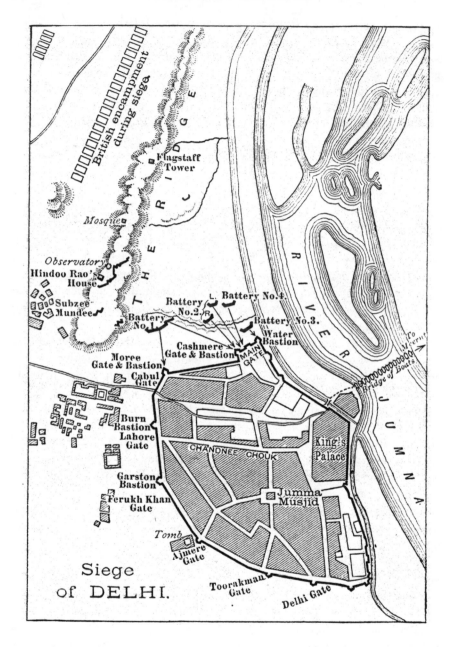

or heard of the atrocities which took place daily whenever the mutineers got English people in their power. Not even rebels who surrendered were spared. When we got before Delhi we found that the city looked formidable enough to withstand a long siege, and this proved to be the case. Delhi at that time was nearly eight miles in circumference, and was surrounded by a ditch and high walls. On one side the Jumna flows, and on the land side were nine gates, the chief of which was the Cashmere Gate. About a thousand yards from the city walls was a ridge of ground, and on this was planted our artillery. On that ridge we had many weeks' thrilling practice in the art of dodging shot and shell, and witnessed many a terrible tragedy. Man is not as swift in his movements as a shot, and often enough a fine fellow would be blown to pieces, or, which was worse, hopelessly mangled. The handsomest fellow in my regiment had both his legs shot away by a cannon-ball from the city.

Nothing is harder to bear than a siege such as we were conducting, and especially for a light cavalryman who has been accustomed to active work. He likes to get in with his lance and sabre, and there was no chance of doing either in a general way at Delhi. I had to grin and bear it, and wait for the time to come when I could share in the work of revenge. There was no need to remind us of our duty in this respect, for now and then we got terrible evidence of the sort of enemy we had to deal with. Some poor creature who had escaped from a massacre and into the jungle would crawl up to our pickets. Then the whole camp would be horrified and maddened by the tales of butchery and outrage that were heard.

One case especially there was which was as rousing in its call for vengeance as the massacre at Cawnpore. By some means a lady escaped from the city and got as far as our outposts – sanctuary at last. She was a gently nurtured Englishwoman, and her tale was this:

When the Mutiny broke out at Delhi, when the monsters from Meerut had joined the rebels in the city, her husband was murdered. Then the mutineers rushed to her quarters, where she was in bed with her two children, a little boy and a little girl. A brutal rebel seized the boy, held him up by the hair, and in his mother's presence cut his throat, and flung the corpse upon her. Then he took the girl and treated her in the same way; but terribly wounded though she was she lived for several hours, crying in her agony for water. The mother herself was wounded, but she survived until she saw a chance to escape and get to our lines.

Can you wonder that our war was one of revenge, and that we never gave quarter? And can you be surprised if at times innocent men in the villages we came across were ridden down and sabred? They were; but it must be remembered that we suffered heavily from treachery, and that often enough the mutineers got into our very midst in the guise of friends. It was almost impossible for us to distinguish them, and the time came when we took no risks of any sort. Things went so far that once when some prisoners were being tried the alarm was sounded, and the members of the court-martial rushed to their posts. The Provost-Marshal was asked where the captives were. 'Oh,' he answered, 'I shot them when the alarm sounded, so as to be on the safe side.' And I don't think anybody blamed him.

It was pound and pound, guns booming from the ridge, artillery flashing from the vast city which reeked and sweltered in the Indian sun. Every crevice in the walls appeared to shelter a mutineer, every bit of rising ground seemed to be a post for gunners.

Day and night we were kept on the rack, about 2500 Europeans and loyal natives against 20,000 rebels in the city. It was so often a case of the alarm sounding, standing to our horses, and saddle and bridle, and nothing at the end of the excitement but disappointment and violent language. And with it all there was the ceaseless suffering of man and beast, the harassing of a constant fusillade, the death that comes from shot and shell and steel, and, worse than all, from disease. There were heavy thunderstorms, but how welcome they were after the insufferable muggy heat!

There were musk-rats and at times poisonous snakes to trouble us, and myriads of flies and other insects, such as flying bugs, settling on your food as you ate it and making your drink black as you swallowed it. And the heat was so intense that men were literally shrivelled up by it. There was no escape from the sun except, perhaps, by crawling under beds, as some of the officers did, or into the shade of any object that gave some. Sickness was always with us, and the camels and horses and baggage animals died by the score, the rotting carcases making our camp intolerable. I used to watch the vultures at their ghastly work, and often enough saw the birds standing on the corpses which floated down the Jumna, pecking at them as they drifted.

Are not all these horrors inseparable for ever from the dreadful story of the Mutiny? And is it not amazing that while they are still fresh in the memories of the veterans amongst us, there should be those who are reckless or criminal enough to try to stir up strife in India and bring about a repetition of the atrocities of fifty years ago?

Nothing is more demoralising, or disheartening than a siege. From day to day, week to week, month to month, you go on with your pounding, your scrapping, your toiling, and your suffering, and you never seem to advance. Disease grips you and thins your ranks, scanty rations undermine your constitutions, and incessant strain saps your strength. The comrade who one day is blithe and bold is the next resting in his shallow grave, and the man whose strength and energy you have envied is a lifelong cripple.

We in front of Delhi felt war's wastage as much as any of the troops engaged in crushing the Mutiny; but just as in Lucknow they kept the banner of England flying, in the sure belief that at last relief would come, so we in front of the ancient capital of the Moguls bombarded and skirmished, knowing that in the end we should get our revenge. Always we remembered the slaughter-wells at

Cawnpore, and such happenings as the murder of little children and the violation of our English girls and women. Let not these things be so readily forgotten by those who talk so glibly of India for the Indians.

To show you how these constant alarms by the enemy affected us, I will recall a tragic little incident. A clever young officer of Engineers was returning to camp at night. Knowing how difficult it was to distinguish friend from foe, he had made the most elaborate preparations for his safe return. But all his plans were upset by one of the accidents that are inseparable from warfare. Instead of coming back to camp and being challenged by a sentry who would have known him, he was hailed by another officer. The Engineer for some unknown reason made no reply, and the officer instantly shot at the mysterious figure, mortally wounding him. The Engineer, after lingering in agony till morning, died.

There was another and more startling affair than that – more startling because it involved a heavier loss of life, and because it was so completely unexpected and unlooked-for. In the night-time you take it for granted that there will be thrills, and that the probability is that in some form or other the enemy will prove a match for you, but in the broad light of day the case is different, and you do not anticipate catastrophe.

The siege was in full progress, and I was out with a picket very near the sun-baked city. The guns were booming and the musketry was crackling, but I paid little heed to either. Custom had made me callous. I gave all my attention to the performances of a body of cavalry which was advancing towards our own. I watched it until it joined our own lines; then, to my amazement, I saw that there was an alarm, and that the horse men, who were supposed to be our own native cavalry, had come from the enemy and were cutting and slashing amongst the Carabineers.

So swift was the descent, so much like our own native cavalry were the rebels, that before the Carabineers could saddle and bridle, the enemy was galloping back to Delhi, gloating over an unexpected little triumph, for he left a number of the British cavalry dead and wounded in their own lines. It was a marvellously audacious movement, and its very boldness gave it the success which would otherwise have been out of the question. There were not many more surprises on the same scale, but frequently the enemy, crafty and resourceful, would get a few men into our camp, because of the difficulty or impossibility of distinguishing friend from foe.

Monotonous though the siege itself inevitably was, yet scarcely a day went by without giving us a thrill of some description. Once an officer who had ventured too near the walls was in peril, and saved himself only by hanging on to the tail of his orderly's horse. The horse was shot dead when fifty yards had been covered, but the officer escaped. Neither officer nor man stood on his dignity when the saving of his life was in question.

At another time three men were seen prowling about in a suspicious manner. They were not armed, but at such a time even unarmed persons were a source of danger. They were captured, and after being examined were ordered to be shot as spies. Pistols were aimed at their heads, and, naturally enough, they bolted, and tried to save their lives. Firearms fifty years ago were not the splendid weapons that they are to-day. The spies fled like the hunted creatures they were, for as soon as they took to their heels a few of our Lancers pursued them and promptly carried out the sentence of death.

Of course these things kept us interested, and we were not without amusement, either, because of the things we did or saw or heard. One of the officers must have been a born wild-beast tamer and snake-charmer, for he literally had no fear whatever of dangerous animals and reptiles. One day he amused himself by making a poisonous snake dart its fangs into some object; then he gripped the reptile by the back of the neck and made it go through a number of performances which were infinitely more comfortable to watch than to be near. At another time the officer was taking what we called a mud bath in the Jumna, deep in the mud and baking in the sunshine. And he passed the time away agreeably enough by trying to catch alligators by the nose! He was an enormously strong man, but I have known many strong men give reptiles in India a very wide berth. I did myself, and I was not by any means a weakling.

It seemed as if our artillery would never make any impression on the city and as if Delhi would never be ours; but the day of vengeance was approaching, even if slowly, and we knew that the time was not far distant when the whole of our force would be hurled against the massive walls and into the far-reaching city. But we got nearer and nearer, and at last within three or four hundred yards of the ditch. For a week we pounded away again; then on the 14th the storming came.

All through the hot, hard months we had been inspired by the spirit of revenge; now, near the finish of the work, we were reminded of the way in which our countrymen and countrywomen had been murdered, and the whole of us fell on the place with a determined ferocity that made it ours, but only after a struggle which lasted nearly a week.

I was with my regiment, mounted, under the walls just outside the Cashmere Gates. The stormers were struggling across the ditch and over the walls, the artillery thundering, the musketry rattling, and the mutineers shouting back defiance at our own people. It was wonderful to see the way in which the ditch was crossed and the great high walls scaled, and to see, too, how furiously the rebels fought when they must have known that all was lost. They did not rest satisfied to wait for our coming; they left the city, many of them, and threw themselves in frenzy against us.

Many were maddened with the native drink, none more so than a man who came towards us by himself. I think we were in column of squadrons at the time, and this solitary individual, supposed to be an officer, charged upon our front squadron. He looked a superb spectacle as he waved his sword, making a cut and sweeping on the foremost of our men.

On and on he came furiously, still cutting with his sword, on until he was at the very points of the lances; then there was a flash of steel points in the sun, a loud cry, a tumble to the ground, and an emptied saddle. The solitary horseman had been speared to death.

'No quarter, no loot!'

That was the spirit of our orders, and I, like many others, carried it out with all my strength, when the time to do so came. That was when the Cashmere Gate had been blown up, and an entrance made for our passage into the city.

The Cashmere Gate had been the scene of one of the most daring episodes of the Mutiny. When the rebels began their massacre Delhi had two magazines, the chief being near the Cashmere Gate, containing nearly a million cartridges, an enormous quantity of shot and shell, and a vast number of muskets. To have allowed this material of war to fall into the hands of the mutineers would have been madness, and Lieutenant Willoughby, who had charge of the magazine, knew it. He determined that, rather than let the rebels have the magazine, he would sacrifice his life. He and a small band of British officers defended the spot to the last extremity; then, knowing that the magazine could not be held, he blew it up, destroying hundreds of the mutineers, and perishing himself.

Again, months after that heroic achievement, the Cashmere Gate was to be blown up, and now a little party under Lieutenant Salkeld, a party which was almost a forlorn hope, was hurrying up with powder-bags

Lieutenant Salkeld belonged to the Bengal Engineers, so did Lieutenant Home, who was with him; and there was Sergeant John Smith, of the Bengal Sappers and Miners, and Bugler Hawthorne, of the 52nd Regiment There were nine natives, and all told the party carried a dozen bags of powder, each containing twenty-five pounds. They dashed for the gate. Four of the natives hesitated, became panic-stricken, and refused to advance. Smith presented his musket and swore that he would shoot them if they still refused. Lieutenant Salkeld ran back, demanding to know the reason of the delay. The sergeant told him. 'Shoot them! shoot them!' he shouted; but two of the natives went on, the other pair being left.

No man can tell to a certainty what actually happened in that terrible storming; but the deed was as heroic as was the blowing up of the magazine by Lieutenant Willoughby. A slow match was lighted, but there was no explosion. Lieutenant Home went forward to re-light it and was blown to pieces, for the powder just at that instant burst into flame; a man named

Carmichael was killed with his powder-bag on his shoulder, Lieutenant Salkeld was mortally wounded, yet they tried to save his life, placing a bag of powder under his head as a pillow. Even as he was dying an aide-de-camp rushed up with a bit of red riband — an earnest of the Cross which the lieutenant never lived to see.

I saw it all take place, yet I cannot tell you the details; all I know is what everyone knew, that because of the amazing courage of this little party the breach was made, the opening through which our infuriated troops could pass into the city itself, fighting their way through the narrow, crooked streets, which were choking with battle-smoke, and pitted with the fire of musketry, destroying the rebels wherever they were met, always remembering what the mutineers had done, and giving no quarter, except to the women and children.

For three months we had been investing the city; for six days and nights we were completing our victory, then at last, on September 21st, Delhi was completely ours. The king, an old man, was a prisoner; his two sons and a grandson, who had fled in panic, were captured not far from the city and shot by Hodson, the famous commander of Hodson's Horse, whom I saw on the walls of Delhi during the storming.

We had been forbidden to loot, and I for one obeyed the order. In the shape of loot I got nothing, and Delhi was a city of palaces, where much treasure was obtainable. Some men got gold and silver ornaments or money, and others laid their hands on all sorts of strange things in the way of mementoes.

I cared nothing for the riches of the city; I was satisfied with the feeling that Cawnpore had been avenged, and was glad when, not long after Delhi had been subdued, I marched away. Many of our dead were left behind; many a man who, when the siege began, was unknown, was a hero, for seventeen Victoria Crosses had been won. On the day of the storming alone, the 14th, ten were gained, and the entire number were secured within a period of a week — that memorable week of incessant fighting to make our conquest certain.

I was one of the men who often mounted guard over the king when we bore him away as a captive. I often saw him smoking his hookah, with his harem around him, and not very beautiful women, considering that in a way they were queens. I used to look rather wonderingly at the jewels, which flashed in his turban, like bits of glass glistening in the sun.

Retribution fell upon the mutineers wherever British troops were met with. It was short shrift and the rope, bullet, or cannon, and my last recollection of Delhi is the picture of a great tree, like a banyan tree, on which we executed some of the rebels who had come into our hands — men who were all stained with the blood of our countrymen.

In bullock-carts, mostly two or three prisoners in each, they were drawn to the tree, and ropes put round their necks. Then the carts were drawn away, and the bodies were left hanging, like evil fruit, with the vultures circling in the air and darkening it.

More than a score of the mutineers were hanging from the branches when we marched away; and so that there should be no hope of saving them by cutting them down, they were shot.

It was terrible enough; but they had shown no mercy to our fellow-countrymen and our womenfolk and little children, and we showed none to them.

Finally, an unusual story from the Mutiny, which suggests something of the hardships troops in the 1850s sometimes had to endure, even before they reached the theatre of operations. Once the Mutiny had broken out, British troops were hurried to India from across the empire. Among them was Private George Diggens of the 54th Regiment, who was among a draft of 368 troops sent from Portsmouth to Calcutta about the iron steamship *Sarah Sands*. Having passed the Cape of Good Hope in November 1857, the *Sarah Sands* ran into severe difficulties.

The Burning of the Transport *Sarah Sands*

We were going out to India to help quell the Mutiny, nearly fifty years ago. And we were going in the *Sarah Sands*, whose voyage was to be one of the most disastrous that any ship ever survived.

For two long, dreary months the *Sarah Sands* slowly forced her way south; then we reached the Cape, and, after being there a week, coaling, we set out again for Calcutta. The voyage had not been without incident of a sort—the sort you would rather be without. For one thing, death came unexpectedly in our midst, and threw a shadow on the ship. There was a fine, high-spirited man amongst the crew—a Dutchman, I think—who was the very life of us. He was always cheerful, always full of sport, which e worked off in merrymaking. One day he was skylarking, when he suddenly fell overboard. Strangely enough, we never saw a sign of him, except his cap, which came to the surface. But we were in the tropics then, and sharks swarmed around the transport. We had a good deal to do with these monsters of the sea before our woes were ended.

Another thing which troubled us was the crew. You must remember that in those days, when so many ships were wanted to take troops to India, any sort of human being who called himself a sailor was certain of employment. British seamen were scarce, and our commander, Captain Castle—he died about a year ago—was forced to ship a miscellaneous lot. They were nearly all foreigners and mutinous scoundrels. This being the case, is it necessary to say that they were also cowards?

Well, there you have a picture of us—about 500 souls, all told, in a small screw steamboat—a mutinous crew, taking our troops to crush a mutiny! Such we were when we left the Cape to make our way past Ceylon, and up the Indian Ocean and the Bay of Bengal to Calcutta.

Bad as the first part of the voyage had been, the second was infinitely worse. It seemed as if a curse settled on the vessel from the very outset. Some of the mutineers were in irons, and had been kept on broad and water for seven days. It has been said—and I, for one, do not disbelieve it—that the mutineers even went so far as to cause the mysterious fire which nearly brought about the destruction of us all.

We were heavy laden when we left the Cape, deep with the coal and fresh water and stores we had taken on board. We drove into bad weather, too, and on November 7th a squall considerably damaged us. But these disasters were trifles in comparison with the great calamity which they preceded.

We were about a thousand miles from the Cape, alone on the sea. We had had our dinner, and the officers and ladies were just ready for theirs. It was about half-past two—they dined early in the Fifties, especially on board ship—and we were smoking our pipes and sitting about, chatting and laughing, and passing the time pleasantly enough, as shipboard life went.

I was rather a favoured person, because, as servant to Dr. O'Donovan, I was allowed an extra pint of porter daily. I went below to get my drink, and was instantly met by an awful smell of burning. I knew too well the terrible danger we were in if fire broke out to lose a minute's time in making known what I had seen. I returned to the deck, and just on reaching the top of the hatchway I met the carpenter. "I believe the ship's on fire!" I told him.

"Sh!" he answered. "You'll be put in irons if you say that!"

But he hurried below and hurried back again, and almost instantly Captain Castle and the chief mate came along.

There was no need to mince matters then, or hide the awful truth. The *Sarah Sands* was burning, and every soul on board knew it. The hatches were closed down, so that no unnecessary draught should feed the fire, but it was soon too clear that the transport was a roaring blaze astern.

Without the slightest warning we had been plunged from peace and safety into tumult and peril. We were fighting a battle in which the odds were crushingly against us. Now came the test of courage and endurance, and proof again, if proof were needed, of the steadying power of discipline. What of the mutineers, the foreigners, who knew neither drill nor obedience, and who had no *esprit de corps* to hold them to their duty? They had rushed for the boats and jumped into them, and, caring nothing for anything except their own skins, had pushed off.

A few of the 54th, who, in the confusion, had jumped from the boats also, were carried away from the ship's side. It had been just possible to get the ladies and children into one of the boats, and in it, covered with blankets and anything else we could lay hands on in the hurry and excitement, they were huddled during those long, awful hours of daylight and darkness in which we struggled to beat the flames and save the ship. Their case was as melancholy as our own, for the weather was proving bad, and the boats were thrown about the seas—one, indeed, was swamped, but no lives were lost. Fortunately, as we were going on active service, there were very few women and children on board—eleven in all.

When the fire broke out, the *Sarah Sands* was carrying sail. The commander ordered this to be taken in, and also that the ship should be got, and kept, head to wind. That was, of course, to try to keep the fire from extending, by confining it to the after part of the transport. This was a hard enough task with so few sailors left on board; but during the long voyage some of us had picked up a little seamanship, and so, under the direction and with the help of the ship's officers, we managed it. Hose-pipes were fitted to the fire-engine, buckets and anything from which water could be thrown were furiously at work. We did everything that mortal men could do to drown the flames, and yet our pumy jets had not the least effect on them.

Merciful indeed it is that at such times great exertions keep us from dwelling over-much on what might may seem our hopeless case. If there had been a chance for thought, for calculating the overwhelming odds against us, there were not many even of the bravest but would have resignedly awaited the end, and prayed for its speedy coming; but every nerve and every muscle in every man was alert and working, and like very fiends the 54th laboured for the preservation of the *Sarah Sands*.

Even at a time of the greatest peril some unexpected incident will force use to the thought of matters other than our personal doings. Here were we, overshadowed by present horrors and the prospect of an almost certain death; yet there arose a strange forgetfulness of self and a concern for the welfare of a fellow-creature. And who was he? Where was he that he should claim attention then, of all times? Where could he have been for his case to be worse than our own pitiful plight?

He was a prisoner below, a mutineer in irons, and he was captive in the heart of that fiery furnace!

This seemed the very crowning horror of our case. He was a sailor—a one-eyed man, called Scottie, the best of the crew; and there he was, helpless below. instantly there were men willing to risk their lives to try to save him; but no man was allowed to make the attempt; all that we were permitted to do was to throw a rope down in the feeble hope that he could help himself.

A rope was lowered, and Scottie managed to seize it. Then we dragged him up to the deck, irons and all, and he got his poor chance of life like the rest of us. But there were few who thought he could pull round, for he was so overcome with exhaustion that he lay on the deck like one dead, and it was fully twenty minutes before he recovered consciousness.

First and foremost to the soldier of the old days came the thought of his regimental Colours. Ours were in the saloon, and the saloon was astern, where the fire was raging. Who would venture on such a forlorn hope as the attempt to save them? Who, indeed? Why, there was an instant dash for them, without thought of personal danger, in defiance of the stifling smoke and scorching flames. First of all, the two ensigns into whose special care the Colours had been given—Lieutenants Houston and Hughes—rushed into the choking saloon and tried to seize the precious folds of silk and bring them out. They failed, and barely escaped with their lives.

Then a gallant fellow named Richard Richmond, one of the ship's quartermasters, vanished into the dense smoke and struggled towards the far end of the saloon, where the Colours hung. he had a wet cloth over his face, and was armed with an axe. With frantic cuts he got the Colours down and staggered back through the suffocating atmosphere. Then, overcome with the heat and smoke, he fainted, and it seemed as if his death were as sure as the destruction of the Colours and ship.

But pluck begets pluck. There was another rush, and Private William Wiles dragged Richmond and the Colours from the saloon and on to the deck. They came out of that awful furnace with just strength enough to hold the Colours up so that the 54th should see them, and in that thrilling act and with our cheers ringing in their ears, they fell down senseless and exhausted. Those Colours are now in Norwich Cathedral.

We were in the very thick of our fight, whetted to continue it by the salvation of our Colours, and the ceaseless encouragement and glorious example of our regimental officers. Their pluck was as wonderful as their endurance. And they were finely supported by the ship's officers and the two or three men—Englishmen, mind you—of the crew who had not deserted to the boats. Courage and an unfaltering lead were needed, too, for we had no human enemy to deal with, no opposing troops who at any moment might break and run; but a grim and ruthless foe who had it all his own way, and with whom the very wind and sea appeared to be in league, for the wind was roaring and the waves were running high.

We were formed in sections—drill, drill, drill, it seemed to be on that rolling, burning parade-ground—and a curious sight we must have been, because we were always counter-marching. We were crowded on the cramped fore part of the ship, and were always facing ourselves, so to speak. That was owing to some of us coming up from below, where we had been sent to work, and marching forward and meeting the sections who were on their way to relieve us.

It seems easy to talk about pouring water on the fire, but no tongue can tell the difficulties we had to meet and overcome. Before we could get below we had to cut holes in the deck with hatches; then to grope and stifle in the dense, hot depths, feeling with our hands for the hottest places on the iron plates, and throwing water on to keep them cool. A ceaseless wetting of the coals was also necessary to keep them from bursting into flames.

We crawled and crept and staggered blindly from spot to spot with our buckets and other things, always to keep the fire to its huge metal grate and prevent it from bursting out into the whole of our home. We never stopped throwing the water down, and never ceased to pump it up again, so that the *Sarah Sands* should not meet her doom from her only means of preservation.

Now that we were accustomed to the first great danger, we were confronted with another and more awful peril, and that was our destruction by the explosion of the powder in our two magazines? We had many barrels of gunpowder on board, and, in addition, there were the ship's rockets in another magazine. Not even the bravest could think of that new peril without fear, but the terror disappeared in the fury and excitement of getting at the casks.

First to be tackled was the starboard magazine, and the 54th fell to their work with all the strength that dread gives—almost, if you like, despairingly. The task was so hard, the means of doing it so slight. Everything was against us, and it seemed as if nothing were in our favour. To get at the powder meant that men had to be lowered with ropes through the holes in the deck into the suffocating, scorching depths, and to fasten other ropes round casks, when these were hauled up. Each cask as it was landed on the deck was thrown overboard. One by one they came, men working until they could work no more—some indeed were drawn up senseless—and at last the starboard magazine was emptied.

Again there was a thrill of triumph, but short-lived, for the port quarter magazine was still untouched, and it was very near the fire. It could be reached only by one hatchway, and that was already belching dense clouds of hot smoke.

Volunteers were wanted again—volunteers were instantly at hand.

The furious fight to get the powder overboard was renewed. Again men went below and laboured until they fainted; but the powder diminished and grew less, until at last there remained only one cask of ammunition which an exhausted soldier had dropped, and some signalling powder which had been forgotten. There were also two large barrels of powder which it was humanly impossible to reach.

Our fate seemed sure at last.

We had so far escaped the fire and kept it to the stern; the ship was still manageable, and might be saved, but the powder was certain to explode, and there was n one who believed that the *Sarah Sands* would survive the explosion. We had been striving for hours, darkness had settled on the sea, and it seemed as if nothing could be done. The boats—can you imagine the feelings of the unhappy women and children in them, separated from husbands and fathers, tossed on the waters and expecting certain death?—were ordered to get clear of the ship so as to escape the force of the explosion, and they were pulled away.

No words can indicate the sufferings of those who waited in the boats and in the ship for the awful end—agonies which were intensified by the enforced partings.

Again desperate exertions kept us employed. We never ceased to try to save the ship. We cut away the deck fittings which might catch fire, and cabins and lumber went overboard; we collected the spars and other things and made three rafts. Two of these were set afloat and the third was left across the deck, ready to be lowered at the very last.

To the glory of the 54th be it said that not even then, in the very face of death, with the conviction that the ship might at any moment explode, did a single soldier rush for the rafts. The troops remained obedient, and the officers continued to encourage and lead them.

It was about this time that Captain Castle, brave though he was, abandoned hope. He was on the bridge—I was there also, with the doctor—and turning to Major Brett, who was in command of us, he said, "You have done all you can; nothing more is possible." Then he took a pair of marine glasses which were slung over his shoulders, and flung them into the heart of the fire, saying, "They're no good now!" But Major Brett answered, "We shall never stop working till we're driven overboard."

In the darkness of the night the flames leapt skyward. The after part of the ship was by that time one mass of fire. The deck was burnt away, the iron beams were red hot, the very sides were glowing, and to the roaring of the fire and wind and sea there was the appalling accompaniment of an unearthly light for miles around—a vaporous and unnatural luminosity. The sky itself was a vast red dome, and the very sea was ghastly with the glare.

Most horrible of all, the water swarmed with sharks, which were quite clearly visible as they leapt and struggled, hungrily waiting for the end.

Would the end never come? Would this nerve-destroying suspense never be broken? Would the fire never reach the powder?

Can you picture the pitiful case of us—the troops still fighting, as we were fighting, against these overwhelming odds of fire and wind and sea? Could there be no mercy of any sort for us?

Even as we watched and waited and hoped the tarred mizzen rigging took fire. The ropes swiftly burnt away and over crashed the mast. Still, in the good providence of God, and because we plied our work with hose and bucket, we kept the *Sarah Sands* head to wind, and so preserved her, keeping the fire connived to the after part, although once or twice terrible blasts of flame and smoke were swept from stern to bow.

We had been striving for many long hours. Man after man had fallen senseless, dropping exhausted on the deck, and the only thing even the doctor could do was to throw salt water on their faces to bring them round. Our uniforms were scorched from our bodies, our skins were burnt and black with smoke, and we were parched with torturing thirst. Believe me, so terrible was this thirst upon us that our tongues were swollen out of our mouths, and could be forced back only by the pressure of our hands. And there was no relief for us, because our very life's sustenance, our food and drink, were being destroyed with our ship.

Suddenly there was the terrifying climax for which we had all been waiting.

Right astern there was a mighty red flash upward, a deafening crash, a crackling as if the very elements were dissolving, then a shuddering, sickening sinking of our water-laden troopship.

The powder had exploded at last, and with it had burst the ship's rockets, making such a firework show as never mortal man had seen, I think, for he had never witnessed it in such a setting—and such a one I have no desire to look upon again.

Not a human being in the transport who felt the shock, not a wretched soul in the boats who saw the awful sight, believed that the vessel would survive, and yet when the shudder had passed through her, when she had recovered from the sickening dip, the *Sarah Sands* stool still, although the wreckage of her stern cabins had been blown out and into fragments and a great hole torn in her port quarter as far down as the water-line. Marvellous to tell, the explosion injured only two amongst us, a lieutenant and a corporal, who were blown down a hatchway, but were rescued.

We were still afloat, then—still favoured with a dismal hope of preservation. And so we went into the fight again with fresh heart of grace, and the buckets were passed and the hoses played, and on to the hot coal and the heated plates of her we threw the water, in the hope that even yet we might prevent the fire from spreading, as for many hours, thank God, we had prevented it.

Thought the unspeakable night the 54th fought on, unaided by the cowards who had mutinied and left the ship. They were hailed to come and take the *Sarah Sands* in tow, in order to keep her head to the wind, but they refused, and it was not until all danger from the fire was over that they came on board again. They got a reception which made their ears tingle, I can assure you. The sharks had tried repeatedly to upset the boats with their tails, and now that they saw the people returning to the ship they made savage and voracious rushes at them.

I have seen pictures of fine people going back to burnt-out homes. So it was with the *Sarah Sands*. Her beautifully dressed women, who had been hurried into the boats with bare arms and necks and shoulders, came to the side again. But how different from the joyous, chatty crowd who were on the point of dining when the cry of "Fire!" was raised! Dresses were torn and crumpled, happy faces had become drawn and haggard, bright eyes were dull with weeping, and white, delicate skins were browned and blistered by the merciless tropical sun. They filled with pity even those of us who had fought the flames, and in looking on their miseries we forgot our own. Captain Castle did what he could to relieve them, and that was to order the sila-maker to get pieces of sail and canvas and much such coverings as he could for the scorched skins. And so upon the delicate finery was put a coarse canvas crown! There was no chance of luxury in such a floating shell, and all that ingenuity could do and decency provide was to rig a canvas screen to separate the ladies from the troops.

It is astounding to think what men can reconcile themselves to do when they are the creatures of crippling circumstances. Here were we, who had been so cooped up in a small ship on a long run to India, that we could scarcely move in our narrow quarters and close imprisonment; yet we were finding it possible to exist in half the space, huddled almost indiscriminately to an iron shell that only kept afloat by a miracle.

The after part of the transport was just a gutted mass of ironwork, open to the air and sea. To look down into it was like being on the top of a building that has been destroyed by fire, with only bare girders and the gaunt walls visible. The cabins had been blown out of the stern by the explosion; all the woodwork had long since vanished, and some of the iron had melted away. How could it be otherwise with a heat which was so fierce that the very glass of the scuttles had melted and hung like icicles now that it was cold? The fact alone will show you how intense was the heat—literally a furnace heat. It is marvellous that the work of man could withstand such a consuming flame, and the survival of the ship was a noble tribute to the stoutness of her structure and the honesty of her build. She had been gutted by fire; now heavy seas struck her repeatedly, and as she rolled helplessly our four enormous tanks of water, which were right below, were hurled from side to side, and we never knew when one or all of them would dash through the iron plating.

Strange and incongruous were the things we did after and resulting from the fire. Most striking of all, I think, was the erection of a tent—for the captain's use and other official purposes—on the iron wreckage, where the stern cabins had been.

A tent on a floating wreck, in that wilderness of tropic sea! And below that tent was the torn, bent mass of ironwork, with the very propeller-shaft showing in the depths. Need a man be a sailor to understand our constant peril from shipping a sea, or even a mass of water which, in ordinary times, would only cause amusement?

The long fight was over and a glorious victory was one. But what was our prize? A mere hull, a ship half burnt away, and which was sound only forward of the mainmast. The smoke had gone and now only clouds of steam ascended and vanished in the air. The *Sarah Sands* had nearly twenty feet of water in her, and was so deep by the stern that every wave seemed as if it would overwhelm and sink her. We had only one sound mast, too, the mizzen having been burnt away and the main damaged.

We had saved the troopship from fire; now we had to preserve her from water, so we set to work again and patched her up, but we pumped incessantly for two nights and a day; we rigged up a steering-gear, we covered over the rent side with spars and canvas, and we got some sail up. That was after floundering and drifting helplessly about in a ship that had nothing to control her.

Then, suffering torture from thirst and hunger, because our fresh water and provisions had been almost entirely destroyed, we struggled on for nine days more, when we got our gallant cripple into Port Louis in the Mauritius. Until that time from the hour we started from the Cape we had seen neither ship nor land, so our deliverance was merciful indeed. If we had vanished, our fate would never have been known, because two or three bottles that were thrown overboard with messages were never picked up.

The irony of our fate was on us to the very last. A pilot came off and told us that he could not take us in till next morning, as ships were not allowed to enter in the darkness. No exception was made even for us, so for the first time since the fire the crazy screw was started slowly, and the *Sarah Sands* crawled off and on. She was nearly wrecked in the night on a roof, but in the morning she got in and we went ashore—some of us wrapped in newspapers to hide our nakedness.

For all the miseries we had suffered there was almost recompense in the things that were said about us, and the kindness which was shown. We had gone through that long-drawn time of peril from fire and sea and mutiny; we had saved our Colours and our ship; we had held to our discipline and maintained the credit of our regiment, and we had not lost a life!

Can you wonder that of all the honours which the 54th has gained there is none it holds dearer than this great triumph that was won upon the sea, and not the battlefield?

The storming of Delhi, and the relief of Lucknow, proved to be turning points in the Mutiny, but did not end the fighting. Indeed, the destruction of the main rebel concentrations in some respects served to spread the rebellion further, as the survivors moved into the countryside in an attempt to avoid British retribution. In particular, the rising spread to two small states south of the river Jumna – Jhansi and Gwalior – which had only recently been taken over by the Company. This gave the rebellion a fresh impetus, and fighting dragged on throughout the first half of 1858. By the end of the year, however, the rebel strongholds had been stormed, and their leaders captured or killed, and the Mutiny came largely to an end.

It had proved by far the greatest test of British arms on Indian soil, and it changed the face of British India forever. By the time it was over, India was entirely under British control, either directly, or through compliant local rulers. The British parliament dissolved the East India Company, and responsibility for administering India passed directly to the Crown. The former Company armies were re-organised, to prevent military insurgency ever proving such a threat again. Even in the British army there were repercussions; twenty-five new battalions of infantry had been authorised by the Duke of Cambridge – the Commander-in-Chief – to ensure there were sufficient troops available to suppress the rebellion and police the Empire, and these became second battalions for the first twenty-five regiments of the line – the first in a series of organisational changes which took place over the next thirty years.

With the suppression of the Mutiny, British fears about India's security once more turned to the west. In fact, the suspicion that the Amir of Afghanistan, Dost Mohammed, would prove unable to resist Russian encroachment proved largely unfounded in the aftermath of the 1st Afghan War. Dost Mohammed had remained determinedly neutral in the 'Great Game', a policy which did not change significantly when he was succeeded by his son, Sher Ali, in 1863.

Nevertheless, by the 1870s, both Russia and Britain were keen to gain some diplomatic representation at the Afghan court, with the result that a seemingly slight diplomatic insult resulted in another major British expedition to Afghanistan. In 1877 a Russian representative was accepted at Kabul; the British demanded that one of their envoys be given equal treatment, but he was refused entry to the Khyber Pass in 1878. A British ultimatum followed, which expired on 20 November 1878 – and the 2nd Afghan War began.

The second Afghan campaign ran a curiously parallel course to the first. The British invaded in three columns, heading for the southern city of Kandahar, and for Kabul itself. The initial fighting was largely distinguished by Sir Frederick Roberts' handling of the Kurram Valley column, and in particular by his successful flank attack on Afghan positions at the Peiwar Kotal on 1 December – an action which largely established his reputation as the leading British general in the Indian theatre. The British occupied Kabul, Sher Ali fled, and the British established a Resident in the Afghan capital.

As in 1839, however, a British presence in Kabul did not imply the compliance of the country as a whole. Two of the British columns were withdrawn, leaving only Roberts in the field. Scarcely two months later, trouble broke out in Kabul, and the British Residency was attacked, and the Resident and his escort killed. Roberts immediately advanced once more on Kabul, defeating the Afghans in a series of engagements outside the city. Learning from the mistakes of his predecessor, Lord Elphinstone, Roberts built a secure cantonment on the outskirts of the city, to protect his troops as winter drew on. For several weeks the Afghan tribes in the surrounding hills mustered their forces, and on 23 December 1879 launched a major attack on Roberts' position. The attack lasted throughout the night and much of the following day, but in the end the Afghans were defeated with heavy losses.

A political stalemate then ensued. Although the British now controlled the main Afghan cities, it proved impossible to extend that control over the countryside. Moreover, the town of Herat, in western Afghanistan, had been untouched by the fighting, and provided a focus for Afghan resistance. In July 1880 a brother of Yakub Khan, Ayub Khan, attempted a surprise attack on the Kandahar garrison from Herat. The local British commander, General Primrose, despatched a Brigade under General Burrows to intercept him. Burrows' force encountered the Afghans outside the village of Maiwand on 27 July. The resulting action would prove one of the greatest British disasters of the 1870s, second only to Isandlwana, with which it had much in common. Burrows had under-estimated Ayub's strength, and his position was over-extended. The British line crumpled under the Afghan onslaught, and almost 1000 men were killed. The Queen's 66th Regiment was almost wiped out and, like the 24th at Isandlwana, lost their Colours to the enemy. A British battery – E Battery, B Brigade, RHA – lost two of its guns. Among those who survived the action was Gunner Francis Naylor.

The Lost Guns and Colours

We had marched out of Kandahar into the heart of the enemy's country, which was Afghanistan, to meet and, if we could – which we did not doubt – beat the Afghan forces. There were not quite 2500 of us, the backbone of our body being a few companies of the 66th Regiment and ourselves of the Royal Horse Artillery:

The right of the line,
The pride of the British Army,
The ladies' delight when dismounted,
And the angels' pride when mounted.

That, at any rate, is an old, proud boast of ours; but there was not much parade smartness in our appearance when, men in khaki, we pitched our tents in an Afghan graveyard until such time as we could get to close and hot business with the enemy. We had the headquarter companies of the 66th, and their Colours were with them, for Colours were still carried into battle by British troops. Maiwand is famous for two things – the loss of British guns and the loss of British Colours. I believe I am not far from right in saying that, owing to the Colours being lost, orders were given that they should no longer be carried into action, and for nearly a quarter of a century these famous rallying points have been absent from our fights. They are now merely symbols of the regimental spirit.

We left Kandahar on July 4th, our brigade being under the command of Brigadier-General Burrows, and in a week reached the River Helmand. We were in the thick of the excitement at once, because some of the native troops who were with us deserted in a body to the enemy, taking with them four smooth-bore guns which had been presented to them by the Government of India, and which an English artillerist had taught them to use. But we crossed the river, and after giving them some rounds of shrapnel and some case-shot we got the guns back. Case-shot, you know, is fired point-blank, without elevating the gun. It scatters instantly, like a fan, and the hundred and eight bullets in the shot do terrible mischief.

The enemy flung their dead into a little stream in the village, which was red with blood, and hurried off; but before they got away the 66th came up and got in a few volleys. The native women were on the flat roofs of their houses, and they managed to wound two or three of the men of the 66th.

We were in for plenty of excitement even at that early stage. One man of the 66th fired at an Afghan who was up a tree and brought him down like a crow. Instantly another Afghan rushed out from a ditch pair, where he had been hiding, and made for the 66th man. But the man was too quick for him, and, although his rifle was empty, he hit his bayonet home, and a dismounted native cavalryman, running up, finished the Afghan with his sword. When the guns were ours the 66th got into the shafts, and with drag ropes drew the guns away until our own horses came up. That was on July 14th, and was a very good beginning to what proved a very bad business.

Another piece of luck attended us on the third, when our two guns and some native cavalry went out, Major Blackwood being in command of my battery. Seeing the enemy at a long distance he ordered a couple of shots to be fired into them. This we did; then, believing that the shots had fallen short, and that precious ammunition was being wasted, the Major shortened the distance. When we limbered up and the cavalry scouts went round, we learnt that the two shots which we had considered wasted had destroyed fifty seven and fifty horses.

These happenings were merely preliminaries to the great day of the disaster, which was on July 27th. On the afternoon of the day before, General

Burrows had learnt that a large body of the enemy had reached Maiwand, which was not quite a dozen miles away. He also heard that the Afghan chief, Ayub Khan, intended to follow with his main body. The General determined to try to prevent the two bodies from joining together, and so on the morning of the 27th, at about 12 o'clock, he struck his camp, and the whole brigade of us, baggage and all, marched off. We had no breakfast, and nothing of any sort to eat, and truth to tell, in view of the information which had been received, there must have been some amongst us who had not much appetite.

We marched on for several miles, crawling cautiously, which, hampered as we were, was the only thing to do. Besides, it was a dull, heavy morning, and the enemy might fall upon us almost unseen and unawares at any place and at any moment. Just think what it all meant to us – a long, straggling body, with not far short of 2000 camels, and many ponies, bullocks, donkeys, mules, and horses, and drivers and transport followers. To have had only British troops, untrammeled, would have been bad enough; to be burdened with these swarms of non-combatants and animals was disastrous.

Four hours after starting we were half-way to Maiwand. Then we heard from a spy that that place, which our General had hoped to reach and hold, was already full of Afghans under Ayub Khan. What was to be done? What road can you take when there is only one to use? We were like a gigantic creature which can only travel one way, and that is, ahead. There was one thing to do, and one thing only, and that was to get the business through – to see what would happen when two thousand five hundred of us were in touch with twenty-five thousand of the enemy.

There we were, pinned and crippled, forced to go ahead, if we went at all, and knowing that to advance meant almost certain death. Pretty much as our own position was, I fancy, is the case of the man who has to battle with a storm and drive his ship through it, or bide his time as best he can until wind and sea have done their worst. Just as the gale strikes the ship, so were we struck by the enemy. In the case of the ship something perhaps goes, some point in her stability is affected. So it was with us, for at the crisis when our strength was most urgently needed many of our native troops bolted. I have heard it put in a gentler way than that; but they went, and they left us to it.

There we were, then, trapped in a valley, with thousands of Afghans hovering and flying about us; and only those who have fought against them in their native hills can really understand how swift they are in their movements. And they are so merciless with it! There were the few companies of the 66th, officers and men who were as brave as any that ever wore uniform, their Colours proudly borne amongst them, with the young subalterns carrying them, full of the fire and spirit which always came to men into whose keeping these sacred folds of silk were given.

The 66th were the right sort. We had had plenty of proof of that, we of the Royal Horse Artillery, who had now been in more than one tight corner with them. Then there were ourselves, and, being what we were, we knew what was expected of us.

It was just before noon when that final chapter of the great disaster opened. Strange things happened early and quickly. We got into action, and we could see trees falling in a wood at which we were firing. Almost at the outset, a shoeing-smith was ordered to fasten a shoe on the wheel-horse of the gun. He was a man who had been remarkable for his strength and freedom from sickness; but he was now ill, and, like most people of the sort, took his ailment very badly. He dismounted, and as he began his work said: 'I hope the first shot they fire will blow me to bits.' Almost as soon as we got into action a shot came and killed him, as well as two or three natives.

That artillery duel had developed suddenly. We had fired three or four rounds out of each gun, and I remember so well hearing Gunner Moorcroft say hopefully, as men like to speak at such a time of stress: 'We'll soon have 'em out of action!' Instantly, as it seemed, the very ground rumbled, and the air was filled with the flashes and thickened with the smoke of thirty-two guns, sweeping upon and into us, and tearing into and through our huddled and disorganised masses.

Picture, if you can, the horrors and consternation of an onslaught like that, in a crowded space, with a cruel enemy in overwhelming numbers surrounding us, and animals wildly stampeding, and transport followers and drivers thrown into panic and confusion. There were Krupp guns as well as smoothbore guns, and these weapons outnumbered us altogether. In addition to our own Horse Artillery guns, we had the smoothbores which we had taken, and these were manned by men of the 66th, in charge of a few of the men of E Battery. They were in the rear of our own battery, but did not do much mischief.

We were now fighting not so much for victory, which there was no hope of winning, as for our very existence. At No. 2 gun, which was in charge of Sergeant Mullane, who later in the day won the V.C., I fired no fewer than 105 rounds. That gun and the other guns became almost red hot, and some of the men had their hands burnt in handling them. It was while serving the gun that I lost my hand. I was taking a tube out of my pouch to fire another cartridge, when a six-pound shot ricocheted on the gun-wheel tyre, which is a broad iron band. The shot tore the tyre as if it had been indiarubber, struck me on the left hand, and then broke one of the bones in one of our officers' arms.

Officers and men were now falling fast. It was not so much a fight as a *mêlée*, and the most we could hope to do was to save ourselves and our guns, and the 66th could not hope to do more than hold their own. They were fighting nobly, refusing to give way, and rallying on their Colours. I believe that all would have fallen where they fought, but there was a rush of our own native troops upon them which threw them into confusion and disturbed their steadiness.

Officer after officer, and man after man, went down in defence of the Colours; but they remained flying until the enemy closed in upon us like a horseshoe, and even the most hopeful of us knew that there was only one chance of safety for us, and that that lay in flight.

The gallant Major Blackwood was amongst the killed by this time. He was wounded in the leg, and went to the rear until he tied a handkerchief round it. Having done that, he came back, dismounted, and getting on one side of the 66th, he rallied them.

The Afghans were then rushing up. Major Blackwood tried to remount, but his leg was so stiff that he could not get into the saddle again. He was overwhelmed and slain, his head being struck off with a sword. Gunner Brown, of my battery, tried hard to save him, but he only just escaped with his own life, having seven sword-cuts on his arms and back. He died afterwards in France.

From that point onward all was horror, confusion, and hopelessness. The very life of our guns, the ammunition, was expended; the valiant 66th were absolutely overwhelmed by numbers, and utter rout was being worked amongst us. In a forlorn effort to do something effective, Lieutenant Maclaine rushed off with his guns and got into action. He kept on firing shrapnel as long as he had it to fire; then he used case-shot, and with terrible effect, too. But he was outnumbered, and his two guns were surrounded, one of them especially.

It was a case of every man for himself. There was no time even to spike the guns – they had to be abandoned. One of our men tumbled an Afghan over by thrusting at him with his rammer, and then managed to get away; another cut through the stirrup-leather of one of the gunners, and ran along with his horse and managed to escape. Nearly half our horses were killed, and of those that were living some were shockingly wounded. We could do nothing for them, not even shoot them in mercy; and they, poor brutes, had to take what chance they could get by fleeing. It was wonderful and piteous to see the way they clung to us and followed us – one, in particular, who had his jaw shattered, and galloped on with us in our terrible retreat.

The two guns were lost – we knew that. The enemy had captured them. They had also made Lieutenant Maclaine a prisoner – which in the case of the Afghans was worse than death itself. That was part of the price which we of the artillery were paying. As for the 66th, they were in as bad a plight.

Desperate though their efforts were to save the Colours – even to the stripping of the poles, so that someone might perhaps get clear of the battlefield with the silk – that failed.

The Afghans captured the Colours. What became of them I do not know, but the poles were used as rammers for our own lost guns – which is, I daresay, an incident that is without parallel in our army. The guns were afterwards recovered.

Well, that disastrous retreat began. It was helter skelter for us all, and a wild confusion. Only the fact that the Afghans, for some reason, did not follow up their success by pursuing us, made it possible for a soul of us to escape. We were all jumbled up together, men, horses, guns, camels, bullocks, and camp-followers and drivers, and we could have been destroyed with ease, helpless as we were through exhaustion of ammunition.

In such a flight a man thinks mostly and almost solely of himself – he has neither thought nor care for anything or anybody else. Of this we had abundant proof in our own battery. I will give you an illustration. Being wounded, I was put in a dooley. A rush of camels tumbled the dooley upside down and threw me out.

The forge of the battery was going by, and the farrier-sergeant shouted: 'Get up and have a ride,' which I gladly did. At the same moment a private who had been wounded in an earlier fight and had just rushed out of hospital – he had only his shirt on – was coming by on a 'tat'; but we took him on to the forge. A native rifleman wanted to get on, too, but there was no room, and so I pushed him off.

He raised his rifle, and the farrier-sergeant drew his revolver, which made the native think better of it. A couple of camels were hurrying past, and the native asked the driver to stop. The driver refused, whereupon the native raised his rifle, shot him dead, tumbled him off, and rode away. I saw no more of him. Maiwand bristled with incidents like that.

There was only one thing for us to do, and that was to get back to Kandahar, which we had so hopefully left, and wait for relief – which came at last through Lord Roberts.

I am not going to speak of the horrors of that long, hard ride throughout the afternoon and night till Kandahar was reached in the morning; but there is one point on which I should like to dwell for a moment. I suppose that in the recollection of all men who have been in battle there remains one outstanding feature, one event which looms above and overshadows all else.

It may be some terrible spectacle of death or suffering, or it may be some grotesque and trivial incident such as you may meet with even on the field of death. In my own case, you might suppose that the wound which cost me my hand would be the chief thing to dwell in my memory; yet that is not so. Whenever I look back upon Maiwand the thing I mostly remember is our terrible and maddening thirst. We had nothing to drink before the fight began, we had not a drop of water during those long hours of pounding, and we had no chance whatever of getting anything to quench our thirst. Parched and swollen-tongued we retreated from the battlefield, and mile after mile in that awful land we and our poor horses strained at the guns to save them.

Thirst!

You may understand what it was when I tell you that some of the natives who were fleeing died as they ran; others, more lucky, got at the medicine-chests, smashed them open, seized the bottles, and, frantically breaking them, swallowed the contents. During our headlong flight one or two wounded men who were on the limbers were constantly crying 'Water, water!' and that added to our misery and agony. At last we came to a stagnant pool, a horrible, poisonous patch of water, still and silent, thick with grass-green slime on the top. The very sight of such a pool at ordinary times will fill you with loathing; yet, with our overmastering thirst upon us, we got off the gun and rushed at it as if it had been the purest, coolest, clearest stream, and drank and drank again of the foul liquid.

I was wearing a moustache then, as I do now, and I so well remember that when I rose and had drunk my fill, my moustache was thick with the green slime. Strangely enough, none of us felt any ill-effects, nor do I recollect that any of the medicine-drinkers came to grief.

Those of us who were lucky enough to be living, even though we might be maimed – my own hand mortified, and had to be removed – got back to Kandahar about eleven o'clock next morning, having travelled something like fifty miles without a stop. The news of our defeat had somehow been flashed on before us; but our own appearance told the sorry truth that we were beaten – and the villagers about the city welcomed us back by firing on us and trying to destroy us. Some of our own artillery and the 7th Fusiliers came out to help us in, and there, in Kandahar, we remained until we were relieved. One of the last to enter was General Burrows, who had had two horses shot under him at Maiwand.

Well, that is the story of the disaster. It was crowned in melancholy fashion, for when Lord Roberts had relieved us, and put Ayub Khan to flight, he rode out to inspect the chief's camp. And one of the first things he learnt was that only a very few yards away was the body of Lieutenant Maclaine, whose throat had just been cut. That was the fate of a prisoner of war in the hands of a blood-thirsty and pitiless enemy.

On such a day there were many deeds of valour – Maiwand gave two men the Victoria Cross, and eight men that next best honour, the Distinguished Conduct Medal – but I think that if I were asked to name the most remarkable act of devotion I should say that it was shown by a private of the 66th.

His was a strange and striking case. Some days before the battle a native saw him drinking rum out of a cask, through a straw.

'I'll tell,' said the native.

'Will you,' replied the soldier, 'I'll make sure you don't.' With that he raised his rifle and shot the native dead. There was some delay in carrying out the death sentence on the man, and he was asked at Maiwand if he would fight.

'Yes, to the very last,' he promised.

He fought gallantly from start to finish, and at the end, when the officers and Colour parties had fallen so thickly, he took one of the silk Colours and folded it round his waist, and in that way, fighting still to save the honour of his regiment, he died.

Interestingly enough, *The Strand* also published the story of one of E/B Battery's gunners, James Collis, who was awarded the VC for his actions during the retreat. His story confirms Naylor's account of the chaos and confusion of the defeat.

The Disaster of Maiwand

On the twenty-seventh of July, 1880, we were encamped at Khushk-i-Nakhud, in Afghanistan. At 4 a.m. that day we – Battery E, Battery B Brigade – marched with the rest of the force on Maiwand to meet Ayub Khan. About 9 a.m. we came in sight of him in position under the hills. We were on the open plain. Major Henry Blackwood, commanding my battery, gave the order 'Action front.' I was a limber gunner that day. We began firing with common shell from the right of the battery. After we had fired a few rounds, their artillery replied. The first shot struck the near wheel of my gun, killing a gunner, wounding another, and Lieutenant Fowler.

The limber box upon my gun was smashed by a shell which also killed the wheel horses, but did not touch the driver. Several riding horses of my battery were killed, and a good deal of damage done to guns and carriage. Four gunners and Sergeant Wood, the No. 1 of my gun, were killed, and two men wounded, leaving only three men to work the gun. I took Sergeant Wood's place.

At about 1.30 p.m., some of Jacob's Rifles, who were lying down about ten yards in rear of the trail, began to be panic-stricken, and crowded round our guns and carriages, some getting under the carriages. Three got under my gun. We tried to drive them away, but it was no use. About that time we ceased firing a little, the enemy having set the example. During that pause the enemy on the left got pretty close. To check them, General Nuttall formed up the 3rd Bombay Cavalry and the 3rd Scinde Horse to charge.

Gunner Smith of my gun, seeing what was going to be done, mounted his horse and joined the cavalry. General Nuttall led the charge, Gunner Smith being at his side. After going about 300 yards, the enemy being about 200 yards off, the whole line, with the exception of the General, the European officers, and Gunner Smith, turned tail, forming up when in line with the guns. General Nuttall with the officers, finding themselves deserted, returned, General Nuttall actually crying from mortification. Gunner Smith dashed on alone, and was cut down.

About 4 p.m. a large body of the enemy's infantry charged the left of the battery, the men of the left division 5 and 6 being compelled to use their handspikes and charge staves to keep them off. Major Blackwood on this ordered the battery to limber up and retire. When Lieutenant Maclaine heard this order he said, as I was afterwards informed, 'Limber up be damned! Give them another round.' We limbered up and retired at a gallop about 2,000 yards. In the meantime Major Blackwood remained behind with Lieutenant Maclaine's guns and was killed, Lieutenant Osborne by his side, Lieutenant Maclaine fighting to the last. At length, seeing no use in stopping, he galloped after us – we had got separated from the right division – and called out to us, only two guns, 'Action, rear.' We fired two rounds with shrapnel. Captain Slade, who had been in temporary command of the smooth-bores, finding Major Blackwood dead, came up with his smooth-bores and took command of all the guns. Colonel Malcolmson a moment later ordered Captain Slade to retire, saying, 'Captain Slade, if you and the Lieutenant keep those two guns, he will lose them the same as he has lost his own.' We then limbered up and went off. Just then a shell burst open our treasure chest. Many of the troops and camp followers stopped to pick up the money and were overtaken and killed. Just after that some of the enemy's cavalry caught up the guns. One of them wounded me on the left eyebrow as he passed. He wheeled round and came at me again; I took my carbine, waited till he was within four or five yards, and let drive, hitting him on the chest and knocking him off his horse. As he fell his money fell out of his turban, and Trumpeter Jones jumped off his horse and picked it up. He escaped, and is now corporal R.H.A., and wears the Distinguished Service medal for his conduct at Maiwand.

It was now beginning to get dusk, and I got off to walk by the side of my gun. Seeing a village close by, and some men at a well, I followed them and got some water. Just as we got to the well the enemy charged and drove us off, killing a good many.

On my return I missed my gun, and picked up with No. 2, which I stuck to till I reached Candahar. It was now dark, and we were with a stream of men of all regiments, camp followers, camels, and waggons. Going along I saw a lot of sick and wounded lying by the side of the road, and I picked them up and put them on the gun and limber. I had about ten altogether; they were all 66th men, and a colonel whose name I do not know and never heard of.

We had been fighting all day, marching all night and next day without a bit of food or a drink of water. I did not feel it so much, as I was so occupied, but I saw several dying by the roadside from thirst and fatigue. About four in the afternoon of the 28th, we came to a place called Kokeran, 7½ miles from Candahar; I saw a village where I could get water for the men who were with me. I went off and brought the water back and the men with me. On going to the village I saw Lieutenant Maclaine mounted; when I came back I saw two horses without a rider. I then went again for more water. I was about 150 yards from the gun when I saw ten or twelve of the enemy's cavalry coming on at a slow pace towards the gun. The gun went off and I lay down and allowed the gun to pass me, and began firing with a rifle which I had got from a wounded 66th man, in order to draw their fire upon myself, and stop them from going forward with the gun. I was concealed in a little nullah, and I fancy they thought there was more than one man, for they stopped and fired at me from the saddle. I shot one horse and two men. After firing about thirty-five rounds General Nuttall came up with some native cavalry, and drove them off. When I first saw the enemy they were about 300 yards off, when they left they had got 150 yards. General Nuttall asked me my name, saying, 'You're a gallant young man, what is your name?' I said, 'Gunner Collis, of E. of B, R.H.A.' He entered it into a pocket-book and rode off. I then followed up my gun, which I found some 500 yards distant by the side of a river. The enemy's fire, which had been going on all the way from Maiwand, now became hotter, the surrounding hills being full of them. Some of the garrison of Candahar met us about four miles from the Fort and escorted us in. I arrived about seven p.m.

On the occasion of the sortie from Candahar in the middle of August, 1880, the fighting was going on in the village situated about 200 yards from the edge of the ditch of the fort. I was standing by my gun on the rampart, when General Primrose, General Nuttall, and Colonel Burnet came up. I heard them talking about sending a message to General Dewberry, who had succeeded General Brooke, who had been killed. I spoke to Colonel Burnet and said that I would take the message over the wall. After a little hesitation General Primrose gave me a note. I was let down a distance of about thirty or forty feet to the bottom of the ditch by a rope. When half down I was fired at but not hit by matchlock men about 250 yards distant, and I scrambled up the open side of the ditch and ran across to the village. I found the officer commanding in the middle of it, and fighting going on all round. I delivered the note and returned. When half way up the rope I was fired at again, one bullet cutting off the heel of my left boot. General Primrose congratulated me and Colonel Burnet gave me a drop out of his flask, for what with not having recovered from the fatigues of Maiwand and the exertion and excitement of this trip, I was a bit faint.

I was recommended for the Victoria Cross without my knowledge about September 10, by Sir F. Roberts, on the report of General Nuttall and Colonel Burnet. It was given to me July 28, 1881.

In the aftermath of the disaster at Maiwand, Burrows' survivors fell back on Primrose at Kandahar. Ayub Khan immediately followed up his success by laying siege to the city.

Roberts was ordered to advance from Kabul to relieve General Primrose. He was given 10,000 men – the pick of the Kabul garrison – and the best transport animals. He set out from Kabul on 8 August 1880, and his subsequent march caught the imagination of the British public, and crowned the reputation he had earned at Peiwar Kotal. Marching across rugged country in extremes of temperature, Roberts' column covered 280 miles in twenty days. Among the troops was Private Samuel Crompton of the 9th Lancers, who recalled the difficulties of the march, and the elation which greeted the relief of Kandahar.

Kabul to Kandahar: The Tale of a Lost Army

It was my birthday when we began the march from Kabul to Kandahar. That is one thing which fixes the start indelibly in my memory. There were 10,000 fighting men of us all told, and more than 8,000 followers – doolie-bearers, servants, and so on. Then we had 2,300 horses and gun-mules, and something like 8,000 camels, ponies, mules and donkeys for the transport. So that altogether we numbered 18,000 officers and men, and 11,000 animals.

By far the greater number of the forces consisted of native troops – 7,000 odd to about 2,500 British. We had eighteen mountain guns, which are carried in sections and put together when wanted for use. You will understand how light we marched when I tell you that each British soldier was only allowed 30lb. for kit, and each native soldier 20lb. Everything had to be carried either by men or animals.

Our object was to make a swift and secret march from Kabul to Kandahar. And why? Because in Kandahar a little British garrison was beleagured by the Afghans, who were glutted with the butchery of Maiwand. You know the awful story of that disaster? Who does not?

General Burrows was commanding at Kandahar, and hearing that the enemy was advancing on Maiwand, only eleven miles away, he marched out to intercept him. That was on July 27th, 1880, when the Afghan War was in full swing. He was about half way to Maiwand when the Afghans fell upon him in overwhelming numbers. The fight began at twelve o'clock, and in three hours, out of 2,500 British troops nearly a thousand had been killed, to say nothing of the missing and wounded and the followers. The survivors struggled back to Kandahar, and were pinned in by an enemy that never showed mercy to any Englishman who fell into his hands. It was necessary to relieve Kandahar, and we were got together for the purpose.

We were called the Kabul-Kandahar Field Force, and every member of it was a picked man. We had a picked leader, too – Lord Roberts (Sir Frederick Roberts as he then was), and desperate as our business was there was not a soul amongst us who supposed there would be anything else at the end of it but victory. How could it be otherwise with a commander whose very name was worshipped and represented countless triumphs?

People talk glibly of a few thousand soldiers; but figures convey no meaning.

Think what a battalion of Guards means in London – how long it takes to march past a given spot. Only a thousand men, with everything in their favour, and no obstacles. What, then, of 18,000 human beings and 11,000 animals, crawling with its sick and footsore through a gloomy, barren land of mountains, intensely hot by day, and perishingly cold at night, ceaselessly harassed by a cruel foe that hung on to it to capture and destroy the stragglers?

If you could have commanded a view of it you would have seen it stretching for miles, just moving over crag and plain, its progress regulated, like a fleet of warships, by its slowest members.

You would have seen the kilted Highlanders, 60th Rifles, Sikhs, Native Pioneers, Ghoorkas, British and native cavalry, doolie-bearers, transport people, and swarms of private and native servants all on the move, all apparently in confusion, but all controlled and kept in hand by the famous soldier, who seemed to be everywhere at all times. A peculiarity of 'Bobs' was that he could snatch a few minutes' sleep at any time, and resume his work as fresh as a daisy. But unless you had such a bird's-eye view you never saw more than part of the column – even we of the cavalry rarely got beyond our own immediate companions.

And yet with all the apparent disorder there was cohesion and discipline. Lord Roberts had got his force together in wonderful fashion; he kept it in hand in wonderful fashion, he commanded it in wonderful fashion, too; and the most wonderful thing of all was that he got it through pretty much as a captain gets his ship from one port to another. No one, except those who took part in the march, can ever really understand what it meant – all you can do is to give an idea of it, and so far as I am concerned, a poor idea at best.

I have heard it said that when we left Kabul there were many who believed that we had bidden good-bye to the world. We were to journey by a route and through a region the very name of which was bound up with suffering and disaster to British troops.

You have already told, in the story of the Kabul massacre of '42, how only one man, Dr. Bryden, lived to tell the story of a lost army which had marched from Kabul. That catastrophe was still fresh in the minds of many people at home. Can it be wondered, then, that the gloomiest prophecies should be made as to the fate which would overtake us in the silent hills, and that when we had marched and communication with us had ceased, when day followed day, and yet no news was heard of us, the belief grew and became fixed that we should never more be seen?

That, they say, was the point of view at home; but we of the field force had other thoughts to fill our minds. Besides, whatever secret misgivings might have troubled us, was there not always the perfect, almost sublime confidence in our commander, and the conviction that, whatever might befall, he would see us safely through? Has not he himself put on record his faith in us, his soldiers, and told how thoroughly we understood and trusted each other?

It was the morning of August 8th, 1880, when we began to march to Kandahar. We of the cavalry brigade – the 9th Lancers and three native regiments – covered the movement at a distance of about five miles. That means, does it not, that while, say, the head of the column would be at Charing Cross, the leading cavalry would be at Greenwich? But, instead of smooth paved roads, there were plains and passes, the like of which you will not find anywhere in England.

Two of our cavalry regiments led the way, and another cavalry regiment was on either flank. Two infantry brigades followed, a mountain battery with them, and the field hospitals, the treasure – precious possession! – and baggage, and so on, came next. The rearguard was formed of the 3rd Infantry Brigade, with a mountain battery, and a troop or two of cavalry.

Hard as the work was which fell on the main body, it was, I think, more severe on the cavalry, because we had to take turns in going to the front and flanks and forming a screen round the main body which was marching in the middle.

There you have the rough details; but you must fill out the picture for yourself – the grumbling camels, the bucking mules, the stubborn donkeys, the wild little native ponies, and the patient, plodding horses, with the baggage, guns, forage, rations, ammunition – and the hundred and one odd things that are essential for an army in the wilderness.

We had bread-stuff for five days, preserved vegetables for fifteen, and rum, tea, salt, and sugar for thirty. Those were the supplies for the British troops. The natives were just as well provided for – indeed, so perfect was the foresight of our chief, that when at last we got to Kandahar, we had three days' supplies in hand.

From the time we began the march we were lost to the world, and the world for us seemed scarcely to exist. Our communications were cut, and the enemy took care that no news should come to us, and that no word from us should reach our friends. He cut the telegraph-wires, and did everything he could to make us what we were for many days – a lost army.

It was a strangely lonely journey, although there were so many of us. What was happening in the district round Kabul, which we had left, and what was going on at Kandahar, whither we were bound? Would the garrison hold out until we came, or would the fierce enemy rush the city and destroy the defenders?

All sorts of possibilities occurred to us, and some of them were reasonable enough, because the entire effective garrison was only about a thousand British and three thousand native soldiers, with fifteen field guns. Add to their small numbers the intense depression due to Maiwand, and you can realise the doubts that sometimes filled and almost overwhelmed us.

We had got to sea, so to speak, and our business was to forge ahead and reach our destination. We soon settled down into the hard, stern graft of it, always looking ahead now, never behind, just as the sailor does who has his port to make. During the first four days we averaged eleven and a half miles a day. That was quick work, because the country was not difficult, and was rich enough to help us with our supplies. Less than a mile an hour seems slow indeed to us at home, but with crawling doolie-bearers and laggard followers it was a good rate of speed for an advancing army. And in such a country, too!

Our position was constantly menaced by three great dangers – attacks from the enemy, disease, and starvation. But here, again, the wisdom and foresight of our chief were evident. In a land where an enemy abounded, he kept him hovering at a distance; where supplies did not appear to exist, he managed to extract them; in a climate which brings the most appalling of illnesses, cholera, he succeeded in keeping us fit and well and in good spirits. The very sight of our commander was a tonic.

Every morning Lord Roberts could be seen galloping up towards the head of the column, accompanied by the four men of the 9th who formed his escort. How well we got to know that sight! There was the chief himself, illustrious throughout the Army and the world, mounted on his famous Arab charger Vonolel, which was his friend and companion for nearly twenty years. It was by special permission of Queen Victoria that afterwards Vonolel was decorated with the Kabul medal with four clasps, and the coveted star which was issued for the march itself.

And our chief did not hop half a mile round to escape a gutter. If he had done that there would scarcely have been an end to our labours in a land which seemed mostly made of gutters and gullies. He went straight up and ahead, and whatever came in his path he took it. That was his way – and he always got there.

When the commander of a force is marching through an enemy's country, as we were marching, he is entitled by the rules of war to do pretty much as he likes to keep his commissariat going, for on his eating and drinking his very life depends – and no man can fight for a bigger prize. We could have taken what we wanted at the point of the sword, and no one could have condemned us – according to the usages of war. What actually happened? Why, that our chief got all he could, which proved to be nearly all we wanted, by the simple, ordinary, unromantic method of paying for it.

Before the march was done he had purchased nearly five thousand sheep for food, and that was irrespective of the supply of sheep which we took with us at the start. Indian corn, too, growing in the fields, was bought when we could come across it, and welcome stuff it proved for our horses. Whatever we acquired was paid for – and that, I say again, was something to be proud of in the midst of the enemy's country. Nor were the women or the peaceful inhabitants that we came across molested.

I want to mention these points now, and specially to show you what a great commander can do in time of war. Mind you, the difficulties in the way of getting food were great, very great, but they were always overcome. Water and fuel were scarcest, and we had to strive hard to obtain either. Water we got by digging or scooping in the ground, and even then it was always salty, so that there was not much relief in taking it. As for fuel for cooking, it was so scarce that Lord Roberts actually bought houses for the sake of the wood in them, which was not much. The wood was taken out for the fires; but often enough we had to be content with little roots. These had to be dug up, and sorry work it was, too, at the end of a long day's march in the broiling sun.

When we were in the full swing of our task there was only one idea in our minds, and that was to push ahead. And push ahead we did. We literally did not, and could not, get any real sleep. When we halted, it was a case of taking off our jack boots and rolling ourselves up in our cloaks or blankets on the ground.

By day we frizzled, and by night we froze. And with all the heat of the march there was the ever-present cloud of sand which the column raised – sand which got into our eyes, our mouths, our ears, our boots, our clothes – everywhere, until with the heat and irritation of it we were almost maddened. But torturing though it was, it was the same for all, and you can get used even to keeping your clothes on for the best part of a month.

When a man looks back on many of the things he has done he marvels that he has pulled through. So it is with this long forced march. There seemed to be no break between one day and another.

Before three o'clock in the morning the 'rouse' sounded, infantry bugles and cavalry trumpets were crashing on the still air, everything became bustle and excitement, and in about an hour we were on the march again. Ten minutes' halt at each hour's end was made, with rather longer breaks for breakfast, dinner, and the day's last meal. Then, if you were on rear-guard duty, which was equivalent to shepherding the scattered flock and getting it safely into the fold, you had to keep up to your work until well into the evening. You would begin at three in the morning, say, and end at seven at night or later – fifteen or sixteen hours of incessant duty.

Work like that will tell on anybody. We saw its effects first and most clearly on some of the weary, footsore native followers. They began to lose heart, and when a man on active service does that the end is not far off, in some form or other. In their cases it took the shape of hopeless lagging behind.

Threats and pleadings were useless. A native would fall to the rear and hide himself. When found he would beg to be allowed to remain and die – although he knew that the Afghans were ceaselessly hovering round to cut the stragglers off. You may watch and threaten as hard as you please, but on such a journey, if a man is determined to elude watchfulness, he will succeed. Some did succeed, and the result was that they fell into the hands of the enemy and were cut to pieces.

Whenever a straggler was lost like that there was always nameless mutilation. You ask, Why? Well, the soldier's story is that once, in Kabul, there was an English Army surgeon who was so marvellously clever that he patched up seemingly hopeless cases. His skill was reckoned miraculous, and by way of circumventing doctors generally the Afghans never rested with mere death. They went to the extremity of cutting their victim to pieces, believing that then not even the cleverness of white doctors could patch him up and make him live again.

When we were really in the thick of it we were in it with a vengeance, I can assure you. Twice we had two 'reveilles' in one day. Any soldier knows what that means, and those who are not soldiers will understand when I liken it to the case of a civilian who is roused say, at three o'clock in the morning, goes on slaving without sleep, and, as a matter of routine, is roused again at the same time next day. In that case he gets two 'reveilles' in the twenty-four hours, does he not? And two such routings out are quite enough for any man, even in the course of a long, forced, desperate march.

But there was no grumbling, no repining. How could there be, when we had such a glorious example set by our chief and our officers? We knew that whatever hardships we endured they also were undergoing them – and that means everything in keeping you at it and up to it.

We settled to the monotony and hardness of our task. Day followed day, each being pretty much like its predecessor.

There was the never-ending choking dust of an army on the march, the constant search for fuel and water, and the everlasting work of keeping the units together, as well as the ceaseless strain of being ready for an onslaught by the enemy.

And all the time we were climbing, scrambling, crawling on our way — now up a hillside, now down a mountain pathway, but always in a dreary, sunbaked, stifling country, which gave the eye no pleasure or relief, and did not allow the mind or body to rest.

Just under a hundred miles from Kabul we reached Ghazni, famous in British military history, and especially interesting to our field force, because our chief's father had taken part in its capture more than forty years before, and had got his C.B. for it. Ghazni was at that time one of the strongest fortresses in Asia. Early one morning, a British force blew in its gates, stormed the place, and after a fierce struggle planted its colours on the shattered ramparts.

Lord Roberts and his staff now entered the fortress and met the Governor; then we drove ahead again, plunging into a country which seemed more depressing and inhospitable than ever. We came to a spot where a little British victory had been won. The natives had given it the fresh name of the 'Resting-place of Martyrs.' I have told you how the Afghans treated British stragglers. They were not more kind to our fallen troops who had had decent burial at this spot, for we saw that our soldiers' graves had been dug up and their bones cast out and scattered.

On again we went until we reached a place called Kelat-i-Ghilzai. Then we learnt that Khandahar was still holding out, and that a sortie had been made by the garrison. And a sorry sortie it proved to be, for General Brooke and no fewer than eight more British officers had been killed. But the garrison was safe — that was the main point, and seemed likely to hold the fort until we reached it.

Our force, already big enough and unwieldly enough, was increased by the addition of the garrison of Kelat-i-Ghilzai, which Lord Roberts decided to take with him. This addition brought up our total to just under twenty thousand men, of whom only 3,200 were Europeans.

We had now marched without anything more than absolutely needful halts for more than two hundred and twenty miles, and to the unspeakable joy of everybody Lord Roberts ordered a day's halt, so that man and beast might get a little rest.

While we rested we were able to make inquiries about our friends in other parts of the force and to learn what had happened to the column generally. Our friends were still alive and well, in spite of cholera scares and such like things, and if any were bad it was mostly their own fault, because in their fear of cholera they had nearly poisoned themselves with medicine, particularly chlorodyne.

Our sick had grown rapidly in number, and the force had now trailing after it a long slow procession of doolies. We did not then know how many men were unable to march and had to be carried, but we learnt afterwards that nearly a thousand had to go into hospital when we got to Kandahar. For them there was no withstanding the hardships of the march, the greatest of which arose from the intense heat of the sun. Lord Roberts himself succumbed to an attack of fever and had to be carried in a doolie, and it was only when we were reaching Kandahar that he was able to get into the saddle again.

We pushed ahead and still ahead, and when Kandahar was very near we redoubled our precautions so that we should not be trapped or taken unawares. When we saw the fortress at last it was very much like the people coming out of the wilderness and beholding the Promised Land. We had emerged from the unknown and got into touch with life again, and I don't know which felt the greatest exultation, the besieged or the relievers. On the last day of the month the principal British officers — General Burrows amongst them — came out from Kandahar to meet us, and Lord Roberts marched into the city with them.

The beleaguered troops — there were a thousand British and three thousand natives — hailed us joyfully as deliverers, and well they might, for they had quite lost heart, believing that the worst had happened to us, and that we should never get through to their relief. You cannot wonder at it, either, because there was always the gloom of Maiwand over everything, and the enemy, strong and fierce, ever watching for his chance to swoop down and take the fortress and destroy the defenders.

The coming of relief, that is to say, the appearance of our chief, electrified them. He was utterly worn out with his march and his illness, but his work was not yet finished. There was the enemy to get rid of, to sweep away, to crush out of existence before the march could fairly claim to be ended. There was communication, too, to re-establish with India, and so with home. Our wonderful commander did both — just as he seemed to do everything. He gave the Afghans battle the very day after we ended our march, and crowned his glorious work by routing them completely and with heavy loss.

At Maiwand the enemy had captured two British guns. They were immensely proud of their trophies, as they had good cause to be. When the fight was done and the dead lay thick about the plains of Kandahar, all his artillery was in our possession, and amongst them was the pair of British guns. They were the greatest trophies which Lord Roberts handed over to the Indian Government, and I daresay amongst the proudest that he ever got himself, for they were given back to him, and in turn presented to the Royal Hospital in Dublin – which is as it should be, because Lord Roberts is an Irishman.

That is the story of the army which was lost in the hills and was found again. But it was only lost to the world in imagination, because the world could not get into touch with it, nor could the force send messages. That it never really was lost I have tried to show.

Lost! How could it be, with such a pilot?

Roberts' actions around Kandahar destroyed what remained of the Afghan army, and brought the military operations of the 2nd Afghan War to a successful conclusion. Politically, however, little had been achieved. At home, Disraeli's government had fallen, and the Liberal administration under Gladstone was reluctant to maintain a strong garrison in Afghanistan. In another telling parallel with the events of 1839–42, it was decided to abandon Afghanistan to its own rulers, and by May 1881 the last British troops had been withdrawn to the border.

One result of the withdrawal was that British attention focused instead on the rugged foothills on the Afghan border – the famous North-West Frontier. For almost half a century – indeed, until the British finally withdrew from India – the British attempted to control the Frontier tribes as a buffer against Russian intrigue in independent Afghanistan beyond. As a result, the North-West Frontier was the scene of dozens of minor campaigns, of risings, sieges and punitive expeditions, which would prove a dangerous training ground for two generations of British soldiers.

3. Policing the Empire

While the grand strategic demands of Empire led Britain into war in the Crimea, on the Indian sub-continant, and, indeed, time and again in South Africa, the steady and often unplanned growth in territorial acquisition led to constant campaigning on the very fringes of the Imperial borders. Between 1839 and the 1880s, British troops found themselves involved in a constant stream of what might today be considered 'police actions'. Some, like the 1868 Abyssinian expedition, were self-contained campaigns, brought about by specific circumstances. Others, like the successive campaigns in New Zealand, were the result of steady settler encroachment on independent territory, for which the Crown had ultimately to pay the butcher's bill.

Each of these campaigns tested the army in different ways. For an institution often characterised – with some justification – as inflexible and conservative, the British army was required to be remarkably flexible in the field, facing a variety of foes, each of whom had their own distinctive ways of waging war, and in a range of equally inhospitable environments. Often, British troops were outnumbered and ill-equipped for the challenge, and the start of each fresh campaign often produced a crop of disasters as a result. Yet the British army invariably learned from its mistakes, and most campaigns were brought to a successful conclusion in the end, the result not only of the technological superiority of British weapons, but of the courage, endurance and fortitude of individual soldiers in the ranks.

In the British were pre-occupied by India's western frontier, they remained at least sensitive to events beyond its eastern boundaries, a sensitivity which brought them into conflict no less than three times with the kingdom of Ava in the steamy tropical rain-forests of Burma. Based on the central reaches of the Irrawaddy river, the kingdom of Ava was militarily robust in the nineteenth century, and pursued an expansionist policy which worried successive generations of Imperial administrators. Burmese troops had occupied the Indian border towns of Assam and Chittagong early in the century, provoking the 1st Burma War of 1824. The British lost almost as many men to heat-stroke – campaigning in jungle thickets in full-dress uniforms – as to enemy action in that expedition, but Ava's policies remained largely unchanged, and by the 1850s tension once again threatened to spill over into violence. The arrest of two British merchant sea-captains by the Burmese was taken by the British as proof of hostile intent, and provoked a fine piece of gun-boat diplomacy. HMS *Rattler* was sent to bombard Burmese stockades along the Irrawaddy, an action which the Burmese not unnaturally resented. Fighting broke out, British troops were rushed to the area, and a two-year war ensued. Ordinary Seaman George Goddard was serving on the *Rattler*, and described the subsequent fighting, which culminated in the British assault on the Golden Pagoda, and the capture of the capital of southern Burma, Rangoon.

Rangoon: The Storming of the Golden Pagoda

To talk about line of battle ships, powder-monkeys, screw-corvettes, and bow-chasers is to carry you back to the navy of more than fifty years ago. I am going to do that, because it is the only British navy that I remember. As a boy I went into the *Prince Regent*, a sailing ship of the line; and afterwards I joined the *Rattler*, a screw-corvette of eleven guns, which was ordered out to the East, where they say the temple bells are ringing, and calling you back.

Well, I saw a good many temples, and they made a ringing noise, but not with bells particularly. They were guns in my time, and they flung their murderous china-shot over the swampy rice-fields and the muddy Irrawaddy, and did their level best to smash the expedition that was sent to punish the Burmese. And the temple that made the biggest noise was the Golden Pagoda, a splendid gilded building, which glowed in the terrific heat of the pitiless Indian sun.

The *Rattler* left Woolwich for Portsmouth at the end of 1851, but did not reach Rangoon until April, 1852. The marvel is that she ever got to the East at all, for we ran into the worst gale I have ever known in English waters. We were three days getting from Woolwich to Portsmouth, and it was thought that we had foundered. Boats were smashed and spars carried away; but when we had refitted we were off again, to make Rangoon by way of Madeira, Sierra Leone, Ascension Island, St. Helena, the Cape, Singapore, and Moulmein.

The night before we reached Sierra Leone we were caught in a very heavy tornado, and many of our spars and sails were torn away. The thunder roared incessantly, and the vividness of the lightning was appalling. We put the helm up and put the ship before the wind, and on she went, dragging a mass of wreckage after her. I remember so well struggling up to the mainyard and trying to stow the canvas, which was ballooning out to such an extent that it seemed impossible to get at it. I really thought that not even the war to which we were going could be worse than this. Afterwards I should have been glad to exchange Rangoon for the tornado. We are never satisfied in this world!

At Moulmein there was an English garrison, and we took on board some troops. Lord Wolsey was in the war—the first of his many campaigns; and, for anything I know to the contrary, he may have embarked with us to go to Rangoon. But I do not remember. You see, in those days he would be an ensign, and naturally you don't expect an ordinary ensign to become Commander-in-Chief of the British Army. There are so many ensigns, and only one commander-in-chief.

We entered the Irrawaddy, and ascended the river till we got within sight of Rangoon. Then we anchored, and found ourselves in a river about as wide as the Thames at London Bridge. On each side of us were swampy rice-fields, with insignificant buildings shooting up from the low grounds.

Most noticeable of all the structures was the Golden Pagoda, which reminded me of nothing so much as St. Paul's at home, rising from a cluster of mean structures, and very near the river, too.

Rangoon was really a city of pagodas, terraced and fortified. Just as in London, from a high building, you can look round on almost numberless churches, with St. Paul's rising in splendid dignity above and dwarfing them, so, it seemed to me, you could look upon Rangoon, with its little temples and the biggest and most magnificent of them all, the Golden Pagoda.

It seems a hard thing to set yourselves deliberately to pound a temple with your guns, but that is what we had to do in the muddy Irrawaddy; and we had to do it because the Golden Pagoda was the most strongly fortified of all the places we had to deal with, and because the gunners who defended it set steadily to work to blow the *Rattler* out of the water. We offered a fine target; so did the Golden Pagoda. But we soon discovered that the structure was beyond the range of our guns. That was lucky for the Golden Pagoda, which in these days would be pounded to pieces in a few minutes.

The *Rattler* was light of draught, and so we had been able to steam up and take our places for the bombardment. In those days steamers were primitive concerns—I have seen engines positively lift themselves out of their beds at every revolution of the crank—and it took them all their time to look after themselves. But the sailing ships were worse; they were absolutely helpless, and so it happened that we had to take the frigate *Fox* in tow. We had to leave her, however, because her draught was too deep for the Irrawaddy. The *Fox* was a forty-four gun frigate, and flew the broad pennant of Commodore Lambert, who commanded the river expedition. I believe we cast the frigate off before we began the bombardment of the stockades which

had been made to defend Rangoon—stockades of mud and cane and stone—
a sort of strong fence to keep an enemy at bay. The stockades were loop-
holed, and from the embrasures peeped the muzzles of guns and muskets. I
do not think that any gun they had was bigger than a 12-pounder, and those
were the days, remember, of muzzle-loaders.

It was Easter Sunday, just before noon, when the Burmese opened fire
upon us from their stockades. Then the fight began which meant an incessant pounding until sunset.

It was a steady, simple sort of battle; gun against gun; steam-corvette
against joss-house.

Marvellous indeed is the change that has taken place in war. Nowadays
you shut yourself up in walls of steel and pound away with weapons that are
terrible to look upon and think about. When a ship goes into action not a
living soul is seen; but guns, officers, and crew were just as visible on board
the *Rattler* as a motor-bus is in the Strand.

The captain and the first lieutenant were on the bridge; other officers,
such as mates and midshipment, were on deck; and the crew were on deck,
too, for the most part, because the guns were on the upper, or spar deck,
and the heaviest of them all was the 68-pounder in the bow—a pivot gun.
We had five broadside guns and the pivot gun, in all eleven. The broadside
guns, which were 32-pounders, were exactly the same sort of weapon as was
used at Trafalgar.

We might, indeed, have been Nelson's sailors come to life again—many
of them were still alive—for we had our powder-monkeys in the *Rattler* just
as the *Victory* had. These little fellows ran between the guns and the magazine hatchway and brought the powder in their cartridge-boxes. They looked
on the business as a glorious game, and revelled in the fighting. I sometimes
think that the youngsters of to-day are not made of the same stern, dare-
devil stuff as the lads who were helping to pound the joss-houses. There are
no powder-monkeys nowadays; hydraulic lifts and electric devices do their
wok. I should be utterly lost on board one of our modern battleships.

I was the assistant loader of one of the broadside guns and wore what we
call a jumper—that is, a sort of white jacket, with white trousers and a white
hat. It was the lightest clothing you could have, even for the tropics; yet it
was too much, and many a man stripped to the waist long before the bombardment ended.

It was insufferably hot, but we pounded away, fascinated by the sight of
the mischief that we did. Our weapons were not formidable, but they were
heavy compared with the Burmese guns, and we saw stockade after stockade destroyed, and exploded powder magazine after powder magazine.

On the bridge the captain watched Rangoon and the havoc of our shots.
He gave his orders by word of mouth to the first lieutenant, who shouted

them to the junior officers on deck, and they in turn controlled the captains of the guns. All was absolutely fair and above board; now, in our warships, the captain gets into the conning-tower, and with the help of his tubes and electric wires directs his ship just as the brain guides the human body.

One by one we shattered the stockades. Sometimes our broadsides blazed; then there was the deeper boom of the pivot gun and the roaring of the shot across the swampy rice-fields, mostly towards the Golden Pagoda. That was the chief target, because it was from the Golden Pagoda that the biggest shots came towards us. It was there that the Burmese had their heaviest guns, although those weapons, as I have pointed out, were not nearly so effective as our own.

Our shots went home with pitiless precision, but the Burmese cannonade was harmless. We had no casualties from the guns themselves—those came later, in the storming—but we suffered many from the terrible sun. We had no small-arm fire, but our muskets loaded, were ready for instant use, and we had our cutlasses buckled on, in the good old Trafalgar fashion, as we served the guns. We got very thirsty, of course, and helped ourselves to drinks from buckets of water which were placed about the deck.

The bombardment went on until nearly sunset; then Rangoon seemed to be burning, and it looked as if the Burmese had had enough of the *Rattler*. The bugle sounded the cease fire, and boats were manned and armed, and I went away in one of the cutters to disperse some of the enemy who had gathered on the bank of the river, rather too near us to be agreeable. They had had enough of us, however, and bolted into the jungle; and I, at any rate, had had enough of them for the time being, and was glad to see them go.

Next day two of the East India ships came up, the *Formosa* and the *Pluto*, with troops on board and guns and ammunition. The guns were landed on the Monday and Tuesday by the simple method of throwing them overboard into the mud. We had to get them out and clean them, so as to be ready for the storming of the Golden Pagoda. There were no artillerymen; all that particular work was done by the sailors.

With the Royal and East India troops leading the way, and the detachment from the Navy bringing up the rear with the guns, drawn by bullocks, we began the storming. I fancied that, as we had escaped in the ship, we should be lucky enough on shore to get clear of the shot; but it was a very different business indeed this time.

On the Easter Sunday the Burmese had only a ship to go at, and not a very big one, with weak artillery; now they could fire point-blank at masses of marching men, with chain shot—that is, shot chained together, and canister and grape shot, which means that the guns were loaded with bullets and pieces of metal which, when fired, scattered and did terrible mischief.

The Golden Pagoda is very much like one of the pyramids, crowned by a structure which looks like an enormous lighthouse, a gilt spire which you can see from every part of the surrounding country. All round the pagoda are smaller shrines, or temples, and in the fifties the building was moated and defended by batteries.

Standing on a small hill, which is the only high ground in the district, the pagoda was an unpromising fort to attack; but the stormers marched across the exposed land, under a burning sun, towards the moat and the draw-bridges.

We sailors had the work of seeing to the guns, and a tough job it proved to be, for when the chain shot and the rest of the scrap-iron began to fly amongst us and cut us up, some of the bullocks fell, badly mangled. The other bullocks, maddened by the smell of blood and the awful noise which the whizzing iron made, either tried to bolt or, which was just as bad, refused to budge.

There we were stuck, open to the full fury of the fire from the pagoda, unable to get the guns nearer because of the stubborn animals. All the same, we served the guns and smashed away at the enormous golden building. It was needful to get nearer, and we beat and pulled and cajoled; but the bullocks would not move; then our commanding officer, the first lieutenant, shouted to us to clear the animals out and drag the guns ourselves; and with plenty of cheering we obeyed and took the ropes and hauled the guns to a more suitable place.

The lieutenant was a magnificent specimen of the old fighting naval officer, the man whose trade was battle, and who did not know the meaning of fear. He saw what was happening; he noticed that some of us—myself amongst them—were ducking and bobbing our heads rather faster, I think, than the flying shot. You couldn't help it; for when you heard that murderous whizz you ducked instinctively. Shame didn't count. The lieutenant was standing on a bit of rising ground, with the scrap-iron whistling and whizzing about him, with his sword drawn, and, believe me, never moving a muscle. He scorned to do it.

"It's no use bobbing and ducking," he shouted at us. "You aren't going to save your skins that way. Hold up to it, men, and face it! And plug in with the guns as hard as you can. The faster you fire, the sooner you'll be through with it.

So we did as we were ordered to do, and having dragged the guns up we pounded away at the Golden Pagoda and, to do them justice, the Burmese blazed away at us.

Ambulances began to come down from the pagoda and past us; but the most singular thing about them was that they contained men who had not been wounded, but had been struck down remorselessly by the sun, the heat of which was perfectly dreadful. More men died of the heat and disease during the war than were accounted for by either gun or musket or robber.

Being in the rear of the stormers I did not quite see all that was passing in front, where the soldiers were, but I saw them going ahead, and I saw them rush the moat and the draw-bridges, and I saw the Burmese bolting across the rice-fields and the cornfields, leaving behind their guns and their Golden Pagoda behind them, and thinking only of one thing, and that was the best way of saving their skins.

At last, I scarcely knew how, I found that I was on the steps of the famous temple, and I sank down exhausted by the heat and the desperate fighting. The dead and dying Burmese, who were around on every hand, in the moat, and on the level ground, showed how fierce the combat had been, and the passing ambulances and the red-clothed figures on the earth told the sorry tale of British loss. Yet even then I could not help noticing the magnificence of the great place, which is said to be the most splendid of all the Burmese temples.

All sorts of dragons and weird idols were around me, and there was a horror hidden in every dark place about the uneven stairs. I believe that even in these days, when British tourists go in perfect safety to the temple which I helped to take, they are awed into silence when they begin to make their way up the dark, uncanny by-ways to the building to look at it, or, like the Burmese, clap a patch of gold leaf on to add to its splendour, and at the same time, I fancy, to rid them of some of their sins.

There had been a lot of talk of loot. Wonderful stories had been told of the riches of the Golden Pagoda, of jewels in abundance, and of precious metals, which were to be had for the picking up. I believe that a good deal of treasure feel to the lot of some of the stormers, but I myself did not come across it; I certainly did not get a share of the riches. They went mostly to the troops; the sailormen were out of it, because they were not quite so well up to the game as the soldiers of those days. I am talking now of the times when the old East India Company was in existence, and when soldiers in the East could make fortunes out of loot, and ships' captains make fortunes, too, out of two or three voyages.

On that famous night I slept on the steps of the Golden Pagoda. The night before I had camped out under the stars. I was none the worse for the fight. A spent ball had struck me in the stomach, but had not done lasting mischief. The Burmese kept up a ragged firing as they retired, which they had done very unwillingly, because the temple was a very sacred place and treasure house, and they did not want it to get into the hands of infidels, as I suppose they called us.

When morning came I went back to the ship, without seeing the inside of the pagoda; but I was not very sorry on that account, because the heat

was insufferable, and the mosquitoes were worse than the heat. They literally swarmed. It was no use killing them, for millions rose up to take the
places of the slain. On board ship it was impossible to sleep for them, and
my legs were swollen with their bites, to say nothing of my hands and face.
I remember going below and passing my hand along one of the beams. It
was wet and warm with the blood from the mosquitoes, which, after their
feast, had got as far as the beam. You could sweep thousands of them away
in a second.

No, there was no East calling me, once I had got away from it, and I
don't think poets would answer the call so readily, or listen so much to the
temple bells if they had had the experience of Rangoon that came my own
way in the early fifties. I daresay things are better in these days; but I suppose
that the Golden Pagoda rises up now, as it did then, from the melancholy
rice-fields and the dismal mud banks of the river, with their untold millions
of shrimps.

We buried our dead and left the fallen Burmese to be looked after by
their own people. Then we had to set to work to clear the country of the
Burmese who had taken to dacoiting or robbing; and hot work it was, too,
especially as the dacoits loved nothing so much as fooling us and then
escaping.

We could track them so closely that we fell upon their very living-places;
but as for the Burmese themselves I seldom saw them. Often enough, however, I was in time, with my comrades, for the dinner that the dacoits had
made ready for themselves. Great pans of rice would be seen on the fire cooking, and the chickens would be plucked ready and roasting. We finished the
cooking and the roasting, and after that, with very contented minds, finished
the dinner, too. So you see, it wasn't all chasing in vain.

I was thankful enough to leave the land of swampy rice-fields and pagodas and blood-thirsty mosquitoes and go further East, this time to the China
Seas after pirates, who swarmed it their junks and lurchers, which were bigger and faster craft than junks.

The pirates were cruel and pitiless. When we caught them in the beginning we handed them over to the Chinese authorities, who put them to death
without mercy. I used to see the poor wretches crucified against walls, or
with their eyes gorged out or their limbs mutilated. The authorities were
even more merciless than the freebooters.

At last we got orders that the pirates were to be destroyed without mercy,
ships and all, and that they were not to be captured. There were two reasons for this—first and foremost, humanity, because it was too terrible to
hand them over to their own judges; and, secondly, because they were a constant menace to the peace and safety of the China Seas.

One day a naval officer and his boat's crew had made a valiant attack on some pirates. The men only carried ten rounds of ammunition, and these were soon exhausted; then they fell to work with the steel and boarded their junk in the good old reckless fashion, slashing at and sweeping away the pirates with the cutlass.

Those of the Chinese who escaped from the boarders ran below, and the lieutenant and his men followed them.

Instantly another junk, whose sweeps were got out, rowed stealthily down towards the captured vessel, and the pirates swarmed on board. Hearing the noise, the officer and his men hurried back to the deck.

They were met with overwhelming numbers, and the lieutenant and three men were killed on the spot, cut to pieces with spears, while the rest were hacked and left for dead. Some villagers found the poor wounded fellows, and brought them and the news of the disaster to us.

Being a steamer, we were soon on the track of junks and lurchers, and, the guns having done their work, we got the boats out, and boarded what were left after the fire and shot had one their duty. One day I and a comrade, cutless in hand, had rushed below, after accounting for all the pirates, so far as we knew.

We were prodding about, trying to turn hidden Chinamen out of dark holes and corners, when we both started and, perhaps, turned rather pale. I, at any rate, felt uneasy enough, for on the deck we heard a most terrible and uncanny noise.

"I thought they were all done for!" exclaimed my comrade. "She only carried a dozen men, and I thought we'd settled 'em."

"There's more on deck," I answered.

In a brace of shakes we had rushed on deck.

We saw no Chinamen, but there, just by us, was the most enormous chest I ever set eyes on—a huge box about three feet deep, the same width, and something like ten feet long.

Chinamen are the most cunning creatures on two legs, and instantly I thought that we had a box chock full of the yellow devils, waiting for a chance to spring out at us.

For one awful moment we stared at the thing; then I whispered:

"Have you your musket ready?"

"Yes," he answered, and there was dew on his forehead which was not caused by the eastern sun.

"Then," I said, "I'll lift the lid up swiftly, and as soon as I do it shoo the first yellow man that jumps out. Then we'll slash in with the cutlass."

He presented his musket, and I jerked the lid up.

I fell back, and the lid fell back too, for the most affrighting yells and squeals greeted our ears.

The chest was full, not of Chinamen, but of pigs.

We carried out our orders, to fire and sink the lurcher, and I fear that a lot of fine roasted pork was wasted, because we had no time to shoot the tenants of the chest.

The success of British arms in the 2nd Burma War typified many of the smaller campaigns, in that military victory caused almost as many political complications as it resolved. The British occupied lower Burma, but this hardly improved their relations with the kingdom of Ava, and in 1885 fear over growing French influence in upper Burma led to a fresh campaign. Although the King of Ava, Thibaw, was deposed, British troops were then faced with a prolonged campaign to suppress Burmese resistance in the countryside.

In China, too, military action was problematic. To acquisitive minds in western Europe, China at the start of the nineteenth century was a rich plum, ripe for plucking, the home of 400 million potential customers for European goods, whose pagan souls were a spur to missionary endeavour. Moreover, to outsiders the administration of the Quing (Ch'ing) dynasty seemed hopelessly introverted and inefficient, while Chinese armies were weak and anachronistic. Yet the Chinese seemed singularly unimpressed by European endeavour, and for the early part of the century resolutely confined European trading concerns to 'factories' (compounds) on the coast. Both the British and the French were deeply frustrated by official Chinese obstruction of their commercial enterprise, and the result was a series of wars fought, whatever the cause of each individual outbreak, with the ultimate intention of opening China to European trade.

Fighting in these campaigns was not continuous, but rather a series of outbreaks of varying ferocity, interspersed with long periods of negotiation. The 1st China War occurred in 1842, when Chinese officials attempted to stamp out the trade in opium, which the East India Company cultivated in huge quantities in central India, and which was one of its most profitable exports. It seems ironic to today's sensibilities that military action was undertaken by a European power in order to force the Chinese to buy a drug which was destroying the lives of tens of thousands of their subjects. The British won the Opium War, and forced the Chinese administration to open more ports to foreigners, but in 1854 the treaty expired, and the Chinese again sought to curtail European trading activity. Another violent outburst occurred, during which combined British and French forces bombarded the Dagu (Taku) forts, which guarded the mouth of the Peiho river, just 100 miles from the capital at Beijing (Peking). While this demonstration was sufficient to force the emperor to accept foreign representation at the court, when Allied ships attempted to sail up the Peiho in 1859, the Dagu Forts fired on them.

The result was a combined expedition against the forts. There were three forts in all, impressive earthworks surrounded by trenches, set with sharpened stakes, and built on mud-flats on either side of the river's mouth. The Allied force – some 11,000 British and Indian troops, and 6000 French – landed further up the coast, and marched across country to strike the Peiho upstream from the forts. They then attacked the forts from the rear. Despite this, however, the assault troops were still faced with a gruelling advance through swampy terrain, and a veteran of the expedition, Private John Dempsey of the 60th Rifles, recalled this aspect of the campaign with almost as much horror as the fighting.

Storming the Taku Forts

Fighting the heathen Chinee strikes many people as a humorous performance, but they are mostly those who have not waged war with 'Johnny' on his own soil – and that soil, I should think, is about the worst in the world for campaigning.

While I was out in China in the war of 1860, I seemed to spend most of my time in the mud, and when it wasn't mud it was water. Put yourself, in imagination, on some of the mud-flats on the banks of the Thames, in London, when the tide is out, and you will get some idea of the sort of ground we had to fight over when we stormed the Taku Forts.

You might carry the idea a little farther, and fancy that the gloomy buildings on the banks of the Thames are forts, and that you have been landed in boats on the mud and have to plant ladders against the walls and scramble up them to the top, with the very good chance of being hurled back or having a spear or knife or sword thrust through you.

That was the kind of entertainment we had to put up with on that August day, nearly fifty years ago, when we rushed to the assault, side by side with Frenchmen, and fought like fiends to be first to plant our country's flag on the ramparts. We all panted to get in, but only as real victors. There could be no half measures with an enemy like ours, because it was worse than death itself to fall into the hands of the Celestials as captives. I shrink even now when I think of what might have happened to me, and when I recall the Temple of Horrors, as we named it – a building which we entered when we had won our battle, and where we saw evidence of what the Chinamen could do in the way of torturing and destroying prisoners – but I will come to that later.

We struggled through the mud and water, waist-deep, after we left the ships in the boats, and were a truly filthy army when we got ashore and made preparations for the storming of the forts. We knew that that would be a pretty desperate business, because we had deep ditches to fight over and there was water to swim; then, at the end of that advance, we had to plant ladders against the straight sides of the forts and clamber up them as best we could.

We had scaling-ladders made of bamboo, which had the advantage of

Roger Fenton's atmospheric study of British troops in the Crimea: NCOs of the 8th Hussars relax at their cookhouse. *(Private Collection)*

The impressive fortifications around Sebastopol, photographed after their evacuation by Russian forces. *(Private Collection)*

Right: The destruction of an army: Afghan tribesmen attack the straggling British column during the retreat from Kabul.

Above: The remnants of the 44th regiment made their stand at Gandamak, on the domed hill in the background, during the retreat from Kabul in the 1st Afghan War. This photograph dates from the 2nd Afghan War, 1879. *(Bryan Maggs)*

Left: Fighting during the Indian Mutiny, one of the most vicious of the early Victorian campaigns.

The ruins of the Residency at Lucknow, pockmarked by shell-fire, photographed after the siege. *(Private Collection)*

A war of retribution: the remains of Indian dead, slaughtered by British troops during the storming of Lucknow. Unlike most Victorian campaigns, the mutual bitterness engendered by the early stages of the Indian Mutiny gave the later fighting many of the characteristics of a race war. *(Private Collection)*

The attempt to save the guns during the disaster at Maiwand.

The Bala Hissar, the impressive fortress which dominated the Afghan capital of Kabul. Lord Roberts reduced the fortress during his occupation of the city. *(Bryan Maggs)*

Lord Roberts' cantonment at Sherpur, outside Kabul, during the 2nd Afghan War.
(Bryan Maggs)

The 9th Lancers, photographed after their victory at Charaisa, in the 2nd Afghan War.
(Bryan Maggs)

An impressive study of an Abyssinian Ras, or chief, in traditional costume. *(Raphael Rugierri)*

Stanley Wood's typically dramatic rendition of the storming of Magdala, in the Abyssinian campaign of 1868.

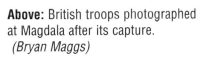

Above: British troops photographed at Magdala after its capture.
(Bryan Maggs)

A Maori chief, wearing traditional flax cloak, and carrying a flat whalebone club. The Maori proved a determined and skilful opponent, who inspired both fear and respect among the British who fought them.

Stanley Wood's illustration of a skirmish in the bush during the fighting in New Zealand in the 1860s.

Above: Maori prisoners captured in an action in 1866, guarded by men of the 18th and 57th Regiments. By the 1860s, British troops in the field in New Zealand had adopted a more practical blue campaign uniform. *(Tim Ryan)*

Right: An Asante musketeer. The Asante military system was ideally suited to its forest environment, but the long guns which were typically used were generally inaccurate and ineffectual. *(Basel Mission Archive)*

Above: Sir Garnet Wolseley coolly directing the fight during one of the battles against the Asante in the forest gloom of West Africa. *(Anne S.K. Brown Collection, Brown University Library)*

Left: Storming the entrenchments at Tel-el-Kebir, by Stanley Wood.

Above: The abandoned Egyptian entrenchments at Tel-el-Kebir after the battle. *(Private Collection)*

Right: The fierce close-quarter fighting at Abu Klea, by Stanley Wood.

Left: A dramatic duel between a lancer and a Mahdist swordsman: an incident during the charge of the 21st Lancers at Omdurman, by Stanley Wood.

Below: Some of the thousands of Mahdists cut down during the attack on the British zariba at Omdurman.

The most famous study of the sinking of the troopship *Birkenhead*, during the Eighth Cape Frontier War. The reality was not quite so romantic, but equally courageous.

The charge of the 17th Lancers at the battle of Ulundi.

The 58th Regiment's disastrous charge at the battle of Laing's Nek – the last time Colours were carried in action by a British regiment.

The ignominious climax of the 1881 Transvaal War – General Colley's troops in full flight from the summit of Majuba hill.

The terrible effects of shell-fire on the exposed defenders of Spioenkop, as depicted by Stanley Wood.

Right: A rare heroic moment to suit Stanley Wood's style amidst the horror of Spioenkop: Colonel Thorneycroft orders 'No surrender!'.

Below: A resourceful and stubborn foe: Boer 'bitter-enders' captured during the guerrilla war phase of the Anglo-Boer War.

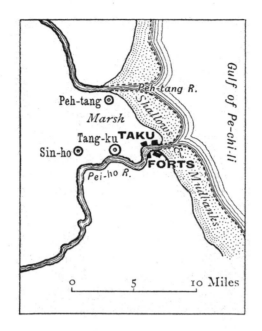

being very light and strong: and we had a special sort of ammunition, a patent, I think, which, it was rightly claimed, would not be affected by immersion in water. That was a lucky circumstance for us, because our pouches became thoroughly sodden. But the great thing was to fight our way into the forts and drive the Chinamen out, and to do that we had to depend mostly on our own nimbleness, and cold steel. The firearms in those days were not much good for storming purposes. They would not carry far, and you could not shoot quickly with them.

I must confess that when I looked upon the Taku Forts I felt that I would a good deal rather be inside them than out. They looked tremendously strong and grim, with guns grinning at us on every hand, and particularly that face which we were to assault. I believe there were nearly four hundred cannon, of different sizes, and besides these the Chinese had all sorts of firearms and spears and swords.

They had fearsome inventions, too, called stinkpots, which they were accustomed to throw at their enemies, and by means of their evil fumes try to put the men out of action. We knew, too, that they had an unpleasant and unsoldierly habit of hurling quicklime, in the hope that the dangerous stuff would burn the face and destroy the sight of the enemy. I think that all the stormers, both French and English, would rather face guns and steel than these barbarous helps to victory.

The Chinese had their own methods of fighting. They had tremendous faith in noise and show, and they had all sorts of devices for creating uproar and striking terror into us. The ramparts were quite gay with flags of all colours, mostly very gaudy, and taken altogether the sight of the Taku Forts was as strange and uncanny as any man could wish to see. But there was nothing gorgeous or inspiriting or romantic about the business. I never saw anything more depressing than that region of mud and wet, and the pluck seemed to ooze out of us as we made our preparations for the storming.

We wallowed in mud, and slept in it. And as for little reptiles, they positively swarmed. After we landed, we turned in for the night, and I lay down to sleep as best I could. My rest was troubled, I did not quite know why, but I had that sensation of oppression which so often comes over one in sleep.

At last I pulled myself together and awoke. Then I wished myself asleep, or unconscious, or in any state that would have spared me the spectacle of what I saw, for I was literally covered with tiny frogs – creatures about half as big as my thumb. They were squatting on me, and jumped away in a cloud as soon as I moved and shook them off. They had made themselves comfortable on us, wanting a change, perhaps, from the monotony of the mud and wet. They were quite harmless, of course, but it was creepy and uncanny to find them using one as a lodging.

When all was ready, and the heavy rains allowed us to make a start, we began the operations of war by assaulting a place named Tangtu. It fell to the lot and honour of the 60th to help considerably in the reduction of the place, for we found a sort of secret passage, after struggling through an appalling double ditch which was really like a canal. I think we must have fairly paralysed the Celestials, because they bolted as soon as we got into Tangtu, and left forty-five guns in our possession. That was an appetiser for the Taku Forts, which were the great objective of our attentions. Until they were reduced, nothing could be done. We wanted to be able to reach Pekin, the capital, and it was as needful to smash the forts as it would be for an enemy who determined to raid London to break down the defences of our chief city.

I for one was thankful when the bugles sounded the advance, and the hosts of us, French and British, marched to the assault. I liked the French. They were good men, and fine men, and I believe that they were moved by a determination to do their best, and to maintain the reputation of their country for military valour.

Those were the days, you know, when we went to our stormings with colours flying and drums beating. All that is a thing of the past, for in these times no man could live who bore a standard. He would be too good a target. I sometimes think that the old-fashioned storming has gone for ever.

In modern warfare there have been some fine performances by British troops. I may be wrong, or prejudiced, or both; but I cannot help thinking that the storming of the Taku Forts was amongst the very finest. But we had some splendid men to do it, if it comes to that, for many of us, including myself, had served in the Mutiny. I had gone from India to China. I believe that of all the soldiers of the 60th who rushed upon the Celestials, I am the only one left in the neighbourhood of the depôt, where we are talking.

We had made a road, by August 20th, to within less than a thousand yards of the forts, and our Armstrong guns, at a range of something more than a mile, had opened fire. The idea was, of course, that the walls should be broken and breached, and that in the openings made we should enter and rout the Chinamen. Things seem so very simple when they are described and laid down for you in orders; but they are so terribly difficult when it becomes a question of putting them into hard practice.

There was mud to be struggled through, and ditches had to be fought across, ditches which, in some places, were so full and deep that the only way to cross was to swim; yet officers and men did not hesitate to hurl themselves into the thick, muddy water, sword and bayonet and rifle and all. The marvel is that at such times troops can get through at all, much less score a victory. They conquer only, I think, because of that fierce lust for fighting which takes possession of every properly constructed British soldier on the field of battle.

Our own guns boomed and flashed, and under cover of them we struggled on – we of the 60th and the old 44th and the 67th. Not many years before, the 44th had been cut up in Afghanistan, where, in the snow-clad pass at Gundamuck, the weak and wounded fell beneath the hillmen's knives. The old 44th – now the Essex Regiment – were known as the Little Fighting Fours, and nobly that day they sustained their nickname. They suffered heavily, and during a day which covered many men with glory none won greater renown than those of the 44th.

Struggling and floundering, burdened with our arms and scaling-ladders, we fought our way towards the forts which had opened fire on us. It seemed ages before we were near enough to plant our bamboo ladders against the frowning walls of the forts, and before we strove, in a confused heap, to be amongst the first to set foot on the rungs which meant literally the rungs of fame.

I know that we in the 60th did our duty – had we not always done it, and have not the 60th more battle honours than any other regiment in the British Army? But the 44th and the 67th were in before us, and it was an ensign named Rogers, of the Little Fighting Fours, who was the first Englishman to gain a footing in the forts.

Ensign Rogers and other officers and men had dashed into a ditch and made for a hole which had been pounded in the walls by our guns. Ladder after ladder had been planted, and almost as soon as the bamboo structures had been placed against the walls they had been thrown over by the Chinamen or dragged into the fort itself. And all the time the guns were crashing, and the enemy were hurling vases of lime, stinkpots, cold shot, stones, and anything else on which they could lay their Celestial hands, while the air, thick with battle-smoke, resounded with the heathens' yells and noises.

Meanwhile, Ensign Rogers struggled fiercely at an embrasure, trying to get a footing, but the enemy was too much for him, and he was driven back. The subaltern rushed to another spot, but there again he was baffled, and it seemed as if defeat for him was certain.

Another young officer – Lieutenant Lenon, of the 67th – saw what was taking place, and dashed to his comrade's help, and then occurred one of the most thrilling incidents of that astonishing assault. With the swiftness of thought Lieutenant Lenon rammed the point of his sword into a crevice of the fort, and using the blade as a step, Ensign Rogers managed to scramble through the embrasure and to be the first Englishman, literally, to get inside the forts. He instantly set to work to help others through, and they say that the brave Lieutenant Lenon was the third to enter.

Ensign Rogers and Lieutenant Lenon got the Victoria Cross, and with them, for the storming, John McDougall, a private of the Little Fighting Fours, Lieutenant Burslem (he afterwards became a captain in the 60th), Private Thomas Lane of the 67th, and Ensign John Worthy Chaplin, of the same regiment, a gallant gentleman who afterwards became colonel of the 107th Regiment, and who is still living, I believe, in Leicestershire.

Ensign Chaplin was the first man to mount what is called the *cavalier* of the fort, and he was badly wounded in doing so. He carried the Queen's Colour of his regiment, and when the storming-party had made a breach, he planted the silken banner there. Another fighter, Arthur Fitzgibbon, a hospital apprentice of the Indian Medical Establishment, won the Victoria Cross at the storming of the forts; so, you see, no fewer than seven Crosses were awarded for the assault. I believe that, except Rorke's Drift. Taku Forts gave more V.C.'s for one event than any other action in the annals of the British Army since the decoration was instituted. The Cross does not mean everything; but it is something of a standard, at any rate, and shows how desperate and determined a business was the taking of the forts. Of those Crosses the 67th gained four, and two went to the Little Fighting Fours.

They say that it was a Frenchman who was actually first to get a footing in the forts, and I am sure that no survivor of the storming will deny the right of his memory to the honour. I believe the Frenchman was a drummer of the 102nd Regiment of the Line. With an agility that seemed incredible, and a luck that appeared to be impossible, in view of the fury of the fire, he gained the summit of the parapet, and there, a solitary figure, he stood, firing rifle after rifle that was handed to him. He went on firing till death claimed him, for he was killed by a spear-thrust through the brain. Then another man, carrying a pickaxe, tried with frantic courage to take his place, and he went on fighting and picking until he was shot.

It seemed as if no human being could live at such a furiously contested place, yet Lieutenant Burslem, of the 67th, dashed forward and continued the work of this brave pioneer.

Just a round two hundred officers and men, in killed and wounded – that was the price we paid on the British side to get our colours planted in the forts, and to see the Chinese flying from us, scattering to any place that gave them shelter. Many of them fled towards the Summer Palace of the Emperor, and many more towards Pekin, while the rest sought shelter in the neighbouring country and villages. Many there were, too, who remained in Taku Forts, for our guns had told heavily upon them, and the storming had been very stern.

I was amazed, on examining the forts, to find that many of the guns were dummies. They were made of bamboo, but from the embrasures they looked just like the real artillery with which the Chinese managed to do considerable mischief. These wooden guns were very tough, in their way, and I daresay they were capable of firing powder, to scare us; but that would be about all. What I noticed most, however, when I got inside the forts, were some poor Chinamen who had been chained to the guns – the real guns – so that they should not be able to run away. Some of the gunners had been killed by our artillery fire and others wounded. The survivors, I am sure, were better treated by the conquerors than they had been by their own people. We were very merciful to the poor fellows.

When we had done our work at Taku Forts we pushed ahead to get the war finished. Not very far away was the famous Summer Palace, a gorgeous building which was supposed to contain untold riches. Our commander-in-chief had made it known that unless the enemy agreed to his conditions the palace would be destroyed.

He told them that twenty-six British subjects had been seized and half of them had been done to death in the most barbarous manner. He insisted upon the survivors being restored at once, and as the Chinese did not agree to his demands he set out to keep his word – and kept it, for he ordered the palace to be burnt. In that famous event the French took the leading part, I think; at any rate they went mostly for the loot, and there were some wonderful hauls of gold and silver goods and precious silks. Of course, a private soldier does not understand the value of things of that sort, but even we were able to appreciate the marvellous beauty of some of the things that were taken. It was pitiful to see such a splendid place put to the fire; but I suppose it was the only way of bringing the Chinese to their senses.

I remember the palace well, but not so vividly as I call to mind the place which we spoke of as the Temple of Horrors, a building which was full of models, mostly in clay, of human creatures who were being punished with all the cruelty for which the Chinese were notorious.

One dreadful figure comes back to mind as I talk – that of a man, firmly bound in a chair, who had been put to death by having boiling lead poured down his throat. The thing was so shocking and real that it was hard to believe that the model was not actual flesh and blood.

Then there were other figures, the sight of which was sickening, and many of which gave us clearly to understand what the sufferings had been of those British prisoners who were restored to us, and what awful things we ourselves had escaped by not falling into the hands of the Chinamen. That was the one thing which most of us were careful not to do – fall into the enemy's hands as prisoners, for to do that, as I have said, was worse than death.

Looking back on the war and that famous storming, I find that the incident in it which is most firmly impressed on my memory, and which I dwell on now, is my adventure in the village of Pehtang and my discovery of a missing French sergeant of the Line.

Our convoy had gone astray, and we were badly pressed for food. Like my comrades, I was a hungry, tattered soldier, and wanted something to eat and drink – especially to eat. There was a good deal of talk just then about loot, but the only loot I craved for was something in the shape of Chinese pork or fowl. My mind did not dwell overmuch on Chinese gods or Chinese art.

At that time I was a corporal, and in my shirtsleeves, with about eight of my companions, I wandered about the village in search of food, and perhaps a pair of boots, I particularly wanted a pair of boots, because my own were worn to shreds.

I made my way into one of the miserable little houses of the village, a sort of mud hut, walking very stealthily and carefully, because although we had defeated the Chinese there were still a good many of them lurking about in strange and unexpected corners. You never knew when the blade of a sword or spear would flash round a corner where you craned your neck, or when a hidden Celestial would spring upon you from the gloom.

This foraging was creepy work, and I stepped into the house as craftily as ever burglar went about his business. I listened, but heard no sound which indicated the presence of an enemy; I pushed the door open and entered softly. Still there was no suspicious noise of any sort to trouble me; only an oppressive silence.

At last I walked in boldly and looked around; then I felt as if my heart had stopped, for on the earthen floor, stretched at my feet, was the form of a French sergeant – a fine figure of a man he was, too.

I would have bent down, but there was that nameless something in the figure which told of death. I seemed to be rooted to the ground with horror, and had that overwhelming fear which comes to one in nightmare. I was totally unarmed, and had no chance whatever of defending myself against the attack of any Chinaman who might be lurking round.

I knew that the Frenchman had entered, just as I had done, in search of food, and that from some unexpected quarter his enemies had fallen upon and killed him. I got into the open air, I don't know how, and found myself in a sort of yard or compound, and there I heard stealthy noises which told of Chinamen in hiding.

I can tell you, the sound did not make me feel very joyful. I knew too well what falling into Chinese hands meant.

A pig-tailed head bobbed up from behind a wall, and a stolid Chinese face stared at me, but there was the gleam of murder in the little almond eyes, and I knew that the Celestial hand gripped a sword or knife. I had nothing whatever to defend myself with except my fist and even the hardest of knuckles come off a poor second against sharp steel.

It is curious how one acts mechanically, even when overcome for the moment by a sense of overwhelming danger.

Almost instinctively I shouted 'Hullo!' and then I put my fingers to my mouth and gave a long, shrill whistle of alarm which made my comrades rush up to see what was happening, and the Chinaman bolt for his life. I do not know whether there was more than one – and being a defenceless shirt-sleeved man. I do not think I should have stayed to inquire if my friends had not joined me.

I had not left the French sergeant in such a hurry that I was not able to have a good look at him and the spot where he was lying. I had taken from him a little pocket-book, with a silver pencil, and was anxious that his people should have it. So I hurried off, coatless though I was, to the French lines, and reached a marquee where some officers were assembled. They soon understood my mission, and the bugle was sounded and the sergeant's company was paraded, for the little book contained the names of his men, and the officers wished to learn if any more were missing.

They were all reported present and correct – except the poor sergeant, who was buried near the spot where he had been murdered – for you could not call a death like his fair fighting.

In those days the French troops had *vivandières* with them – women who wore a sort of military uniform and followed the army, carrying little barrels of wines and spirits to give to the wounded and exhausted. One or two of these feminine warriors came up to me and gave me a drink, and in the shattered state of my nerves I was very grateful for the attention. The picturesque women were very kind to me, and I always think of them with gratitude.

I have told you that my own boots were worn to tatters. When I examined the French sergeant I saw that he was wearing a pair of fine new boots. I coveted them, even in that awful little Chinese house; but I did not touch them. I could not rob the dead. The only things I brought away were the notebook and the silver pencil – the book from which the roll was called to which no answer could be given by the sergeant of the Line.

The capture of the Dagu Forts paved the way for an Allied advance on Beijing itself. Reluctantly, the emperor agreed to accept Anglo-French demands for greater foreign representation at the Imperial Court. The success of the expedition led to forty years of peace between the Allies and China, but European intervention within the country at large continued to be resented. In the 1860s China was wracked with a major internal rebellion – the Taiping revolt – in which foreign troops supported the Imperial government. Nevertheless, by the end of the century popular dissatisfaction with the obvious presence and influence of westerners led to the greatest popular revolt of them all – the Boxer rebellion. This uprising, a genuine expression of discontent which started among the rural poor, eventually won the support of the Imperial government, but provoked international intervention on an unprecedented scale. Combined British, French, German, Italian and American forces ultimately broke up the Boxer concentrations, and defeated the Imperial armies, bringing a century of western intervention to its logical conclusion.

In New Zealand, too, decades of resistance to settler encroachment on the lands of the indigenous people – the Maoris – was only resolved by military means. The Maori possessed a robust tribal society, and had occupied almost all of New Zealand at the time of the arrival of the first whites in the eighteenth century. They were courageous and inventive warriors, who frequently resorted to violence to resolve inter-tribal quarrels. While their fighting techniques were, in many ways, individualistic, and involved the skilful use of close-quarter weapons – tomahawks, stone axes and wooden clubs – they were also expert military engineers, whose standard method of defence was a complex entrenchment known as a *pa*. Conflict between Maori groups and settlers first led to violence in the 1840s, and sporadic outbursts continued until 1870, by which time most of the Maori tribes had been reduced, and their land opened up to white settlement.

Not that the Maori were easily dispossessed, however. They quickly adopted European weapons, and adapted their fighting techniques to meet the challenges offered by the British. In particular, they remained highly skilled guerrilla fighters, and used New Zealand's rugged terrain, its mountains and forests of fern, to good effect. Private George Rose of the 65th Regiment was certainly impressed by Maori warriors – and their women – when he encountered them during the most bitter phase of the fighting, in the 1860s.

The New Zealand War

In the sixties it was a far cry to New Zealand, especially for the soldier who had to get there by sailing ship. And news did not travel very quickly either, but fast enough for us who were in the Army to know that our comrades twelve thousand miles distant were not having it all their own way with the Maoris – especially the Maori women. It seems strange to have to consider women in relation to a war; but I think my clearest recollection of New Zealand forty years ago is in association with its dusky belles.

I had seen many drafts go, and at last, in 1863, when the rebellion was at its height again, I sailed from Cork. In ninety-six days I landed at Auckland, in the North Island. I gloried in the change from salt water to dry land. Besides, there was the excitement of the unknown to keep me going, the attractions of a country about whose people and marvels I had been told so much.

I had heard a great deal about the Maori women, and had been, I fancy, something of a doubting Thomas, because the stories were so singular; but I was soon to find that they were not exaggerated. Many a soldier in those days, I fancy, had his curiosity whetted because of what he was told concerning the dusky and alluring ladies of New Zealand.

From first to last the war was essentially a campaign in the bush, and the most nerve-racking sort of fighting you could have. The vegetation was wonderfully luxuriant, the ferns growing to an enormous height. There were what are called tea-trees, too, bushes which, with the dense ferns, made perfect cover for the Maoris, so that we were everlastingly expecting to be attacked, always apprehensive of a swift and overwhelming swoop from the bush. The natives swarmed, and more often than not the first tidings we had of their presence was when we saw the gleam of their spears and tomahawks and heard the ping of their bullets amongst us. You could not see them until they fell upon you in a mob. Then it was mostly a case of which side could do the most with steel – ourselves with the bayonet and the Maoris with those deadly weapons which they handled with such marvellous skill and quickness.

The war had broken out afresh in a very dramatic way. Two British officers were seen by an escort to be in danger of massacre by Maoris. The escort – it consisted of only half-a-dozen men of the 57th Regiment, with a prisoner – hurried up to support the officers, but the whole party was fired on by the natives, who were hidden behind a bank, and all were shot or tomahawked except one man, a private, who escaped into the bush, wounded, and hid there till he was rescued by a relief party.

That was the sort of thing the Maoris did, and they were just as swift and merciless in dealing with individuals as they were in tackling these small, isolated bodies. They went in for the sniping with which in these days British soldiers are so familiar, and often enough a sentry would find a Maori trying to brain him and steal his rifle. There was one instance of a native stealthily attacking a British sentry on his post. While he tried to tomahawk the soldier with one hand he attempted with the other to snatch his rifle; but Tommy was too much for him, and he stuck to his weapon and preserved his life. But he had a thumb cut off, and the worst of it was that the Maori slipped back into the bush and wasn't hurt at all over the business.

Now these are the incidents to make you keep your eyes skinned, so to speak, and however young a soldier was he kept very wide awake, and often enough felt a creeping of the scalp. It was my luck, very soon after landing, to be in at one of the most desperate affairs of the campaign.

I had marched from Auckland into very rugged and dangerous country, and had got as far as a post which had been named Cameron Town, on the Waikato River. Commissariat supplies had been taken by friendly natives to Cameron Town and stored there, but the enemy rushed the place, captured it, murdered a district magistrate, and fired the post.

When this lurid little affair was in progress we were at a place called Tuakau, a few miles up the river, but near enough to enable us to see what was happening. Captain Swift, of my regiment, one of the best and bravest of officers, instantly determined to set out for the post and support the friendly natives, and, before we quite knew what was happening, the captain was marching off with a mixed little band, with Lieutenant Butler of my own company, and a splendid non-commissioned officer named Edward Mackenna.

Through an almost impenetrable bush, across some eight miles of the hardest country you could wish to see, we forced our way to Cameron Town, and at last got to the very spot where the triumphant Maoris were assembled. This was a little open space, and it seemed as if we fairly had them at our mercy. At any rate, Captain Swift must have thought so, for he ordered us to charge in amongst them after giving them a volley.

Nowadays it is hard to believe that the firing of a volley could be such a slow business as it was in the New Zealand war. It was a case of biting a cartridge, ramming it home, getting the bullet in after it, and putting a cap on before you could take aim and fire. Even then the cap might miss fire, or your bullet would go wide of its target. Before you could load again you would be in the thick of the spears and tomahawks.

'Let's go for them!' shouted Captain Swift, and we dashed upon the Maoris with wild cheers.

There was a blaze of fire from the clearing and the whizzing of bullets amongst us, and the captain fell, mortally wounded, almost as soon as he had shouted to us to charge the enemy.

Instantly Captain Swift directed the lieutenant to take command, and the subaltern obeyed; but just as he was leading us he also fell, shot in the body. He went down, but before he collapsed he killed two Maoris with his revolver.

We were in a desperate plight. Fifty strong when we started, we had been reduced to about thirty fighting men in a few minutes. A dozen members of the party had got adrift in the bush and could not regain us, and already several men were employed in removing the wounded, because we dared not leave them to the mercy of the Maoris. The enemy fought most bravely; not only the men, but the women too, for I saw to my amazement that the women were sharing in the war with their husbands and brothers, as I took them to be.

We knew that our captain was shot, and that there could be only a slight hope of his recovery, yet there was not one amongst us who thought of leaving him in such a place to such a foe. John Ryan, a lance-corporal, one of our most splendid fellows, and two privates, named Bulford and Talbot, took charge of Captain Swift, and in defiance of the bullets, spears, and tomahawks, caring nothing for the hordes of Maoris who swarmed around them, they removed him to the shelter of the bush, and for the time being the enemy lost sight of them.

Meanwhile, we were soldiers without an officer, wanderers, almost, without a leader. It was the time when a non-commissioned officer has the chance to show the sort of stuff he is made of.

Mackenna saw his opportunity. His captain had fallen, the subaltern, too, was not of action. The colour-sergeant dashed to the front of us. With all the valour and resourcefulness of a born leader, he hurled us against the strongest part of the enemy's position, and, inspired by his example, we fought our way from the spot where we had been so suddenly ambushed and so nearly annihilated. We found shelter in the bush, and the welcome night came and gave us protection from the Maoris until reinforcements arrived and we were relieved. That night in the bush was the longest and most anxious of all the hard and trying nights I have ever spent.

Throughout the night Ryan, Bulford, and Talbot remained by the side of their captain, refusing to leave him, although it was clear enough now that he was mortally wounded. It was a noble act, and rightly enough Ryan got the Victoria Cross for it, while his comrades received the Distinguished Conduct Medal. The Cross was also awarded to Mackenna, and I do not think it was ever more deservedly given. It was hard on Ryan that he did not live very long to enjoy his honour. Before the war was ended he lost his life, again in trying to save another; but this time there was not the excitement of battle to encourage him. We were crossing a river by means of a bridge of boats, and Ryan was drowned while attempting to save a man who had fallen into the water.

Captain Swift was got into hospital, where he died. I believe that the two men who were killed were never found.

There were during the war some wonderful displays of valour, and none more noticeable than that by Sergeant John Murray of the 68th Regiment, which is now the Durham Light Infantry. Experience had made the Maoris very artful in fighting. They saw, just as more civilised people see, that it is no good to waste the lives of warriors; and although they did not shrink from battle in the open, still they recognised that it was well to get as much protection as possible. For this reason they constructed rifle-pits, and it was in these dug-out places that many a fierce encounter happened. The pits had to be stormed and the natives routed out of them.

One day – it was on June 21st, 1864 – a position was being stormed at Tauranga, which is in Auckland, on the shore of the Bay of Plenty. Murray was one of the stormers, and he performed the extraordinary feat of tackling, single-handed, a rifle-pit in which ten men were sheltering and firing. He took the little affair entirely on himself; and when he had finished he had either killed or wounded every Maori in the pit. Most men would have been satisfied with such an achievement, but the sergeant dashed ahead, and did not rest until he had settled several more of the enemy with his bayonet.

The Maoris were splendid specimens of humanity, and grand fighters, too. They had their own methods of warfare, and I suppose you cannot blame them for campaigning according to their lights; but their ways were not always our ways, and it was an ill thing to fall into their hands, living or dead. Their firearms were bad enough; the old muzzle-loaders and the flintlocks made terrible wounds, and both these weapons were used in New Zealand. But the spears and the tomahawks were infinitely worse than the muskets, and some dreadful wounds were inflicted with them.

The most remarkable thing about our enemies was that they were women as well as men; and I assure you that there was hardly a soldier amongst us who did not prefer fighting the men to the women. Somehow, when a woman is roused, she is such a desperate and irreconcilable creature; and the Maoris were no exception. The women could handle the tomahawk just as skilfully as the men. I saw many a fine Maori dead on the field of battle; and sad though it was to see our brave male enemies stretched lifeless under their beautiful sky, it was far more distressing to come across their women-folk. I was always badly upset when I saw such spectacles.

Ah, those Maori women! How frequently I think of them! Often enough, in our marches and foragings, we would come unexpectedly across them – handsome creatures they were, with the scantiest of coverings, and with such beautiful eyes, and teeth, and skins. It was always a delight to see them, except when they had their tomahawks. We would suddenly find ourselves near the native dwellings, 'warris' we called them, and discover perhaps forty

Maoris in each warri – Maoris of all ages and both sexes, the men as scant-
ily clothed as the women, with nothing more than a loin-cloth. They looked
very much like Hindoos, but were far finer specimens.

The women were very wild. Almost invariably, when they saw us on the
march, they would run away as fast as their legs would carry them, anxious
only to put the biggest distance between themselves and us; but in time of
battle it was very different, for then they were perfect fiends, and all they
wanted was to get near enough to ply their tomahawks. I tell you, some of
the most quaking moments I spent in New Zealand came when these
Amazons were unpleasantly close to me in scrimmages. Some of my saddest
hours were those which followed seeing them lifeless on the ground which
they loved so well, and which they had perished in defending. Would not
many Englishwomen do the same to keep their own beloved country out of
the clutches of an enemy?

I got to know the Waikato River well. The affair at Cameron Town was
enough to impress its recollection on my mind; but there were harder, brisker
times in store, for at Rangariri, a Maori settlement on the bank of the river,
we were to fight one of the most stubborn battles of the war. Rangariri is
the native word for 'angry heavens,' and it is a very appropriate description,
too, the district having as one of its famous features the active volcano,
Tongariro. The enemy was in force at Rangariri, and General Cameron determined to attack him and rout him out.

Rugged country, dense bush, swampy ground, and a fine flowing river –
these were some of the natural advantages which the Maoris enjoyed, and of
which they made the best use in defending themselves against our assault.
It was to be a storming business, and to the 65th was to fall some of the
hottest of the work. Scaling-ladders and planks were served out to us, and
I was chosen to be one of the stormers. We were a mixed force, of course,
amongst us being men of the Royal Navy and the Royal Engineers.

The enemy had made himself snug in a very strong square redoubt. Before
you could reach the redoubt you had to cross a ditch a dozen feet wide, and
then swarm up a parapet nearly twenty feet high. The redoubt was a sort
of surprise-box, and we knew a good deal more about it at the finish than
we knew at the start.

Our guns, both on land and afloat – two gunboats were in the river –
paved the way for the advance by shelling, but although for the best part of
two hours there was a heavy fire from the artillery, there did not seem to be
any great impression made on the enemy's position.

It was getting late, and the officer commanding saw clearly enough that
if we were to do our work before darkness came we must get ahead with it.
So the order to assault was given, and with ringing cheers we swept on,
always remembering that the sooner we got to the redoubt the better it

would be for us. Even the most valiant soldier fights none the worse for a bit of shelter.

We were met with a furious fire. Some of the skirmishers and ladder party fell, and the bullets found their way amongst the supports, too. Still, we swept on with our planks and ladders, rushing for the ditch.

How we got across the ditch I cannot tell you, nor have I any clear recollection of the means we adopted to climb the sides of the redoubt; but the way to do it was to plant our planks and ladders and struggle up as best we could, and that is what we did. I do know that the fire seemed terrific, and that officers and men went down under it, and I do remember that we had a desperate task to drive the Maoris out of the redoubt and rifle-pits.

We fought in the waning light, struggled till darkness fell – then we had to stop for the time being; but we had good reason to be satisfied. Although we were not perfect masters of the place, still we held the most important positions, and the first thing in the morning our victory was made complete by the surrender of the enemy.

So it happened that when we should have been killing and maiming each other again we were hobnobbing, and the Maoris were swearing eternal friendship for us. But there was not a chance for all of us to be so amiable, for our dead had to be buried and our wounded carried on board the steamers in the river; while the Maoris had their own dead to dispose of, and their wounded to succour. It was the invariable custom in the war for each side to deal with its own dead.

Considering the smallness of the force engaged we had lost heavily, four of our officers having been killed and eleven wounded; while thirty-seven men were killed and eighty wounded. What the Maori loss was I do not know, and I do not think it was ever ascertained; but a good many of their dead were buried, and in fleeing across the swamps to escape more were either drowned or shot.

An extraordinary thing about the affair was that we did not come across any wounded Maoris, and we could only suppose that under cover of the night they had been removed.

The fight produced its heroes, none greater than the man who did as much as any, and yet was not to see the fruits of his success. This was Captain Mercer, who led the Royal Artillery in the assault which they made with sword and revolver. He was heading an attack on the redoubt when he was shot through the face and mortally wounded. Capt. Mercer, like the other officers and men, was in an exposed position, and a heavy fire was being turned upon them. It was almost certain death to try to help them, and time after time men who tried to reach them were either killed or wounded. Lieutenant Pickard, of the Artillery, and Assistant-Surgeon Temple managed at last to reach the wounded, but not before a little opening in the redoubt, through which the Maoris kept up a deadly fire had been masked with planks and earth. The subaltern repeatedly crossed the fire-swept zone to get water for the wounded, and it is a remarkable fact that in spite of the danger he ran he was the only rescuer who was not killed or wounded.

Both he and Surgeon Temple got the Victoria Cross. Captain Mercer could not be saved. He was dying fast in the very hour of victory. Shot through the tongue and jaw he could not speak, but he was conscious, and when they sent for his wife to see him – those were the days when often enough women went almost on to the battlefield with us, which is a mistake – he scribbled a farewell note to her in pencil. This was one of the saddest incidents that I remember in connection with a war that had many distressing features.

Glorious climate, splendid country, fine men, and handsome and attractive women – there were many things to cause the war to remain in one's memory. How often since those far-off days have I wished that Fate had been as good to me as it was to some of our fellows, men who could see ahead a bit and recognise the possibilities of the colony. And men, too, who by some means discovered that the Maori belles had comfortable little fortunes, and were not always likely to look with the eye of disfavour on the white man.

As a matter of fact, not a few of the British soldiers were very powerfully affected by the spirit and alluring qualities of the Maori women, and when the war was over they took their discharges and settled in New Zealand, with former enemies as wives. And very good wives they made, too, I believe. That, at any rate, was more natural and agreeable than having the poor creatures unprotected in front of your terrible musket bullets, and lying wide-eyed under the blue heavens they could not see.

It is astonishing to notice how careless we become when we are constantly confronting danger. It is, indeed, a case of familiarity breeding contempt. You might suppose that having been so long in New Zealand, fighting against cruel and crafty savages, I should have been everlastingly on the alert, especially when I remembered their practices towards our dead and wounded; yet the very commonness of peril made me reckless, and that recklessness brought me as near to my death as ever I have been in all my life.

There had been a skirmish – one of the brushes with the enemy which were so common that I cannot recall exactly where this took place. But it was the same old story of losses on both sides, and the hoisting of the white flag to proclaim a truce, during which the fallen could be buried. I and a few comrades were told off to bury our dead, and we went towards the spot where our own poor fellows lay. A handful of Maoris were there, with their tomahawks, and just in front of them was a chief.

By this time some of our soldiers had picked up a few words of the native language, not many, but enough to make themselves understood to the Maori men, and perhaps pay a compliment or two to the women. The British soldier then was just as ready as he is now to bid his mortal enemy good day, and when we got up to the chief we noticed that he did not look very well.

'What's the matter with you?' cried one or two of our men as well as they could.

The chief looked as if he might have had a pain in the region where his waistcoat would have been, if he had worn one, and answered: 'Too much the matty, matty.'

Exactly what he meant I do not know, but while I was laughing at the question and the chief's way of answering, I heard a loud shout of warning.

'Look out, George! Look out! He's going to kill you!'

I turned swiftly round, and then I saw a thing which almost made my heart stand still – and I was a strong, big young fellow then, not easily scared.

One of the Maoris had slipped away from the place where he was standing behind the chief, and unheard by me, unseen, he had got to within a few inches and raised his tomahawk above my head. At that very instant it was poised in the air, and in a second more –

But there was a flash and a crack and a twirling figure near me, and the Maori and his hatchet tumbled to the ground together.

One of my comrades had shot him dead – and can you wonder that in view of such treachery not even the chief himself was spared?

While British troops were mopping up in New Zealand, an Anglo-Indian force was required to mount an expedition in a terrain which could scarcely have been more different – Abyssinia (modern Ethiopia). The Abyssinian expedition of 1868 was in many ways a typical punitive expedition; the British had no great territorial or trading interests in the 'horn of Africa', but were provoked by an insult to Imperial pride. In the 1850s, King Tewodros (known to the British by the Anglicised version of his name, Theodore) had united Abyssinia's disparate tribal groups to form a kingdom. A Coptic Christian, Tewodros seems to have been driven by a desire to modernise his country in the face of internal opposition, and he looked to Europe for support. In particular, he invited the British to send him a representative. This they duly did, but the first envoy was unfortunately killed by Abyssinian rebels. Another was sent, and with his help Tewodros compiled a letter of friendship to the British government. Sadly, this letter seems to have languished unread by the Colonial Office, and Tewodros, feeling himself slighted, promptly arrested the British envoy, who was soon joined by further European prisoners.

To the British, Tewodros soon became known as 'Mad King Theodore', and while this undoubtedly reflected a sense of Imperial indignation at his actions, there does seem something self-destructive about Tewodros' actions, for he seems to have relished the impending conflict with a power whose military capabilities he much admired. A force of British and Indian troops was assembled in

India under the command of General Sir Robert Napier, and despatched to the port of Zula on the Red Sea coast. Napier's greatest challenge was Abyssinia's terrain; Tewodros' mountain capital, Magdala, was over 400 miles from Zula, and Napier's men would have to make their own roads, and carry their own food and water with them. As George Dunlop, who served throughout the campaign with the Sappers and Miners, commented, Napier's greatest achievement was bringing his army to a point where it could confront Tewodros at all.

The Abyssinian War: The Storming of Magdala

If you expect me to tell a tale that reminds you of the Chicago stockyards – and I know them well, because I have worked in them – you will be disappointed. Nor must you imagine that you are going to listen to a recital of marvellous deeds with sword and carbine. But if you want a story of amazing marches in a land of hills and lions, snakes, scorpions, centipedes, and every filthy thing that creeps and crawls, of terrible sufferings by baggage animals of all sorts, of floggings of British soldiers for small offences, and of a triumphant victory at the end, and in spite of all, then I can give you the framework for one. It is for you to do the rest of the building.

Theodore, who ruled things in that dark country, was a cruel tyrant, and one of his performances was to keep in chains and in prison a number of British subjects. Now, Great Britain does not allow that sort of thing to be done with her people, and the Emperor was plainly told that the captives must be set free. He refused to listen; he was defiant, and all the more so because he lived in an amazingly strong place in the hills called Magdala, four hundred miles from the coast. His Majesty had good reason for deluding himself into the belief that he could not be touched or punished by a British army, even if England sent an expedition out against him. He was to learn by experience what a bitter mistake he had made. He flouted the demands of our Government, and accordingly we set to work to teach him manners. It was one of the costliest lessons ever taught by England.

India was the nearest and best place to get troops from who were needed for work in a hot, hard country, and from India we sailed to Annesley Bay, which is on the shore of the Red Sea.

Abyssinia is a land of mountains, some of which rise to a height of 15,000 feet. In the centre of the country, perched on an enormous, lonely precipice, is Magdala; and it was there that the Emperor calmly awaited our coming – calmly, for the very good reason that he did not suppose we should ever reach him. But when a British army in the old days – I am talking now of forty years ago – set out for a certain place, it got there, particularly when it was commanded by such an old-school soldier as Sir Robert Napier, who afterwards became Lord Napier of Magdala.

We had a wonderful transport service; legions, as it seemed, of elephants, camels, mules, ponies, donkeys, and bullocks – half-a-hundred elephants, more than seven thousand camels, thirteen thousand mules and ponies, nearly a thousand donkeys, and over seven thousand bullocks – not far short of thirty thousand animals all told; not to mention thirteen thousand sheep for use as food.

Imagine what it meant to give all these animals food and drink in a barren country where water was only to be got by sinking wells: Lucky were the brutes that were drowned, as many were, in the heavy surf through which we had to force a landing on the coast. It was all the troops could do to get ashore; as for the animals, they were thrown overboard and had to swim for it. The best swimmers of all were the elephants; they were too 'fly' to get into trouble, and all landed safely. I have often seen them in India take to the water rather than use the pontoon bridges.

I had had some pretty tough marches in India, but they were child's play to this work of toiling through a mountainous country, at a crawling pace, from the coast to the interior. Some days we could not do more than seven miles, and we started early at that. For every drop of water we had to bore, to make wells; and for this purpose we had with us some American boring apparatus which answered very well. But what are you to do with so vast a number of animals which need so much water? – to say nothing of the European and Indian troops and followers, human beings who must be kept alive at any cost, so that the fighting can be done. Animals perished on every march, and from start to finish of the expedition our track was marked by their decaying bodies or their bleaching skeletons. The air was rank with the smell of them.

As we advanced the enemy skedaddled; we scarcely ever saw them; we seldom seemed to know where they were. We wanted so badly to come into touch with them and to have a fight – anything to relieve the hardship and monotony of the marching by day under a fierce sun and the strain and irritation of our camping at night. We were ceaselessly on the alert, and anything like refreshing sleep was impossible.

I had seen something of snakes and reptiles in India, and thought I understood what it meant to have to deal with them – cobras and the rest of such deadly creatures – but I had a vast deal to learn in Abyssinia. Snakes of all sorts, almost without exception very deadly; scorpions, centipedes, lions, and many other four-footed brutes, had to be contended with, especially at night. Wild beasts carried off numbers of our people, mostly natives, and poisonous reptiles added to the total of our casualties.

The campaign was nothing but suffering and hardship, with plenty of

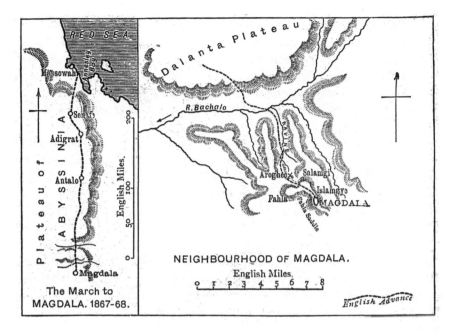

NEIGHBOURHOOD OF MAGDALA.

English Miles.

The March to
MAGDALA. 1867-68.

English Advance

discipline thrown in to flavour it. For ourselves, we were on ship's rations —
and ship's rations forty years ago were most appetising when they were taken
on trust. I remember, though, that we had Australian mutton, tinned, and
very good stuff it was.

The advance was not exhilarating. Men were dying of fever, animals of all
sorts were perishing of thirst and hunger, and pitiful it was to see them die,
knowing that we could not do anything to save them. At the end of the
campaign very few of them were left alive.

Skirmishes we had, it is true; but we wanted something more thrilling
than that; we longed for a fight, so that we could get our work done and
clear out of the country. Variation on the day's work of heavy labour we got
certainly, but it was of the kind that one would rather not become acquainted
with, because it consisted of terrible punishment for offences which in these
days are treated very lightly.

Our Commander-in-Chief was a stern soldier of those earlier days when
men were considered simply as fighting machines, and when the private was
looked upon as being something that was scarcely to be accounted human.
If a soldier went wrong, however trivially, he had to undergo the punishment of the lash, and in Abyssinia there were many cases of the infliction of
the cat. Discipline had to be maintained, and that was a favourite way
of keeping it up — a survival of the system of the Iron Duke.

A man named Coleman tried to get at the rum, which was under guard.

Some men will do anything to quench their thirst, especially when the slaking liquid is alcohol, and this was the case with us, although it was known that judgment would be swift and heavy. Coleman was caught, and sentenced to fifty lashes by a court-martial, sanctioned by Sir Robert – there was none of the chocolate or feather-bed soldier about him, and I do not believe that flogging in the Army would have been abolished if the matter had rested with him.

Flogging was inflicted in the cavalry by farriers, and in the infantry by drummers, and in the case of Coleman two drummers were told off to do the disagreeable work.

The troops were paraded, and the culprit was fastened to a wheel of the treasury-chest, which was always under guard. The treasury-chest was exactly like a gun-carriage, except that where the ammunition-boxes should have been the money-boxes were placed.

The drummers plied the lash, and we were forced to look upon the degrading and terrible ceremony. I may be wrong in my recollection, but I feel pretty certain that although he had been primed for the performance Coleman did not take it very well. Perhaps the exhilaration had evaporated too quickly.

We had reached Annesley Bay on January 4th, 1868, and on April 2nd we had got as far as Magdala, ready to storm and take the place. Meanwhile Theodore had come to his senses to the extent of setting the British captives free; but, as a set-off, he had massacred three hundred native prisoners. Some of his troops had mutinied, too, so that he was not in anything like an enviable situation. But he was plucky – let that be remembered in his favour. He stuck to his city and his people long after the time when he knew that all was lost, and could have saved himself by flight.

Any properly constituted man has a peculiar pleasure in feeling that a given piece of work is done, and I know that I rejoiced when I knew that that appalling march to the black monarch's capital was finished, and that at last there was to be some real, good, hard fighting.

As we advanced the natives had fled, and had given us a very poor show for our money; but here in the mountain fastness they were standing at bay, believing, I am certain, that we should never have the audacity to attack them, and that if by any chance we were so foolish we should be hurled back with enormous losses. The Abyssinians, remember, are good fighting people when it really comes to a crisis, and they were completely cornered now. They had to make their choice between abandoning their capital and all its treasures and driving us away or destroying us; and they took the latter chance.

As a signaller I was with the advance body, and reached the fortress the night before the main body arrived. The signallers took up a position on the outskirts of the city, and throughout the night which preceded the assault I was restless with excitement, like a man who goes to see a thrilling play.

It was wonderful, when day had broken and the attack was being formed, to see the eagerness and courage of our people – men like the old Thirty-third, now the West Riding Regiment, and the Forty-second, the Black Watch. And the odds seemed so hopelessly against the assailants; it seemed so impossible for any troops, however desperate, however valiant, to storm and capture such a strong-hold.

It was a hill perched on hills, a fortress almost in the clouds, to which there was admission by one gate only, and that gate so well defended that, with resolute troops behind it, there was only the most shadowy hope of successful storming. First there was the gate to reach, by scrambling and climbing; then barriers made of thorns and boughs and stones – anything and everything that came handy – to break away, and then the gate to burst in before our soldiers could force an entrance.

The actual place which was to be stormed and taken, the central object to be gained, was an oval-shaped platform, about a mile and a half long and three-quarters of a mile wide, rising something like five hundred feet above a surrounding plateau, and approachable, as I have said, only by one way. First of all there was to be a bombardment, and when the big guns, which had been brought up by the elephants, had paved the way, the British and native troops were to hurry to the assault.

It was Easter Monday morning when the drums and bugles sounded in the hills and the stormers sprang to arms. Rain began to fall, but nothing could depress the spirits of the men, who were now as keen to seize the city and bring away the prisoners as a tigress is to get her prey.

The big guns boomed and crashed, making a wonderful echo in the mountains, and by way of answer came the little spits of fire from the hilltop, which told of men who held their ground and challenged us to come on. Lucky it was for us that they did not know how to use the artillery they possessed. because a single well-served gun could pretty well have destroyed us.

For fully two hours the artillery hammered at the defences, then the booming ceased, and a strange silence fell upon the fortress, in which the musketry had been overpowered. It was literally the calm before the storm, for the Thirty-third, the Forty-second, and other troops were forming for the assault, to deliver the last and biggest blow of the campaign.

Suddenly, as I watched, I heard the sounds of cheering, and saw the waving of colours as the storming-parties began their advance. They rushed on to the final attack, and forced themselves very near to the last of the defences, almost to the gate of Magdala itself.

Whatever his faults were – and they were many – Theodore was at least a brave man. He must have known by this time that the fortune of war was against him, and that he was doomed; but instead of bolting he encouraged his people, and personally directed the defence of the gate. He saw the British troops approaching, regardless of the fire which was poured upon them; advancing up those steep rocky slopes which had been reckoned unclimbable.

There was, indeed, something here to strive for, and the men of the Thirty-third and the Black Watch knew it. So far, no white soldier had ever set foot in Magdala, and there was a noble struggle to be first within the place.

It was a marvellous sight to see them forcing their way up the hill to the fortress, and made the more impressive because, just at the most stirring stage of the assault, heavy rain began to fall, the lightning to flash, and the thunder to bellow — and it bellowed indeed in that land of mountains when it began to play its tune at all.

Who would be the first within the fortress? Whose colour would be the first to float in token of victory? By whose hand would the king be slain or taken — the monarch for whose body, dead or living, a big reward was offered?

I daresay some such questions had passed through the brains of the men who were struggling and panting up the slopes of Magdala, rushing for the gate and barricades behind which Theodore and his faithful remnant were at bay.

There were amongst the very foremost of the stormers two young soldiers of the Thirty-third named Michael Magner, a drummer, and James Bergin, a private. They were rushing on, separated only by a few paces, towards the very top of the defences, into the thickest of the fight and the deadliest of the danger. They had tried to reach a particular gateway and had failed; but they climbed up a cliff, and forcing their way through a barricade of thorns, they hurled themselves upon the nearest of the Abyssinians, and in a fierce hand-to-hand encounter either slew or scattered them. Then they struggled into Magdala itself, the first of all the stormers to enter the fastness of the king.

Redcoats streamed in after them, and as if to emphasise the splendour of the victory, the sun burst out from behind the dark clouds and shone on the triumphant troops and reddened steel. If this was not one of those daring deeds which are so often done in time of battle for salvation of human life, it was at any rate an act of such especial bravery that the Commander-in-Chief recommended the two heroes for the Victoria Cross, and each received it. These were the only crosses given for the whole of the campaign.

When the troops were pouring in to Magdala, furious because of what they had seen and heard of the cruelty of the king — that very morning more than three hundred mutilated corpses, fettered, had been seen at the foot of one of the precipices — a solitary figure was observed near a stack of dried grass. In his hand was a revolver, and, as a rush was made towards him, the weapon, pointed at himself, was fired, and the man fell to the ground, mortally hurt and at the point of death.

They drew him more into the open, and then the startled report went round that this very man, now dead, was the king himself. He had committed suicide – with a pistol presented to him by Queen Victoria in 1854 – rather than fall into the hands of those conquerors from whom he had no right to expect mercy, and from whom in all probability he would have got short shrift.

There was a fluttering of silk regimental Colours, the waving of helmets, and the roaring of triumphant British cheers. The sounds of victory rang down the hill and travelled along the plateau for a distance of two miles or so, until all the force was made aware that Magdala had fallen. Then a chorus of joyful sounds was heard, and the hills re-echoed 'God Save the Queen,' which the bands struck up – bands which not so long before had played the troops to the beginning of the storming with stirring tunes like 'Cheer, boys, cheer,' and 'Garry Owen.'

Few of us who went into Magdala failed to see the body of the man who had defied us, who called himself not only King of Abyssinia, but also Lord of the Earth, King of Kings, Saviour of Jerusalem, and I know not what else. We had no pity for him, but this I do know – there were few indeed of us who did not in our hearts admire the man who had made a gallant stand at the end and was not afraid to die.

The main thing that enters a soldier's mind when he gets into such a place as this is the desire to loot, and most of us went in search of spoil. Most of us were disappointed, too. There were many extraordinary articles and ornaments, but very few were of real value, not by any means the precious metals that we had expected to find.

The palace of the king itself – if you can call a two-storeyed thatched barn a palace – was disappointing, and as for the huts, the general buildings, you might as reasonably expect to find riches in an East End slum as there. Many things that looked like gold – they glittered bravely enough – were merely gilt; but there was a mitre of pure gold which weighed several pounds, and three or four royal crowns.

I was either lazier or less greedy than my comrades, because nothing in the way of loot came into my possession – not even a bit of the blood-stained clothing of the king, for which there was such a struggle that when he was finally left he was naked.

I was curious to set eyes on the prisoners for whom we had suffered so many hardships, and I was amazed to find that there were so few of them, and that they were by no means all our own countrymen. Perhaps it was because they were so excited through their freedom, perhaps it was because they were merely human, or it may have been that they wanted an early chance of getting level with their gaolers; I do not know what the motive was, but a few of them at any rate were very active when it came to laying hands on loot.

Next day the king was buried in a church with scant ceremony, and then it became a question only of crowning our work of vengeance. That took some time – three more days – during which we prepared the city for destruction by fire. That in itself was no very hard task, seeing that the three thousand houses or so which formed it were slightly built, with straw roofs, and that enormous quantities of very inflammable articles were strewn about the alleys which served as streets.

Every living creature having been forced to go, the Engineers blew up the towers, defences, and magazines; then torches were placed against the huts, and very soon, fanned by a strengthening breeze, the city was a blazing mass.

Awed, and with something like a feeling of compassion, I watched the growing fire, a mass of flame and smoke on the summit of that frowning hill. By nightfall what had been the city of a monarch was a smouldering furnace – the funeral pyre of the man who had claimed to be the King of Kings.

It had been a terrible country to get into, and it was almost as bad to leave. Yet there was always the cheerful knowledge that we were on our way back to the coast and India, which was a land of comfort compared with Abyssinia. We had, as our Commander-in-Chief told us in General Orders, succeeded in our task. We had marched over four hundred miles of mountainous country, and had stormed Magdala and burnt it so that it remained only a scorched rock. We had also got something in the way of prize-money from the sale of plunder, but very little.

Before we reached the coast our victorious army endured what was, I think, the most appalling thunderstorm I ever saw. The very skies seemed to burst to let the water down, and the thunder and lightning were terrific. Men and animals were drowned in torrents that subsided as swiftly as they had been created. I really think there were those amongst us who would far more readily have stormed Magdala afresh than go through such another performance of Nature.

We had released the captives and brought them away with us. I did not know how much a head they had cost the country, or I daresay I should have looked at them with deeper curiosity. They were certainly the costliest prisoners that were ever liberated, for there was only a handful of them, all told, and from first to last, to set them free cost England nearly nine million golden sovereigns.

In its triumph over environmental challenges and logistics, Napier's Abyssinian campaign had much in common with another short, sharp expedition in the 1870s

– Sir Garnet Wolseley's advance on Kumase, the capital of the Asante (Ashanti) kingdom in West Africa.

British involvement in West Africa – the so-called Gold Coast – dated back to the hey-day of the slave trade, a trade so lucrative that it brought most of the major European powers to the area, despite its reputation as 'the White Man's Grave'. Rival European trading enclaves clung to the coast, reluctant to venture into the steamy interior, and conducted their commercial activities through lines of African intermediaries. Although the British had abandoned the slave trade early in the nineteenth century, there was still enough profit to be made from gold and other goods for it to be worth her while to maintain a presence on the coast. Twice, during the century, however, this brought Britain into conflict with the dominant African power in the interior, the Asante.

The Asante were a confederation of forest groups, ruled by their king – the Asantehene – from his capital at Kumase. Militarily strong, the Asante were nonetheless compelled to conduct all their trade with the Europeans through the agency of another group, the Fante, who lay between them and the coast. This led to prolonged rivalry between them and the Fante, which broke into occasional violence. In 1824 a British representative had attempted to organise Fante resistance to Asante influence, and been soundly defeated as a result. In 1873 a dispute over the ownership of several trading ports led to a fresh invasion of Fante territory, and a threat to British interests.

General Sir Garnet Wolseley – who was then just establishing his reputation as the Young Turk of the British military establishment – was sent to put the Asante in their place. Like Napier, he approached his task with a logistical thoroughness which ensured its success and made his reputation. He ordered the troops under his command to abandon their impractical scarlet uniforms, and devised instead loose-fitting garments in a neutral grey. Realising that the climate and the terrain were his greatest enemies, he expended prodigious amounts of energy organising transport and medical facilities, and wrote complex instructions on the complexity of forest fighting. By the beginning of January 1874 he was ready to begin his advance, and pushed forward through Fante territory, up the forest track which led to the borders with the Asante kingdom. When the Asantehene, Kofi Karikari, refused to comply with Wolseley's demands, he crossed the border and made a dash for Kumase.

Most of the subsequent fighting took place in the dense gloom of the tropical rain-forest, a succession of fights made eerie by the almost total invisibility of the enemy, and by the unnerving Asante practice of human sacrifice. Both aspects of the campaign made an impression on Sergeant J. Flynn, of the Rifle Brigade.

The City of the Death-Drum

When we were wallowing in the swamp, and slime, and gloom of the Gold Coast, on our way to Coomassie, I used to listen to some of the young soldiers grumbling and growling, and telling all about things they did not understand.

'The trenches aren't in it with this,' they said.

Well, I had been in the trenches before Sebastopol, and they hadn't. I had seen what Russian guns, slushy snow, bitter frost, cholera, rags, and starvation could do, while they were babies in cradles, and I told them they didn't know what they were talking about. But although the swamp and jungle weren't quite so bad as the Crimea – I don't think any modern war was – still Ashanti was bad enough, and in some ways it was worse even than Sebastopol.

I will admit now that Ashanti, while it lasted, was worse than the trenches. In bitter cold you can often enough keep warm, but in such a deadly climate as that of the Ashanti swamps you could not by any possibility keep cool.

We went straight away from an English winter, and yet in a few days we were toiling, sweating, and suffering in an awful, deadly climate, in a swampy bush as gloomy as night, full of pestilential smells, and with all sorts of nasty, dangerous animals and insects about. The animals did not trouble us, though, for by day our numbers scared them, and by night our watch fires kept them at a distance.

But it was not the wild beasts or the snakes we cared about so much as the Ashantis themselves. They were the hardest nuts to crack, for they had a stealthy way of hanging about in the dense vegetation, and firing at us and potting us, or suddenly falling on stragglers, and braining or knifing them before they could defend themselves or call for help.

A sergeant I knew went into the bush, and that was the last I ever saw of him. He vanished, and I should think some prowling Ashantis clubbed him before he knew what was happening. Just imagine yourself in a region where you had to cut your way through dense vegetation, in a steamy heat, struggling in inky slime, and expecting every moment that a club would crack your head, or a slug or a charge of buckshot hit or riddle you, and you will understand what our marching through Ashanti to Coomassie meant.

There were native troops with us – Fantis and Haussas; and some of them were not much good, though others did splendidly.

From the thunderous surf of the Gold Coast we forged ahead through the dismal jungle – the 23rd, the 42nd – the Royal Welsh Fusiliers and the Black Watch, to give the good old numbered regiments the names they have now – and the Rifle Brigade. We had guns, light, handy field-pieces, which could be man-handled by natives from one place to another, and rockets.

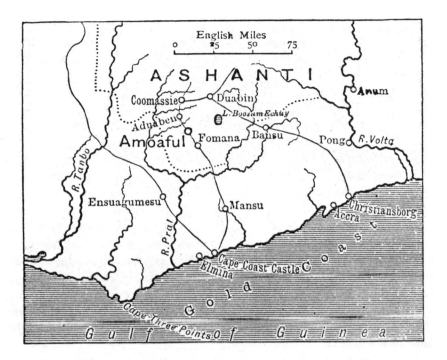

We had our own Snider rifles, too, and we had Sir Garnet and two other officers who became very famous, one as Sir Redvers Buller and the other as Sir Evelyn Wood.

With such a leader as Sir Garnet, you could not go wrong, even in such a forsaken place as Ashanti. Like him, I was an old Crimean soldier; so was Colonel Wood, as he was then, and Captain Macdonald, who was one of the staff of Lord Raglan, Commander-in-Chief in the Crimea. Lord Raglan was an old Waterloo officer, so we almost had a sort of link with Wellington and Napoleon with us in the Gold Coast swamp.

Of course, you know that the Rifle Brigade – the old 95th – has more battle-honours than any other regiment in the Army, except the King's Royal Rifle Corps – the 60th Rifles – and that is saying a good deal. I am always proud to know that I helped to win the honour of 'Ashanti' for the Rifle Brigade.

There were three companies of us, and mine was D. Company, commanded by Captain Macdonald. We had our own company bugle-calls, and each company would respond only to its special call. We fitted words to each, our own being: 'Dirty, Dirty Number Four.' But the same word 'dirty' would have applied to A., B., or C. Company just as well as to D., for in that pestilential swamp and jungle everybody, officer and man, was as dirty as dirty could be.

There was damp enough of sorts – slimy, inky, spongy undergrowth, and water of a kind, in the narrow River Prah; but there were no means of keeping clean and fit as we understand these things at home. Our drinking-water was carried with us by natives, and when we took it we drank it through a purifying device – tubes of charcoal which acted as filters. There were pools of water everywhere, but they were foul, stagnant patches, covered with rotting vegetation and the leaves of trees. The only safe thing to do with them was to give them a wide berth and march on.

The chief event of the march was the battle of Amoaful, and I am going to tell you about it, because the affair is, I think, something uncommon in the annals of war, and there are not many left of those of us who fought in it nearly forty years ago.

There was no highway to march on, no ordinary road to use, not even honest ploughed fields or meadows to cross, but just the thick jungle to pierce. We had to make headway as people might force a passage through a dense plantation, with hardly air enough to breathe, in a suffocating atmosphere and constant twilight. There was no chance of even seeing your enemy, and the first sign of his presence was the crack of his old gas-pipes, or the thud of the slugs and buckshot, which he sent into you, or, worse still, his knife or knob-kerrie.

It was a merciful thing for us that the Ashantis had not better arms and proper bullets, instead of slugs and buckshot. If they had had our own guns and rifles, for instance, and had known how to use them, I don't suppose that anyone would have been left to tell the story of the march through swamp and jungle to Coomassie. Lots of us felt the thud and 'winding' of a slug; but it often did no more harm than that. If a rifle bullet had come in place of a slug, it would have done more than just make a bruise, or knock the breath out of a fellow's chest.

The New Year had come in, and the last day of the month of January was with us. We were all in the swampy bush, forging slowly ahead towards Coomassie, and in the morning we heard a shot or two from the bush around us, the cracks being mingled with battle cries and the racket of war drums. We knew that the Ashanti warriors were out to meet us, and that a tough day was in front of us.

I think that fight was one of the queerest and hardest that any British troops have taken part in, because we were constantly peppered and harassed by an enemy that we could not see. We went out in skirmishing order, and made our way ahead as best we could; but our only guide was the flash of fire from the bushes, or the snap of an old firearm.

It was a confused sort of fight – sometimes the skirmishers going ahead and blazing away, then the black men hurrying up with the guns and booming into the bush. These weapons did a lot of mischief, and scattered the

Ashantis; but the things that were most useful and terrifying were the rockets. Nothing has more effect on savages, who believe in all sorts of strange spirits and gods, than an uncanny row, and the rockets gave them all the noise and spectacle they wanted.

They would rush off howling after an explosion, thinking, maybe, some fetish worse than their own was after them. The 23rd, the 42nd, and the Rifle Brigade, with the black troops, had a stiff, hot stifling time in that dense jungle, and one of the strangest sounds ever heard in West Africa was the skirl of the pipes as the Highlanders charged into the bush and went for the enemy who could hardly be seen.

Amoaful was a hard, long fight, and cost us dear, for when it was over we had lost nearly two hundred in dead and wounded. The dead were buried where they fell – and quickly, too, and the wounded were put in litters and carried by the bearers. The doctors did all they could, but there was many a wounded man who never got away from the region of the slimy swamp and gloomy jungle.

No soldier can die a nobler death than on the battle-field, and none can have a greater honour than that which was paid, by the Commander-in-Chief. A very fine young officer named Eyre was killed by a bullet, and even while the battle was raging Sir Garnet himself helped to bury the body in the shallow grave which was hurriedly dug. It is not often you hear of an incident like that, even in war – of a soldier being buried actually while a fight is going on. After most actions there is always a truce for the burial of the dead; but you cannot make truce with an enemy like the Ashantis, who don't understand the meaning of civilisation.

This was only one of the many exciting incidents that occurred during the Ashanti campaign. Soon after we began our march, a Haussa non-commissioned officer was badly wounded.

Now, a British officer is a British officer all the world over, regardless of rank. He may be a peer or a commoner, but that makes no difference to his pluck. If he sees a man in danger he goes to help him, and Major William Sartorious saw the black sergeant in peril. He rushed out and saved him, in spite of a deadly fire, and they gave him the V.C. for it. Not long afterwards Lieutenant Lord Gifford got the Cross for doing all sorts of brave things that helped Sir Garnet wonderfully; and another officer, Lieutenant Bell, received the decoration also.

A fourth Cross was won by a lance-sergeant of the 42nd, for bravery at Amoaful, the chief fight on the advance to Coomassie. He was badly wounded, but during the whole of a long and awful day he led his handful of men through the bush. His name was Sam McGaw. He died three or four years later – suddenly, I think, from sunstroke.

Five days of almost incessant fighting, crowned by the victory of Amoaful and other triumphs, and we reached Coomassie, about a hundred and fifty miles from the Gold Coast, just before dark. By that time we were utterly weary; but above all things we were almost mad with thirst and rushed towards the women who came to meet us carrying immense gourds or earthenware pots filled with fresh water. Poor souls! I daresay they came out of their squalid houses in fear and trembling, expecting to be killed, but they soon found out that that was not the reason why the British soldier had been led through the bush to King Koffee's terrible capital.

Coomassie stood on a sort of hill, and was the place where the palace of the king was built, and things were done which were past belief in their barbarity and horror. When that night was over we had a chance of looking round the place, and no words can tell the horrors we saw on every hand. Bad as the swamp had been on the march it seemed to be worse in Coomassie. It surrounded the awful place – a place of human slaughter-houses.

The killing was done wholesale. I believe that at one time as many as two thousand victims were offered up. Great numbers of them were executed on a thing called the sacred stool, a kind of butcher's block, to all sorts of hideous, drunken cries and mad music, one of the principal instruments being what they called the death-drum, or execution-drum.

When the Ashantis knew that we were sure to get to the capital, they offered up, I fancy, some special sacrifices to their gods or fetish, because the sacred stool was sodden with fresh blood, and the death-drum – an immense affair about five feet in diameter – was dreadfully decorated. This drum looked exactly like a large ale cask, or a big tub standing on end. It seemed to me that the way the thing was handled was to leave it standing and then thump on the top and make a horrible commotion while the king's executioner plied his enormous decorated sword and chopped heads off almost as fast as you could count. In the wretched place they called the king's palace there was a fetish-corner, a kind of altar for sacrifices, with all sorts of skins and objects nailed up as charms against evil spirits. The place was almost like a blacksmith's smithy, the pile of heads and bones and oddments taking the place of the fire.

We could not move in that city of dreadful death without coming across signs of human sacrifices and suffering.

I am not dwelling on these things because their remembrance is a pleasure, but to show what wrong things we had to put right. When we went out to Ashanti there were so many kind-hearted folk who had such a lot of unnecessary pity for the poor heathen we were going to fight. Poor heathen, indeed! What about his cruelty towards those poorer than himself and his wholesale massacre of them!

It was a glad sight indeed when the good old Union Jack was run up a long staff, and fluttered out in the death-laden air. There was a symbol of freedom and fair dealing for you – waving over the horrid sacred stool and the awful drum that had beaten so many death knells. The eyes of some of the well-meaning people at home would have opened wide enough if they could have seen what it meant to the slaves and the down-trodden wretches of Ashanti to have British soldiers in the place and the Union Jack floating from the tall pole.

But there was a brighter side to our entrance to Coomassie – where our stay was astonishingly short, for we were no sooner in and had settled our affairs than we were out again, the General fearing for his troops in such a reeking atmosphere.

We had heard wondrous tales about the gold and riches of the capital, and some of the stories were true. It was amazing to see how lavishly gold was used in Coomassie. The Ashantis used it just as we use cheap metal at home. I saw door-knobs of solid gold – fancy putting your hand on a thing like that! And I saw all sorts of common cooking articles made of gold, too – a wonderful rich-coloured gold with a red tinge in it, not like the yellow metal we see in sovereigns.

But the Ashanti gold was the pure thing, just as it was got from the beds of the rivers, and had no alloy to make it harder and wear better. More than once, when we were on the march, crossing rivers, I scooped up the sand and saw yellow particles of gold in it. That was the way, I suppose, the Ashantis got some of theirs; then melted the metal and made it into knobs and pans and such-like articles.

It was no good trying to carry any of the gold with us from the river beds because apparatus was needed to extract and purify it – and when you are on the march like that, always having to be ready for a fight, you don't want to be burdened with anything that isn't eatable.

There was, as there always is, a lot of wild talk about the big sums of money made from booty; but, as a matter of fact, the private soldiers got very little. My own share of prize money came to £2 2s. 6d., and in addition to that I got £8 10s. 8½d. as 'hardlayin' money – just over ten guineas in all. Of course, it seemed a fair amount to an ordinary soldier, especially one of the old Crimean school like myself; but it was little enough when you remember the sort of country we were fighting in and the kind of enemy we had to fight.

Oh, yes! Some of us had gold with us when we were marching from Coomassie. There were gold ornaments and rich embroideries piled up in what you would call the chief street of the place, because Sir Garnet was setting fire to the palace and the town generally, as part of the king's punishment.

King Koffee had bolted to a place some miles off, and I think that a good many of his wives – he had more than three thousand of them, they say –

had gone with him. A lesson had to be taught him, and this destruction was Sir Garnet's way of teaching it.

The gold and silver ornaments were collected before the buildings were set on fire, and strict orders were given that no soldier was to help himself to loot. It was given out that a strict search would be made. There was to be prize money at the proper time, and so there was, but very little. It needs something more than frail human beings, however, to obey orders at a time like that, and I saw men wrench precious door-knobs off.

I did not go quite so far as that, but I managed to get a few little articles, such as bracelets and rings – beautiful, pure gold – and bring them away with me. I have not one of them left; I parted with them all long ago.

There were other men, though, who came away with good hauls of precious articles, because, after all, no search was made when we were clear of Coomassie. The great thing to do was to get out of the awful, death-dealing, pestilential region and back to the good air of the sea and the open sky.

The capture and looting of the Asante capital enabled Wolseley to claim that the expedition was a great success, and certainly he had succeeded in his main objective of defeating the Asante in open battle. Yet in truth it was impossible to maintain an army of European troops in such an exposed and unhealthy position as Kumase, and Wolseley's hurried retreat enabled the Asantehene to emerge from the forest, and revive his administration.

Like many colonial expeditions before and after, it was a curious type of victory; one which salvaged Imperial honour, but had little political impact. By the end of the century, British troops were compelled to march once more down the road to Kumase, and impose British authority by force.

4. Egypt and the Sudan

Throughout the 1880s and '90s, the British army was heavily involved in one of the most inhospitable terrains in the world – the deserts of southern Egypt and the Sudan.

Typically, it was British concern for the wider safety of India which led to the Egyptian entanglement. Until the 1860s, the principal maritime route to India lay around the southern tip of Africa – a fact which, incidentally, also shaped British involvement at the Cape of Good Hope. In November 1869, however, the Suez Canal was opened, shortening the sea-route to India by several weeks. Secure access to the canal became an immediate British concern, and led to Benjamin Disraeli's audacious financial coup in 1875, in which he secretly bought out the bankrupt Khedive of Egypt's shares in the canal, securing British interests, and forestalling the French.

With interests in the canal, however, inevitably came involvement with the Egyptian government. Nominally run by the Ottoman empire, the Egyptian government was deeply unpopular with native Egyptians, and the Khedive's growing dependence on European finance did not improve matters. This resentment soon crystallised around the army, where a charismatic Egyptian colonel, Ahmad 'Urabi, emerged as the leader of a protest movement. 'Urabi was an eloquent speaker, who damned not only the incumbent Khedive, Tawfiq, but the European powers who appeared to be propping him up. Rioting broke out in the streets of Alexandria, and a purely internal protest soon turned into a demonstration against westerners. Worried that this might affect British access to the canal, the British government decided unilaterally to adopt a strong line. On 11 July 1882, a British fleet bombarded Alexandria.

The bombardment of Alexandria provoked a direct conflict with 'Urabi and his supporters. 'Urabi called out the Egyptian army, and moved out of Alexandria, establishing a base on the road to Cairo. Sir Garnet Wolseley was given command of an expedition to defeat 'Urabi, and return Egypt to the control of the compliant Tawfiq. Troops were despatched from both Britain and Egypt, and with typical precision, Wolseley laid a trail of false information as to his plans. A series of feints from Alexandria convinced 'Urabi that the British intended to advance directly up the Nile to Cairo. In fact, however, Wolseley's British contingent landed at Port Said, and the northern end of the Suez Canal, and his Indian contingent at Suez, at the southern end. Before 'Urabi realised what was happening, the two forces had met mid-way along the canal, and turned inland, following the course of the Sweetwater Canal towards the Nile. 'Urabi attempted to muster to stop them, but was defeated in a sharp action at Kassassin on 6 September 1882. From there, Wolseley advanced on 'Urabi's main position at the far end of the Sweetwater Canal, at Tel-el-Kebir. Private Robert Tutt of the Royal Marine Light Infantry recalled the peculiarities of desert fighting, and the desperate nature of the climactic battle of the campaign.

The Desert Battle of Tel-el-Kebir

A moonless night of dense Egyptian darkness. Overhead the black sky, pitted with faint stars; underfoot the sand of the desert; softly crunching over it 14,000 British soldiers, steady and silent, to fall with the bayonet on 26,000 sleeping, unsuspecting Egyptians in their intrenched camp.

There, in a few words, you have a picture of the first act of the swiftly played, decisive drama of Tel-el-Kebir.

We were all pretty well used to fighting and enduring. For myself I had been at Mahuta and Kassassin with the Royal Marine Light Infantry, and had got on terms of more than welcome intimacy with bad food, poisoned water, myriads of flies, and the ravages of dysentery, to say nothing of that sweltering, fatal weather which the tourist up the Nile knows only by repute. Let him be thankful that he can allow other people to make its acquaintance for him.

Kassassin was a stiff, hard struggle on August 28th, 1882, far and away a more strenuous battle, reckoned as a battle pure and simple, than Tel-el-Kebir, because it lasted many hours, while the latter was over in fifteen or twenty minutes. We were quietly at breakfast when shells began to fall in amongst us from the Egyptian garrison at Kassassin. We left our meal and sprang to arms, and during the whole of that hot, blazing day we were rushing here, there, and everywhere, fighting and suffering torture from thirst.

When the day ended, the enemy, who had attacked us, abandoned Kassassin and hurried off to fortify himself at Tel-el-Kebir, a very few miles away. The cavalry did splendidly, and there are those who say that if the action had been properly followed up the Egyptians would have been destroyed completely there and then. But, of course, there are always so many people who are wonderfully wise when a thing is over.

Arabi had had sixteen days to do his work in, and thousands of first-rate men to do it, and he had carried out his plans with astonishing completeness. So had our own Commander-in-Chief, Sir Garnet Wolseley. It seemed like drawing up a time-table, and carrying it out as if it had been a programme. At such a time, said Sir Garnet, such a thing was to be done – and at such a time it was finished. That is the way of the men who have made Egypt. He had some fine soldiers with him, and fine sailors. There was an almost unknown soldier, an Engineer, who knew his business amazingly well, and I doubt not, was even then looking far ahead and seeing strange things with those cold, calculating eyes of his. That was the present Lord Kitchener.

Everybody believed in the star of Sir Garnet's good fortune, and the desert battle justified our faith. He had prepared his plans, and we were now to put them into execution in a thrilling fashion.

You can picture the scene without much difficulty. Take a vast stretch of hard gravel and sand – the desert; put an army of twenty-six thousand men on it, with guns, horses, camels, mules, stores, ammunition, and the hundred and one odd things that are needed for soldiers in the field; inclose that army in intrenchments of low walls made of mud, sand, and gravel, and bound together by wattles – an intrenched camp, with a front face four miles long and a flanking face of two miles. At intervals in the wall, which was about four feet high, put bastions, mounting guns, and in front of these place deep trenches. Dispose the attackers in two divisions of two brigades each, with forty-two guns and cavalry, and arrange them in two horns of a crescent, with orders to advance and close in on the camp and take it.

That was what the Commander-in-Chief directed us to do.

That was what we did.

Our business was to march straight across the desert for something like five miles, and not to fire a shot until we reached the enemy's works. We were to advance in two enormous lines, two deep, so that when we got to the intrenchments there should be no crowding of men at certain points. We needed plenty of elbow-room, and with such a formation this was possible, because of the great extent of the wall which rose from the desert, and over which we had to fight and climb to reach the camp.

There could be no possibility of confusing or misunderstanding our orders, because only two were to be given. The first, which was to be by word of mouth, and in whispers, was to fix bayonets, which would be just before we reached the trenches, and the other was to be a signal on the bugle to storm.

To me, as a young marine, the work was just as exciting and attractive as it could be. It was a change from ship life – and there was always the ambition among the Marines to do things rather better than anybody else. The spirit of rivalry counted for a good deal, seeing that every branch of the Navy and Army was represented, and that the Indian native forces had sent contingents. Fine fellows they were, too, especially the mounted troops, like the Bengal Lancers. The Marine Light Infantry, my own corps – I belonged to the Portsmouth Division – formed part of General Graham's brigade, which was a splendid body of picked cavalry, artillery, and infantry. There was no mistaking the Marines, for we were the only infantry in blue serge, all the other infantry wearing red – the colour associated with all the heaviest fighting in the British Army. That was before the days of khaki.

On the evening of the 12th we made completely ready at Kassassin for our desert march and battle. We were to leave behind the 50th West Kent Regiment to guard the lock – hard luck for them, in a way, as it proved, because they are the only corps that did not get the bar for Tel-el-Kebir. Each of us had a hundred rounds of ammunition and two days' rations, and the regimental transports had two more days' rations and thirty extra rounds per man. Our water-bottles were filled with cold tea, which some of us thought was poor stuff to fight on. I think so still.

We struck the tents where we had been camping, just as quietly and orderly as if we had been changing stations and were making ready to pitch them somewhere else. There was, however, that excitement which is always present when an army is getting ready for battle. It was particularly notice-able in this case, because many of the troops were quite young fellows, and not a few of the officers were mere lads. They were all eager to start and get to close quarters with the Egyptians. We did not by any means expect a walk over, because the enemy had shown that he could make a very stub-born stand even against white troops.

Our last meal before the battle was eaten just as the swift darkness fell. I am sure that the spirits of not a few sank with the sun, because the solemn thought came that for some of us the sun had set for ever.

The night was fully with us, and everything was still and peaceful when we started on our stealthy march, high-strung and excited, knowing, even the rawest of us, that it would not be easy to keep ourselves under that perfect control which was essential for the success of the undertaking. You cannot enter on a task which makes a heavier call on your courage than such a march as this. Such vast results depend on such trifles – and who can tell what trifle in the darkness and the desert may bring about an army's doom?

We advanced a little way across the sand and gravel, finding it a desper-ate and trying business to keep in proper touch with each other and to main-tain our formation. There was bound to be straggling to some extent, yet it is astonishing, considering the intense darkness and the excessive strain on everybody, that the army kept together as well as it did.

We had not gone far before a halt was ordered and we piled arms. There was still plenty of time before us, and it would be madness to hurl an exhausted army against Arabi's strong intrenchments.

At half-past one o'clock in the morning we were on the march again, and even the low, nervous laughs and subdued talk died away as we got nearer and nearer to the sleeping camp. When we first started there was something like a little freedom in the ranks, but this was soon rigidly suppressed, and we were forbidden to make a sound.

The officers of the Intelligence Department rode ahead, guiding us by compass, which, on such a dark night, was the only way, and it was a very difficult thing indeed to keep straight for the intrenchments.

Cannot you picture the terrific strain on those pilots, who knew how easily they could take 14,000 men several miles away from the spot which it was necessary to reach, and thus utterly destroy our leader's plans, prepared with so much anxious care?

Occasionally a short halt was made, so that the regiments could keep in proper touch with each other and maintain the formation of the advance.

To the north were the Cavalry and Horse Artillery; on the right was my own brigade – Graham's – with the Guards to support us; on the left was the Royal Artillery, and between it and the fresh water canal to the south was the Highland Brigade; in a truck on the railway, which ran past the camp parallel with the canal, was the Naval Brigade with a forty-pounder; and to the south of the canal was the Indian Brigade of Cavalry.

You will understand from this short description how minute and complete were our Chief's preparations. He was staking everything on a surprise attack with the bayonet – a swoop in the night on a vast, sleeping camp, a rousing and a routing, and then a crowning with the cavalry and artillery of the work which the infantry had begun.

There was nothing in the way of speech but hoarse, excited whispering in that overpowering darkness. Sometimes it would be a careless, jerky remark, accompanied by a snappy little laugh of nervousness – the kind of noise that people often make when they are afraid and ashamed to show their terror. At other times it would be a muttered order to the men to keep their mouths shut and preserve silence in the ranks. You could hear men talking in low tones to themselves, too, and sending, God knows, many a fond message to those distant homes which they might never see again.

You may try to laugh and jest as you will, but you can never overcome the deep solemnity of a silent desert march like that. You are awed into dumbness, and your very body seems to shrink into quietness. You are afraid to breathe, for fear you should raise some mysterious alarm which would let loose every muzzle that you know is facing you, ready to blaze, and blast and sweep you off the face of the desert.

The tension was terrible and unbearable – like that which overpowers many people during a dangerous thunderstorm, when, fascinated, they gaze at the black sky, watching for the vivid flash and waiting breathlessly for the thunder. So were we – piercing the darkness ahead, expecting every second to see the red bursts of light and to hear the booming of the guns.

The strain was almost at breaking point when an agitated voice whispered in my ear. We were marching on, crunching softly into the desert sand, and, in spite of all our care, tumbling into and colliding with each other.

'Bill!' I heard the voice whisper hoarsely.

'Hello!' I whispered back. 'What do you want?'

It was my front-rank man who had turned suddenly in the darkness to address me.

'Bill,' he answered hurriedly, 'do you mind changing places with me? I've come over a bit queer.' He had been suffering from dysentery for some time.

Now, as you know, it is against all orders to do a thing like that, especially when you are marching into action, and are almost on the enemy; but in battle many a place is changed, either by accident or design, and nobody is much the worse for it.

Well, I was young and dare-devil, and did not care a straw whether I was at the mouth of a gun or the breech, so I whispered back:

'All right, mate, I'll swop; but front or rear rank won't keep you from being shot, if it's your luck to get a bullet.'

It was all done in a second or two. I just edged to the right and passed ahead into his place, and he slipped into mine, and for the time I thought no more about it.

Everything that a gallant general and brave, far-seeing officers had it in their power to do had been accomplished, so that our plan should be carried out. It seemed, indeed, as if we should be able to rush in with the bayonet and literally throw the enemy out of his intrenchments before he could recover from his amazement and confusion.

The crisis of our advance had come – the whispered orders to fix bayonets, and the last words of encouragement and exhortation had been uttered.

Then came one of the unexpected happenings of war.

The silence was broken by the crack of a single rifle in the intrenchments – a startling signal in the night, which showed that our presence was known. Concealment was useless now, and there was no need to sound the bugles for the storm.

With appalling suddenness the guns of the intrenchments crashed upon us, and there was a blaze of rifle fire in the darkness which showed up the enemy's defences, and revealed the figures of some of the artillerymen and infantry.

Everything was in favour of the Egyptians, and against ourselves. They were sheltered, and had only bullets and bayonets to reckon with; we were in the open desert, with the fire of the guns themselves to meet, and afterwards rifle and steel to overcome.

If the guns had been well aimed and served, if the rifle-fire had been properly directed and well maintained, few, if any, of the British troops could have reached the intrenchments. They would have been mown down by regiments, they would have melted as they advanced across the desert, for when we were discovered we were still about three hundred yards from the earthworks – and that space, short though it was, was enough for practical annihilation. But the guns had too much elevation, and the result was that when, in panic, they were fired at us, their shot and shell went overhead instead of through our ranks. Need I dwell on the havoc which even a single missile could have wrought, with nothing to stop its point-blank force but human bodies – or hint at the destruction which a discharge of grapeshot could have done? Very recently in the campaign one of our own shells had destroyed a dozen men in a cluster, and in another case nearly thirty dead were found in a heap, killed by gun-fire.

Officers and men amongst us were killed and wounded instantly, and were lying dead or dying on the sand which but a moment earlier they had been treading in the vigour of a splendid health. The gloomy fears of some at least had been fulfilled, and for them the sun would rise no more.

The perfect silence of the advance had been followed by the roar and turmoil of a fierce and bloodily contested action. Orders which had been whispered before were shouted now, and there was the loud, steely rattle of bayonets which were being plucked from their scabbards and fixed on to the rifles – the old three-cornered bayonets, and the fine Martinis which all fighting men loved and understood so well.

It was a furious rush towards the wall of fire across the desert, and a mad spring at the intrenchments. These were not much to speak of – earthworks about four feet deep and six feet wide. These were the trenches proper, which we had to pass; then there was a breastwork on the other side, which had been formed of the dirt and sand from the hollows of the intrenchments.

The dawn in Egypt seems to come as quickly as the daylight enters when you draw your blind at home. It is dark, then the sky flushes in the East, and before you can understand things, day is with you.

When we reached the trenches the blackness was vanishing, and the day itself gave us the fighting light which for a few minutes had been afforded by the gun-bursts and the rifle-spits.

I dashed along with my comrades, running and cheering, in a whirl of excitement and frenzy. Before I could realise what was happening, I was at the intrenchments, making ready to swarm up the low defence and get in amongst the Egyptians.

I looked up, and saw against the sky a white-clad Egyptian with a short, brass-hilted sword. He must have been a bugler, for he had a bugle hanging from his shoulder. He was bending down, with the weapon ready for a cut or thrust. He was about four feet above me, fighting downward, and slashing at me savagely.

I drove my bayonet swiftly upward, and the weapon went through his chest. He tumbled down upon me as I drew it out, and we rolled to the ground together. I was on my feet instantly, twisted him over to the right, drew my bayonet out, and scrambled as hard as I could to join about a dozen of my comrades. I left the bugler where he fell, and I never knew whether he lived or died.

I do not suppose that anybody who was in that amazingly short and effective fight could give you a clear and connected idea of what really took place. It was all so swift, so bewildering, and yet there was such a clean and splendid sweep of everything. We had not been used to this sort of thing – you remember that at Kassassin we were fighting for many hours on end, and in other actions we had been led to know that the Egyptian stood his ground and made a stiff, long fight for it.

At Tel-el-Kebir, protected as he was by his trenches, with immense supplies of food, stores, and ammunition, and everything in his favour, we believed that he would never turn tail until he had made us pay an awful price for our victory. Yet it was clear to a good many of us, as soon as we had swarmed over the earthworks and got in amongst the defenders, that they would not have much staying-power or stomach for the fight. It was a confused *mêlée*, a desperate jumble of opposing soldiers, and the pitting of cold steel against fire and sword. But, above all things, the Egyptians were demoralised and disheartened by the suddenness of our assault.

The greatest peril of all – the artillery fire – was soon put behind us, and we got to close quarters and hand-to-hand fighting, which was just what most of us were best fitted for and craving to do. After a long and desperate tension you need a special outlet for your energies, and in the intrenchments we got it.

Everybody was now firing wildly and anywhere, and British and Egyptians were mixed up in what seemed like hopeless confusion. But the men on our side never forgot their task, which was to drive the dark men in white clothing out of the trenches and take or destroy as many as they could.

I was fighting near and with a married man named Sindin, who came from my own native place, Hastings. His rifle was loaded, but so far I had not had time to slip a cartridge into my own. I was too busy with the bayonet.

Already the Egyptians were on the run; but many were at bay, and, like all cornered creatures, were dangerous to tackle. A couple were very near Sindin and me, and the four of us were together almost before we quite knew what was happening. My comrade shot one, and I bayoneted the other; then we rushed on and another fell to each of us.

I would like to pause for a moment here to say two things – one in praise of the gymnasium practice at home, and the other in praise of that service which, like a Red Marine, I reckon is the finest in the whole wide world. What would I not give to live my life afloat and ashore over again! It was my gymnasium training at home which stood me in such splendid stead, because I had now to rely entirely on steel, as I found it impossible to load. My breech-block was clogged with sand – choked, I suppose, when I fell into the trench with the Egyptian bugler.

I mention these personal incidents of the battle, not because I glory in them, but to show how savage the carnage was, and how it came about that, in a short space of time, we, who trusted almost entirely to the bayonet, accounted for a large number of the Egyptians. It was wonderful and terrible to see the way in which many of the assailants handled the defenders, and especially some of the Highlanders, who on that famous day distinguished themselves greatly.

The Cameron Highlanders did brilliantly. The regiment claims to have been the first in at the storming, and to have lost the first man in the battle on our side – a private who was killed by a bullet as he reached the top of an earthwork. Certainly Colonel Leith, commanding them, waved his sword and shouted 'Come on, 79th!' and the men broke into double time and cheered as they charged. Their pipe-major, Grant, stirred their blood to boiling point by playing as they sprang forward the rousing strains of 'The March of the Cameron Men,' which is the regimental quickstep of the old 79th.

Before we could grasp what had happened, the first line of the defences was ours; but the worst was not over. There was a harder task to fulfil, and that was to get to the stronger fort which lay behind, and then to rush line after line of shelter trench until the enemy was fairly on the open desert and either captured or destroyed.

It was a time of wild confusion and fury, the ceaseless, savage plying of butt and bayonet, and the driving forth of a dispirited and panic-stricken horde. There was a hideous clamour – the shouts of the combatants, the rattle of musketry, the clash of steel, the crash of artillery, the cries of the wounded, and the despairing screams of the dying masses. And above all there arose that sound which you can never mistake – the skirl of pipes, for as soon as the Highlanders were in the trenches and on the tops, their bagpipes rose in wild strains and fired the kilted troops to great achievements.

Tel-el-Kebir was, like Inkerman, a soldiers' battle, and an infantryman's at that. When we had done our work with the bayonet the rest was left to the cavalry and artillery. It was marvellous to see the way in which the British gunners rushed their weapons over obstacles and swept the flying masses down, and terrible to watch the British and Indian cavalry pursuing and destroying the fugitives. There was no escape for them, and recognising this they surrendered and were made prisoners – and it was pleasanter work to take their bodies than their lives.

Cairo had been threatened, and it was feared that the beaten enemy, or at least that part of him which escaped from Tel-el-Kebir, might hurry on and take his revenge on a practically defenceless city. If he had any such hope or scheme both were shattered by the swiftness of the British cavalry movements. General Sir Drury Lowe, after finishing his work on and around the battlefield itself, took his brigade straight across the desert to Cairo, never stopping until he reached the city, fifty miles away, and insuring its safety. This is justly reckoned one of the finest cavalry performances on record. We ourselves gradually went to Cairo, where Arabi was a prisoner.

When the battle itself was over there was a rush to the canal to drink, and to slake that thirst which was the most dreadful part of the whole campaign. The water was thick and dark – filthy, in fact, and we knew it, but a desert thirst is splendid training for overcoming squeamishness.

We drank our fill, and then looked at the canal. Some of us instantly wished we had left that action unfulfilled, for the water, just a little higher up, was choked with the carcases of dead animals and the corpses of men.

When I returned to the battlefield I set to work to find out how my comrades had fared.

I made a strange discovery, and one that shows how curious is the luck of war.

The man with whom I had exchanged places – the front-rank man – had been shot in the left arm as he twisted it round to hold the scabbard while he drew his bayonet. The bullet struck him in such a way that the arm never set properly – it was always twisted and awry, just as if he were constantly holding his scabbard. He got a wound pension, so, you see, that exchange of places in the darkness on the desert was a nice bit of luck for him.

Tel-el-Kebir broke the back of Egyptian resistance. 'Urabi surrendered, and British troops entered Cairo in triumph. Tawfiq's authority was restored, and the Egyptian army reorganised under British officers. Control of Egypt effectively passed to the British.

While this secured the future of the Suez Canal for the British, however, it brought with it other problems. Even as the British took over, the first stirrings of revolt were beginning in the southern Egyptian province of the Sudan.

The Sudan is a vast inhospitable tract of desert and semi-desert. Any form of communication and administration was almost entirely dependent on the life-line of the Nile, but the Egypt of the Khedives lacked the resources to govern the Sudan efficiently. Egyptian rule was resented as foreign – Turkish – corrupt, and inefficient.

The rising, when it came, crystallised about the person of a mystic from the

Dongola province, in northern Sudan, Mohammed Ahmad ibn al-Sayyid Abdullah. Mohammed Ahmad's early life was characterised by a scholarly devotion to Islam, and in 1881 he proclaimed himself *al-Mahdi*, 'the chosen one', a prophet whose coming was foretold in some Islamic sects. The Mahdi's initial supporters were from the poorest sector of Arab society, for whom the prospect of paradise had an immediate appeal, but the movement spread rapidly, offering as it did fundamentalist religious certainty, and nationalist rejection of foreign influence. The Mahdi, guided by a divine vision, strove to drive the Egyptians out of the Sudan, and to that end proclaimed a *jihad*, the Islamic holy war. His first successes were so spectacular that his followers readily saw the hand of God in them.

In January 1883 the Mahdists were strong enough to storm El Obeid, the capital of Kordofan province. The Egyptian army sent a strong force against them, under the command of a British officer, General William Hicks. The Mahdi met Hicks at Shaykan in the desert wastes in November 1883, and utterly destroyed him. Encouraged by his success, new followers declared themselves, particularly among the Beja peoples in the Red Sea littoral.

The Mahdi's rise caused the British government some concern, but the Gladstone administration was reluctant to commit British troops to what it regarded as a purely Egyptian affair. Instead, it appointed a special representative to travel to the Sudanese capital at Khartoum, and supervise the evacuation of Egyptian officials. The representative was Colonel Charles 'Chinese' Gordon, RE, who had already earned a reputation for determination and resourcefulness. Yet Gordon was a complex character, driven by a strong faith, and an acute sense of conscience. Once in Khartoum, he refused to abandon the Sudan to the Mahdi, and bombarded London with alternative suggestions. In March 1885 the Mahdi advanced on Khartoum, and set up camp at Omdurman, across the Nile. Almost symbolically, the two rival administrations had moved into conflict, and Mahdist troops began to lay siege to Sudan.

In London, the British government was exasperated by Gordon's attitude, and refused to send troops to his assistance. Yet Gordon's story was taken up by the British press, and he became a public hero, the epitome of British pluck and defiance, a lonely figure standing resolutely on his palace roof, scouring the desert through his spy-glass for signs of relief. Reluctantly, in August 1884, parliament finally granted the funds necessary to assemble an expedition for Gordon's relief.

Command was given to Lord Wolseley, the victor of Tel-el-Kebir, then at the height of his reputation. Yet the task ahead of him was daunting enough. Firstly, Wolseley had to assemble his forces on the Sudanese border, at the furthest limit of the creaking Egyptian infrastructure. Then he faced a march across several hundred miles of extremely difficult terrain, presumably in the face of Mahdist opposition, while his enemy would no doubt try to cheat him of his prize by overrunning Khartoum. In the event, Wolseley decided to transport his entire command up the Nile in a flotilla of small boats as far as it was practicable. This proved a slow business, and by January Wolseley had only reached Korti, two hundred miles from Khartoum. Worried that Gordon might not hold out, Wolseley despatched a flying column under Brigadier-General Stewart to strike out across the Bayuda desert – a more direct route.

Stewart's advance followed a line of wells across the desert. His men were acutely aware that the fate of a national hero rested in their hands, while the Mahdists were equally determined to cheat them of success. Private William Burge of the Guards Camel Corps told the story of the desperate fighting which ensued – and of the heartbreak which awaited their arrival at Khartoum.

The Broken Square at Abu Klea

I was jogged and jolted on a camel's hump across the Bayuda Desert, by the solemn waters of the Nile, for something like two hundred miles. I made the return journey on a stretcher carried by natives, with my right foot and part of the ankle missing. I had done my share of marching and fighting, for the fuzzi-wuzzies had put me beyond the power of doing either for a long time. I can laugh at the artificial substitute now; but nearly a quarter of a century makes a vast difference to a man's point of view. The loss of the foot was a terrible thing at the time; but now, when I recall the battle of Abu Klea, I dwell more on its amazing brevity and fierceness, and the astounding daring of the Arabs, than on my own loss or suffering.

It is so strange to think of the black children of the desert, with only spears and rifles as their weapons, having the audacity, to say nothing of the pluck, to sweep across a vast plain of sand in the broad light of day, and hurl themselves against a British square so furiously that some of them actually got inside and planted their banners and shouted their prayers of victory. But they did not get out again.

The Guardsman on active service is very different from the Guardsman at home, and he is very wonderful indeed when you stick him on the hump of a camel, which is the most awkward and ill-conditioned beast you can tackle. Ride him once and you will never forget it; be bitten by him, and you will give his mouth a wide berth for ever.

I had left my bearskin and smart tunic and trousers far behind in England, and I was in the land of history, as I suppose it is, wearing a thin red serge jacket, brown riding-breeches with putties, and a helmet and pugaree which had been white; but I had dyed them brown with the help of mud and boiled bark stripped from trees. I was just about six feet high in those days, and, like the rest of the two hundred big fellows who were in the Guards Camel Regiment, looked an odd spectacle when perched in the saddle of a clumsy camel that was crossing the desert, and showed a wicked inclination to steer any way on earth except the right one.

There was the Heavy Camel Regiment, the Light Camel Regiment, and the Guards Camel Regiment. There were some Marines with the Guards, and they made a very fine mixture. The riding was rough and hard, but the clothing itself was not oppressive. The one thing that seemed to grow in weight and tightness – to grow in everything except grace – was the ammunition bandolier. The belt became a positive vice around your chest and shoulder in the course of a long, hot march – and all the desert marches were that.

Arab guides and cavalry scouts headed the desert column which marched from Korti. They were commanded by a remarkable British officer, who could so cunningly disguise himself that it was impossible to tell whether he was a native or an Englishman. I often saw him walking about, and believed him to be a real son of the desert. It was Major Kitchener, now Lord Kitchener of Khartoum. The natives looked upon him as a god, and positively worshipped him.

Two thousand camels stretched out their necks into the hot air of the desert, and their ungainly legs moved swiftly as the thick, padded feet thudded softly in the yielding, glaring sand, and sent up a blinding, suffocating dust. It was a broad, mile-long column, and was perhaps the strangest fighting force that had ever been organised in connection with a British campaign. But no other animal was fit for the work, and it was pitiful to see how even the camels suffered, hardened though they were to desert work.

There were just over two thousand officers and men, under Sir Herbert Stewart. He was to march to Metemmeh, after resting the camels at Gakdul. At Abu Klea a post was to be established, and garrisoned by a few men of the Suffolk Regiment. General Stewart was then to return to Gakdul, and continue sending stores to Metemmeh. From Metemmeh a force, which included Lord Charles Beresford and some sailors, was to push on to Khartoum, to relieve or rescue General Gordon. There was no if or doubt in the matter. The thing was to be accomplished. Sinister reports from Khartoum came in from time to time, but General Gordon himself had sent a messenger saying that he was all right.

In high spirits we began the march; but the laughs and jokes became weaker and weaker as we got into the solitude of the desert, and began to understand the grim meaning of warfare with fanatics. The worst of all privations was the lack of water. We carried as much as we could, and it would have done for us on our meagre allowance of two pints a day; but the skin bags in which it was carried leaked badly, and the precious, priceless fluid was lost on the parching waste.

It was terrible to see the fierce struggling for a drink as soon as a so-called well was reached — a drink of a foul and muddy concoction which would make you ill to look at in ordinary times. I assure you that time after time, when I had filled a kettle with water from a well and boiled it, there was a deposit of at least two inches of mud and sand at the bottom of the vessel. Yet this sweet, sickly liquid was the most acceptable drink that ever man could have.

In the solitude of the desert we came abruptly upon a man and his wife and family tending some animals. The guides and scouts had them to deal with, and the commander of the guides and scouts was not the man to let a captive go. The prisoner was brought in, and proved to be a notorious hill thief, who had intercepted many messages from Khartoum. I daresay that some nations would have given him a short trial, and a quick volley, or good length of rope, but we kept him as a guide, and he remained with the British for many weeks. His wife and family were sent home, though where that was exactly I can't say. The Soudan is not a very homely place.

The camels that fell by the way had to be killed and left. Their bones soon became white on the desert sand; so also did the bodies of the enemies who fell. The vultures were always with us — and they are wonderful scavengers.

I do not know what mysterious force is at work in time of war to tell opponents that a fight is coming on; but that force was in operation in the Soudan. True, we constantly saw little bodies of the Arabs, but it was not supposed that they would have the courage to make a serious attack upon us. We were expecting to carry out our time-table without much serious opposition, and to end our journey at Khartoum.

We might, perhaps, have known better, because we had had previous experience of what a desperate fellow the fuzzi-wuzzi could be in time of intense excitement. He scorned death, encouraged it, in fact, because by way of death he could make sure of Paradise and everlasting joy. Nothing could be happier than to slay an infidel, and gain as a reward the delights of Heaven.

New Year's Day came and went, and we got into the middle of January and the heart of the enemy's country simultaneously. By day sometimes we saw the gleam of spears — cruel weapons, with heads like masons' trowels, which made the most ghastly and fatal wounds; and by night we listened to the hideous howls of the fuzzi-wuzzies and the thumping of their tom-toms. These primitive drums made a doleful and discouraging sound — and your melancholy fits were not helped away when you had the chance of a scorpion bite as a relish to the tune.

We got to Abu Klea at last, burnt brown — some of us as black almost as the Soudanese; caked with the sand of the desert and dirt that could not be removed. There was no washing water, no shaving time even. There was a general belief in a coming fight, and a zareba was made.

We built it swiftly – a mere breastwork of mud, boxes, stones, brush-wood, and branches, anything that came handy. The enemy had only rifles and spears, but they were at least five to one against us, and a rush would be an ugly thing. We all knew that, but I do not think there was one amongst us who anticipated for a single moment the disaster that actually happened; not one of us believed that the square could be broken. We expected that the Martinis and the field-guns and the Gardner would mow the fuzzi-wuzzies down, and make such barriers of their own dead that the advance would be impossible.

The zareba was a snug sort of refuge, and I was hoping that it would be my luck to remain in it; but I and about sixty more men were told off to spend the night in a mud hut to guard the wells. I never spent such an excit-ing night in my life, and may I be spared from ever knowing another like it. We were a little isolated band. The night, as usual, was bitterly cold, especially by comparison with the burning day, and all around us were the hordes of fanatics, thumping their tomtoms and howling, rousing themselves, I suppose, for the attack on the morrow. I dreaded an assault on the hut, but I think the enemy could not have known of our existence, for they might have swept down and annihilated us.

In the morning I went back to the zareba, and the fuzzi-wuzzies made ready to attack us.

The camels were in the centre – a huddled, groaning mass, a prominent target for the enemy's rifles; and the four sides were solid walls of the finest men in the British Navy and Army. At the rear were three guns of the Royal Artillery; in front was a Gardner; thrown out on each side were skirmishers. Mounted infantry was in readiness to pursue the foe when he began to fly.

A square mass of men and camels in the open desert; around it enormous bodies of Arabs, and the two forces on the point of hailing bullets into each other. That was the state of affairs on the morning of the 17th of January, 1885.

I looked around me and saw that the yellow desert and some little hills were alive with white and coloured-robed Arabs, that they were massed in their thousands, and were sweeping on towards the square. It was a tense and terrible strain, to watch them coming – an appallingly solemn sight. The chiefs amongst them were mounted, and many of the Arabs carried ban-ners. The sun shone on the forest of spear-blades, and the quiet air was rent with the frantic shouts of the fanatics and the recital of their prayers.

On they came, ever getting nearer. Still, no shots were fired. Then, when their own small arms rattled out on the desert, our Martinis crackled and our Gardner ripped, while the field-guns of the Artillery flashed and sent their shells into the living, moving mass.

It was terrible yet fascinating to watch the enemy advance. They were led

by men on horseback, and it seemed as if a solid wall of steel were coming
irresistibly towards the square. Our fire was awful and destructive. You could
see the Arabs falling; horses were shot, and flying banners were riddled with
bullets.

'Aim lower, men, aim lower!'

That was the cry which came from our own officers as the fuzzi-wuzzies
swept across the desert. We had been firing high, and many of our bullets
had buried themselves harmlessly in the sand. Outside, some distance from
the square, were camels that had been abandoned by the frightened drivers.
Camels are stubborn beasts, and these had refused to obey their masters.
They fell victims to the Arab spears. The skirmishers had rushed and tumbled in, and now it was a case of the square holding itself together till the
battle was decided, reconciling itself to the fact that for some almost unendurable moments, at any rate, it must be made a target.

The sides of the square literally blazed with fire; the air was thick with
flying bullets and deafening with the cries of man and beast. It was a
furious and incredible turmoil in the desert, and all the more dreadful
because it had come so suddenly. It was like an awful storm bursting on a
calm sea.

There was a sudden cessation of one of the sounds – the Gardner had
jammed, and a weapon which might have saved the square was useless. A
quick-firing gun like that can do such a vast deal of havoc in such a brief
time.

It is hard to tell you exactly what happened – the thing was so sudden,
so overwhelming. It was all begun and finished in a few minutes. That makes
the battle so amazing, so memorable. But I know that I went on firing
steadily, and aiming as low as I could, because I wanted to stop some of the
desperate, murderous fellows who were positively leaping towards us.

I saw the gleaming spears, and I knew what they were capable of doing.
They were worse than bayonets, and almost as bad as shells when once they
got to work. Those trowel-like tips of the long staffs are amongst the things
I most vividly remember of Abu Klea.

Everybody was doing magnificently. The sailors, now that their gun was
jammed – they were working the Gardner, under Lord Charles Beresford –
were joining in the general firing, and making ready to receive the shock of
the charge, which was inevitable.

Somehow, I cannot tell you quite how it was done, the rear rank of the
Guards Camel Regiment was faced about, so that we were firing both in
front and behind us. Indeed, we seemed to be blazing blindly at anything
and everywhere, for the desert appeared to be alive with Arabs, all swoop-
ing on the square.

The weakest point of a square is considered to be the left corner, and it was to this part of the massed British force that the fuzzi-wuzzies rushed. We had mown them down by hundreds, yet they charged unchecked, and within what seemed only a period of seconds they had hurled themselves with furious shouts upon the square.

You know what it is to feel the rush of an ordinary crowd of people against you; how speedily you fall, how difficult it is to get upon your feet again. Picture the power of thousands of Arabs dashing upon you with all the ferocity of their warlike nature, bent on your destruction, and absolutely defying death.

How could the thin line of a square withstand such an attack? How could hundreds of men survive the shock of thousands?

The living avalanche swept on – and the square, at its weakest spot, collapsed. White man and black man mingled in a bloody struggle for the mastery.

Bayonets were plunged out and about – and some of them, to the everlasting shame of the makers, crumpled up like lead. Martinis flashed and cracked, and some of them did splendid service in stopping rushes; but there were others which were as useless as the twisted blades of steel. Ought not the makers themselves to have been out there in the desert, at the butt-end of the rifles, with the soft metal bent and twisted at the muzzles?

Reckless of death, defying shell and bullet, scorning even the wall of steel which pointed towards them, the fuzzi-wuzzies had rushed upon us, and by the very daring of their onslaught had succeeded for the moment.

I cannot even tell you whether I myself shot or bayoneted any man that came against us. I suppose I must have done. I do not see how it was possible to aim at such a mass and miss, or to ply the steel and not strike home; but I did as most of my comrades did – fought blindly, and with the sole object of driving off the hordes of foes who were in and amongst us.

The terrible spears were doing their awful work, the bullets had killed and wounded many officers and men on all sides of the square, and there was heavy loss in the centre, where the screaming camels were huddled.

The seamen by the disabled Gardner were speared as they fought. Lord Charles himself was hurled to the ground, but he sprang to his feet again and slashed about him with his sword. Other officers did the same, and what the leaders did the men copied.

Very near me was a man who was reckoned the finest specimen of a soldier serving in the Army. He was of gigantic stature and corresponding strength, and in that short fight already he had done tremendously well. His powerful right arm swung a great sword about like a toy blade, and many an Arab had fallen before it. They were valiant Arabs, too, for many of them had not been sabred or bayoneted until they were quite through the living wall and inside the square itself. One magnificent chief, indeed, had rushed on horseback into the very centre and planted his banner there, and he was shouting his song of victory when he was slain.

It was at the most critical and dangerous period of the fight that the mounted giant rushed outside the disorganised square and shouted to some of the men to wheel back. That was when the hordes of fuzzi-wuzzies were mixed up with us. Almost as he shouted his horse fell, killed or wounded, and in the twinkling of an eye, as it seemed, the giant himself was no more. One of the terrible spears had been plunged into his neck, and he was dead.

That happened very near me, just under my eyes, and I knew that the Army had lost one of its most brilliant and valiant soldiers, for the fallen warrior was Colonel Burnaby.

For some few moments there was mad, inexpressibly wild confusion. Men and camels and horses were driven upon each other, and made a hideous, struggling mass, smothered in the rising sand of the desert, and almost choked by the smoke and fumes of the powder. Some of the Arabs had thrown their rifles away and depended solely on their spears. They plunged madly with the deadly blades, and there was scarcely a thrust which did not mean a life.

So terrible was the onslaught, so sudden the swoop, so inevitable the confusion, that I believe it is a fact that one or two of our own officers and several of the men were killed by British bullets; but in such a fight a calamity like that was inevitable, for the firing seemed to be all ways at once, and while the battle lasted it was impossible to tell friend from foe.

The end came as swiftly as the start.

The square had been rushed and broken, and some of the fuzzi-wuzzies had penetrated it as far as the centre, but not one of them who went in got out. All were shot down or bayoneted. Some feigned death and came to life again when they saw a chance of rising for a moment and killing a British soldier. No mercy was shown to them.

Almost before the shock of the charge was over, and before the fact was realised that the enemy was amongst us, the fight was done.

The fuzzi-wuzzies recognised that there was no hope of final victory for them, and they withdrew almost as swiftly, it seemed to me, as they had advanced. I saw them drawing off in their thousands, and dotting the little hills about us just as they had dotted them before their frantic rush across the desert. They were allowed to go in peace. No shots, at any rate no general firing, pursued them, although they could have been destroyed as they retired.

I, for one, was glad that they went away unmolested. Of their kind they were the bravest of the brave. They did not know the meaning of fear. I was glad and relieved, too, and I do not think that there was either officer or man in the broken square who had not a feeling of thankfulness to see the backs and not the faces of them.

I looked around and about me, and saw that the desert was literally strewn with the dead and wounded. In those few minutes, nine of our officers and sixty-five men had been killed, and eighty-five wounded, while in and near the square itself, to say nothing of the ground beyond, nearly a thousand Arabs were lying dead.

Only when the fight was over, and it was possible to think, was I able to form a correct impression of the event. Details came back to my mind, and I remembered that as we were marching down in the square one of our colour-sergeants, Kackwich, of the Coldstream Guards, was shot. He was placed on the side of a camel, but when riding towards the Nile he was again struck twice and mortally wounded. In the hospital tent where I was lying there were four men who were maimed for life – Trooper McLeod, of the Royal Horse Guards, who had lost a leg; Private Renton, of the Royal Marines, who also had a leg missing; myself, less a foot; and Private Clark, of the Scots Guards, who had both arms amputated. Wounds were bad to treat and slow to heal in the desert, especially when they were inflicted by the fuzzi-wuzzies' spears.

Not long afterwards I repassed Abu Klea, and saw the whitening skeletons and ribs of camels. By that time I had been in another action, where the Arabs had again tried to rush and break a British square. But this time we were craftier than they were – and we recollected what the spears had done – and we drove them back into the hot desert from which they came. Again they suffered heavy loss. Like most of us poor human beings, they paid bitterly for their experience. That was at Gubat, two days after Abu Klea, and the fight cost me my foot and ankle.

While I was wounded and helpless I craved for water, but it seemed as if not a drop existed in the world. I craved and prayed for it, and my longing was at length gratified. Just when I had reached the stage when death itself would have been welcome as a release from suffering, I became aware that someone was offering me a sip of brandy-and-water. I took it thankfully, and pulled round enough to see that my benefactor was an officer, but I did not know till afterwards who he was; then I learnt that it was Lord Arthur Somerset, of the Heavy Camel Regiment.

In a stretcher I set out to recross the desert.

General Stewart was with us, and I saw him when we started. When next I met him it was at Gakdul. I was being carried in as he was borne out to his last resting-place. He had died that morning at four o'clock.

It was just such burial as every soldier had who fell in that pitiless desert warfare. There was no music, no beating of drum. The little ceremony was terribly sad and impressive, but I think by that time we had become acquainted with sadness, for General Gordon himself, only a few days after the square was rushed and broken a Abu Klea, was murdered at Khartoum.

With the death of Gordon and the fall of Khartoum, Wolseley had little option to abandon the Sudan to the Mahdi. For nearly a decade, there was desultory warfare along the Egyptian/Sudanese borders, and around the Red Sea port of Suakin. It was not until 1896, however, that public pressure, combined with increased French and Italian interest in north Africa, prompted thoughts of reconquering the Sudan. Some 18,000 men were assembled in southern Egypt under the command of General Sir Herbert Kitchener. Kitchener's plan was to undertake the task piecemeal, beginning with the northern Sudanese province of Dongola. In June 1896, after months of careful preparation, Kitchener advanced into Dongola, and defeated a Mahdist force at Firket.

Kitchener intended to use Dongola as a stepping-stone. Here, he assembled fresh forces, and in early 1898 he advanced further into the Sudan. The Mahdi had died – curiously, he died just a few months after Gordon – but his successor, the Khalifa Abdullahi, realised the importance of halting the British advance. He despatched an army of 12,000 men to oppose Kitchener, but Kitchener attacked and over-ran their camp at Atbara on 8 April 1898. By August, he had advanced to within sight of the Mahdist capital of Omdurman itself, and the stage was set for the climactic confrontation of the war. Inspired by a vision, the Khalifa opted to attack Kitchener on the banks of the Nile, in the shadow of the Kerreri hills. Sergeant George Hamilton of the Royal Army Medical Corps was present during the subsequent battle.

The Crushing of the Dervishes

I was stationed in a very quiet little Irish town when the Sirdar was carrying out the first part of that marvellously successful campaign of his which ended in the smashing of the Mahdi's power in the Soudan. Every day, with a soldier's eagerness and interest, I got the newspaper to see how things were going at the seat of war. One morning I opened the pages and learnt that a severe and brilliant action had been fought – the battle of the Atbara.

To my wife, who was with me, I read some of the details of the fight. Woman-like she exclaimed: 'How thankful I am that you are not there!'

Almost before the words were spoken there was a rat-a-tat at the door – the postman's knock.

I responded to the signal, and took in an ominously official letter. I opened it, and found that I had got my marching orders for the front. I was to go to Aldershot at once, and thence to Egypt. It was a hard wrench, but soldiering is soldiering; and within twenty-four hours I had got the sadness of farewell over, and was hurrying as fast as boat and train could carry me to my first destination. Then it was rush and bustle for embarkation for Alexandria, and an excited voyage across the Bay of Biscay and up the

Mediterranean, wondering all the time how the war was proceeding, and speculating upon the chances of getting to Egypt before all the fighting was done.

Having been ordered out I naturally wanted to see something – not that I was unacquainted with campaigning, for at the age of sixteen I had marched with the Servian Army against the Turks, and in 1884 I was within reach of Khartoum. Any fears of disappointment vanished on reaching Cairo, and learning the latest news.

I had had a good deal to do with Eastern people, and was intensely interested in the workings of the Oriental mind, and the convictions of the people with whom I came in contact in the famous capital. I had travelled extensively, too, and had. amongst other things, acquired a conversational knowledge of Arabic.

I mingled with the natives, and asked them what they thought of the prospects of the campaign.

'We have made a good start,' I told them, 'and shall soon smash the Mahdi.'

I was not, however, particularly surprised when I learnt that the downfall of the religious impostor and oppressor was the last thing in the world they expected or believed in.

'You will never conquer the Dervishes,' they solemnly assured me. 'They are invincible. Besides, they cannot be killed in battle, because they wear charms which will protect them.'

This was in allusion to the little snake skins which the Dervishes wear round their arms, and which were supposed to keep them safe from all evils of fire and sword.

The natives held to their conviction, and I did not depart from mine. I joined the Howitzer Battery and left Cairo for Upper Egypt, which at that time of the year was insufferably hot. It would have been bad enough to journey through the country even if we had had the best of food and drink and the greatest of comforts, but now, marching with the Sirdar, the man of iron, under the harassing conditions of a campaign against a brave and ruthless enemy, the work was trying and dangerous even to the strongest and healthiest.

It was not so much battle as disease that we had to dread; and many a fine fellow who left Cairo and escaped the sword and bullet of the fanatic, marched back, or was carried, only to die and find his last resting-place in Egypt.

I eventually reached a little island in the Nile about twenty miles from Khartoum, and was one of eight favoured men who were chosen by the officer commanding to push on to that strange city which was so closely associated with the tragedy of General Gordon. There was no doubt by this time that we were very close upon a desperate and probably final meeting with the enemy, who had already given proof of his splendid fighting qualities, and I was eagerly anticipating developments.

For everyone engaged it was ceaseless hard work, marching against time, and it was with a feeling of relief as well as excitement that I found myself in view of Khartoum and at what proved to be the battlefield of Omdurman.

That was on September 1st, a day which, for many and varied reasons, will never fade from my recollection. It was about noon when the gunboat in which I had sailed up the Nile was stationed with other similar vessels in the river not very far from the bank, and commanding the vast stretch of yellow desert which was broken by mounds and rising ground.

Within twenty-four hours a bloody battle had been decided, and the British had established themselves as the conquerors of Upper Egypt and the saviours of the oppressed.

A strange force it was that was gathered for the struggle – a strange army on either side. The British were such a mixture as you will find in no other army in the world – for there were the English, Irish, Scotch, and other regiments, mingled with the black troops, those Egyptians and Soudanese who from the most unpromising material had been turned into such fine fighting stuff.

We were in a very good position for awaiting that attack which was certain to be delivered. A long stretch of the bank of the Nile formed the rear of the encampment, and sweeping out from it, in the form of a gigantic semi-circle, was the zareba, a wall or barrier of stones and mud, tins and boxes – anything that comes handy and can be spared – which is so intimately associated with our desert warfare.

When the daylight had died away – which it does in those regions very quickly – the severest test of courage came.

Would there be an attack by the Dervishes under cover of the darkness? Would the fanatic hordes sweep resistlessly upon that enemy which they so greatly outnumbered, and force him to endure the horrors of a struggle in which it would not be possible to tell a friend from a foe?

These questions were constantly and eagerly asked, and even men who had been tried and proved in battle fervently expressed he hope that the struggle would be postponed till daylight, saying that if it came to fighting in the darkness the chances in favour of the defenders would be small indeed.

For the most part, the black troops who were with us were reliable, but there were some on whom too much dependence could not be placed at such a crisis, and who might easily give way to panic and cause the rout and downfall of our forces. Of course, it proved otherwise – but I am now only attempting to describe to you what our feelings were on the eve of that eventful struggle.

The night was so extraordinarily dark, indeed, that I really believe myself that if the enemy had attacked us it would have been all over with us. So convinced were some of the men of the gunboat that an attack would be made, that they stripped themselves of everything except their pantaloons, ready to jump into the water as their only means of escape. They preferred to take their chances with the crocodiles and hippos rather than with the fanatics.

The Sirdar, whose marvellous caution, courage, and foresight provided for every possible contingency, apparently recognised the peril, for it was rumoured that he caused spies to be sent out into the midst of the enemy to spread the report that it was the intention of the British to attack them during the night. The statement doubtless had much to do with the freedom from molestation which we enjoyed. On the general question, however – that of the result of the battle if fought in broad daylight – there was no difference of opinion whatever. Every soldier was satisfied that short work would be made of the fanatics, brave to recklessness though they were.

'We shall give 'em beans!' 'We shall make short work of 'em!' and many expressions of the same sort showed the perfect confidence which Tommy had in his wonderful commander – the man of iron.

The night, besides being intensely dark, was full of that mystery and wonder which you only find in perfection in that particular part of Egypt – a region where, up to that time, few white men had been seen, although now – marvellous change within a decade – it is regularly visited by train and steamboat tourists. Does not Cook, who still largely rules Egypt, take them out and bring them back again, according to time-table, and with every luxury that money and experience can provide? – but only in the glorious, perfect winter months, not in the heart of the blazing, deadly summer time.

I had left the gunboat and gone ashore, to do a little reconnoitring on my own account, and to compare this present fighting with the many strange experiences I had gone through in other parts of the world. I was overtaken by Mr. Frederick Villiers, the war correspondent, who asked me if I could direct him to Prince Christian Victor, who was with the expedition. I happened to know where His Highness was, and told Mr. Villiers that he would find him in a boat which was moored not far from my own. 'Thank you,' he answered, and added that he hoped the enemy would not attack us during the night.

We parted, and I continued my way as well as I could over the sand of the desert. It was so dark, however, that I literally could not see a yard ahead, and having no wish, I can assure you, to walk into a trap, I began to find my way back to the boat. It is astonishing how, in spite of yourself, you imagine evil things at such a time. To me every bit of rising ground concealed a Dervish whose sole aim was to secure a place in Paradise at the cost of my life – an aspiration which I had not the least wish or intention to gratify, and every sound was that which came from some advancing enemy. I certainly believed that I heard noises which, as a matter of fact, had no existence; but at last, abruptly, I heard the unmistakable sound of footsteps.

What was it? Who could it be? What should I do? Perhaps in my heart of hearts I longed to show a clean pair of heels; but I pulled myself together and shouted 'Who goes there?' No answer came, which was enough to confirm my suspicion that it was not, at any rate, a friend, for a friend would have answered the challenge.

I shouted again, this time in Arabic, '*Stana, ye kelp!*' which is effective, but not complimentary, for it means 'Stop, you dog!'

Still there was no reply, and I can tell you that in spite of the heat of the night I felt a sudden chill all over me. The least I imagined was that it was a Dervish spy, with a spear, who was crawling towards me, and who was on the point of winning a sure triumph. I could see nothing in that actual Egyptian darkness, but I knew that the thing, whatever it was, almost touched my face.

I could endure it no longer, so I struck out right and left – and I think that as an Army athlete and boxer I can strike pretty hard. Instantly there was a strange, mysterious reply – a hideous '*Heio! Heio! Heio!*' and I was immensely relieved, even if utterly ashamed, for my unseen companion proved to be only a wandering donkey. I hurried to my boat, and as I rolled myself up in my blanket told myself that my invisible companion was not the only ass at large that night.

Morning came suddenly, and the battle began almost as abruptly as the day had broken.

It was a deeply impressive thing to gaze upon the field of battle and the opposing forces for a few moments before the action began. Many of our own splendid fellows had already distinguished themselves at the stern struggle of the Atbara River, and they looked the very apotheosis of the fighter. Other regiments were perfectly fresh and had been hurried up to the front without any previous experience of warfare.

Then there were the black troops, many of whom were fighting against their own relatives, or, at any rate, their own flesh and blood; and the fanatic hordes, clad in their *jibbehs* – white robes, with black and coloured patches – and carrying banners, spears, and in many cases huge, two-handed swords, with which they knew so well how to do appalling execution.

On the one hand was the great, placid Nile, with the picturesque but filthy cities of Omdurman and Khartoum in sight, and on the other was the far-reaching yellow desert. Here, where civilisation was opposed to barbarism, the British forces calmly awaited the desperate onslaught of the masses of Dervishes, who neither gave nor took quarter.

Suddenly in the distance, against the perfect blue of the sky, I saw flashes of flame and little clouds of smoke; then I heard the boom of guns, and knew that the battle had been opened in real and desperate earnest.

The howitzers were firing across the river into the town of Omdurman. Shortly afterwards I saw at a distance of about two and a half or three miles the Dervishes advancing towards us in skirmishing order, and a marvellous sight it was, for the brave fellows made a line which was three or four miles in length and consisted of men about ten deep.

It has always been a matter of conjecture as to how many of the fanatics advanced over the desert on that great day on what they believed would be a triumphant and annihilating charge; but I think myself that the number was not far short of 80,000.

After the style of the Mussulman they advanced with their banners flying, and chanting their prayer or hymn of victory, and even then it was terrible to realise that they were marching on to their inevitable doom.

Destruction was certain, because they had to advance for a long distance over the desert to attack steady troops who were armed with Maxims and magazine rifles, and had the great additional protection of artillery fire.

The Dervishes were swept down as they marched, but they neither halted nor deviated. They had a purpose to fulfil, which was the destruction of the infidel, and after all, perhaps one ought not to wonder overmuch at their reckless valour, seeing that their faith taught them that they were proof against sword and bullet, and that if by any chance they should fall they were assured of the joys of Paradise.

Being on board the gunboat I was, of course, exceptionally fortunately placed, because I could see the whole of the battle from start to finish.

With the help of a pair of first-rate field-glasses I swept the field of battle, following all the movements as they were carried out. I saw clearly the bursting of our shells amongst the huddled forces of the enemy, and it was inexpressibly terrible to observe the havoc which these missiles wrought. A shell would strike against the Dervishes, and make a breach in that human wall, reddening the yellow sand, and covering it with dead or wounded fighters. When this happened the fanatics were scattered literally like packs of cards.

Yet in spite of this ruthless and inevitable butchery the Dervishes came on, and it seemed as if not even the merciless rain of bullets from our rifles and Maxims would ever keep them back; it appeared certain that in spite of their enormous losses they would have survivors enough to reach the British troops who were formed in square and were mowing them down. It is certain that if by any chance the ammunition had become exhausted there would have been such a hand to hand struggle that no one could have foretold the end of it.

You would have supposed that before such a remorseless and destructive fire the enemy, however brave, would have broken and fled; but for fully three-quarters of an hour these courageous fellows, who did not know the meaning of defeat, marched on to the attack, doing everything that was humanly possible to get to a death grip with their opponents. But they literally melted, and never did they succeed in getting nearer to the zareba than five or six hundred yards.

One of the most thrilling and audacious things I witnessed that day was the charge of a body of Dervish cavalry. They swept furiously towards us over the desert, but there was no human possibility of success, and horses and riders were destroyed as they thundered on, rolling over on the sand in hideous confusion. A few, recognising the futility of the attempt, turned and retired, and in that way saved themselves.

There was one desperate and heroic rider who galloped about two hundred yards ahead of his companions, and it seemed almost as if he bore a charmed life, and would actually force himself as far as the zareba, but many a British rifle was turned deliberately towards him, and many a bullet hit the flying target.

Horse and rider were destroyed, and I do not think it is too much to say that no man that day showed greater valour than this unknown dark warrior. He was almost the last to fall, for soon afterwards there were signs that the Dervishes had lost heart and recognised that Fate was against them, and that they could not hope successfully to stand against the Sirdar's conquering army.

Meanwhile there had been the famous charge of the 21st Lancers, a brilliant swoop of British cavalry against enormously superior numbers of the enemy, who had the immense advantage of cover. This charge was productive of many acts of valour, and it was the cause of many a terrible sight, for, as you know, the Dervishes, like other barbarous warriors, made a practice of mutilating their fallen enemies, and when we afterwards collected our dead horsemen it was utterly impossible to recognise them.

After the charge I met one of the troopers of the 21st, who, luckily for him, had only been slightly wounded and was able to ride back. He told me that when the charge was delivered he thrust his lance through the chest of a Dervish, and that so terrible was the force with which the weapon had been driven home that he could not withdraw it. Even then, literally like a fly on a pin, the Dervish raised his sword to kill his assailant, who, for the moment, was completely powerless; but one of the officers of the 21st dashed up and slew the brave fanatic.

By noon the battle was ended, and a complete and momentous victory was ours. The British loss was slight, but the Dervishes had suffered to an appalling extent. On that wide battlefield they were lying dead in thousands, and great numbers more were hideously and indescribably mangled. Not even the most seasoned soldier or the most callous man could go over the ground without shuddering and feeling intense pity for the vanquished. The killed were estimated at 10,000, and it was calculated that the wounded numbered 14,000.

A thing which shows the extraordinarily different points of view of black and white troops was the conduct of our Soudanese battalions after the fight, when we entered Omdurman. They walked straight in'o the houses from which the Dervishes had marched to battle, and sat down and devoured the meals which the wives had prepared for their husbands on their return as victors, just as if they themselves had been the triumphant menfolk.

There were many wonderful things to see in that strange city of misery and suffering. We marched in as conquerors, and the first thing the Sirdar did was to set at liberty many a wretched captive who had lingered in what appeared hopeless captivity.

One man in particular I noticed, because something about him told me that he was a white man. He seemed to be literally mad with joy at his unlooked-for deliverance, and well he might be, for he proved to be Mr. Charles Neufeld, who for ten years had been one of the Mahdi's prisoners.

There were many sad sights in Omdurman itself. True, captives were rejoicing because they had regained their liberty, and many who had been oppressed throughout their lives knew that at last they would enjoy real freedom under the protection of the British; but on the battlefield just outside thousands of husbands, brothers, and sons were slain, and the air was filled with bitter wailings and lamentations.

Omdurman itself, too, had been under fire, and pitiful as were the sights on the battlefield itself, infinitely more moving was the spectacle of little children who had been unavoidably wounded by our fire in the city. You may be sure that we did everything we could for them.

It was not all sorrow, however, for we, at any rate, were rejoicing at the finish of the war; and, as a sort of celebration of our victory, thousands of us, British and Soudanese, bathed in the Nile, and it was one of the most extraordinary sights imaginable to watch the immense numbers of white and black bathers in that famous river.

I was thankful to bid good-bye to Omdurman and Khartoum and get back to Cairo.

The natives utterly refused to believe that in such a short time we had not only met the enemy, but had completely vanquished him.

'No, no,' they said, 'you are not the winners! You have run away!'

It was indeed an amazingly swift and decisive campaign.

Within five months after the postman brought that fateful letter I was back in the little, quiet Irish town, grateful to be at home again. And had I not cause for profound thankfulness when I remembered how many a gallant fellow who had been ordered from home in exactly the same abrupt way was sleeping under the yellow sand?

I see that you are looking at my medals. Yes, I have six of them, with eight clasps, and, in addition, I have been twice mentioned in dispatches.

Yet in all the fighting that they represent I have not been wounded, nor, with the exception of five days, did I ever go sick during the whole of the time I was in the Army.

The battle of Omdurman was enormously destructive to the Mahdists. Over 10,000 are thought to have been killed, for the loss of just 100 of Kitchener's men. Kitchener ordered the Mahdi's tomb to be shelled – rumour has it he wanted to take the Mahdi's skull as a souvenir, but was prevented by Queen Victoria's disapproval – and held a service of remembrance on the ruins of Gordon's palace. Imperial honour had been restored, and a martyr's death avenged; it remained to Kitchener merely to march to the frontier town of Fashoda, to over-awe a French outpost, and reinforce Britain's claim to the region.

The Khalifa, meanwhile, fled to the desert; it was not until November 1899 that Egyptian troops caught up with him. He met his death calmly, sitting on a prayer mat until riddled with bullets.

By that time, Britain's attention was already focused on a new and yet greater conflict elsewhere.

5. South Africa

By the time Queen Victoria came to the throne in 1837, British Imperial entanglements at the tip of southern Africa had already produced a bitter crop of conflicts. Furthermore, the region would continue to remain problematic throughout her reign, to the extent that by the time of her death, in 1901, the British army was engaged in the most prolonged, costly, and testing war of her reign.

British interests in southern Africa were largely dictated by her need to secure the shipping route to India. Until the creation of the Suez Canal, all maritime traffic from Europe to the Indies had to make the long haul around the Cape of Good Hope, and control of the Cape effectively offered control of that traffic. It was this need which had first brought Europeans – the Dutch – to the Cape in the fifteenth century, and in 1806, as part of the twists and turns of the Revolutionary Wars in Europe, Britain displaced Dutch authority. This created the first of two common threads which bound the conflicts of the following century together. Many of the original Dutch inhabitants – who called themselves Boers, or farmers – soon became disillusioned with British control, and trekked into the interior to create their own independent republics. Anglo-Boer rivalry would thereafter prove a potent source of violence. So, too, would that second thread; the reaction of the indigenous African groups to white expansionism, from whatever source.

The indigenous peoples of the Cape, the Khoi and San, had possessed a fragile semi-nomadic lifestyle which had been easily displaced by the whites. Not so the stronger African groups of the interior. As the white settler community expanded slowly up the coast, following the pattern of good grazing land, it ran into African groups already in possession. From 1779 there were no less than nine wars of varying severity along the eastern Cape frontier, fought in succession between Boer farmers and British soldiers and the amaXhosa people (known to the whites at the time as 'Kaffirs'). Later, as white groups penetrated further into the interior, they would encounter new African societies, such as the Zulu or BaSotho. Each contact brought with it its bitter crop of bloodshed.

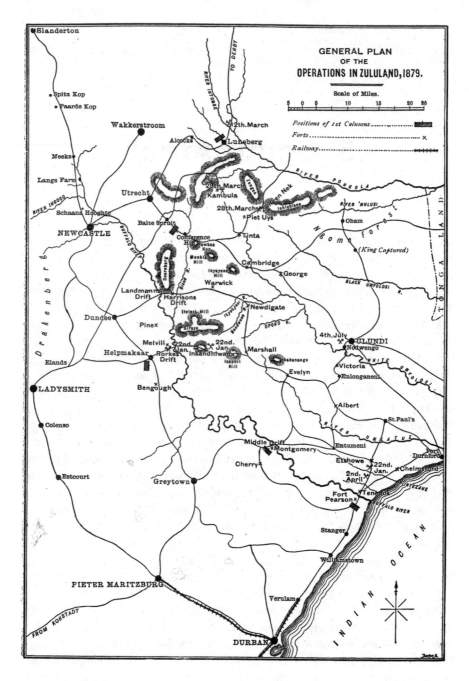

GENERAL PLAN
OF THE
OPERATIONS IN ZULULAND, 1879.

Yet the story of the struggle for the Cape frontier made no great impact on the British popular imagination in the manner of, say, the Anglo-Zulu War. Even the longest and bloodiest struggle, the 8th Frontier War (1850–53) was remembered largely for one unusual incident. On 26 February 1852, the troopship *Birkenhead*, carrying a draft of reinforcements for the Cape Frontier, struck a submerged reef of Danger Point, two miles off-shore near Cape Agulhas. The ship quickly broke up and sank, and it was impossible to take most of the men off in time. Instead, the order was issued to save women and children first, while the troops fell in on deck. The image of British troops, disciplined to the last, struck a deep chord with the Victorian public, and the incident was the subject of a number of famous paintings. One of those who survived the wreck, Corporal W. Smith of the 12th Regiment, recalled that the truth was rather different from the popular myth, but his story remains one of enduring courage none-the-less.

The Loss of the Troopship *Birkenhead*

I am an old man – old in body, if you like, but young in memory and spirit, and I can still march with some of the best of them, in spite of my seventy-five years. I can recall many things that I did in my long years of soldiering on home and foreign service, and can picture many scenes that my eyes have witnessed.

But one event stands out with awful clearness, one memory will linger when all other impressions vanish, and I parade for the last muster – and that is, the picture of the sinking of the *Birkenhead*. From time to time the papers tell us that the only survivor of the troopship has died – that neither man nor woman nor child who was in her when she struck on Danger Point, and broke her back and sank, is left: but some of us die hard, and there is still a handful of officers and men who were hurled into a shark-infested sea in the darkness of an early morning, and heard the last hopeless cries of soldiers as the steamer disappeared. Aye, and worse than that – the wails and screams of heartbroken wives who had been torn from husbands' arms and the piteous cries of little children who were forced into the boats and rowed away, leaving to a sure and awful death those who were sacrificed that they might live.

The old King of Prussia commanded that the story of the *Birkenhead* drill and fortitude should be read to every regiment in his army; artists have painted pictures of the troops drawn up in steady ranks on deck, and poets have sung of the way the bugles rang and the drums beat; but there was no sound of bugle and no roll of drum; there was none of the stiffness of parade which pictures show – and yet there was a falling-in, a last muster, a standing shoulder to shoulder as the end came, and many a handshake and many a sobbed farewell. And how, at such a time, can even the bravest do otherwise, swept, as they were swept, from perfect peace and comfort to an unexpected doom?

Sometimes, aye, often, I wake suddenly from sleep, or start up as I smoke in my little cottage in the quiet country, and wonder whether the vision that has come again is only dreaming or reality; and I have to take my papers out and cast my mind back over the half century before I am satisfied that I have not imagined it. The whole terrible catastrophe returns as fresh and vivid now as it was then – for such a thing as that makes the same scar in your memory as an ugly wound will leave upon your body – and I know what both are.

I am in the old regiment again, the 12th Foot, which became the Suffolk when it lost its number, and I am back in the early fifties, when the British soldier's duty was to obey every order, without wondering, as they do nowadays, why it was given and whether it was right. They were the days of iron discipline and not overmuch considerations for the private soldier, who was still only a machine for fighting purposes.

There is a strong draft of us of the 12th for the Cape, where we are going out to fight the Kaffirs, and there are drafts for other regiments – Lancers, Highlanders, and Rifles amongst them.

On January 7th, 1852, we embark in the *Birkenhead* and sail for the Cape. We are in a famous ship, for the *Birkenhead* is of big size for her day, and has already made the run to the Cape in forty-five days, while other vessels in the Navy have been as long as sixty-five. Think of that, you soldiers of to-day, who grumble because your steamer takes a month – but very rarely – to do the same distance.

But, after all, we are cooped up in a ship that is no bigger than many a fine ocean-going tug nowadays. She is not much more than two hundred feet long, but broad of beam and of nearly fifteen hundred tons. She has engines of 564 horse-power, and is of course driven by paddles. She has been made from a frigate into a steamer, and a heavy poop and forecastle have been added to her to increase her accommodation as a troopship. Even then we are packed like sardines in a box, and have to eat and sleep and get through the time as best we can, and trouble nothing about the many little comforts that we enjoy ashore.

We start at a bad time of the year, and after leaving Cork run into a lot of heavy weather which puts the crowning touch to our miseries afloat. Life and death are busy with us at sea, just as they are ashore. The weary days go past, and the only thing that marks one from its fellows is a birth or death. One woman dies of consumption, and our spirits are depressed by the awful solemnity of her burial at sea. Three children are born – but at what a cost! Each mother dies – and what more striking evidence can you have of what it meant for women to sail in troopships fifty years ago?

The days pass slowly, and the *Birkenhead* steams steadily towards the south. Week follows week, and we have entered our seventh at sea when we are gladdened by the sight of Simon's Town. We reach it on February 23rd, after a voyage of forty-seven days. Now the weariness of the sea is forgotten and we are all alive with eagerness to reach the very end. Some, more lucky than the rest – how lucky they are so soon to learn – are landed, amongst them the handful of sick and more than half of the women and children. We learn definitely what we are to do, and find that the *Birkenhead* is to go at once to Port Elizabeth and East London, and that the drafts will join the forces of the Commander-in-Chief in South Africa, Sir Harry Smith, for service on the frontier of Cape Colony.

Who need describe the joyful expectation of those who fill the troopship? Not a man is there who does not burn to get ashore and march to the front, and there is not a soul who is not glad to think that there is only a pleasant little run along the coast before our long voyage is ended altogether. We are in perfect spirits as we steam out of Simon's Town at about five o'clock in the afternoon of February 25th.

How vividly that final run comes back again over the half century that has passed! The sea is calm and the night is clear, the daylight quickly fades and gives place to a glorious darkness. The lights are twinkling ashore, a grateful sight to us who have been so long surrounded by the tumbling seas. The stars, too, are shining brightly.

All is well.

From time to time as we thud bravely on from the Atlantic to the Indian Ocean we hear the sullen murmur of the surf which breaks ashore about two miles away, rising above the ever-present roar of the machinery which we no longer notice. A good look-out is kept, the leadsman is in the chains, and the watch on deck have little else to do but watch the lights glide past as the *Birkenhead* makes nearly ten miles an hour. The captain of the ship, Captain Salmond, has gone below, so has the commander, and the *Birkenhead* is in charge of Mr. Davies, second master.

I go below at last and turn in, never so much as thinking of danger. I discuss the latest news with my comrades. The gossip is that Captain Salmond is pressing the ship hard, for two reasons, one of which is that he wants to get ahead of the steamer *Styx*, which is carrying stores of war, and the other that he wishes to make a quick passage so that he can land the troops for the Commander-in-Chief, who is concentrating his forces for a grand attack upon the natives. And so that he may make his run as short as possible, Captain Salmond is keeping very near the coast.

We have gone to sleep on the crowded lower deck. Midnight has passed, one o'clock comes and goes, and the ship's bell strikes again. But I do not hear the strokes or the melancholy voice which rises in the night and proclaims that all is well. I am fast asleep and unconscious.

What is that? Why this appalling shock? Why these terrible cries, this sudden panic, this staggering confusion? Why are men crowding and struggling and all making, as if by instinct, for the companion-ladder, to swarm on deck?

Why ask the question, for we know, even we who are landsmen, that the *Birkenhead* has struck; we know that even now some of her people are dead, drowned in their hammocks by the rush of the sea upon them.

I do what my fellow soldiers do, what nearly every soul on board does – struggle to the upper deck and clamour to know the worst. There are others like me, rushing up and crowding the deck – small space indeed for so many human beings. And it is dark, too.

What need to ask the question which the simplest soul on board can answer? The ship has struck on a sunken rock, and not even her water-tight compartments, of which she has no fewer than a dozen, can save her. The *Birkenhead*, with her resistless weight, driving hard, has been impaled upon a cruel, submerged fang, and she is ripped just as you might rip a drum of paper with your finger.

Panic, you ask? Confusion? Yes – both. And how can it be otherwise when, like a flash, sentence of death has been passed upon the *Birkenhead*, and in the twinkling of an eye serenity and safety have given place to overwhelming peril?

There are times when even the bravest of the brave succumb to their emotions. Was not the Iron Duke himself overcome with grief at the loss of so many of his troops at Waterloo? No wonder, then, that the men of the *Birkenhead* are in want of steadying when the first shock of the disaster falls upon them. Remember that most of them are very young – and then there are the men whose wives and children are on board. Put yourself in their places, then you will understand.

Even now, with the ship abruptly stopped, with that awful sound of rending asunder in our ears, it seems impossible to believe that she is doomed. How can she be, the stout vessel that has borne us so far through such troubled waters without disaster of any sort? And so near the shore, too?

I know that even now, so far as I am personally concerned, there is no suspicion that the end will be what it proves to be. I see that things are bad; I am aware that already many lives are lost; but there are the boats, the coast is very close to us, and, above all things, there is the discipline – that spirit of obedience which proves stronger than the love of life itself.

I have spoken of the panic, the confusion. They have been born suddenly,

but their death is just as swift. Now come the excited voices of the officers
– the men who are heard in the darkness, but are not seen.

It is 'Steady, lads, steady!' and if there is a tremor in the tones – what of
it? If at the first, before the drafts have found themselves, there is something
of a rush for the boats, what of that, either? Does not the panic die away at
the word of command? Is not the rush stopped at the very outset? Do not
the men make some pitiful attempt to fall in on that sloping deck, which is
already breaking under their very feet?

And why? Because there are women and children on board, and the women
and children are to be saved, whatever happens to the rest.

I seem to tell the story slowly; but however fast I spoke I could not do
more than talk haltingly of a thing that happened with such fatal swiftness.

Lieutenant-Colonel Seton, of the 74th Highlanders, commanding the
troops on board, gathers all the officers about him, and tells them that at
any cost order and discipline must be maintained. He specially charges
Captain Wright of the 91st to see that Captain Salmond's instructions are
obeyed, because on him alone, as a sailor, we can depend for safety.

Instantly sixty men are told off to work the chain-pumps on the lower
deck, and I am one of the sixty. I go below again, and the stoutest heart
might shrink from such a task. It is like descending into a dark well, for the
water is already flooding the deck. But we strike out for the pumps, and in
reliefs we man them and work with frantic energy. We might as well spare
all our strength, because we do not make the least impression on the flood.
How can we, with such a yawn in the troopship's side? She has been caught
on the port side, between the foremast and the paddle-box, and the waves
sweep in just like a heavy running stream.

We are up to our waists in water; but we work away at the pumps, cheering each other, saying that we shall soon be out of it and landed. But within
touch of us are men drowned in their hammocks.

Officers are everywhere, steadying encouraging, and directing. The rest of
the troops are on the poop, and the women and children are there, too, drawn
up in readiness to be put into one of the boats, the cutter.

Blue lights are burning, making a ghastly illumination in the darkness,
and rockets crash on the stillness of the night. But no answer comes to our
signals of distress. The lights are not seen, and the sound of rockets does not
carry far.

What of the guns? you ask. Aye, guns would have boomed deeper, and
could have been heard ashore; but we cannot fire them, because the ammunition is in the magazine, and the magazine is under water now, so that it
is impossible to reach it.

Captain Salmond, like the brave commander he is, tries to repair his terrible mistake of hugging the coast too closely, and he forgets himself entirely

in his wish to save his people – always the women and children first, remember. We hear his voice as he issues orders – he swings a lantern in his hand – and we know that the engines, which are still workable, have been turned astern.

Fatal error again! and this time final. There is more hideous grinding and tearing, and the rent in the hull is made bigger as the *Birkenhead* is backed. There is a mightier inrush of the sea and a furious hissing as the boiler fires are drowned. But for the present we have no orders to leave our places, and we work unflaggingly at the useless pumps.

On deck they are throwing the horses overboard – the few officers' chargers which the troopship carries; and the women and children are being driven and helped into the cutter. Can you understand what it means – that tearing away of wives and children from husbands and fathers – unhappy creatures who beg that they may die with their own loved ones rather than be saved without them?

Sixty men are at the chain-pumps, sixty more are struggling to lower the paddle-box boats. The other boats, too, are being handled.

What happens? The tackle is rotten, the boats themselves are ill-found and in bad condition, so that the very means by which alone we can hope for safety are not to be relied upon in our desperate extremity. In this furious effort to get the boats away, Mr. Brodie, the master, and a number of men are lost.

There is a long swell running towards the shore, and the *Birkenhead* is rolling heavily. Her foremast is tottering, her funnel is threatening to collapse. It leans dangerously over towards the starboard side, and as the fight with the boats goes on the smoke-stack thunders down and crushes a little host of human beings on the paddle-box.

Everything now happens with paralysing swiftness. The funnel has fallen – a great, high mass of metal; the foremast has come down, and the *Birkenhead* herself has snapped in two, her fore part dropping down into deep water and her stern tilting high in the air.

Half a hundred men perish instantly at the chain-pumps, and those who do not die rush up to the deck to hear the order given that all who can swim must jump overboard and make for the boats, which have got clear and are waiting at a safe distance so that they shall not be drawn down into the vortex.

The order is given by Captain Salmond, but other voices are heard immediately – Captain Wright's and Captain Giradot's – begging that the men will stand fast, as the boats are full already with the women and children, and will be swamped if the soldiers make for them.

Discipline again! And always the women and children! The men stand fast, in the very grip of certain death, and not more than two or three jump overboard and try to reach the boat, which safely gets away.

During the whole of this time, the agonies of which no man can describe, Cornet Bond, of the 12th Lancers, and Ensign Lucas, of the 73rd, have been superintending the removal of the women and children to the boat, and handing some of them to the gangway with a politeness and attention which is so wonderful that, sore as my own strait is, I cannot help smiling.

Cornet Bond, you say, is still alive – now Captain R. M. Bond Shelton – and you have met and talked with him? Then he has an old *Birkenhead* soldier's best wishes for continued life as a gallant officer and gentleman! of Ensign Lucas I can speak myself, because I lived to serve under him. Here is a letter from him, sent to me only the other month, and a box of cigars, 'for all old soldiers smoke,' he says.

Not twenty minutes have passed since we were sleeping peacefully and safely; now, with terrible noises, the troopship disappears, settling on the rock which has destroyed her, and with only her mainmast rising above the water.

For some minutes there is a scene which I cannot picture, there are sounds that I dare not recall; then there is something of quietness, because the sea has claimed most of these desperate bidders for existence.

Where am I now? What new terror has been added to this great tragedy of a sailor's mistake?

I am overboard and in the water, clinging to a spar, a bit of wreckage which I have reached, I know not how. I have rushed on deck in my shirt and greatcoat, just as I have been roused from sleep, and in this clothing I am adrift in the Indian Ocean, a non-swimmer, and doomed to an eighteen hours' struggle in the sea to keep myself alive. I do not know that my fight will be for so long or so terrible, or I could never see it through; but I still have faith in my salvation, and grip my spar and look about for help.

And what do I see – what do I hear?

All around me are men who have been hurled to a pitiless death, some struggling fiercely, some clinging to any floating object from the wreck. There are awful sounds which I come to know well as the last groans or screams of men who sink to rise no more – and still more terrifying outbreaks which I do not for the moment understand, but the cause of which I quickly learn. They are the hopeless cries of victims who are seized and killed by sharks. Remember, we are in southern waters, in the southern summer, and the Indian Ocean thereabouts is swarming with these cruel monsters.

And yet, in all that time of suffering and terror, I am strangely undisturbed in mind. I cannot swim, but I have my spar to keep me up, and the knowledge that I am so near the land is wonderfully comforting and helpful. I have a feeling, too, that, having escaped so far, when so many have been swept to death, I shall be saved at last – and this conviction grows upon me even as the number of my comrades lessens.

Picture for yourself the long-drawn agony of those hours of darkness, in spite of all the hope fills me, and the senses which are growing dulled; and imagine, if you can, the scene when the night is passing, and the tropic dawn comes quickly.

The daylight shows me dangers which the gloom has mercifully hidden. The mainmast of the sunken *Birkenhead* shoots upwards from the sea, and its spars and rigging are crowded with men, clinging, fly-like, to the ropes and timbers. With bits of mast and wood from the deck, trusses of hay, cabin furniture, and anything and everything that will float, men are holding their heads above water, casting yearning glances towards that shore which is so near and yet so far, and always looking for a sight of sail or help.

What is that strange object which is moving steathily and swiftly through the water near me? It disappears suddenly, and I know that it is the fin of a shark, which has turned on his back for his savage and always sure attack. There is a piercing cry, and a tinging red of the sea – and the number of survivors is lessened. Time after time that awful drama is played, and the senses are dulled until even such a death is robbed of terror.

Yet even now I cannot help wondering why some are taken and some are left by these monsters of the deep. I do know – and I am thankful for it – that they do not molest me, nor throughout my stay in the water does a shark so much as make a rush at me. They say that the sharks that night and day seized mostly those who were naked, while I had still my greatcoat on, and I keep it on for some time. But it goes at last.

The hours pass slowly, and I am parched with thirst; but I do not let the hope within me die. I am drifting to the land, inch by inch only, because I am held a prisoner in a mass of sea bamboo, which is worse than any weed, and proves the death of many a poor fellow who might otherwise escape. It is like a floating jungle. Through this enveloping obstruction I and my spar are driven by the tide towards the coast, and at last I am within a stone's throw of the land.

All this time the men, exhausted, are dropping from the mast into the sea, and are letting go their frail supports; but I am absorbed in my own position, full of my own miseries, able only to think of my own salvation. I have reached the limit of my endurance, and am the plaything only of the sullen swell which rolls ashore.

And now, just when salvation seems assured, I am met by my greatest danger. I am hurled into the heavy surf, which is like to break or crush me. It is as if the ruthless sea was making one last effort to claim me, who have defied it so long, and is determined to wrench me from my spar. But I struggle desperately still, and at last, just after sundown, I am thrown, like flotsam, on the beach, bruised and bleeding, hungry, thirsty, almost senseless, utterly exhausted, and stripped of every scrap of clothing – after eighteen hours in that remorseless sea.

I lie where the waves have thrown me, caring nothing, and fall into a log-like sleep till morning, when I join some of my unhappy comrades who have been saved also.

There – that is my old man's story. What else is there to tell? What else can there be?

I join my regiment, and march and fight as if there had been no *Birkenhead* disaster. It is soldiering – and it is discipline.

Yes, that all-conquering discipline – for of all the women and children not one is lost.

Because of that, and because we obeyed – I and the rest of us are satisfied.

If the Cape Frontier Wars made little impact on the minds of the British public, the Anglo-Zulu War of 1879 transfixed them. The Zulu, whose territory lay on the eastern coast of southern Africa, had emerged during the 1820s as one of the strongest groups in southern Africa. British interests in the region had originally been limited to a small trading enclave at Port Natal – now Durban – but in 1843 the British had annexed Natal, the area lying immediately south of the Zulu kingdom. For thirty years Anglo-Zulu relations remained cordial, but by the 1870s the British had adopted a new expantionsist policy in southern Africa. Called Confederation, it was designed to resolve the area's festering conflicts by brining the disparate British colonies, Boer republics and African kingdoms under loose British control. To the British, the Zulu, with their centralised political system, strong army, and only marginal involvement in the European economic system, offered a major block on the road to Confederation. Anticipating a quick and easy campaign, the British High Commissioner at the Cape, Sir Henry Bartle Frere, provoked a war with the Zulu king, Cetshwayo kaMpande, and in January 1879 British troops entered Zululand.

The campaign went wrong almost immediately. On 22 January one of the British columns was all but wiped out at the foot of a distinctive rocky outcrop known as Isandlwana. Over 1300 British troops and their African allies were killed, and the British invasion was effectively repulsed. Later that same day, however, part of the Zulu reserve went on to attack the British border post at Rorke's Drift, which was defended for more than ten hours by little more than 140 men. Coming on top of Isandlwana, the gallant defence of Rorke's Drift seemed all the more heroic, and reassured the British public that their soldiers could still be relied upon when the chips were down. Rorke's Drift, indeed, became one of the great epics of Victorian military achievement, and it is still remembered to this day, when other similar incidents – the defence of Ambigol Wells in the Sudan, or the siege of Chitral – have been long forgotten. The *Royal*

Magazine was lucky enough to be able to interview one of the most articulate of the Rorke's Drift VC winners, Private Alfred Henry Hook, of B Company, 2/24th.

How They Held Rorke's Drift

What Rorke's Drift means in British history is told in a sentence. For thirteen hours a handful of Englishmen, outnumbered by thirty to one, defended themselves and their sick and wounded against the furious assaults of Zulu warriors, glutted with victory and plunder at Isandhlwana, and saved an army, if not a colony, from destruction. Of the defenders, seventeen were killed, and fifteen wounded; of the Zulus, 351 were buried, and almost as many more were left where they had crawled to die.

Rorke's Drift was a little farm on the Natal side of the Buffalo River, which had been used as a Swedish Mission station. At the farm there is a 'drift,' which means ford, into the Zulu country, called Rorke's Drift. Ten minutes' walk from the drift were two houses, which, being considered useful for military purposes, were acquired by the British when invading Zululand. A large outhouse, 80ft. by 20ft., which had been used as a church, was converted into a store-house; a dwelling-house, about the same size, was turned into a hospital. Rorke's Drift was a large camp and depôt, and therefore had plenty of stores and ammunition, including bags of Indian corn – 'mealies' – and boxes of biscuit. On January 12th, 1879, the British marched off, and formed camp at Isandhlwana, leaving a small garrison to guard the stores and the sick and wounded at Rorke's Drift. Lord Chelmsford advanced in force from Isandhlwana before daylight on the 22nd. Before noon 20,000 Zulus had swept on the weakened camp, and within an hour killed more than 800 officers and men, including regulars, police, and volunteers. So much is necessary by way of preliminary to the story of Sergeant Henry Hook.

Sergeant Hook is a Gloucestershire man. He was born in 1851, and served five years in the militia before enlisting in the 24th Regiment. He left the army as a private, with the V.C. and a yearly pension of £10. He is now employed as cloak-room attendant at the British Museum reading-room, and is in by no means good health. Two campaigns in South Africa have seriously affected his constitution, and he will probably get the full £50, which can now be awarded with the Cross. His rank of sergeant comes from his twenty years' association with the Volunteer force.

'Everything was perfectly quiet at Rorke's Drift,' he told me, 'after the column had left, and every officer and man was going about his business as usual. Not a soul suspected that only a dozen miles away the very men that we had said "Good-bye!" and "Good luck!" to were either dead or standing back-to-back in a last fierce hand-to-hand fight with the Zulus. Our garrison consisted of the B Company of the 2nd Battalion of the 24th, under Lieutenant Bromhead, and "details," which brought the total number of us up to 139. Besides these, we had about 300 men of the Natal Native Contingent; but they didn't count, as they bolted in a body when the fight began. We were all knocking about, and I was making tea for the sick, as I was hospital cook at the time.

Suddenly there was a commotion in the camp, and we saw two men galloping towards us from the other side of the river, which was Zululand. Lieutenant Chard, of the Engineers, one of the finest officers in the world, was protecting the ponts over the river, and, as senior officer, was in command at the drift. The ponts, floating bridges, were very simple affairs, one of them being supported on big barrels, and the other on boats. Lieutenant Bromhead was in the camp itself. The horsemen shouted, and were brought across the river, and then we knew what had happened to our comrades.

'They had been butchered to a man.

'That was awful enough news – but worse was to follow, for we were told that the Zulus were coming straight on from Isandhlwana to attack us. One of the horsemen was Lieutenant Adenhorff, and the other was a Natal carabineer. The lieutenant stayed behind with us, and the carabineer, who was in his shirt-sleeves, dashed on to Helpmakaar, twelve miles away, to take the news to two companies of the 24th there. At the same time a note was received by Lieutenant Bromhead from the 3rd Column – that which had left the drift, and part of which had been cut up – to say that the enemy was coming on, and that the post was to be held at all costs.

'For some little time we were all stunned, then everything changed from perfect quietness to intense excitement and energy. There was a general feeling that the only safe thing was to retire and try and join the troops at Helpmakaar. The horsemen had said that the Zulus would be up in two or three minutes; but, luckily for us, they did not show themselves for more than a hour.

'Lieutenant Chard rushed up from the river, about a quarter of a mile away, and saw Lieutenant Bromhead. Orders were given to strike the camp and make ready to go, and we actually loaded up two waggons. Then Mr. Dalton, of the Commissariat Department, came up, and said that if we left the drift every man was certain to be killed. He had formerly been a sergeant-major in a Line regiment, and was one of the bravest men that ever lived. Lieutenants Chard and Bromhead held a consultation, short and earnest; and orders were given that we were to get the hospital and storehouse ready for defence, and that we were never to say "die" or "surrender."

'Not a minute was lost. Lieutenant Bromhead superintended the loopholing and barricading of the hospital and storehouse and the making of a connection of the defences between the two buildings with walls of mealie-bags and waggons. The mealie-bags were good big heavy things, weighing about two hundred pounds each, and during the fight many of them were burst open by assegais and bullets, and the mealies (Indian corn) were thickly spread about the ground. The biscuit-boxes contained ordinary army biscuit. They were big, square wooden boxes, weighing about a hundredweight each. The meat-boxes, too, were very heavy, as they contained tinned meat. They were smaller than the biscuit-boxes.

'While these preparations were being made, Lieutenant Chard went down to the river and brought in the pont guard of a sergeant and half-a-dozen men, with the waggons and gear.

'The two young officers saw that every soldier was at his post. Then we were ready for the Zulus when they cared to come.

'They were not long. Just before half-past four we heard firing behind the conical hill at the back of the drift, called Oscarsberg Hill, and suddenly about five or six hundred Zulus swept round, coming for us at a run.

'Instantly the natives – Kaffirs who had been very useful in making the barricade of waggons, mealie-bags, and biscuit-boxes around the camp – bolted towards Helpmakaar, and, what was worse, their officer and a European sergeant went with them. To see them deserting like that was too much for some of us, and we fired after them. The sergeant was struck and killed.

'Half-a-dozen of us were stationed in the hospital, with orders to hold it and guard the sick. The ends of the building were built of stone, the side walls of ordinary bricks, and the inside walls, or partitions, of sunburnt bricks of mud.

'These shoddy inside bricks proved our salvation, as you will see. It was a queer little one-storeyed building, which it is almost impossible to describe; but we were pinned like rats in a hole, because all the doorways except one had been barricaded with mealie-bags, and we had done the same with the windows. The interior was divided by means of partition-walls, into which were fitted some very slight doors. The patients' beds were simple, rough affairs of boards, raised only about half a foot above the floor. To talk of "hospital" and "ward" conveys the idea of a big building; but, as a matter of fact, this hospital was a mere little shed or bungalow, divided up into rooms so small that you could hardly swing a bayonet in them.

'The half-dozen of us who had been told off to defend the hospital were put in corners where we could shoot best through the loopholes which we had made with picks. I was a good shot, being a "marksman," and was able to clip more than one Zulu at a good distance before we came to the hot fighting at close quarters. In the hospital there were about nine men who could not move; but altogether there were about thirty. Most of these, however, could help to defend themselves.

'As soon as our Kaffirs bolted, it was seen that the fort as we had first made it was too big to be held, so Lieutenant Chard instantly reduced the space by having a row of biscuit-boxes drawn across the middle, above four feet high. This was our inner entrenchment, and proved very valuable.

'The Zulus came on at a wild rush, and although many of them were shot down, they got to within about fifty yards of our south wall of mealie-bags and biscuit-boxes and waggons. They were caught between two fires – that from the hospital and that from the storehouse – and were checked; but they gained the shelter of the depôt cookhouse and ovens, and gave us many heavy volleys.

'During the fight they took advantage of every bit of cover there was – anthills, a tract of bush that we had not had time to clear away, a garden or sort of orchard which was near us, and a ledge of rock and some caves which were only about a hundred yards away. They neglected nothing, and, while they went on firing, large bodies kept hurling themselves against our slender breastworks.

'But it was the hospital they assaulted most fiercely. I had charge, with a man that we called "Old King Cole," of a small room with only one patient in it; and two men named Joseph Williams and John Williams had charge of another. There were two men named R. Jones and W. Jones in a different part of the hospital. One was an old soldier, the other a young one. Cole kept with me for some time after the fight began, then he said he was not going to stay. He went outside and was instantly killed by the Zulus; so that I was left alone with the patient – a native whose leg was broken, and who kept crying out: "Take my bandage off, so that I can come!" But it was impossible to do anything except fight, and I blazed away as hard as I could.

'By this time I was the only defender of my room. Poor "Old King Cole" was lying dead outside, and the helpless patient was crying and groaning near me. The Zulus were swarming around us, and there was an extraordinary rattle as the bullets struck the biscuit-boxes, and queer thuds as they plumped into the bags of mealies. Then there were the whizz and rip of the assegais, the spears with which the Zulus did such terrible work during the war, and of which I had had experience during the Kaffir Campaign of 1877–78. We had plenty of ammunition, but we were told to save it, and so we took careful aim at every shot, and hardly a cartridge was wasted. One of my comrades, Private Dunbar, shot no fewer than nine Zulus, one of them being a chief.

'From the very first the enemy tried to rush the hospital, and at last, although they failed to take it, they managed to set fire to the thick grass which formed the roof. This put us in a terrible plight, because it meant that we were either to be massacred or burnt alive, or get out of the building. To get out seemed impossible; for if we left the hospital by the only door which had been left open, the others having been blocked up, we should instantly fall into the midst of the Zulus. Besides, there were the helpless sick and wounded, and we could not leave them. My own little room communicated with another room by means of a frail door like a bedroom door. Fire and dense choking smoke forced me to get out of my own room and go into the other. It was impossible to take the native patient with me, and I had to leave him to an awful fate. But his death was, at any rate, a merciful one. I heard the Zulus asking him questions; and he tried to tear off his bandages and escape.

'In the room where I now was there were nine sick men, and I was alone to look after them for some time, still firing away, with the hospital burning. Suddenly, in the thick smoke, I saw John Williams, who had rushed in through a doorway communicating with another room, and above the din of the battle and the cries of the wounded I heard him shout: "The Zulus are swarming all over the place! They've dragged Joseph Williams out and killed him!"

'John Williams had held the room, with Private William Horrigan, for more than an hour, until they had not a cartridge left, The Zulus then burst in and dragged out Joseph Williams and two of the patients, and assegaied them. It was only because they were so busy with this slaughtering that John Williams and two of the patients were able to knock a hole in the partition and get into the room where I was posted. Horrigan was killed.

'What were we to do? We were pinned like rats in a hole. Already the Zulus were fiercely trying to burst in through the doorway. The only way of escape was the wall itself – by making a hole big enough for a man to crawl through into an adjoining room, and so on until we got to our inmost entrenchment outside. Williams worked desperately at the wall with the navvy's pick, which I had been using to make some of the loopholes with.

'All this time the Zulus were trying to get into the room. Their assegais kept whizzing towards us, and one struck me in front of the helmet. We were wearing the white tropical helmets then. But the helmet tilted back under the blow, and made the spear lose its power, so that I escaped with a scalp wound, which did not trouble me much then, although it has often caused me illness since.

'Only one man at a time could get in at the door. A big Zulu sprang forward and seized my rifle; but I tore it free and, slipping a cartridge in, I shot him point-blank. Time after time the Zulus gripped the muzzle and tried to tear the rifle from my grasp, and time after time I wrenched it back, because I had a better grip than they had.

'All this time Williams was getting the sick through the hole into the next room – all except one, a soldier of the 24th named Conley, who could not move because of a broken leg. Watching for my chance I dashed from the doorway, and grabbing Conley I pulled him after me through the hole. His leg got broken again, but there was no help for it. As soon as we left the room the Zulus burst in with furious cries of disappointment and rage.

'Now there was a repetition of the work of holding the doorway, except that I had to stand by a hole in the wall, instead of a door, while Williams picked away at the far wall to make an opening for escape into the next room. There was more desperate and almost hopeless fighting, as it seemed; but most of the poor fellows were got through the hole. Again I had to drag Conley through, a terrific task, because he was a very heavy man.

'We were now all in a little room that gave upon the inner line of defence which had been made. We – Williams and R. Jones and W. Jones and myself – were the last men to leave the hospital, after most of the sick and wounded had been carried through the small window and away from the burning building; but it was impossible to save a few of them, and they were butchered.

'Privates William Jones and Robert Jones during all this time had been doing magnificent work in another ward which faced the hill. They kept at it with bullet and bayonet until six out of the seven patients in that ward had been removed. They would have got the seventh – Sergeant Maxfield – out safely, but he was delirious with fever, and, although they managed to dress him, he refused to move. Robert Jones made a last rush to try and get him away like the rest; but when he got back into the room he saw that Maxfield was being stabbed by the Zulus as he lay on his bed. Corporal Allen and Private Hitch helped enormously in keeping up communication with the hospital. They were both badly wounded, but when they could not fight any longer, they served out ammunition to their comrades throughout the night.

'As we got the sick and wounded out they were taken to a verandah in front of the storehouse, and Dr. Reynolds, under a heavy fire and clouds of assegais, did everything he could for them. All this time, of course, the store-house was being valiantly defended by the rest of the garrison.

'When we got into the inner fort, I took my post at a place where two men had been shot. While I was there another man was shot in the neck, I think by a bullet which came through the space between two biscuit-boxes that were not quite close together. This was at about six o'clock in the evening, nearly two hours after the opening shot of the battle had been fired.'

Pause for a moment to picture the scene from this time onward. The field of battle itself is luridly illumined by the flames of the burning hospital. Behind the little fort a hill like a sugarloaf stands lonely on the plain; a few miles away the fallen 24th are stretched on the bloody field of combat, plundered and mutilated, and near them are many black ridges of Zulus. At the Drift, too, are rows of dark corpses, like waves, for the whirlwind swoops have been checked by rifle fire at a distance of several hundred yards, and the assailants have been mown down in ranks. Time after time the Zulus have rushed to the attack, time after time they have been driven back.

Blood and fire and sickness and suffering are everywhere around – with such a life and death struggle how else can it be? There are many terrible sights, but the merciful darkness veils them. Every soldier is at his post – there is one especially who is resting on the mealie-bags, with his rifle presented to the enemy, and his face staring, fixedly. He never moves; he is like a figure carved in stone.

More than one long bayonet has been twisted or doubled; more than one Martini has become jammed or useless through repeated firing; more than one stock has been snapped from the barrel, for when a shot has been discharged there has been no time to reload before a valiant Zulu has come, and so he has been killed with a butt instead of a bullet. Boots are redsodden, helmets are smashed and torn, greatcoats, kerseys, and trousers are ripped, slashed, and stained. Not a face that is not grimy with the smoke and sweat of battle; not a hand that is not black, not a body that is not weary – and not a heart which falters.

That is the secret of the holding of the Drift. There is no surrender – there is only death or victory. It is the three-century-old story of Grenville and the *Revenge* over again. It is all very hideous and very terrible; but the horrors of the combat are lightened by the valour and humanity of the defence. Men are wounded and helpless – they cannot be left to die. Away in Natal, just over the river which divides the colony from Zululand, are unprotected people and women and children. If the drift is lost the victorious hordes will swarm into the colony, and there will be horrors worse than Isandhlwana. So the drift must be held – and the fight goes on.

'We were glad enough to be in the shelter of the little inside fort,' continued Hook. 'Every now and then the Zulus would make a rush for it and get in. We had to charge them out. By this time it was dark, and the hospital was all in flames, but this gave us a splendid light to fight by. I believe it was this light that saved us. We could see them coming, and they could not rush us and take us by surprise from any point. They could not get at us, and so they went away and had ten or fifteen minutes of a war-dance. This roused them up again, and their excitement was so intense that the ground fairly seemed to shake.

'Then, when they were goaded to the highest pitch, they would hurl themselves at us again. We could sometimes, by the light of the flames, keep them well in sight, so well that we could take steady aim and fire coolly. When we could do this they never advanced as far as the barricade, because we shot them down as they ran in on us. But every now and then one or two managed to crawl in and climb over the top of the sacks. They were bayoneted off.

'I need hardly say that we were using Martinis, and fine rifles they were, too. But we did so much firing that they became hot, and the brass of the cartridges softened, the result being that the barrels got very foul and the cartridge-chamber jammed. My own rifle was jammed several times, and I had to work away with the ramrod till I cleared it. We used the old three-sided bayonet, and the long, thin blade that we called the "lung" bayonet. They were fine weapons, too; but some were very poor in quality, and either twisted or bent badly. Several were like that at the end of the fight; but some terrible thrusts were given, and I saw dead Zulus who had been pinned to the ground by the bayonets going through them.

'All this time the sick and wounded were crying for water. We had the water-cart full of water, but it was just by the deserted hospital, and we could not hope to get at it until the day broke, when the Zulus might begin to lose heart and to stop in their mad rushes. But we could not bear the cries any longer, and three or four of us jumped over the boxes and ran and fetched some water in.

'The long night passed and the day broke. Then we looked around us to see what had happened, and there was not a living soul who was not thankful to find that the Zulus had had enough of it and were disappearing over the hill to the south-west. Orders were given to patrol the ground, collect the arms of the dead blacks, and make our position as strong as possible in case of fresh attacks.

'One of the first things I did was to go up to the man who was still looking over our breastwork with his rifle presented to the spot where so many of the Zulus had been. I went up to him, and saw that he did not move, and that he looked very quiet.

'I went nearer and said: "Hello, what are you doing here?"

'He made no answer, and did not stir. I went still closer, and something in his appearance made me tilt his helmet back, as you sometimes tilt back a hat when you want to look closely into a face. As I did so I saw a bullet-mark in his forehead, and knew that he was dead.

'I went away, and was walking up the dry bed of a little stream near the drift, with my own rifle in my right hand and a bunch of assegais over my left shoulder. Suddenly I came across an unarmed Zulu, lying on the ground, apparently dead, but bleeding from the leg. Thinking it strange that a dead man should bleed, I hesitated, and wondered whether I should go on, as other Zulus might be lurking about. But I resumed my task. Just as I was passing, the supposed dead man seized the butt of the rifle and tried to drag it away. The bunch of assegais rattled to the earth.

'The Zulu suddenly released his grasp of the rifle with one hand, and with the other fiercely endeavoured to drag me down. The fight was short and sharp; but it ended by the Zulu being struck in the chest with the butt and knocked to the ground.

'The rest was quickly over.

'After that we were not allowed to go on with our task except in twos and threes.

'When we had done this work we went back to the inner line of defence, sad enough, even the most cheerful of us. But we had no time to dwell on the awful scenes about us. We did not know how soon another assault would be made, but we did know that if the Zulus kept on attacking us it was only a question of time before we were cut to pieces, as our comrades a dozen miles away had been destroyed.

'The roof of the hospital had fallen in by this time, and only the store-house was standing. We were ordered to put ropes through the loopholes of the walls of the hospital, and pull them down. This we did, and the walls, which had already been weakened by our picks, partially collapsed. Then we tore away the thatch from the storehouse, so that the Zulus could not, even if they wished, set fire to it, as they had fired the hospital. With the ruins of the walls we strengthened our little fort, and again waited for the Zulus – if they cared to come. But they had finished their attack.

'We looked about us everywhere for signs of relief, but saw nothing, and our hearts sank. Then came an awful time of suspense. Two of our men had been on the roof of the storehouse signalling with flags when the Zulus meant to attack us. This gave us time to make ready for them. The signallers were still able to stand above the ground, so that they could be seen at a good distance. We saw their flags going wildly. What was it? Everybody was mad with anxiety to know whether it could be friends to relieve us, or more Zulus to destroy us. We watched the flags flapping, and then learnt that signals were being made in reply. We knew we were safe, and that friends were marching up to us.

'We broke into roar after roar of cheering, waving red coats and white helmets, and we cheered again and again when, at about six o'clock in the morning, Colonel Russell rode up with some mounted infantry. We saw them come in, and at the same time we saw that the Zulus had once more got ready to sweep round the mountain to attack us. But it was too late, and on seeing that we were reinforced, they turned silently away, and only their dead and a few wounded were left with us.

'Lord Chelmsford and what was left of the 3rd Column came up to Rorke's Drift soon after. There was no time to sit down and mope, and there were the sick and wounded as well as the rest to look after. So when the Commander-in-Chief arrived I was back at my cooking in my shirt-sleeves, making tea for the sick.

'A sergeant ran up and said:

'"Lieutenant Bromhead wants you."

'"Wait till I put my coat on," I said.

'"Come as you are – straight away," he ordered, and so in my shirt-sleeves, and with my braces hanging about me, I went into the midst of the officers, and Lord Chelmsford asked me all about the defence of the hospital, as I was the last to leave the building. An officer took our names, and wrote down what we had done. He was the first officer to be killed in the last South African war – Major-General Penn-Symons, at Dundee.

'When the relief had come up the men of the column were sent out to bury the Zulus. There were 351 dead blacks counted, and these were put into two big holes in front of the hospital. The column made the Kaffirs who were with them dig the trenches; but although they dug the holes, they positively refused to bury the bodies. There were only a few badly wounded left, as the Zulus had carried off their wounded as they retired. A great many dead were found in a mealie field not far from the hospital.

'As for our own comrades, we, who had fought side by side with them, buried them. This was done the day after the fight, not far from the place where they fell, and at the foot of the hill. Soon afterwards the little cemetery was walled in and a monument was put up in the middle. The lettering was cut on it by a very clever bandsman named Mellsop, who used bits of broken bayonets as chisels. He drew a capital picture of the fight. Those who had been killed in action were buried on one side of the cemetery, and those who died of disease on the other side. A curious thing was that a civilian named Byrne, who had taken part in the defence and was killed, was buried outside the cemetery wall. I don't know why, except that he was not a regular soldier.

'I was at Rorke's Drift for six months after the fight, but we were moved about a quarter of a mile away from the storehouse and hospital. On August 3rd, at Rorke's Drift, where I was the only recipient of the Victoria Cross, the others having left, I was decorated with the Cross by Lord Wolseley, at a special parade. It was curious, but until then I had scarcely ever thought about the V.C. – in fact we did not know or trouble much about it, although we had a V.C. man in the regiment – Griffiths they called him. He was killed, with the rest, at Isandhlwana.'

[The Zulu War was ended with the decisive victory of Ulundi on July 4th, 1879. Soon afterwards the chiefs submitted, and Cetewayo, the king, was captured, and peace was declared.]

There was, of course, more to the Anglo-Zulu War than Isandlwana and Rorke's Drift. Fresh troops were hurried out to Zululand, and six bitter months of fighting followed, before the Zulu were eventually defeated at King Cetshwayo's royal homestead at Ulundi. Trumpet-Major Henry Wilkinson of the 17th Lancers was among those reinforcements, and he recalled both the final stages of the war, and the lingering horror of the defeat at Isandlwana.

The Fight for Natal

The Death or Glory Boys were hurried off from Hounslow Barracks to South Africa when the dreadful news came of the butchery of British soldiers at Isandhlwana, or Sanwana, as we called it, not far from the Buffalo River. Fifteen thousand Zulus had attacked the camp, and wiped out more than eight hundred officers and men, mostly of the 24th Regiment, which is now the South Wales Borderers. Amongst the dead were Lieutenants Melville and Coghill, whose bodies were found ringed in by fallen Zulus, and covering the Queen's Colour of the 1st Battalion of the 24th.

From Sanwana the Zulus swarmed to Rorke's Drift, ten miles away, and would have overrun Natal and killed hosts of English men, women, and children if it had not been that they were driven back by the handful of heroes who defended the burning buildings at the Drift throughout the afternoon and night. I remember well how terribly the nation felt the disaster of Sanwana, and how, at the same time, it exulted in the valour of the two brave officers who perished in saving the Colour.

About four months after this reverse – which was on January 22nd, 1879 – I was looking at Sanwana's awful field. The 17th had landed in South Africa, and passed through Rorke's Drift. The hill of Isandhlwana, which means the 'Little Hand,' I think, was hard by the battlefield, on which the British dead were still lying as they had fallen, and unburied. It was the most ghastly and pitiful spectacle that ever eyes beheld. Carrion birds and prowling animals had done their work, and time had been very busy; but wherever we looked we saw the remnants of the officers and men who, as even the Zulus declared admiringly, had fallen in their places like the stones of walls. The high, rank jungle covered rotting helmets, tunics, and skeletons of men and horses. Broken rifles, twisted bayonets, smashed waggons, and all sorts of tinned provisions were lying about, and everywhere were signs and proofs of the deadly nature of the savages' attack, and the heavy price at which the 24th had sold their lives. In a very small space three thousand black and white men had been killed, and all the British had been mutilated hideously.

The battalions of a regiment rarely meet; but both battalions of the 24th were in South Africa, and just before Sanwana the officers of the 1st and 2nd were dining together. It was very near the anniversary of the battle of Chillianwallah, in India, when, thirty years before, the 24th was cut to pieces.

The officers of the 1st, who were entertaining the officers of the 2nd, had a few bottles of wine left, and the toast was drunk: 'That we may not get into such a mess, and have better luck this time!'

A few days later not a soul of the 1st who drank the toast was living, and of the 2nd five officers had fallen. I saw the remnants of the gallant soldiers who had drunk the toast, as they were lying in the shadow of the Little Hand four months after the massacre.

It was not our duty to bury the dead – that was done by other parties and native levies – but we took two guns back to Rorke's Drift. The carriages had been dragged some distance before being abandoned by the Zulus, who found that they had no use for them. At the Drift several things were recognised by a handful of fugitives who had escaped from Sanwana. I took away, as a relic, part of the big drum – the bass drum, which struck my fancy as a musician. It was a bit of the shell part, with some of the letters of the battle-honours of the 24th showing. I kept it for a long time, but gave it away in India.

The Martinis had been carried off by the Zulus, who used them in many a fight with us, especially at Ulundi; but they had not touched a lot of the boxes of provisions, thinking, I suppose, that they contained explosives, though some of the boxes had been assegaied. It proved a lucky thing for us that the Zulus did not really know how to use our ammunition effectively, for though they could load with it all right they could not aim straight.

Amongst the volunteers who had gone out to the war was the young Prince Imperial. He was a great favourite with everybody, and I often saw him walking about and chatting with the officers, and sometimes the men. He was a very keen soldier, as you might expect from a descendant of the great Napoleon, and there was nothing that he was afraid to try to do in that dangerous country. He was particularly good at understanding and describing the geographical features of the country, and one morning – it was the first of June – the Prince rode off with an infantry officer and a small escort of only a dozen troopers to select some camping ground which we were to occupy the next day.

We had been out, and at about eight o'clock at night had returned to our camp, hungry, thirsty, and tired. We were getting supper ready, and that was a far simpler matter than during the last South African war, because we had not over much going in the way of provisions. Sometimes we would have biscuits issued, and at other times flour. On the night of the first we had received flour, and we were mixing this with water in our canteens, so that we could put it over little fires which we made in small holes in the ground by digging with our heels.

Everything was calm and peaceful, and we were looking forward to the evening meal, when we were startled more than we should have been if a thunderbolt had fallen in our midst.

Suddenly, and with intense excitement, the voices of the adjutant and the sergeant-major rang in the camp with the orders, 'All lights out,' and 'All fires out.'

We obeyed the orders instantly, thinking, most of us, especially those who had seen Sanwana's field, that the Zulus must be in immense strength around us and on the point of rushing the camp. But it was something even more startling than that, for, almost instantly, the whisper went round – 'The Prince Imperial is killed!'

Not a soul in the standing camp could believe the news, still less the circumstances of the Prince's death. It was a terrible blow to the Commander-in-Chief, who had been superseded already by Sir Garnet Wolseley, and who seemed to have changed greatly since the disaster of Sanwana. Yet the tidings were true enough, and, at four o'clock next morning, we rode off to bring the body in. We knew pretty well where to find it, because the escort had given us the locality. For about eight miles we went; then, at the edge of a mealie field, we found the body of the Emperor's son.

He had died fighting like a soldier, and, as the Zulus said, like a lion at bay. He was riddled with assegai wounds, and near him, also speared to death, was his pet, a small white terrier. He carried a sword which his father had borne through the Franco-German war; but he had not been able to use it. Two troopers of the escort were lying near him, where they had fallen in the surprise attack.

We found the Prince between six and seven o'clock, and while the 17th were formed up in line, so as to be ready to meet instantly any rush by the enemy, he was put on a mule stretcher. That was a sort of pannier on the side of a transport mule, a very strong animal, the pannier on the other side being balanced with a living man. We took the Prince back to the camp, where everything seemed terribly still and gloomy; then the body was sent down the country to Maritzburg, with an escort, after which it was conveyed by train to Durban and shipped to England for burial.

There were many things, indeed, to trouble and depress us in that war in Zululand; and there were some very strange happenings, too. I reckon amongst these the loss of our adjutant, Lieutenant Frith, a very smart officer. The regiment was formed in line, and was near a very high ridge of hills. The adjutant was on the right flank, and a peculiar thing about him was that he was riding a Cape horse. Our commanding officer, the famous Colonel Drury-Lowe, also rode a Cape horse, and as both were creams, and the rest of the horses were English, and had gone out from Hounslow, the colonel and the adjutant were very conspicuous.

The Zulus were potting at us, at long range, from the hills and the surrounding country; but it did not seem in the least likely that they would do any mischief. To me it is a mystery to this day that the adjutant should have been struck; but he was, and in dramatic fashion. He collapsed suddenly in the saddle. We all wondered what had happened, because we were supposed to be quite out of range.

The trumpet-major, Dunn, a fine, tall fellow, dismounted quickly and lifted the adjutant bodily out of the saddle. Then it was seen that Lieutenant Frith was dead. He had been shot through the side, and killed instantly, and without uttering a word. That was our only casualty in the skirmish, but it made more impression upon us than a much heavier loss would have done, because the fatal shot seemed to come from nowhere.

Cetewayo, the Zulu king, had retired to his kraal, or village, of Ulundi, and we pushed on towards it in tremendous expectation of a desperate fight and a splendid victory, with a prospect of all sorts of booty at the finish, for wonderful stories had been told of the wealth of the royal city of huts. Like most yarns of the same calibre, there was not much in them, and precious few of us got anything in the way of booty. I fancy that those who did come across anything in the shape of gold kept their mouths shut.

Just over five thousand of us, mostly Europeans, with two Gatlings and a dozen field-guns, were making for Ulundi. There were with us two very famous soldiers, besides our own Commander-in-Chief, Lord Chelmsford, and our colonel, Drury-Lowe; and these were Colonel Evelyn Wood, V.C., an old 17th officer, now a field-marshal, and Captain and Brevet-Colonel Redvers Buller, who had recently won his Cross. He little foresaw, then, that twenty years later, in that very country, he would witness the tragedy of Colenso River.

Ulundi itself did not give any Victoria Crosses, but the day before the battle three were won, by Captain Lord William Beresford, of the 9th Lancers, and Captain D'Arcy and Sergeant O'Toole, of the Frontier Light Horse. We were in camp very close to the White Umvolosi River, and the three were taking part in a reconnaissance across it. They had pushed towards Ulundi, where swarms of Zulus were known to be assembled, mostly hiding in hollows, behind rocks, and in the thick, high grass. All at once the Zulus opened fire, and there was nothing for the little band to do but to make a bolt to safety.

Just as they were dashing off, a sergeant of the 24th was thrown from his horse, and it looked as if the Zulus would get him, for they swarmed around only a few yards away. Lord William saw what had happened, and instantly he cut his way through the enemy, got hold of the sergeant and hauled him into the saddle, and rode off with his burden. He was nearly pulled out of the saddle, for a wounded man is a heavy weight to handle; but Lord William never let him go, and while he bore him off O'Toole shot down the nearest Zulus with his carbine.

Stunned and almost senseless, the sergeant reeled and rolled in front of the captain, who was slashing away with his sword, and as he fired his carbine O'Toole helped the officer to keep the sergeant in the saddle. At last O'Toole had to throw away his carbine, and bear a hand to bring the sergeant away.

At the same time Captain D'Arcy was doing pretty much the same thing as Lord Beresford. As they were retiring, a trooper of the Frontier Light Horse fell from the saddle. Here also the Zulus were swarming around; but the captain waited till the trooper mounted behind him before he started to ride off. Then one of the unexpected things happened – both officer and man were kicked off by the excited horse, and the Zulus rushed up for the slaughter. The trooper was almost senseless, and unable to look after himself.

It was an awful situation, but the captain held heroically and grimly on to his forlorn hope. Time after time he tried to get the trooper back into the saddle; but he did not succeed, and it was not until the Zulus were actually ringing him round that he rode away. The trooper was assegaied. Oddly enough, the captain's own life was saved during the war by one of the brave V.C. men I have mentioned – Sir Redvers Buller.

Well, we saw that thrilling little skirmish from the other side of the river, and I think it put heart of grace into some of us when we thought of what the real thing might mean.

The Zulus were at least four to one, and they had the tremendous advantage of remembering that they had fallen on and wiped out the British force at Sanwana, just as they expected to rush down on us and give us the same dose of the gun and the assegai.

All through the night before the battle of Ulundi the Zulu warriors howled and danced and drank and worked themselves up into a frenzy; but we were not unduly disturbed. We had profited by the bitter experience of the war, and were drawn up in a square which it was not likely that even the Zulu impis would succeed in breaking.

Impi means a brigade or big body of warriors, and it was the Zulu plan to swoop down on us in crescent formation and annihilate us. These huge living half-moons were to close in on us, just as they had closed at Sanwana.

I do not think that in the modern history of the British Army there has been a grander or more inspiring sight than that which met the Zulu impis on the morning of Ulundi. The little British force was drawn up in square – an immense four-sided wall of scarlet-coated men, with field-guns at the corners, Gatlings on the left flank, native troops and ammunition carts and waggons inside, and King's Dragoon Guards – not many of them – and the Death or Glory Boys behind the infantry, ready for a dash with sword and lance when the time came.

The Colours were flying and the bands were playing as we advanced, and the sun shone on the glittering bayonets, lances, and rifle-barrels. That was just before we were actually and finally disposed in square, waiting for them to come on; and then, of course, we were silent enough, for we were out for business.

Ulundi itself was only a few hundred yards away, and we had burnt it as we passed through it, after fording the White Umvolosi, which was then low. The place where we were in square was a plain, surrounded by high and low hills, and it seemed as if we were standing in the middle of a basin, with the river behind.

When the day had broken fully, the Zulus could be seen completely surrounding the square, at a considerable distance to begin with. They were armed with all sorts of rifles, from an elephant gun to a Martini. Some of the guns were frightful things; they would break your back or shoulder to fire them, for they had a bullet nearly the size of a two-shilling piece.

The cavalry had been ordered to dismount and stand-to – that means, stand to your horses and be ready to mount instantly. We were told to crouch down, too, so as to escape the bullets as much as possible; but when the fight began and the Zulu impis were rolling down on the square, we bobbed up constantly to see how things were going.

It was a wonderful and awful sight to see the big regiments of black men, with their shields and assegais shining and flashing in the sun, gathering in around us, and not the pleasantest of sounds to listen to their savage and excited yells.

When they were about two thousand yards off, they began to plug away with their elephant guns and Martinis, and our own artillery and Gatlings and rifle, started in with the chorus.

At first the field-guns had the lead; then as the impis rushed towards us, the smaller arms began to crackle and the smoke to thicken about, for those were not the days of smokeless powder.

The roar and din of battle grew; on came the Zulu impis; from both sides rose a deafening commotion of fire. Officers' voices were heard encouraging their men to be steady, and to fire low; gunners were furiously serving their artillery; the infantry were blazing away with the good old Martini, ready with the bayonet if the enemy came near enough to taste the steel; and the cavalry were lying low, waiting to mount and sweep out of the square to the charge and put the crowning touch to the battle.

Yet on and on, nearer and nearer, the hordes of frantic Zulus came, fearing nothing and defying death. Their regiments, the human moons, were cut and torn by shot and shell, and rifle bullet; still they advanced, running, springing, and jumping towards the four human walls which were now faced with solid fire and enveloped in a dense smoke.

It seemed as if nothing could stop or check that mad and brave assault;

but the Gatlings were pouring their destructive and incessant fire into the black regiments, and the Martinis were mowing the Zulus down.

Less than a hundred yards separated the foremost of the Zulus from the square, and it seemed impossible that they could be driven back, except by the bayonet. The ground was covered with fallen men; still the Zulu impis rushed on.

For half-an-hour there had been a perfect hail of fire; then the impis began to waver, they began to break – then, knowing that the fight was hopeless, they bolted, swarming in disorder in all directions.

And well they might, for they knew that the dreaded 'long assegai' – the lance – would soon be at work amongst them.

'*Stand to your horses!*' '*Mount!*'

The orders were rapped out; but almost before they were uttered the Death or Glory Boys were in the saddle, and the sweating, blackened infantry were opening out to let us through to reach the flying Zulus.

There were storms of cheers as we swept through the redcoats, and each squadron formed up in line. Then came the order to gallop.

The trumpet-major sounded the 'Charge,' and like a living avalanche the 17th swept over the ground which was black with the broken enemy.

We were met by a murderous fire as soon as we were clear of the square, for half an impi, which had been hidden in the long, thick grass, rose up like a phantom body and blazed away at us, while some of them stabbed and ripped the horses cruelly. The Zulus were pinned with the 'long assegai' or cut down with the sword until there were no more left in the region of the square.

One of the first to fall was a brave and fine gentleman, Captain the Honourable E. V. Wyatt-Edgell. He was shot through the throat while leading his men in the charge – and if we needed anything to madden us more than we were already maddened we had it in the sight of his emptied saddle. His terrified horse bolted amongst the Zulus, and you could see it quite plainly, because the Zulus had no mounted men, except a chief or two.

A troop of the King's Dragoon Guards, under Captain Brewster, had dashed after us out of the square, and when we had rallied the officer said to me:

'There's a fellow moving about over there – lend me your carbine.'

A good many of the Zulus were shamming death and suddenly coming to life when they could get a shot in or a rip at us, and this warrior was one of them.

I lent the captain my carbine and gave him two or three rounds of ammunition. He advanced to within a couple of hundred yards of the Zulu and got the shots in, but whether he dropped his man or not I don't know.

The 'long assegai' had done its deadly work, and by putting the finish to the Zulu rout at Ulundi ended the war.

Our fallen captain was buried in his cloak on the battlefield, but soon afterwards he was taken up and brought to England.

Cetewayo had bolted, but he was pursued and taken, and England heard a good deal about him till he died a few years later.

I myself went to India with the regiment, taking my Sanwana relic with me, and it was in Lucknow that I got promoted trumpet-major.

In many respects the defeat at Isandlwana brought an end to the Confederation policy which had spawned it. Rather than being quick and easy, the Zulu War proved to be long and bloody, and it caused the home government to question the wisdom of Confederation. Moreover, the Zulu War was followed by another war in southern Africa, and one which was destined to provide more than its fair share of disasters.

In 1877, as part of the Confederation plan, Britain had annexed the Boer republic of the Transvaal. To outsiders, the Transvaal administration seemed hopelessly inefficient, and its Treasury bankrupt, and the British made a highly selective canvas of opinion which suggested that the republic's white citizens would welcome British intervention. In fact, however, most Boer farmers – who carried the greatest political weight within the kingdom – were deeply opposed to British rule, and while British troops were preoccupied with the Anglo-Zulu War, a fervent republican movement gained strength. In December 1880, 7000 Boers gathered under arms and proclaimed the Transvaal once more a republic. British garrisons across the country were besieged, and a column marching to the capital, Pretoria, was attacked and cut down by accurate rifle-fire.

The revolt caught the British authorities by surprise, and a column was assembled in northern Natal to march to the relief of the beleaguered garrisons. It was commanded by General Sir George Colley, who was widely regarded as the best-educated soldier of his day, although he had little experience of commanding troops in the field. Colley's route took him through the foothills of the Kahlamba (Drakensberg) mountains, where Boer forces had gathered to oppose him across the Laing's Nek pass. Colley decided to take the pass by force, and the mournful events which followed were described by Corporal William Clark of the King's Dragoon Guards.

The Tragedy of Majuba Hill

I landed in South Africa in the gloomy year of 1879, when the Empire was ringing with the mournful tales of the annihilation of a British force at Isandhlwana and the thrilling stories of the valiant defence of Rorke's Drift.

I was a cavalryman, and marched straight into Zululand, to the fatal spot where the 24th had fallen under the rifles and assegais of the savage warriors.

Three months had passed since the butchery, yet even then our slaughtered troops remained unburied. They were lying where they had been shot down or speared, and all were mutilated, according to the custom of the Zulus. Every tin of preserved food, too, had been pierced — which showed that some white man had told the savages how to make it worthless.

It was a stern, terrible beginning to my soldier's life. The dead were buried about a week later; but so slightly that, when I visited Isandhlwana again, two or three years later, the field of battle, which was also the place of sepulchre, was white with bones that had become exposed.

Within a few months the Zulus were crushed at Ulundi, and the British troops were ordered down into the Transvaal, where the Boers were giving a lot of trouble. The Transvaal was then annexed and under British rule, and many of the Boers objected strongly to this system of dominion.

I was able to know exactly what their feelings were, because I was in the police during the whole of the time I was in South Africa, and as my duty was to accompany the Sheriff to collect taxes and preserve order generally, I was constantly visiting the Boers in their homes. I know that there has been long and bitter controversy on the subject of Briton versus Boer, and I would like to say in favour of the Boers that repeatedly I received kindnesses from them for which they refused to accept any payment or acknowledgment whatever. Those were the real Boers, the patriots who were fighting only for their country, and who were to wage a war which was to give them many victories, and, greatest of all, the overwhelming triumph of Majuba.

For a little while the clouds seemed to disperse — had there not been a great review of the British forces in Pretoria, to impress the possible enemy, and was not that army crowned with its victory over the Zulus?

Peace seemed to be assured, and most of the troops were accordingly sent home. My own regiment went to India, a few of us, about forty, being left behind to go to England to the depôt. All our horses were sold, and I believe they were, nearly without exception, secured by the Boers. Our accoutrements were given into stores and sent away down country. As for us, we marched to Pietermaritzburg, a strange sight indeed, for we were literally in rags. We wore anything we could lay hands on, and looked more like wandering tramps than British cavalry.

Again I was in the police, and lived in the fort, which was used as a prison. In spite of all I heard to the contrary, I knew that the Boers would fight. The actual truth came home in sudden and dramatic fashion. One day I was returning to the fort from some quarries where the prisoners — they were mostly English soldiers who were punished for such crimes as looting — had been working, when an Afrikander galloped past us on a horse. He was intensely excited, and waving a paper over his head he shouted: 'It's all over with you! We've done for the 94th, and we'll do for you when we're ready!'

That was a startling enough threat, because a detachment of the 94th Regiment had been massacred by the Boers at Bronker's Spruit.

The threat was carried into the fort like a flash, and General Sir George Colley, Governor of Natal, who had been appointed Commander-in-Chief, ordered a parade that very evening. He was full of fire and hope, and had the reputation of being a brave and resourceful soldier – which he had fully earned in that land of wars.

Cavalry would be badly wanted, if the worst came to the worst – and Sir George made this clear when he addressed us.

'I shall have to form a regiment of cavalry,' he told us, 'and I look to the King's Dragoon Guards to help me to raise one, as quickly as possible. That regiment will be established, I know – and I will promise you one thing, men – that it shall never be taken by me into any corner out of which I cannot get it!'

Brave words by a brave man, and spoken almost under the shadow of Majuba! And how we cheered him when he spoke! We were wild with eager enthusiasm, and even the maimed came forward as volunteers. Amongst them was a gallant fellow named Cutler. He had only one eye, but he insisted upon joining, and was taken. What would you have when men are scarce and danger presses?

Horses were needed badly, and we got them in as best we could. They were mostly Cape horses, awkward, untrained, unsatisfactory brutes; but I was lucky enough to get one of our old chestnut mares, which required no drilling. Volunteers came from all classes. Some could ride, but most could not. That, however, was not a very serious matter, because we had a few horses which had belonged to the artillery, and did finely for the recruits, because they were as comfortable as old arm-chairs, and ambled round in a way that could not hurt anybody. The old stagers amongst us were interspersed so as to leaven up the regiment – and I can assure you that when it came to drilling with drawn swords, at the trot, we would rather have faced the enemy than the recruits.

In a month or so we started for the Front, and plunged straightway into disaster after disaster. First of all came Laing's Nek on January 28th, 1881, then our defeat on the Ingogo River on February 8th, and after that, on February 26th – a terrible Sunday – the overwhelming calamity of Majuba.

Our first sight of the Boers was at the pass called Laing's Nek. Eager as they were to meet us, we were more impatient to fight them, and can you wonder at this when you remember how great a trust was put in us, and our faith in ourselves?

If such a thing can be a distinction, then I can lay claim to seeing the very opening of a most unhappy war, for I was on outpost with a man named Todd when I saw a company of Boers galloping round with the purpose of cutting us off from our main body. We made a dash for camp and got safely back, to the intense surprise of Captain Brownlow, our commander. All was excitement and commotion, with hurried calculations as to what the enemy would do. It seemed as if we should be rushed, but for the time being the Boers began to withdraw.

Instantly our captain ordered some infantry who were near him to lie down and fire, giving the range at 800 yards. He chose them, I suppose, because he thought they would be better shots than the cavalry. They did very well, too, because two or three horses dropped.

I cannot say whether human life was claimed in this first firing of the war, because we were not near enough to the enemy to see the full effect of our practice. We had not done much, perhaps, but it was enough to win praise from General Colley. 'Owing to your able scouting,' he said, addressing us, 'I have been able to give the infantry more scope than would otherwise have been possible,' meaning, I suppose, that he had taken them over a larger area of ground. That was encouraging, but infinitely more satisfactory was his intimation that next morning he would lead us to attack the Boers and fight the first battle of the war.

Few of us could sleep during that anxious night of preparation, and no sound of trumpet or bugle was needed to make us ready for the advance. We went out, and with what seemed like appalling swiftness plunged into fighting.

The first real challenge screamed into the quiet air, not from gun or rifle, but from the Rocket Brigade, which was furnished by the officers and men of the *Dido* and the *Boadicea*, warships on the Cape station.

To that shrill hiss and crash of invitation the Boers responded instantly and crushingly. I cannot describe to you what I actually felt, but I do know that the reality was far and away more stirring and dramatic than anything I had expected. Much as I knew about the Boers, I was not prepared for such a struggle as that which confronted us. And in this I was not alone.

But there was no time for thought. We were in for a desperate business, and the only thing to do was to get it finished as quickly and triumphantly as possible. I do not think I exaggerate when I say that even then, at the very beginning of our battle, the most pessimistic of us anticipated speedy victory, and probably an instant finish to the war.

Our handful of cavalry got away to the right of the Nek, not in very brilliant fashion, perhaps, but you could hardly look for that from such a scratch mounted body. A good cavalryman is not created in a month, and some of the ready-made troopers were so unaccustomed to the saddle, and – reasonably enough – so chary of a fall, that instead of jumping an obstacle, they would walk their horses round it!

If, while we were fresh and eager, we could have been led straight into a charge, or to carry out some stiff and stirring work, it would have been more agreeable to some of us than being forced, as we were forced, to halt and endure a very heavy and demoralising fire. There we were, a fair target for the enemy, and a target that was seldom missed.

With startling abruptness a shell plumped into the very thick of us. Now, not even a band of raw soldiers will be wanting in smartness at a crisis like that. The shell was there, and every instant we expected it to burst and spread death around. We did not stand on ceremony or wait for orders – we inclined – that is to say, we opened out – and did it as smartly, too, as I ever saw that particular evolution performed.

But the puzzling thing was that the shell did not explode. There it lay, and before we could fathom the mystery of it another came, but this did not burst either. We could not understand it at the moment, but soon enough we learnt that the missiles came from our own artillery, so that at the very opening of the battle we were being bombarded by our own people. The Boers had no artillery.

Our captain was a little distance away, and did not at first realise what was happening. When he saw us scatter he shouted: 'What are you men inclining for?' By way of answer we pointed to the shells.

The captain turned to me.

'Clark,' he said, 'gallop to Colonel Deane, and ask if we are to attack.' Colonel Deane was then leading a storming party of the 58th Regiment.

It was a desperate, almost forlorn undertaking to ride across that bullet-swept ground, but I spurred my gallant mare on, and dashed towards the stormers. As I galloped I met a staff officer belonging to the Rifles – Lieutenant Inman, I think it was.

'What do you want?' he shouted.

I answered that Captain Brownlow had ordered me to ask Colonel Deane if the cavalry were to attack, and so support the stormers.

'Colonel Deane is down.' replied the subaltern. 'Yes, certainly, go on.'

I turned my mare to gallop back to my superior officer, and almost as I did so Lieutenant Inman was shot dead. His words to me – the order to 'go on' – were probably the last he uttered.

As best I could I made my way back, but the fire and energy seemed to have left my mare. She struggled bravely on, but I knew from the way she galloped that she was hit somewhere – and no wonder, for by that time the enemy's fire was so furious that it seemed impossible for anything to escape being struck.

At last I rejoined my commander, who was anxiously awaiting me, and I hurriedly delivered the order to advance.

'Bugler,' cried the captain, turning to a little boy who belonged to the Army Service Corps, 'sound the Charge!'

The boy raised his bugle and put it to his lips. Only the first wild note of the 'Charge' had sounded when the poor little fellow fell dead, shot through the brain.

Tragedy succeeded tragedy. Scarcely had the bugler fallen when the captain went down, with his horse shot under him. Then fell Sergeant-Major Lunney, who commanded the first squadron, because the non-commissioned officers amongst us had been given commands, owing to the shortage of officers. I think the Boers must have aimed at him deliberately, as he was riddled with bullets.

Who in such a fusillade could escape? I myself became a marked man, doubtless owing to the fact that I was wearing a blue patrol jacket, and at a short distance looked like an officer. Two shots struck my bridle arm, shattering the elbow. The reins dropped and my startled mare dashed away, and just cleared the croup of my captain's horse. Both horses stumbled and struggled on the ground together, and there for some awful moments we lay, in hopeless confusion, with death threatening from the bullets which hailed around us, and a not less awful fate from the driving hoofs of our maddened mounts. I do not know how I managed it, but I seized the reins in my teeth, then took them on my sword-arm, the sword hanging by the knot.

Confusion, which was almost panic, reigned. Saddles were emptied, horses were kicking on the ground, shot and mangled, and men were lying all around. Some of the horses, terrified, were galloping away without riders. Captain Brownlow's was shot dead. We were in the thick of the fight now, and mixed up with the enemy.

My commander's position was one of the gravest peril, because he was lying helpless and at the mercy of the enemy. His danger was seen by Private John Doogan, a trooper of the King's, who was his servant. Doogan himself was shot through both arms, and therefore as a rider was useless; but one thing he could do, at any rate – stand by his captain under fire.

He did it, too. He gave his own horse to the captain, who did his best to rally his troops, then took the reins under his arm and led him into safety. Badly wounded though he was, yet he refused to take refuge in the ambulance. For this brave action Doogan won the Victoria Cross, and never, I think, was that decoration more thoroughly deserved. Another Cross was given for Laing's Nek – to Lieutenant Alan Richard Hill, of the 58th, who picked up a wounded subaltern and tried to bear him off the field of battle. The young officer was again shot in his rescuer's arms, this time mortally.

Lieutenant Hill, undaunted, defying the deadly musketry, rushed back to the open ground again twice, each time bringing in a wounded man. So, you see, though Laing's Nek was a disaster, it was redeemed from shame by many a noble act.

I bled excessively, and felt as if I should faint. My mare, too, staggered, and as I could not control either her or myself, we collapsed together, and tumbled in a heap on the earth. For several hours I knew nothing, then Corporal Smith, of the Army Service Corps, and some Kaffirs picked me up, gave me brandy, and took me down to the ambulance – which was worse than all the fighting I had seen.

A field officer of the 58th, one of the defeated stormers, was brought in and placed alongside me. He was shot through the chest and was dying; yet he was perfectly conscious. The doctor bent down and said sadly: 'I am very sorry, but I can do nothing more for you, major.'

'No,' replied the major, 'it is all over with me.'

I turned round and looked at him, with an awful fascination, and even then he asked huskily, with the kindness of a brave, unselfish gentleman: 'And where are *you* hit, corporal?'

I told him, but he never answered, for even as I spoke he passed away.

They removed him when the end came, and put in his place a seaman of the *Dido*, who, like so many of our poor fellows, was badly wounded in the chest. He was perfectly conscious, but from the time they brought him in until he died he never spoke.

I was carried from the ambulance to the camp, and heard General Colley address the troops. 'Men,' he said, 'you have not been beaten; you have simply been repulsed. With the number of troops at my disposal it is impossible to renew operations, and I must wait for reinforcements. I hope the wounded will do well. I can say no more. I wish you all good-night.'

Hard things have been said of Sir George, but I know myself that he was a kind and gallant gentleman. Next day he came up and asked me if there was anybody to whom I should like to send a letter, and I told him that I would be glad to have one posted to my sister, who lived at Sandgate. The General had a letter written, which he signed himself – and to this day she treasures it.

Words cannot picture what our camp was like. We were hemmed in, and cut off from all medical comforts and necessaries – bran, for instance, was used in poultices. Marquees were filled with wounded soldiers, many of them dying, and blood was on everything you touched. The very stretchers were stiff with it. Sailors from the warships served as nurses – and splendid nurses they made, I can assure you.

I will not dwell on the reverse we suffered in the stubborn fight of the Ingogo River. For twelve hours we were under a withering fire, then the night came and we knew that we had been repulsed again, with terrible losses. To add to our gloom the night brought the most appalling storm of thunder, lightning, rain, and hail that I ever saw. In the thick of it, Captain Wilkinson, of the 3rd Battalion 60th Rifles, was drowned while trying to cross the swollen river with medical comforts for the wounded.

This second and unexpected check meant that we were in more desperate case than ever, hopelessly pinned in, as it seemed.

Perhaps some foreboding of the crowning disaster oppressed our general, for he never addressed us again. There was no short speech of encouragement or hope for us, and we knew nothing till the coming of that dismal Sunday which will always be connected in my memory with Majuba Hill.

The hill by this time was a familiar object, rising like a colossal sugar-loaf from the Drakensberg Mountains, and about ten miles from the Nek.

Our camp was at Mount Prospect, and, as I have said, we were completely locked up. We knew that only a dozen miles away Sir Evelyn Wood was getting reinforcements for us, and we had already been strengthened by the arrival of more than 600 of the Gordon Highlanders, fresh from victory after victory in India, amongst the triumphs being the Kabul to Kandahar march. They were all hard veterans, and the world could not show finer soldiers than these and our own troops who had been through the strain of war in Zululand and the Transvaal.

You may be in the thick of things in time of war and yet know very little of what is going on around you. The first I learnt about Majuba was that the great, bare hill was ours! That astounding fact was revealed to me by Dr. Babington, the surgeon in whose care I was and to whom I owe so much.

I was outside the marquee when the doctor spoke. 'Look here, Clark!' he said, 'it's all over with the Boers now! We've got the hill!'

In amazement I looked towards Majuba Hill, and then I saw that British troops were in possession of it, and that the Boers were already advancing to that attack which ended in such an unexpected and amazing triumph for them.

I rubbed my eyes and marvelled. How had the seemingly impossible been accomplished? How had our men got more than six thousand feet up the hill? And why? My own wits and other tongues enlightened me. Not long before midnight on the previous day (Saturday) Sir George had ordered a secret parade of a mixed force of about 550 men – a handful of King's Dragoon Guards, Rifles, Gordons, and the 58th, and a small Naval Brigade – with three days' rations and seventy rounds of ammunition. But they had no water – and there is no water on Majuba's barren heights!

The general had marched forth to seize the hill, believing that in doing so he was commanding the Boer position and insuring his own salvation. He had left 200 men at the base of the mountain to secure his communications with our camp, and in the dead of night had taken his mixed band of 350 fighting men to the very top, an almost incredible achievement. No wonder the Boers were thunderstruck next morning when they discovered that a lonely and almost inaccessible peak had been silently seized and was dotted with men who in theory, at any rate, could pick off their enemy at pleasure.

I watched the whole of that world-moving tragedy from a distance of only a few hundred yards – through the doctor's field-glasses, which he had lent me, and with which I had taken myself to a spot not far from the marquee. That was one advantage of being an invalid, with freedom of movement; and perhaps no survivor of the war was more fortunately placed as an eye-witness of Majuba than myself.

The small, heavy-laden band which had climbed up the narrow, rugged pathways of the hill in such an astonishing way – it had been an incessant struggle in dense darkness, for about six hours – was in fancied security on a flat piece of ground about a mile in circumference. I say fancied, because the result proved that it was the most fatal spot that could have been selected. No water was available on the hill, none had been taken up – and water is the most essential of all things in battle, when a destroying thirst assails the combatants. Yet Sir George definitely and more than once announced that Majuba Hill was to be held for three days! I am not offering explanations or expressing opinions – that is no part of my wish; I am telling simply what I saw and heard.

The general first of all had ordered that not a shot should be fired; then he changed his mind and a rifle cracked at his command. This was the first intimation to the Boers that the British held Majuba, and from that moment they set to work deliberately and patiently to wrest it from the captors.

They knew their work, and did it with a mere handful of picked men so far as the real capture of the hill was concerned. From their main body of some 2000 they detached 200 stormers, and these took such complete advantage of the cover offered, which they knew so well, that they ascended the mountain unseen by the defenders and undetected till the very moment when their withering rifle fire revealed their closeness.

Already the war had shown what deadly shots the Boers were, and now every British figure was a target, every helmet that was seen was riddled. It was not so much a battle as a *battue*, because the British troops could see no enemy to fire at, and yet they were themselves fatally exposed. They shot away their ammunition – such as they could get at from their pouches and the boxes; but many of the boxes could not be opened, and the cartridges were therefore useless.

Still watching through my glasses, I saw the wildly-moving figures on Majuba, but the idea of disaster never entered my mind until I noticed – what? British troops, the finest in the Army, men of twenty years' service, not bare-faced boys, veterans, hurriedly retreating from the hill which they had so laboriously ascended in the dead of night!

Then I knew that all was lost, and that it was a case of every man for himself. The plateau, even in that short space of time, was littered with our dead, and the line of retreat was cumbered with the wounded.

General Colley was already down, shot, not by his own hand, as some have said, but by Boer bullets, as a man who saw him die assured me; and other officers had been killed. Of the little band which the general had led up the hill nearly a hundred were left dead, some died as they tried to crawl back to the refuge of our camp, more than a hundred were wounded, and, as for the rest, they were made prisoners. Not many more than half a hundred got away when the order to retire was given. Amongst the captives was Hector Macdonald, then a second lieutenant who had just won his commission. He fought furiously at the head of a little section, until every man except himself was either slain or wounded.

I watched until the fight was ended; then, sick at heart, I went back to the marquee and the camp and heard, first-hand and hot from the lips, the details of the tragedy. Next day a burial party went up the hill, and put the dead to rest in one huge grave.

You ask me what I think was the cause of the disaster. Well, my business is not to theorise – I leave that to more responsible people; but I was talking of Majuba with a very distinguished officer, and he put it this way: 'You simply tried to bounce the hill – and you failed!'

There are one or two things I should like to add by way of finish to my sad tale. Only a year or two after Majuba, Boers themselves told me that when they saw us on the hill top they were satisfied that we could hold it, and accordingly they began to inspan, so that they could get away.

They suddenly changed their minds, however, and resolved to make that attack which they accomplished with such marvellous success.

But the bitterest blow of all came in a last shot, which was worse than all wounds – a taunt published in one of their chief newspapers. It ran:

'We fought you and beat you in the hills, and we beat you in the open; yet we had no artillery, and you had all the appliances of war.'

The defeat at Majuba and the death of Colley undermined the will of the home government to pursue the war. In the peace negotiations which followed, the British allowed the Transvaal to regain its independence, subject only to a vaguely defined British suzerainty. Yet, over the following twenty years, the pace of Imperial expansion accelerated to the extent that the British were once again drawn into conflict with the Boers.

The immediate cause of the Anglo-Boer War was the discovery of gold in the Witwatersrand district of the Transvaal in 1885. Foreign miners flocked to the region, but the hard-line republican government, under Paul Kruger, was reluctant to grant them political rights, for fear that control of the country would pass out of Boer hands. This took place at a time of growing British interest in the region, and of the Empire-building of the diamond magnate, Cecil Rhodes. Rhodes became increasingly frustrated at the republic's attitude towards the exploitation of the gold fields, and in 1895 encouraged his associate, Dr Jameson, to lead an armed raid into the Transvaal. It was hoped that the miners would rise to support it, but in the event they failed to do so, and Jameson, isolated, was defeated and arrested.

The Jameson Raid marked a shift towards open conflict between the British and Transvaal. Kruger took the opportunity to import large quantities of modern arms from Europe, while diplomatic exchanges between the two became increasingly frosty. Argument over the issue of miners' rights led to a complete breakdown, and in October 1899 the Transvaal presented an ultimatum demanding the withdrawal of British garrisons from the republic's borders. When the British failed to comply, the Boers moved their commandos into the British colonies.

The main Boer thrust took place in northern Natal. Here, after a stiff fight, the British decided to abandon their outpost at Dundee, and fell back instead on the town of Ladysmith in the Natal midlands. The Boers immediately followed them up, and took possession of a commanding ring of hills around the town. Thus the main British force in southern Africa was besieged within a month of the war beginning. Reinforcements were hurried out to South Africa from the UK, and placed under the command of Sir Redvers Buller, a soldier of enormous experience who was regarded as a national hero.

Buller's troops landed at Durban, and marched inland. A large concentration of Boer troops lay between them and Ladysmith, along the line of the Thukela river. This was a formidable natural barrier, since the country was open and exposed on the British side, but rose steeply in a series of terraces on the Boer side. By holding the heights, the Boers effectively dominated the entire Thukela line. General Buller made a first tentative attack on the Boers in December at Colenso, but his initial deployment suffered so heavily from Boer fire that he called the assault off. Instead, he attempted to outflank the Boers by marching to his left, and by trying to force a way across the river upstream. In particular, he attempted to carry a distinctive hill, known to the Boers as Spioenkop, which dominated the enemy line.

In many ways, the attack on Spioenkop had much in common with Colley's attack on Majuba nearly twenty years before. From the foot of the hill, the tactical advantages of its capture seemed obvious, but once on the summit, the position proved cruelly exposed to Boer fire. Private Thomas Humphreys of the Middlesex Regiment left a terrible account of what was to prove one of the most hard-fought, destructive, and ultimately pointless actions of the war.

The Fight for Spion Kop

They call my old battalion the 'Pothooks,' because of its regimental number, the 77th. The 1st Battalion is the 'Die Hards,' for at Albuhera, in the Peninsula, the colonel kept on shouting: 'Die hard, my men! Die hard!' And they did.

You needed human pothooks for the fighting on the rocky crags at Spion Kop; and diehards to hold a place at all on the terrible plateau which was swept by the fiercest of the shell and pom-pom fire. There are many who say – and, of course, having been there, I agree with them – that of all the heavy fighting in South Africa the storm and capture of Spion Kop was the worst.

We were marching on to Ladysmith, about twenty thousand infantry, three thousand cavalry, and sixty guns of various sorts, big and little, long and short. I was in Coke's Brigade, which was made up of Imperial Light Infantry, the 2nd Somerset, the 2nd Dorset, and the 2nd Middlesex – the 'Pothooks.'

Buller's army was near enough to Ladysmith to see the beleaguered people signalling for help; to watch the winking of the heliograph in the burning sun. They wanted us to meet them, and we were just as keen and fierce to join our hands with theirs. Few there were amongst us who had not had enough already of the almost unendurable privations of marching, and the incessant harassing of an enemy that never seemed to rest or sleep, and had a way of hiding and remaining invisible that would have done credit to a marmot.

But of all that vast procession of British troops, only a very small proportion had a share in the struggle for Spion Kop – I mean the actual combat on the barren hill itself. The country round about the Kop was held by a brave and stubborn opponent, and he barred our way in the most determined fashion.

In an advance like this there comes, first of all, the artillery duel; and I do not think that in modern warfare there has been anything to beat the pounding of our guns, big and little. Hour after hour the cannonade continued, the yapping of the small weapons mingling with the deep, terrific roar of the long naval guns and the bellow of the howitzers. Yard after yard we forged ahead, until at last, after two days' ceaseless effort, we were near the point where the final dreadful contest for the Kop took place.

During all that time the shot and shell had whizzed and whistled over us, and under cover of the hail of metal we had laboured far enough to make ready for the storming of the trenches which the Boers had made on Spion Kop, and out of which it was imperative to drive them before we could continue our advance to the relief of the soldiers and civilians who were bottled up in Ladysmith.

A day of rest came on January 22nd – rest on the ground which had been so laboriously won after many hard days' work. Then at night the first part of the assault was made, and it ended in the capture in the most gallant and brilliant manner of the crest of the Kop.

That bit of work was done by the Lancashire battalions.

In the dead of a dark, rainy night they had climbed and crawled up two thousand feet of almost hopeless hill; and in the morning, when the heavy mist had cleared away, they stood triumphant on the summit.

They had done at Spion Kop what the Boers accomplished at Majuba.

General Woodgate, who was in command, was in possession of a great part of a plateau, an enormously long but narrow ridge, so narrow that it was not possible for troops to form up in large bodies, but only in very small numbers – tiny clusters, in fact. But it was soon clear that the plateau was about the worst of places to have won, for it was open to a terrible and deadly artillery and rifle fire from the Boers, and a cross fire at that.

Soon after the General had looked round from the height which he had gained he was mortally wounded by a bullet which struck him in the head, near the right eye. As they carried him to the dressing-station he ordered that an urgent message for help should be heliographed. He was obeyed; but a shell smashed the instrument as it flashed its terrible appeal, and the gallant signaller finished with his flags.

Now it was that I and my comrades, with the 2nd Dorsets, began the scaling of the Kop. We were the nearest to give help, and, in answer to the message from the plateau, General Warren had signalled that he was sending two battalions up.

'Hold to the last,' he ordered, 'and no surrender!'

It is hard to make you understand what that storming meant.

I had served seven years in India, and had done some pretty tough work in the hot weather; but it was as nothing compared with this assault of Spion Kop. There had been the days of long, hard marching, the want of proper rest and sleep, the incessant pounding of the guns; and now, with rifle, bayonet, and eighty rounds of ammunition to carry, we were to struggle up the rugged hill, from rock to rock, to reinforce men on an open space which had no artillery to defend it, and which was swept at leisure by Boer gunners and marksmen, who could not be seen.

It was only the rifle against the gun, and the odds seemed hopeless; yet with fierce enthusiasm we began the storming.

Pothooks we were called by nickname; pothooks we became in very truth, for we had to climb and clutch to make ascent at all. When there was a bit of fairly level ground we scrambled over it; when the ridges barred our way we had to overcome and win them with a wonderful display of gymnastics. It was more like an acrobatic performance than an assault by British infantry.

Bodies were bent and used for supports in getting up; then the man who was on the ridge bent down and lugged a comrade up, while the men below gave him leg-lift. Our officers, wonderfully lithe and active, armed like us, and dressed like us so closely that you could not tell them, at a distance, from privates, cheered and encouraged us, and showed us how to do it, as they always do in time of action. They know how to lead, and we, I think, know how to follow.

Staff-officers, shorn of all their glory, on foot like us, because that was the only way on Spion Kop, hurried past us, excited, anxious, strained, and troubled. Who could be otherwise in face of such a desperate situation?

'Keep up to it, men!' they shouted. 'Go ahead and keep on climbing. Mountain guns are being hurried up. We shall get them to the plateau!'

To a man who knows India, and what the little mountain guns can do – the *kutchi* batteries, as we call them in the East – you cannot offer better encouragement than the promise of their wonderful assistance. They can be hauled up the most unpromising eminences; and I for one, at any rate, knew that if we had the help of them we should be infinitely better off than with rifle-fire alone. But I had my doubts as to whether they could get even the handy small weapon up Spion Kop – the gun that takes to pieces and can be conveyed pretty well anywhere. You see, if it was necessary for men to pull each other up the Kop, it was scarcely likely that gun and gear could be handled and carried or dragged up to the plateau. As a matter of fact, not a mountain gun was taken up the Spion slopes. They could not even get a Maxim to the plateau.

We toiled upward, slowly, in the sweltering heat, almost cursing the very weapons on which we had to rely for our existence. We had left our great-coats at the foot of the hill. We were free of the weight of them, but many a man, when the bitter night came, who was lying helpless on the barren heights, would have given almost life itself for the despised covering which he had looked upon as a burden.

I do not exaggerate when I say that, on reaching the plateau, as we did at last, we were in the thick of a very hell of fire – not rifle-fire, but the infinitely more merciless and destructive shell-fire. It was terrible to see the havoc which had been wrought already; pitiful to notice the dead, and unendurable to look upon the wounded. It was marvellous that human beings could live at all; yet the valiant men of Lancashire were holding grimly on, despite what looked like certain death. As soon as I could get to work with my Lee-Metford I began to fire. Wherever I saw a sign of man in the distance I let a bullet go. For the most part, I am sure, the ammunition was wasted; but in many shots some are sure to be effective. You can empty a magazine swiftly, and each man had eighty rounds; besides, fresh supplies came up, and the pouches were refilled, emptied, and refilled again.

I believe that during the day I myself fired at least two hundred rounds. Other men did the same, so that, although the band of soldiers on the plateau was small, yet the total number of rounds of ammunition used was very large.

I should not like to calculate the weight of the shot and shell which swept the plateau, nor how many came each minute. Not everyone did mischief; if that had happened there would not have been a living soul on Spion Kop. Rifle bullets are terrible things as wound creators, bayonets are worse; but neither of them can be named in the same breath as a shell wound. This is too awful yet most of the injury on Spion Kop was caused by shell.

It was a bitter, merciless battle. Men on both sides fought to kill, and so to win. It was the only way. May I be evermore spared from looking on such a scene, and sharing in such a struggle.

Tragedies occurred on every hand, and on every hand, too, were seen such deeds of heroism as you sometimes think and dream of, but never expect to witness; and such endurance and tenacity as you can get only from men who are stubbornly and heroically led.

We had got used to shell fire by that time; but not to such a withering cannonade as we were forced to face on Spion Kop. Hot, sweating, tired, mad with thirst, we gained the plateau, and set out to hold it. Water was wanted, but it was not to be had, and so, with parched mouths, we went on firing.

If you can get very near your enemy and use the bayonet, there is at any rate some satisfaction; but there we were, mere targets, scarcely seeing a Boer, although at times they got so near us, under cover, that I do not think more than fifty yards separated the two forces. Nor could we get at our food, although within easy reach were Irish stew rations – one for every two men. They were 'iron' or emergency rations; but we left them where they were. They were not worth shell fire just then. If it comes to that, we were in a big enough stew ourselves, without falling back on the Maconochie productions.

The bursting shells made a veritable hell of the plateau. It was miraculous that men could live in such a fire, and that troops could hold the ground they had won, especially with such sights to look upon as they saw on every hand.

Torn by the shot and shell earlier in the morning, the Lancashire Fusiliers had suffered terribly. My own battalion was baptised in blood as soon as it reinforced the north countrymen.

Captain Muriel, one of our company officers, stopped for a moment to give a wounded man a cigarette. He was shot through the cheek while doing it. Undaunted he held on to his post, and led his company until he was struck by a bullet. This time he fell and did not rise, for the bullet had gone through his brain.

Very near me was my own sergeant – Murphy. I heard one of the awful sounds which told of somebody being struck by a shell, then a cry of 'My God'!

I looked at the spot where I had seen the sergeant standing, and saw that the shell had torn both his legs away. What was left of him was lying on the ground, where he bled to death.

More pitiless still was another shell, which came and killed four men in a cluster. They literally seemed, when I saw them, as if they were on fire, and their clothes smouldered. Corporal Cakebread was amongst them.

In front of me also was a man of the Lancaster Regiment named Mallow. We were all mixed up by that time, irrespective of regiments. We clustered and huddled as best we could. There was no ceremony about it – we simply and solely wished to get as well out of the way of the shells as possible.

A pom-pom screeched past me. I looked and saw a ghastly sight. Mallow was staggering on a bit, just two or three steps, without his head, for the pom-pom had carried it away.

It was death, or worse, to be in the open, and an almost certain fate befel the man who, being under shelter, dared to show even so much as his head. Shell or bullet would account for him. I saw a man of the Durham Light Infantry peep round the corner of a little kopje where he was sheltering. Instantly a pom-pom smashed his head against the side, and he fell to the ground.

Even the dead were struck or riddled as they lay, and it was not possible for the wounded to escape.

I saw two Natal refugees, as we called them, carrying off a wounded Engineer – those splendid Sappers who did such fine work in making trenches – on a stretcher. Both of them were struck, and became as helpless as the burden they were bearing.

It was all terrible beyond expression, yet we held on. We had been sent off with the order of 'No surrender!' and we were doing our utmost to obey. And in that attempt we had one of the finest and most thrilling examples that ever fell to the lot of British troops in action.

General Woodgate had fallen – I saw him borne away to the dressing hospital – and his place had been taken by Colonel Thorneycroft. Men were wavering – of some it could be said that they were missing, which meant that the enemy had got them. Ammunition had been shot away or could not be obtained.

It had taken us three hours of incessant toiling to reach the plateau and to get within the zone of shell fire. The pluck had vanished from a mere handful of soldiers – three dozen or so – and they had gone so far towards caving in that they had thrown their rifles down and were making their way towards the spot where the enemy was to give themselves up.

The Boers were coming on to take the fruits of what they thought would be their victory and the capture of the hill.

It was a moment of the gravest, sternest peril. If these men surrendered, who was to say that the day would be ours, and that Spion Kop, won at such a dreadful sacrifice, would be kept?

Suddenly a man of gigantic stature, himself wounded, hurried after the handful who were giving themselves up.

The men in khaki were on the very point of putting themselves into the hands of the Boers, who were armed, and waving white flags or rags.

The big man rushed to the front and roared to the leader of the enemy, telling him to take his men back with him and go to— 'I'll have no surrenders here!' he shouted. Then he added: 'Follow me, men!'

They obeyed, and he led them back to where the good old Pothooks were lying, and put heart of grace into the lot of them and us.

That was Colonel Thorneycroft. He was a valiant leader, and where you get a British officer like that you have men who don't surrender while there is a chance at all of life and victory.

Throughout the whole of that appalling afternoon we went on fighting. I settled down to it in the most dogged manner. I was caked and choked with dust and parched with thirst, and I was hungry; but food didn't count at such a time. I only wanted something to drink – and there was no water or other liquid to be had.

I had been marvellously, miraculously fortunate. Men had been killed and maimed all around me, yet so far I had escaped without a scratch. I began to think that it would be my luck to get away from Spion Kop with a sound skin.

So certain was I that I was safe that I turned to a comrade and said laughingly: 'We're lucky to be here all the time without being plugged. It's nearly dark, and as soon as the "Cease fire" sounds we shall be able to celebrate our escape from a jolly hot hole. Besides, they'll send reinforcements.' Reinforcements never came, as a matter of fact; but I needn't dwell on that. They couldn't get where they were wanted.

You see, amongst other things, a shell had come and struck the ground at the very feet of four of us, yet we had escaped without a scratch. It could not have been a shrapnel, because it never burst; I daresay it was a common shell in which the fuse would not act. There had been some wonderful escapes, too, amongst them that of Sergeant Phillips, who was struck by a bullet which buried itself in his report-book. Another man had been hit on the nose by a bullet – which, luckily for him, was a spent one. He picked the bullet out and made a joke about it.

The day was waning and the swift night was coming on.

I was thankfully looking forward to the ending of the firing, till the day at any rate, when I felt a queer, dull thud on my left leg.

I looked to see what had happened, and sank to the ground, for a fifteen-pound shell had taken off the leg completely, trousers, puttie, sock, and boot. I never saw it; I don't know where it was carried – and I didn't wish to learn. The same shell took off the leg of another man of my regiment called Pasby and smashed his other foot.

I was perfectly conscious. I knew what had happened; but, believe me, I did not feel any real pain. There was only a strange numbness, and the horror of knowing that the dreadful thing had happened.

I dragged myself away from my comrades and crawled instinctively to a place of shelter, just as a wounded animal would have done. I got into a little place of refuge which was made by a couple of small kopjes – a sort of crevice. As I reached it another shell dropped at the very side of me.

For nearly an hour, as far as I can tell, I lay in my hiding-place, craving for water, hoping for help. I knew that unless I could be quickly taken into hospital I should die of exhaustion and loss of blood. The wonder is that I lived at all; yet at last, when it was dark, a surgeon and a sergeant came, and their arrival was at the very moment when another shell buried itself in the hard ground. It was only shells that seemed to have the power of penetrating the rocky face of Spion Kop.

'Are you all right?' shouted the doctor to the sergeant.

'Yes, sir,' the sergeant told him.

'Then you're a lucky man,' replied the doctor. 'It seems to me that these poor, wounded fellows are drawing all the rest of the fire on them.'

The doctor stopped the bleeding with a tourniquet, and I watched him do it, strangely fascinated. Then they made an ambulance for me – a couple of rifles and slings, and two of my own comrades began to carry me down the Kop.

They were utterly worn out and exhausted and the task was too much for them. They turned to an officer who was leading away what was left of the Scottish Rifles, and he ordered a dozen of his men to take charge of me in turn.

'Put me down, and let me die, for God's sake!' I begged them piteously, for it was terrible now to be carried and jolted down the rocks. Every movement was a torture to me; but they held on with their task, and at last my own two comrades again took charge of me.

I became unconscious at last, not because of my pain, but owing to the spirits with which they supplied me on that awful downward journey. I remember, however, being outside the operating tent, waiting in a pitiful crowd for my turn to come. After that I knew nothing till next day, and then I found that it was all over and that my leg was represented by a stump.

That was the end for the time being to something like ten days of the most terrible hardships you can imagine; but the finish did not come even then. I made the close acquaintance of a Scotch cart and a bullock waggon; I knew what it was to have to lie almost unattended on a stretcher, because fighting was still going on, and the army which had been victorious was being drawn away by its leader. Once only in seven days was I dressed, and that was when I was sent to Mori River with the wounded.

I had the personal attention of some of the ablest surgeons in the world – Sir Frederick Treves, Sir William McCormack, and Sir William Stokes; and the devoted care of a nurse who was afterwards in attendance on the King himself. At one time I was rigged up in a suit of pyjamas which a kind lady had sent out for the use of sick and wounded troops.

There are funny incidents even in such dreadful times as those. I had lost my left leg; another man had parted with his right foot. Each of us was in need of a boot, and the authorities, who have no sentiment, divided a pair between us. I took the left and the other man got its brother. The country saved something on the deal.

I knew as I was being carried down the rugged, merciless face of Spion Kop that we were not going to hold what we had won, for the order to retire had been given.

In time I was home again, luckier than the poor fellows who were buried in the trenches on the Kop, and the years that have passed have brought us into friendly touch with our brave and stubborn foes.

Last year I was working at Olympia. Many of the Boer leaders visited the exhibition and took a deep interest in the old soldiers who were present – the men who had been wounded in the war.

While Ladysmith was besieged, Boer forces, too, invested another British town, the dusty frontier outpost of Mafikeng (Mafeking) in Bechuanaland. Although the siege of Mafikeng had little of the strategic weight of the struggle for Ladysmith, it nonetheless captured the imagination of the British public, largely because of the spirited actions of the garrison's commander, Colonel Robert Baden-Powell. George Tighe was a civilian who joined the Mafeking Town Guard, and described the distinctive character of the Anglo-Boer War on the remote western reaches.

How We Defended Mafeking

In the native lingo, Mafeking means 'stony place,' and it is very well named, because if you start digging in a garden there you will probably fetch up more stones than mould. Eleven years ago – how time flies! – when the Boers so swiftly formed a ring round it, the town was not a mile square, and consisted of streets of low buildings, few of which were two storeys high – indeed, practically the only two-storey structure was the Convent.

Mafeking rises from an absolutely flat plain, and the Molopo river runs past it two or three hundred yards away. The flatness is broken by a small mound which became of great interest during the siege. This was called Cannon Kopje, and the Boers concentrated their efforts upon the occupation of this place, which was the only commanding defensive position outside the inner defence works. If the enemy had routed us out of Cannon Kopje, we should have been forced to cave in. It was not a very formidable place, although it was strong compared with the poorly constructed houses and hotels and stores, with soft brick walls and roofs of corrugated iron, to say nothing of the huts in which the Kaffirs lived.

Mafeking was a new, crude, defenceless town, with nearly ten thousand men, women, and children as a population; but the great majority of those were natives, people who had to be fed and defended, and could not do much in the way of help. There were only about 700 partly-trained soldiers; the rest of the garrison consisted of civilians who, whether they liked it or not, had to take up arms in the defence of the town. These numbered about 300, and were called the Town Guard. Most of them had never used a rifle in their lives, but they showed amazing cleverness in handling the magazine weapons that were served out. A few of them became expert snipers, and picked off their enemies at wonderfully long and difficult ranges.

I had had three years' volunteering in the Cape Garrison Artillery, and when commands were given to likely civilians, I was asked to take charge of the Hospital Redoubt, which was in the extreme northern section of the Town Guard defences. I accepted the offer, and immediately set about the construction of my redoubt. In its earlier stages this was simply a piece of bare ground, but with grain-bags filled with sand, of which there was plenty available, we soon made a rude fort, piling up the bags as a bricklayer lays bricks.

What I was doing was being done by every able-bodied white man in the town. There was no shirking. The natives, too, did their share, fetching and carrying splendidly, and as for the small boys, they had the time of their lives, then and afterwards. They were the pioneers of the Boy Scouts of to-day, and their leader was the same, too. If the day ever comes when England knows the horrors and sufferings of sieges, the nation will recognise what it owes to Colonel Baden-Powell, the commander-in-chief at Mafeking.

Almost as soon as war had been declared we were shut up in that small shanty town in the desert, cut off from all communication with the outer world, unprepared for a siege, and with only a handful of men who had been trained in the art of war. But they were fine and enthusiastic teachers, and I think they found very promising pupils.

Mafeking had jumped into fame. From being a small, insignificant town in the heart of a desolate country, it had assumed the importance of a garrisoned stronghold which had to be held at any cost. And in the face of the

Boers' most desperate onslaughts we more than held our own.

The main object of the defence was to keep the Boers sitting round Mafeking, and to prevent them from carrying out their own purpose, which was to control the line north and south, and so prevent Lord Methuen's force from relieving Kimberley.

Colonel Baden-Powell and his men sacrificed seven months of liberty to keep the Boers sitting outside the town. During the first six weeks of the siege we had 12,000 Boers around Mafeking, doing their best to rout us out, and not only failing in that but also being kept away from other operations in the war.

It is always hard to make people understand what a marvellous change is wrought by war. Mafeking had been a busy little town, with its hotels, houses, huts, and stores – shops where you could buy almost anything, from a broom to a bassinette – its convent, and, of course, its gaol.

War had been declared, though not unexpectedly, and, as if by magic, the place had been transformed. Business was crippled, martial law reigned, peaceful citizens became warriors, and the quiet air was torn with the din of strife. We had made forts, dug trenches, constructed bomb-proof shelters, and had developed the cunning of the fox in finding refuge from danger.

There was much and inevitable suffering, but with it great bravery, especially amongst the women. No one can speak of the defence of Mafeking without dwelling on the courage of the women, who were cooped up in their bomb-proof shelters during the week, and only allowed to come out on Sundays, generally speaking, when, by mutual consent, hostilities ceased.

How we loved and welcomed that day of peace and rest! The women showed the old Mutiny spirit, the valour of Lucknow, and as little thought of surrendering as the garrison itself. And just as the women in those awful times in India suffered, so they suffered in the siege of Mafeking. One of the very first of the inhabitants to be killed was a woman – Mrs. Graham. She was wounded, and died in hospital.

Throughout the siege the women and children had a dreadful time, for they had to lie in rows in their trenches and hide. You can imagine what that meant, away from the fresh air and sunshine, and living on very scanty and dwindling rations. The commonest things of life became luxuries, and food which, in ordinary circumstances, would have been revolting became quite palatable. The very husks which were formerly cast away as refuse were gladly accepted as food, and horse-flesh and donkey-flesh took rank as delicacies.

Prices rose enormously. The editor of the *Mafeking Mail* needed a chicken to make broth for his invalid daughter. He had to pay eighteen shillings for a wretched bird – a sum for which, in ordinary times, he could have bought a coopful of full-grown fowls.

Then, as time went on, we had a raffle for a case of whisky, because we wanted to do something to show our appreciation of the constant kindness and devotion of the Sisters of Mercy at the Convent of the Sacred Heart. We bought the case, containing a dozen bottles, at Weil's Stores for £30, which was 50s. a bottle.

When we put the case up for auction, we sold it for £120, which worked out at £10 a bottle, so that we had a balance of £90 to hand over to the nuns. No present was ever more gladly made, and none was ever more thoroughly deserved. Wherever sickness and suffering needed them during those seven long, weary, dangerous months, there the Sisters were, veritable angels in their tender ministrations.

Other prices were in proportion. As a special favour, you could get a bottle of beer for 4s. 6d. An egg would readily fetch sixpence. There was no fresh milk, as the cows were required for beef. The person was lucky who had stores which could be legitimately disposed of; but most things, of course, were commandeered for the good of the community, fair prices being paid. I had three bottles of whisky, and was offered £5 each for them; but I refused the money, and broke the bottles up amongst my boys in the Hospital Redoubt.

The commanding officer and his staff are the very life and soul of a beleagured garrison. Everything depends on them, and particularly on the chief. In that respect we were almost miraculously fortunate, because we had in Colonel Baden-Powell not only a brave soldier but also a most resourceful man, one who was thoroughly able to beat the Boers at their own 'slim' game.

There was no fear of becoming either rusty or depressed under his leadership, and, often enough, after a hard day's pounding, we would gather at a concert and listen to the chief's performances. He was a very clever vocalist and entertainer, and it was wonderful to see him at times, cheering and encouraging us with quip and crank and song, and to think that on this apparently light-hearted leader depended the safety of the whole of the town and its people. This was the chief whose word was law, and at whose bidding the place could fall. But there was never a thought of surrender – not even when the two hundredth day of the siege had been reached.

That was a Sunday, and we were having a cricket match, because on the seventh day we rested on both sides from our fighting labours. A Boer came in with a flag of truce and a message for the chief. It was to the effect that we were not behaving like Christians in playing cricket. We were invited to surrender – and not for the first time. To that invitation Colonel Baden-Powell replied: 'I am batting – I am two hundred, not out – and I mean to stick at the wicket.' How could you fail to have faith in a leader like that?

Another thing which won for him the confidence and affection of every member of the garrison was his determination to share and share alike with the men. Once he was offered white bread, which was a great luxury, but he refused to take it, saying that what was good enough for the men was good enough for him; and he expressly intimated that in future no distinction was to be drawn between him and anybody else in that respect.

In artillery the Boers hopelessly outranged us. They were well equipped, and could do pretty much as they liked with us. We had to be content with any sort of gun that we could find or make – and we did both. Amongst other weapons we dug up an old muzzle-loader which was supposed to be an obsolete naval gun. It had been buried, and my own theory of its hiding-place is that in the old days, when the freebooters used to operate between the Transvaal border and Mafeking, a distance of about seven miles, they had to abandon the piece, which they buried, in the hope that some day they would be able to dig it up again.

Ordnance like that, however, was utterly useless against modern artillery – we might as well have used bows and arrows against the Boers' Mausers. The extreme range of our own guns was two miles; but the Boers had a weapon which would do heavy mischief at three times that distance. That was the celebrated Creusot gun, which discharged at 94 lb. shell – a monster of destruction. I knew something about the beast, which we called Long Tom, Creaky, and other fancy names, because I had been in the Cape Garrison Artillery, and I had seen it brought up, to bear against us, with a team of sixteen oxen. They set great store by the gun, and had a detachment of the Staats Artillery to work it.

The bigger the gun the less danger there is often enough, for you can see the operations of the creature and have warning given of what is going to happen. Long Tom used black powder and, being so huge, we could tell where it was aiming. When we had become used to its performances we had a regular system of giving the alarm.

The ringing of a bell told us that the gun was being fired, and there was a frantic rush to the refuge of the bomb-proof shelters. Often enough, of course, the mighty shell exploded without doing very much mischief, but when it did get home it created havoc. Far greater damage would have been done if Mafeking had been a substantially built town, for in that case there would have been much more heavy material to wreck and scatter, and a far greater loss of life. As it was, never a week passed without its toll of killed and dead of wounds and disease. Enteric told dreadfully upon us in the little community.

One can get used to most things in this world, and we accustomed ourselves to the cannonade; but there are a few exceptions, and the rifle-fire was one of them. We never got so used to that that we could afford to ignore it. The cannonade became almost a hobby with some of us – the watching of the gun-fire, and the scurrying and scuttling to shelter when the warning had been given; but there was no dodging the Mauser and Martini bullets.

Apart from the awful velocity and accuracy of the modern small arm the Boers were amazingly good marksmen.

As the siege went on we became more and more resourceful in all directions, particularly that which dealt with the preservation of our lives and the keeping of the little town. We even manufactured artillery. There was amongst us an old Cornishman named Gerrans, a blacksmith. He was asked by the Colonel if he could make a gun, and promptly replied that he could. He kept his word and evolved a marvellous work in the shape of a muzzle-loading implement which sent a missile trundling over the country like a spent cricket ball.

I do not think that it was ever dangerous, except to those who fired it; but the moral effect of the weapon was great. It made a loud noise when it was discharged, and showed plenty of smoke, and generally made the Boers believe that we had a good deal more artillery than we really possessed.

The siege dragged wearily on, giving us many dull and unhappy days. The thing we felt most was the entire absence of news from the outside world; but we had to do as best we could without that intelligence, and make the most, as we did, of our own little affairs. The monotony, however, was relieved by many exciting happenings, of which I will mention one or two.

The most rigid care was taken to ensure a fair distribution of the food and stores, and anyone found guilty of wrongdoing in this respect was severely punished. One case I remember particularly – that of a non-commissioned officer of long service who had almost qualified for a pension. It was proved that he had stolen a bag of meal and he was quickly and severely dealt with.

All ranks, regulars, irregulars, and Town Guard, were paraded on the Market Square. The sentence was handed over by the Commander-in-Chief to the chief staff officer, who read it aloud. The prisoner had been brought into the centre of the square by the troop sergeant-major. His decorations were stripped from him, he was then reduced to the ranks, dismissed from the army, sentenced to five years' penal servitude, handcuffed, and handed over to the common gaoler. It was a terrible and moving spectacle, and a drastic measure; but it put a stop to stealing food – and without food the town could not have held out. Wellington hanged men in the Peninsula for less serious offences.

Mafeking had the honour of getting the first Victoria Cross awarded during the Boer War. It was the first of three which were granted to Mafeking men. This decoration was won three times over by one of the most dashing

officers of modern times – Captain Charles FitzClarence, of the Royal
Fusiliers. Four days after war had been declared he rushed out of the town
with a squadron of the Protectorate Regiment to succour an armoured train.
He had everything against him, even to the extent of poorly trained men
who had had no experience of fighting; but he routed the superior force of
his opponents, fifty of whom, it was reckoned, were left dead upon the
field.

Two weeks later, Captain FitzClarence headed a cold steel night charge
into the Boer trenches. His force was small, but it did its work with amazing thoroughness. Steel only was to be used – that was the order – and steel
alone was employed by the plucky band who threw themselves into the
trenches and routed the Boers so thoroughly that a hundred of them were
killed.

Of all the warriors there, none more greatly distinguished himself than
the leader, who slew four of the enemy with his own sword. He was wounded,
but not seriously, and had six of his brave followers killed. Not a shot was
fired by the attackers; but the Boers blazed madly at them, and incidentally
amongst themselves, for they had a whole-some terror of the bayonet.

On Boxing Day Captain FitzClarence led a desperate assault on Game
Tree Fort with a force of a hundred men, against four times that number.
The fort was not taken, because a spy had given warning of the attack, but
it was a victory for us – and dearly bought. Three officers and twenty-one
rank and file were killed, and Captain FitzClarence and twenty-two rank and
file wounded. Four men were taken prisoners by the Boers.

I watched the attack through a telescope, and it was one of the most
thrilling affairs that you could possibly witness. Few such assaults have been
made at such heavy cost, for you will see that nearly one man was killed for
every man wounded. No other Cross, of all that were given in that long and
costly war, was more bravely earned than Captain FitzClarence's.

Before that great day came when the relieving forces entered Mafeking,
we had had another fierce fight, for the Boers, led by Eloff, Kruger's grandson, made a furious attempt to seize the place. It was known, at that time,
that the relieving force was near at hand, and no words of mine can tell you
what it meant to feel that help was so near, and that at the very end of our
sufferings we might have plucked away from us the prize that we had fought
so hard to keep.

One great truth was recognised by every man amongst us – that there
should be no surrender. I imagine that even the Boers themselves scarcely
hoped to capture Mafeking. But they made a valiant onslaught. By way of
the bed of the Molopo River, which led past a fort about an eighth of a mile
beyond our fighting line, they advanced stealthily and cautiously.

The route led past the native town, and to this the Boers set fire; then, under cover of the smoke and flame, they rushed on – there were about seven hundred of them – and so furiously that they stormed and took the fort. But they did not hold it for long. The whole of our garrison was turned out, every man who could hold a rifle or wield a bayonet was taking a hand in the defence. Even the gaol itself had been emptied, and the prisoners were fighting with the best of them. Amongst the prisoners was an officer who had been condemned to death for the murder of a newspaper correspondent – a sentence which had been commuted to penal servitude for life.

There had been telephonic communication between this outlying fort and Mafeking, and when this communication ceased, the Boers having cut it off, the Commander-in-Chief suspected what had happened. He took prompt and decisive measures, for he brought two seven-pounders up to within 400 yards of the fort, and declared that unless the Boers gave it up he would destroy the place and them, even at the cost of his own people who were prisoners within. He allowed Eloff till daylight to decide.

Meanwhile, however, a plan was formed which, it was hoped, would prevent such a sacrifice and yet force the Boers to surrender – and it was to cut off the water supply. There was no drinking water available in the fort, the supply being kept in a tank about forty feet from the entrance. A few sharpshooters were chosen to pot the tank, and this they did so thoroughly that the vessel was riddled like a sieve by the bullets.

We allowed the Boers to cross the open space between the tank and the fort, and to their dismay they saw what had happened. I was about twenty yards away, and saw their faces very clearly. I gathered that they knew that they had got into Mafeking, but that there was no getting out of the place. There was no help for it – they had to surrender, and so, with the relieving force almost at the very gates, we made the assailants prisoners.

It is no good denying the fact – we 'mafficked' in Mafeking as madly, apparently, as you 'mafficked' in London, and the very air was rent with crazy cries of victory and snatches of song about the Queen and the rule of Britannia.

That affair was the most desperate struggle of the siege, and no wonder we went off our heads a little – they were not over strong, perhaps, after so much starving and suffering. Next day, the relieving troops really entered Mafeking, the first to join hands with us being Major Karri Davis and about half-a-dozen men.

We were on the shattered roofs and in the wrecked streets to meet them – the tiny advance party, and soon afterwards the main body – and I don't quite know which of the two lots of us felt the meeting most. Anyway, we were satisfied and proud – we had held out for seven long months, and had kept the flag flying all the time.

Then came a day of thanksgiving. It took place at the cemetery, where, this being a fortified position, many a man had fallen. The survivors of the garrison assembled and took part in it.

Three farewell volleys were fired over the graves of the dead, who had given their lives – and surely they lived again when, in their honour and to their memory, the bugles rang out the 'Last Post'.

Eventually Buller broached the Thukela line. Both Ladysmith and Mafikeng were besieged, and the British advanced to capture the capitals of the Boer republics. By the middle of 1900, it seemed that a British victory was guaranteed. Yet in fact, the war was about to enter a new phase, as Boer forces, stripped of the need to defend strategic objectives, took to the bush, and waged an increasingly bitter guerrilla war. For nearly two years they hounded and harassed British forces, until the British were compelled to divide the countryside into sectors with barbed wire and block-houses, and sweep through the veld, as if on the hunt. The war became directionless and formless, as the Boers simply strove to cause the British as much damage as possible, and the British strove to catch the Boers.

Private James Dunning of the Northumberland Fusiliers fought in one of the last actions of the guerrilla war, when a convoy he was escorting was attacked by one of the most daring Boer leaders, Commandant de la Rey. Dunning's account provides a vivid contrast to the great set-piece battles which began the Victorian era, and suggests not only how far the British army had developed across the Great Queen's reign, but also something of the horror of modern weapons, and the ruthless accuracy of the Boer marksmen. His account is a fitting end to the story of the experiences of the Victorian soldier.

South Africa: Chasing a Phantom Army

There is one thing a soldier always likes to see – and that is his enemy. He soon loses the taste for being potted by invisible marksmen, and for seeing men fall dead, as I have seen them, killed by the bullets of riflemen who are hidden more than two thousand yards away. A soldier, too, likes to have a pitched battle, to go ahead with his work, and get it done with. He soon gets utterly weary of the pursuit of a flying foe that he seldom or never sees, and rapidly tires of the sport of chasing a phantom army.

You know, of course, about the Northumberland Fusiliers – the 'Ever Fighting, Never Failing Fifth,' as Wellington called them in the days of the Peninsula – and that both battalions went out to South Africa to the war? A wonderful feature of the regimental spirit was that not a single reservist, I believe, failed to return to the Colours when the call came. Of the 2000 officers and men who were on active service, 1200 were reservists. The war cost the regiment, in killed alone, 13 officers, and 229 non-commissioned officers and men, to say nothing of the sick and wounded and the permanently damaged.

I jumped from an easy-going, monotonous Aldershot manœuvring existence to a round of battles – out to Cape Town in the *Gaul*, up to De Aar, and on to Orange River, and there we had a little reconnaissance, which told us something of the kind of work that we were in for. I saw the Boers for the first time, and the Fifth began its sacrifices in the campaign. The first to fall was Lieutenant Bevan, shot through the thigh so badly that he could not move. Colonel Keith-Falconer, our chief, sprang up from behind cover to save the subaltern. He was shot dead – and rests in a soldier's grave in the lonely veld. He was a brave officer and gentleman. It is a strange but inspiriting fact that his successor, Major Ray – 'Young Ray,' he was called affectionately – was also killed in action, soon afterwards, while doing the same thing – giving his life for a friend. South Africa had its days of gloom; but it has given us many glorious memories.

Then, in six days, we had three battles – Belmont, Graspan, and Modder River. Not a man of the Fifth fell out on the advance to the little farm which has given us the victory of Belmont – yet the heat was awful, and we were loaded up with 'oddments,' such as soap, canvas shoes, flannel shirt, towel, socks, and greatcoat; to say nothing of sidearms, rifles, and ammunition. In that fierce fight at Belmont we fired upon each other at a distance of only about a hundred yards. Here again we lost a gallant gentleman – Captain Eagar, who was shot dead while tending a wounded man – the third officer in the Fifth who, in a few days, had died in the attempt to succour a comrade. There is a grave in Belmont Farm Cemetery in which fourteen of our officers and men are sleeping. After the battle we heaped it up with rocks and earth, made a big cross, planted a prickly pear-tree, and marched on.

At Modder River we had a long and desperate struggle of fourteen hours. For nearly twenty hours the Fifth had nothing but a cup of coffee, and we had to use our emergency ration of cocoa. Lord Methuen in his official dispatch said that the action was one of the hardest and most trying fights in the annals of the British Army.

I was shot through the hip, and was ordered home; but I wanted to remain, and I was allowed to stay. There would have been more left of me now if I had taken my chance and returned to England.

I thought I knew, by the time I was fit for service again, what marching and enduring meant; but that was mere child's play to the life I led when we began the pursuit of the phantom army and its 'slim' commander, Delarey. At first we thought it would be sport; but when we had become like a column of ragged tramps, and as lean and gaunt as greyhounds, we changed our minds. There was not a man, I think, who did not yearn for a proper fight, just to get the wretched, harassing business settled once and for all.

It is hard to put in words the toil and suffering of it all. But imagine a tremendous tract of sterile country, baking under a blazing sun by day, freezing under a bitter sky by night, and offering no supplies. Pit the vast expanse with swiftly moving-figures, which know every nook and crevice of it and change their quarters with unerring judgment when a time of crisis comes. See your comrades fall victims to disease or bullets from invisible opponents; start in the early morning in the high and burning hope of meeting your enemy, who has been reported in front of you, and halt at night, utterly wearied and discouraged, only to learn that he has vanished and is probably somewhere in your rear, ready for a swoop in the darkness. I would rather fight a score of pitched battles than go again through the pursuit of a phantom army.

Yet, in a way, I was spared. I did at last go into action again – and what is left of me is here to tell the tale. They call me, with fine humour, the armour-plated man. I wish I had had some armour on in February, 1902, when we unexpectedly came across Delarey in the flesh.

For some time we had heard and seen nothing of the commandant; but we were not so unwise as to suppose that he had forgotten us. As a matter of fact, he was biding his time, waiting for his chance, and it came when I was in the rearguard of a convoy near Klerksdorp, in the Transvaal, just over the border of the Orange River Colony.

How many miles we had covered in that tremendous trek under Lord Methuen I cannot tell – I hardly care to remember; because there are so many things in this life which it is better to forget. But we had been at it long enough to know the meaning of thirst and hunger, heat and cold, rags and tattered boots, and swarming vermin. On February 1st I was at Klerksdorp, and after a joyful rest there I was off to Wolmaranstad. From that place, on the 23rd, an empty convoy was sent back to Klerksdorp. It never got there.

We had only about fifty miles to march. That was nothing to men who had become known as the Salvation Army and Methuen's Mudcrushers, and who at one time, for fifteen consecutive days, had marched on an average more than fifteen miles a day. That was done, too, under a blazing sun, in a land of dusty road and burnt veld, on half rations, with snatches of food and sleep, and burdened with a weight of from thirty-five to forty pounds. Sometimes four miles meant a dozen, for Tommy Atkins did not travel like the crow.

There were about a hundred and twenty waggons in the convoy, which covered an enormous stretch of country. The escort numbered rather more than 600, and was commanded by Colonel Anderson. It was made up of three companies of the Fifth, some Paget's Horse and Imperial Yeomanry, a pompom, and two guns of the Royal Field Artillery.

We were going steadily ahead – a long, straggling, clumsy, slow procession. Forty of the fifty miles had been covered, and already, from the hills around Klerksdorp, the British sentries could see us coming. There was no suspicion of death in ambush – in fact, Paget's Horse had been sent on, and they went away in the night. They were well out of the fatal morning which followed.

After a black and rainy night we struck our camp and resumed our crawl. It was then daybreak – a grey and cheerless morning. Near us was the deep Jagd Spruit and a long mass of scrub and high grass.

I wasn't thinking of any subject in particular; certainly not about the enemy. I wasn't troubling my head about the general plan of things. A private soldier never does, and, for that matter, he doesn't care. He goes ahead with his firing, and then, when the time comes, with the bayonet. He is like his civilian brother – wants to see the end of things as soon as possible.

I was marching in the open, away from rocks and ferns and things of that sort.

Then, like a bolt from the skies, the swoop came upon the convoy. The phantom army had reappeared in the flesh.

A single shot was fired – a vicious little crack which I took to be a signal of attack.

I saw a man in front of me who had sprung up out of the vegetation or from behind a rock – a Boer, whose rifle was presented point blank at us at a distance of something like twenty yards. It was not a comfortable sight to those who were not expecting it. But it was very thrilling.

The solitary marksman fired. Then a lot of his comrades appeared in just the same swift, stealthy, mysterious fashion. I think – I am sure – that they must have been hiding in the spruit and the scrub. I for one saw nothing of them till they were upon us.

Confusion at such a time is inevitable; but there was no panic. We tumbled instantly to the real meaning of things, and settled down to hard, stern work.

'Hands up!' I heard them shouting; but if it comes to that they didn't give a man much time. They might as well have told us that they were going to fire, and then plugged into us.

'Hear that, Tommy?' asked a comrade near me. My name isn't Thomas at all, but that's what I was called. It doesn't much matter to a soldier, so long as he has a name of some sort to identify him. 'Hear that? Hands up!'

'Not hands up,' I answered. 'We'll fight for it!'

'Good for you, Tommy,' he shouted. 'We will!'

I had scarcely got the words out of my mouth when I saw, a little in front of us, a Boer kneeling and taking aim. I rushed towards him and struck him with the butt of my rifle, and he tumbled over.

I dropped on my knee. 'Now,' I told my friend, 'we have to stay and fight for it. It's life for life to-day.'

There was loud and hoarse shouting near me, and a lot of commotion amongst the panic-stricken drivers and the mules.

I saw a mounted man with a *sjambok* in his hand, trying, I suppose, to drive off some of our waggons.

'I'm going to shoot at him!' I said, and I got on my knee at the side of a tree and took steady aim.

I fired and saw the horseman fall.

'That's done it, I think!' I said to my friend. Then I cried: 'Keep down!' for I heard a rattling noise very near us, and knew that a volley was being fired by the enemy.

That was merely the beginning of things. The fight had started and went on in such a way that you might have supposed that it would never finish.

All sorts of sounds assailed me, all kinds of voices rose in the confusion. But I think that the chief note in all that was said was one of hope and encouragement. We were ambushed and overpowered – the enemy, it is calculated, was three to one against us – but we kept on fighting furiously, believing, some of us, that help would come from Klerksdorp. Surely the sentries could see what was taking place, and surely an alarm was raised.

There was time for one thing only, and that was to try to save the convoy and one's own life. It was soon clear enough that the convoy was lost, and as to a man's own life, what could he suppose when he looked around him and saw his own comrades lying dead or wounded?

Another rattling volley came – just as, in a thunderstorm, you hear the vicious crackling of the storm-clouds after the vivid lightning flash.

'They've got the guns!' I shouted.

An officer near me cried: 'They've claimed the guns, I think!'

Then the ominous word was passed along – 'Retire!'

I heard it. The order came from a good and brave officer, and I think that the word was the last he uttered, for almost instantly he was shot dead.

But there was still no immediate withdrawal. We were even yet animated by the spirit of our watchword – no retreat, and no surrender.

I went on firing, steadily, I believe, and as calmly as one can at such a time. Service hardens a man marvellously, and I had been in two little campaigns before I came to South Africa. And in South Africa itself I had had a pretty generous baptism of Mausers.

There had been heavy losses amongst us. I knew that, but I could not tell what the casualties were. I could only judge from what I saw about me – and I knew that many of my comrades would never answer to the roll-call.

As a matter of fact, you can be in action, in the thick of it, and know nothing of what is happening beyond the narrowest possible circle. It may be, and probably will be, months before you know the extent of what they call the butchers' bill.

Sometimes a whisper of surrender would come – and can you wonder at it when you remember what it means to be without ammunition or real hope of final victory? In these days of magazine firing a man soon gets rid of his cartridges, and it is the hardest thing in the world in time of action to bring up fresh supplies.

And death is so demoralising, too. A comrade near me said: 'Jeps is killed – shot dead. We'd better surrender, Tom.'

'No,' I answered, 'we'll fight for it. There's no surrender, and no turning back. That's what the general said, you know.' It is wonderful what influence a saying like that has on the private. He doesn't know much, as I have said, about the plan of things, or the way that schemes are carried out; but he does understand the meaning of an inspiriting message, and a good many of them were issued during the South African war.

So we kept at it, fighting confusedly. At their own particular game the enemy were almost unmatched. They knew so well how to take advantage of cover, and a man with a rifle who is sheltering behind a rock, or hidden in a trench, has infinitely the best of his opponent who is in the open, as we were. He can pick and choose, while his adversary has to take his chances.

You must remember that in such a case as this there is not much chance for using that weapon which probably the British soldier knows better how to wield than any other fighter in the world – the bayonet. The Boers would never face it – and I am not belittling a brave enemy in saying that. No man who has seen the dreadful work of cold steel in battle can fail to have a feeling of horror for the results of it.

So far we had used the rifle solely, answering, as best we could, the merciless bullets from the unseen marksmen. Then something like an electric shock went through us; for the bugle rang out the 'Charge!'

There was a lull in the firing, followed by the rattling of the bayonets as they were snatched from the scabbards and fixed; then, with the glittering, deadly tips levelled we rushed towards the spot where the enemy seemed to be hidden most thickly.

What followed was a confused and wild mêlée. The spruit was glutted with the frenzied mules, the broken waggons, and the demoralised drivers. Some there were, of course, who took to their heels, and they were lucky, for at any rate they saved their skins.

Meanwhile the Boers were cutting up the convoy, destroying it on all sides ruthlessly. Delarey himself was present, and fought like the brave and chivalrous chief which a good many of us knew him to be.

We were a terribly lessened band, but we were not conquered yet, and there was still hope that if we held out a little longer reinforcements would arrive.

I had settled into the way of the battle, and so far had escaped unhurt. It really seemed as if I should escape entirely free; but apparently it was ordained that my peppering should come thickly.

All at once, in the very thick of the action, I felt a strange, searing sensation in my side. I knew what it was, because I had been bullet-struck before. Still, I held on with the fighting; it is amazing what you can do when you are supported by the excitement of battle. And I did not want to fall, either, and endure the torture of thirst and inevitable neglect on the burning veld.

I was hit a second time, and fell to the ground, lying on my wounded side.

A sergeant bent over me. He saw, without asking, what had happened, and set to work to do his best for me. Every soldier carried a roller bandage, a piece of waterproof, a couple of safety-pins, a pad of wool, and a pad of gauze. So, you see, we had something to set us up as amateur doctors. Besides these things we had an identification card. Extraordinary mistakes arose when a tunic was thrown away, and some other man picked it up, wore it, and was killed. I myself was returned in the list of the departed.

The sergeant must have used or lost his bandage; at any rate, he took off one of his putties, and having picked up a stone he wrapped it in the cloth, and then did his best to place the object to my side, to staunch the bleeding.

I can hardly bear to recall the terrors of that dreadful period, and I will pass lightly over the harrowing incidents that followed.

I remained where I had fallen, utterly helpless, but perfectly conscious. I did my best to keep quiet, resting on my side, with my arms over my head, as one places them in sleeping.

A bullet entered my right forearm; a second also struck the limb, so that I had four of the missiles in me.

I had already had my share of attention, quite as much as I wanted or could carry.

Surely I might have been spared; but war is merciless.

A fifth bullet struck me in the left arm.

A sixth entered the right hip.

There was a resting space. Then my unhappy target of a carcase was again the recipient of a bullet, this time through the left calf.

To crown all, an eighth bullet struck my right heel.

It is one of the marvels of modern warfare that so many bullets can enter a single individual, and yet make it possible for that individual to live. But the Mauser and Lee-Metford bullets were far different from the old Martini missile, or the dreadful explosive bullets that were sometimes used during the war in South Africa. More than once I saw the terrible havoc which they wrought.

I lay in agony where I had fallen – an agony which was all the more acute because I was conscious, and all the more terrible because, although I was conscious, I was not able to speak or make a sound. My mouth was choked with blood.

All the time there were the fierce but lessening sounds of the battle around me, then a growing silence, then a swimming of the senses, and I knew no more until I was roused to consciousness by men handling me. I managed to move and make some sort of sound; then the men left me. I knew afterwards that it was supposed that I was dead, and that the Boers were beginning to strip me.

Hour after hour I remained where I had fallen – nine in all before I was carried off the field of battle. It is hard, impossible almost, to tell you anything like my real sensations when I was lying wounded; nor can I recall many of the strange and terrible things I witnessed. But I do remember that one picture which impressed itself clearly on my memory was the sight of a sergeant running about quite naked. I do not know what had happened to his clothing, or how he came to be in that condition. I merely recollect that it was so. It is one of the extraordinary incidents of warfare.

Another man I saw, a noble specimen of health and strength, a sergeant who was here and there and everywhere – the perfect picture of a fighter. I lost sight of him in South Africa, and when next we met I myself had almost risen from the dead, and he was being wheeled about in a chair in hospital, a life-long, helpless cripple, for both his legs, because of wounds, had been amputated.

Seven operations put me more or less right, and now my steel-strengthened corsets hold together what is left of me.

Somewhere in the world there is an old comrade, a sergeant, who carries a relic of me about with him, a trifle in the way of a rib.

Fastened to her watch-chain, an old lady, who happens to be my mother, carries a silvered Mauser bullet, the first of the eight with which I was riddled when I was fighting in the rearguard of the captured convoy.

Index